THE GREAT MIGRATION

Illustrated London News, 1849

TEA-TIME AT SEA

On the better ships passengers might obtain tea-water from the cook at six bells.

THE GREAT MIGRATION

The Atlantic Crossing by Sailing-ship Since 1770

BY
EDWIN C. GUILLET

UNIVERSITY OF TORONTO PRESS

Originally published in 1937
by Thomas Nelson and Sons

Second edition © 1963
University of Toronto Press

ISBN 978-1-4875-9932-4 (paper)

Reprinted 2017

To the Memory of My Father

PREFACE

History records three great migrations: the Barbarians who swept over Europe and captured Rome; the Mongols under Genghis Khan; and the Atlantic Migration to the New World. Anglo-Saxon colonization made its most spectacular growth between 1770 and 1890, when eleven million people came from the British Isles to North America, and this book tells the story of the transition.

It is the great period of the sailing-ship, and the slowness of navigation made the Atlantic crossing unpleasant even for those who could afford the best accommodations; while the poor and wretched made the passage in vessels generally unsanitary, verminous, and unseaworthy. But many came with health and high resolve, and tales of heroism and devotion stand out against the murky background.

The conditions under which the great mass of emigrants left the Old Land were a reflection of the times. Famine, unemployment, poverty, and the brutal arm of the law hastened the exodus, and the unwary were exploited and cheated at both ends of the journey and frequently bullied and starved aboard ship as well. But there is a sense of racial destiny in the march from the Old World to the New, and we observe at first hand the adjustment of the immigrant to strange conditions as he proceeded to the interior of the continent and entered upon the hardships of pioneering.

The author has made every effort to locate records never previously consulted, and much of the most valuable material has come from the more obscure sources. A study of the files of periodicals yielded excellent contemporary descriptions not previously used, while similar valuable material is presented by diaries, narratives, letters, and emigrant guidebooks, many of them accessible only in museum and archives collections.

In presentation and arrangement the point of view of the student of history, as well as of the general reader, has been kept in mind, and the source material upon which the work is based has been appended in a form in which it will be of greatest service. The illustrations are all from contemporary sources and provide in themselves an authentic and comprehensive picture of the times.

PREFACE

The author is indebted to several persons who have kindly permitted the use of manuscript material in their possession; these items are acknowledged and described in detail in the bibliography. His thanks are also extended to librarians and archivists in both the United States and Canada who have facilitated research. Among collections of what are somewhat loosely termed Americana and Canadiana, those of the Public Archives of Canada at Ottawa, the Toronto Public Reference Library, the Legislative Library of Ontario, the New York Public Library, the Buffalo Historical Society, and the Detroit Public Library have proved of outstanding value.

EDWIN C. GUILLET

Toronto, Canada.
May 1, 1937

CONTENTS

I	THE BRITISH BACKGROUND	1
II	STATE REGULATION OF PASSENGER VESSELS	10
III	ASSISTED EMIGRATION	20
IV	UNASSISTED EMIGRATION—PREPARING FOR A NEW LAND	34
V	PROCEEDING TO THE SEAPORT	43
VI	ARRANGING FOR THE VOYAGE	47
VII	FAREWELL TO THE OLD LAND	58
VIII	DAILY LIFE IN THE STEERAGE	66
IX	STORM AND MISERY	81
X	CHOLERA AND SHIP FEVER	89
XI	THE TANG OF THE SEA	99
XII	THE CABIN PASSAGE	109
XIII	SHIPWRECK AND DISASTER	124
XIV	NEWFOUNDLAND AND THE GULF	138
XV	"PURIFICATION" AT GROSSE ISLE	145
XVI	QUEBEC AND MONTREAL	155
XVII	ASCENDING THE ST. LAWRENCE	164
XVIII	ENTERING NEW YORK	179
XIX	THE HUDSON ROUTE	192
XX	PROCEEDING TO THE SETTLEMENT	204
XXI	THE PROMISED LAND	215
XXII	THE PASSING OF THE SAILING-SHIP	233
	SUPPLEMENT	287

ILLUSTRATIONS

	Page
Tea-Time at Sea	Frontispiece
Exterior of Cottage, Isle of Skye	Facing 20
Interior of Cottage, Isle of Skye	" 20
The Deserted Village of Moveen	" 21
Distribution of Clothing at Kilrush	" 21
The Priest's Blessing	" 36
On the Way to the Seaport	" 37
Liverpool Packets Leaving Cork	" 52
The Emigration Agent's Office	" 53
Loading the Baggage Aboard	" 68
Departure from Liverpool	" 69
Towing Out	" 69
The Roll-Call	" 84
The Search for Stowaways	" 84
Emigrants in the Steerage	" 85
Emigrants at Dinner	" 100
Dancing in the Steerage	" 101
Tracing the Vessel's Progress	" 101
On Deck at Sea	" 116
Saloon Cabin on the *Great Eastern*	" 116
The Burning of the *Ocean Monarch*	" 117
The Wreck of the *Edmund*	" 132
The *Martin Luther* Saved by the *Tagus*	" 133
Grosse Isle Cholera Hospital	" 148
Icebergs off the Grand Banks	" 148
Poling Boats Upstream	" 149
Quebec in 1830	" 149
Winter Stage on the St. Lawrence	" 164
Stage-Coach at Waterloo Inn, near Washington	" 164
Andrews' Tavern, above Brockville	" 165
Cobourg, Upper Canada, in 1840	" 165
New York Harbor in 1847	" 180
The *Sovereign of the Seas*	" 181
The *Dreadnought* off Tuskar Light	" 181
The Palisades, Hudson River	" 196

xii   ILLUSTRATIONS

		Page
Albany in 1837	"	196
"Low Bridge!"	"	197
The Erie Canal near Little Falls	"	197
The Public Landing at Louisville	"	212
Midnight on the Mississippi	"	212
St. Louis during Migration to the Far West	"	213
Railway-Building in Nebraska	"	213
Emigrants Crossing the Plains	"	228
Beginning a Home	"	229
Our Home in the Woods	"	229
The *Great Britain*	"	244
Saloon of the *Great Eastern* in a Storm	"	244
The *Britannia* and the *Queen Mary* in New York Harbor	"	245

CHAPTER I

The British Background

"Houseless near a thousand homes,
And near a thousand tables pine for want of food."
"Oh shame that BREAD should be so dear, and HUMAN LIVES so cheap!"

Among the most remarkable incidents in the history of the human race is the great exodus from northern Europe to America during the nineteenth century. Although emigration from the British Isles commenced soon after 1600, for over two centuries it was very limited. Official returns were not made before 1815, but shipping records and other sources indicate a gradually increasing migration from various parts of the United Kingdom after the middle of the eighteenth century. In the 1770's there was a considerable movement from Scotland, especially from the Highlands. The repression following the rising of 1745, depriving the Highlanders of their arms and garb, eventually produced the decadence of chieftains. A contemporary chief, General MacLeod, believed that "the fond attachment of the people to their patriarchs" would have yielded to no laws had not the chiefs themselves degenerated into mere landlords who "became as anxious for increase of rent as the new-made lairds—the mercantile purchasers of the Lowlands."*
As a consequence many small tenants were displaced by higher bidders, and those who contracted to pay the excessive rates soon fell into extreme poverty.

About 1771 emigration commenced, quickly reaching the proportions of an epidemic, particularly in the Hebrides. The inducements of property and independence were played up to the full by agents who reaped handsome profits from the transport and settlement of emigrants. The exodus was not restricted to those who had a real grievance, but included large numbers whose condition left little to be desired. General MacLeod successfully led a reactionary movement in his own clan, relieving, wherever possible, the impoverished tenants at the expense of mortgagees and creditors, and impressing upon them the difficulties and dangers of emigration. As a

* The footnotes in the body of the book give additional information or comment. Detailed references to all citations or quotations may be found on page 249 ff. They are arranged by chapter and page, and are given in the order in which they appear.

result few members of this clan left for America. References to this early migration are found in two famous travel books—Boswell's *Journal of a Tour to the Hebrides*, and Johnson's *Journey to the Western Islands of Scotland*. An innkeeper in Glenmorison told Boswell in 1773 that seventy men had left the vicinity for America that year, and "that he himself intended to go next year; for that the rent of his farm, which, twenty years ago, was only five pounds, was now raised to twenty pounds. That he could pay ten pounds and live, but no more." Dr. Johnson observed at the same time "the general dissatisfaction which is now driving the Highlanders into the other hemisphere," a movement which he denounced as the "epidemical fury of emigration."

The greater number of some 20,000 per year who landed at Montreal or Quebec in the early 1770's were Irish. Emigration declined during the wars with Napoleon, because the British Government discouraged any efforts to leave. In 1814 it was estimated that ten persons emigrated to the United States for every one to the British colonies, and the Secretary for the Colonies took steps to divert the flow to Canada. The excess population which led to this decision had existed for many years, but the press gang and the army had absorbed many who had lost their livelihood through the revolution in industry and agriculture. The Napoleonic wars had also caused an inflated condition which had the appearance of prosperity; but when the career of Napoleon ended at Waterloo, so, too, did Britain's comparative monopoly of the world's commerce. The British manufacturer's war contracts disappeared and his foreign orders collapsed. The wartime prices of corn dropped almost one-half, and wage rates receded still more. The weight of colossal war debts fell most heavily upon the farmer, and poverty was soon the lot of a large part of the middle and laboring classes throughout the Kingdom. The demand for coal had so fallen that in some districts the miners had no more than a day's work a year. The enclosure of waste and common land continued, and the small landowner was fast becoming a rarity. Parish relief became for many the only alternative to starvation, and in 1819 Parliament first voted in favour of emigration as a method of relieving distress, although not until 1824 was it legal for artisans to leave the country.[1]

In Scotland the hand-loom weaver was as badly off as the evicted tenant. In 1803 in Glasgow he was receiving 25 shillings a week,

---

[1] The law prohibiting the emigration of artisans was as much to hamper the development of American manufactures as to foster British.

but by 1819 his wage had fallen to the starvation rate of 5 shillings weekly. Working in their own houses far into the night, the weavers' families attempted to offset low wages by greater production; but the decreased demand soon resulted in a surplus. Emigration was the only means of escape, and many settled in Lanark County, Upper Canada, in 1820. It is no wonder that one wrote back: "I really do bless God every day I rise, that he was ever pleased, in the course of his providence, to send me and my family to this place. Were you here and seeing the improvements that are going on among us, you would not believe that we were once Glasgow weavers!"

The lot of Scottish farmers was no better. Evidence given before committees of investigation contains instances of actual starvation:

"We were asked by a person almost starving to go into a house. We there found on one side of the fire a very old man, apparently dying; on the other side a young man of about eighteen, with a child on his knee, whose mother had just died and been buried; and evidently both that young man and the child were suffering from want. . . . We went upstairs, and under some rags we found another young man, the widower, and turning down the rags, which he was unable to remove himself, we found another man who was dying, and who did die in the course of the day. I have no doubt that the whole family were actually starving at the time."

In Ireland conditions were even worse. The population increased rapidly, and the greater part lived in misery on little but potatoes. Absentee landlords had their agents wring all they could out of their impoverished tenants, and when disorders and risings became widespread, evictions followed. Rioters were executed or transported to the penal colonies. In 1817-1819 there was great distress from famine and fever, and the failure of the potato crop in 1821 because of excessive rains made robbery a commonplace. "Ribbonmen," "Whiteboys," and members of other secret lawless organizations[2] were continually being transported to Van Diemen's Land, but the situation was one which even the military found almost impossible to face. In 1822 the shortage of potatoes caused the price to quadruple, and millions were practically reduced to starvation. In Great Britain £350,000 was raised privately to alleviate this distress; collections in Ireland itself amounted to £150,000; and Parliament added £300,000. But these funds hardly made an impression amid such widespread destitution. It was finally decided to relieve distress in some measure by removal to America. Suspicious at first that they were being transported as a punishment,

[2] An interesting sidelight on the nefarious activities of Irish "White Feet" in forcing one family to emigrate may be found in the *Cobourg Star* of October 24, 1832. Under the caption "The Drowned Emigrant" is described the death of one of these men on the lake shore lot of the very person he had persecuted.

4 THE GREAT MIGRATION

many of the Irish were glad to set out for Canada, provided, as some suggested, that they were assured of priests and potatoes in the new land!

In the 1830's conditions became steadily worse in Ireland. Opinions might differ as to whether the universal pauperism was due to misgovernment, the ignorance of the masses, too great a dependence upon the potato, or the subdivision of farm land, but there was no doubt that some 6,000,000 peasants were habitually impoverished, and as a contemporary reviewer states, "Whenever the potato crop becomes even in a slight degree deficient, which is found to be the case once every five or six years, the scourge of famine and disease is felt in every corner of the country." The general course of events when families were ejected from their small holdings in Clare or Mayo was most terrifying: a murdered agent, the new tenants burned in their beds, a Rockite insurrection, the reading of the Insurrection Act, and half a dozen executions. Destitution prevailed while several million pounds' worth of provisions were annually being exported:

> "Those who have never travelled in Ireland can form but a very imperfect idea of the distress that generally pervades that unhappy country. Often have I seen in one miserable, nearly unroofed dwelling, with scarcely a window remaining, from ten to twelve, *and in some instances more*, families, pent up together, with not an article of household furniture save the shattered remains of an old oak table, or a solitary chair without a back, or a broken stool. And for culinary utensils an iron pot not unfrequently serves the threefold purposes of tea kettle, *if they are able to raise the tea*, a pot to boil the potatoes in, or stirabout, *meat they have none*, and a vessel to wash the tattered remains of their wretched garments in; these, with *perhaps* a broken cup and saucer, make up the sum of the whole of their moveable effects. In every street and alley are to be seen groups of human beings in a state of half nudity; women with their almost lifeless infants struggling to obtain a portion of the scanty nutriment from their exhausted mothers, while their reckless and infuriated fathers wander the streets, lost to all hope, and maddened with hunger and despair. Nay, I have frequently seen women with the lifeless bodies of their infant children in their arms, prowling from street to street, and begging from the casual passengers the means of depositing the remains of their departed offspring in the grave!"

As a sidelight on the misfortunes of Ireland it may be mentioned that there were in the country twenty-two Protestant bishops drawing £150,000 a year, and the rest of the Establishment, which Disraeli termed "an alien church," and Lord Macaulay "the most absurd of all the institutions of the civilized world," was receiving £600,000 more, largely from Roman Catholics, many of whom, supporting their own church as well, were in no position to contribute to any. The most abject could not emigrate at all; while many who could never raise the funds to take them to America were at least able to cross to England and Scotland, where they aggravated the already existing oversupply of unskilled labor.

The Industrial Revolution created an unfortunate condition among a large part of the inhabitants of Great Britain. Machinery frequently displaced five-sixths of the "hands," while agrarian consolidation caused such distress that over one-third of a parish population were frequently classed as paupers. The dissatisfaction of the oppressed and idle showed itself on every side. In the manufacturing towns machines were smashed and factories burned by mobs who imitated the activities of the Luddites of 1811 and subsequent years; while the starving gangs of "Captain Swing" and his associates terrorized the rural districts as they destroyed threshing machines and barns and burned thousands of ricks, at a time when grain was scarce and dear owing to the protection of the Corn Laws. Some of the most miserable poor even poisoned people for the paltry sums obtained for dead bodies.

Agitators and reformers in various parts of the Kingdom formed no small part of the quota of emigrants in the period prior to the Great Reform Bill. Tradesmen who ventured to suggest that there might be something more in Jacobihism than the guillotine not infrequently found their town too hot to hold them, and made haste to put the Atlantic between themselves and their more placid neighbors. The land of Magna Charta was for nearly a generation controlled by a reactionary government which could by no stretch of the imagination be termed democratic. Habeas Corpus and the freedom of speech and public meeting were almost entirely suppressed; the press was either throttled or gagged; while all but the most eminent Whigs were liable to intensive persecution in a day when statements like Bishop Horsley's—that he did not know what the mass of the people of any country had to do with the laws except to obey them—went almost unchallenged. Political agitation for the amelioration of conditions reached its height with the passage of the Reform Bill of 1832, which many thought would prove a panacea for all the grievances of the lower classes. Political unions rioted at Derby, Nottingham, and Bristol; and illuminations in celebration of the passage of the Bill indicated great popular enthusiasm, which was dampened only by the ravages of cholera. The new Poor Law Act of 1834 altered the deplorable practices which had long degraded the poor by practically placing a premium on vice, immorality, and dishonesty of every kind, and for a few years there was an improvement in general conditions.

In the 1840's destitution again became widespread, particularly after the severe winter of 1842-1843. Riots frequently accompanied the activities of Chartists and Anti-Corn Law agitators. In Wales hundreds of toll-gates were destroyed by "The Daughters of Rebecca"[3]—sturdy fellows in petticoats. There was, too, the railway mania, a period of illusory prosperity and plenty of work which was followed by the inevitable bursting of the bubble. Meanwhile the condition of millions of men, women, and children who labored in factory and mine was but little removed from slavery. The few were credited with building up British industry and commerce while enriching themselves and degrading their fellow-beings. In commenting on Lord Brougham's speech in the House of Lords on August 2, 1842, relative to the abolition of the trade in slaves, the *Illustrated London News* suggested that the crying evils of the times indicated that reforms were long overdue at home:

"The execrable tyranny of the New Poor Laws—the degrading thraldom of our factory-toilers for wealth—the wretched and semi-brutalised condition of the unhappy workers in our collieries and mines—are too palpable evidences that in spirit, if not in name, we have a practical slavery existing in the heart of England, and poisoning those beautiful streams of liberty from which all the land should drink alike—as the very waters of the health and life and light of its noble constitution. Pauperism, too, and the goading exigencies of distress, have latterly so afflicted the general body of the people that among the suffering lower-classes there have been deprivations and wretchedness hardly inferior to what has been endured within the fetters of foreign slavery, although the cruelty has been less frequent with torture and the reckless savagery of inhuman disregard. . . . The wrongs and distresses of our own poor do cry to Heaven, and work for remedy upon every impulse and passion of the human heart."

Under such conditions it is not remarkable that emigration literature contained numerous panaceas. James Buchanan announced his plan as calculated "to receive the whole pauper population of England"; while another writer, John William Bannister of Rice Lake, Upper Canada, advanced a visionary scheme to settle some 6,000 persons by having them first engage in public works for two years. His plan was that they should be sent to the Rice Lake region in three emigrations, where they were to be engaged in the construction of a canal from the Bay of Quinte to Rice Lake *via* the Trent, and possibly to continue the undertaking to "the carrying-place in Smith Township" and "the shallow lakes." However impracticable such plans might be, their advancement indicates how deep-seated was the belief that the great remedy for the ills of mankind was emigration to the New World. To some, no doubt, advice of the following nature was appropriate:

[3] The Rebeccaites took the name in allusion to the reference in Genesis XXIV, 60.

THE BRITISH BACKGROUND

"Let no one in a spirit of restlessness and discontent leave home on slight grounds, or without well weighing the consequences of the eventful step he may be about to take, voluntarily exiling himself from all he may hold dear. The pang of parting with old and familiar faces is very severe, and nearly as painful is leaving for ever the home of our youth—even without its loved tenants—the peaceful Cottage with its garden and aged trees, the warm, bower-like village with its grey church, round which our forefathers may be mouldering in the hallowed dust, the pleasant banks of the clear and glancing stream, the smiling fields and the wild moor or heath-clad hills."

But such thoughts of the home land were foreign to many emigrants, for the fates had never permitted them to experience any such happiness. In Ireland the abundant crops of 1842 and 1843, when the poorest beggar refused potatoes and they were commonly used to manure the land, were followed by the blighted crop of 1845 and the total destruction of that of 1846. Famine and disease stalked through the land, mitigated by British and American charity and by a system of relief public works which made the tax bills of the gentry much more onerous. Soon it was considered that heartless eviction[4] and enforced emigration was the way out, for the expense of such a policy was less than the cost of support in a workhouse. Destitution and the cholera so increased that, as a contemporary newspaper observed, "Nothing like the misery of the Irish people exists under the sun." They died by the thousands in their miserable hovels, in the poorhouses,[5] in England, *en route* to America, or after arrival there; while hordes of others, forced to steal to keep body and soul together, were committed to overcrowded Irish jails or transported to Bermuda. Over a million emigrants left for America in the eight years following 1846. A very human document is that sent by eighty-six inhabitants of County Sligo to "Lord Monteagle, House of Lords, London." Entitled, "A Petition from the Poor Irish to the Right Honourable Lords Temporal and Spiritual," it contains a highly illuminating description of the destitution of hundreds of thousands who had watched their potato crops rotting in the fields:

"We, the undersigned, humbly request that ye will excuse the liberty we are taking in troubling ye at a time when ye ought to be tired listening to our cries of distress; but like beggars we are importunate. . . . We thank ye and our Gracious Sovereign and the Almighty for the relief we have, though

[4] In the period 1849-56 some 50,000 Irish families were evicted and practically forced out of the country. Lord Macaulay, who travelled in Ireland in 1849, observed along the route from Limerick to Killarney and thence to Cork "hundreds of dwellings in ruins, abandoned by the late inmates, who have fled to America; the laboring people dressed literally, not rhetorically, worse than the scarecrows of England; the children of whole villages turning out to beg of every coach and car that goes by. . . . Between the poorest English peasant and the Irish peasant there is ample room for ten or twelve well-marked degrees of poverty." (Trevelyan, *The Life and Letters of Lord Macaulay*, II 230 fn.)
[5] It is estimated that half a million Irish died of famine or pestilence.

one pound of Indian meal for a full-grown person, which has neither milk nor any other kind of kitchen, it is hardly fit to keep life in them; but if we got all that we would be thankful. But if we have reason to complain, there is others has more reason to complain, for in the Parish Townagh they are getting but half a pound. . . . So we hope that ye will be so charitable as to send us to America, and give us land according to our families, and anything else ye will give us (and we will do with the coarsest kind). We will repay the same, with the interest thereof, by instalments, as the Government will direct. . . . And we will bind ourselves to defend the Queen's Right in any place we are sent, and leave it on our children to do the same. So we hoped for the sake of Him gave ye power and England power, and raised her to be the wonder of the world, and enabled her to pay twenty millions for the slaves of India, that ye will lend us half the sum, which we will honestly repay, with the interest thereof, for we are more distressed than they; and hope for the sake of Him that said, 'He that giveth to the poor lendeth to the Lord, and He will repay it,' that ye will grant our petition. And may He grant ye heavenly wisdom, with temporal and spiritual riches also, is the earnest prayer of your petitioners. . . . We hope that ye will make allowance for deficiencies of this, for the writer is a poor man that knows little about stiles and titles, for we are not able to pay a man that could [do] it right."[6]

For many months over 3,000,000 Irish had been subsisting by state aid, but in the summer of 1847 this policy was suddenly abandoned when crops appeared likely to be satisfactory. The hope was that wheat, turnips, peas, and beans had replaced potatoes to a considerable extent, for rot was reappearing in that crop in some districts.[7] The immediate result of the withdrawal of relief, however, was mass migration, much of it induced and arranged by landlords whose interest lay in the expulsion of their tenants; and as no adequate preparation had been made for the exodus, ship fever and other horrors attended it, which the London *Times* considered "an eternal scandal to the British name."

Abject poverty among needlewomen and sempstresses in London, and the starvation (or a bare existence upon limpets, periwinkles, and other sea food) which was the lot of thousands in the Western Islands of Scotland are but two examples which might be multiplied up and down the Kingdom at the middle of the century. A correspondent of the *Morning Chronicle,* who noted the cheers which arose as emigrant ships left Liverpool docks, observed that the passengers on the *Star of the West* "did not present

---

[6] "A Petition from the Poor Irish to the Right Honourable Lords Temporal and Spiritual," in *Report of the Select Committee of the House of Lords on Colonisation from Ireland,* 1847, appendix 25. The sufferings of the Irish people are best shown by the enforced migration of half the nation. A population of 8 millions in 1841 dwindled to 6½ millions in 1851 and about 4½ millions in 1901.

[7] Among organizations which aimed to relieve distress in Ireland was one with branches in America which peculiarly combined charity and self-interest. In Canada West it went by the grandiose name of "Provincial Ladies' Society for the Encouragement of Industry among Indigent Irish Females," and contributors had merely to state what articles of home manufacture they wanted in return. Ladies in the vicinity of Peterborough sent £40, and the subscribers received in due course "Curtains, Counterpanes, Shawls, Socks, Stockings, Lace, Children's Woollen Dresses, etc." (See the *Cobourg Star,* February 9, 1848.)

THE BRITISH BACKGROUND

a very favorable specimen of the genus man. Destitution and suffering, long-continued, possibly for generations, had done their work upon the greater number of them. It was not alone their personal uncleanliness and their wretched attire, but the haggard, sallow and prematurely aged expression of their faces that conveyed the idea of degradation and deterioration." Perhaps there were among the 360 Irish on this vessel some who believed the statement of Thomas Mooney, writer of *Nine Years in America*, an emigration tract:

"I have seen a thousand times the two growths of children from the same Irish parentage present a remarkable difference. Those born in America were brave, beautiful and intellectual-looking—high foreheads, bright eyes, quick and intelligent. Those of the *same* parents, born before they left Ireland, wearing still the stamp of sorrow on their brow, and the stoop of suffering in their gait."

However unlikely such observations seemed, it appeared unbelievable that the hordes of destitute could be worse off in a land advertised as literally "flowing with milk and honey" than they had been in the home of their fathers.

CHAPTER II

State Regulation of Passenger Vessels

"The medical examination consisted of 'What's your name? Are you well? Hold out your tongue. All right.' It was all said in one breath, and lasted one or two seconds."

Vere Foster to Lord Hobart, 1850

The policy of laissez-faire, so characteristic of the last half of the eighteenth century, applied to conditions of ocean travel just as it long prevented the alleviation of crying abuses in industry. Emigration was sporadic, however, and the accommodations were fairly satisfactory, as there was competition for a comparatively small traffic. In the 1790's the exodus to America increased, and it was no longer necessary for masters to offer a comfortable passage. Ships became overcrowded, and an agitation to ameliorate conditions gradually gathered headway. The first government regulation, the Passenger Vessel Act of 1803, resulted largely from the investigations of the Highland Society of Scotland. It aimed to protect Highlanders from the rapacity of emigrant agents, and in its representations to Parliament gave several notable examples of the unscrupulous manner in which vessels were crowded. In 1773 a British ship of 300 tons sailed for North Carolina with 450 passengers, of whom twenty-five had no sleeping accommodation until twenty-three who had had berths died. One hundred Highlanders died on an overcrowded brig *en route* to New York in 1775. In 1791 a 270-ton emigrant ship left the Isle of Skye with 400 passengers, who were provided with most miserable accommodations. The berths were only 18 inches high and two feet wide, and they were arranged three tiers high. Two pots, each of 24 pints capacity, comprised the cooking facilities. In 1801 two ships of 550 tons carried 700 passengers each, and while ostensibly they had the usual two tiers of berths, they are believed to have erected a third after putting out to sea. On one of these ships 53 died, while the sufferings of the survivors were severe. Investigators concluded that the law regulating conditions in the transport of slaves rendered their accommodations preferable to those of many an emigrant ship.

As the Canadian timber trade to Britain developed, timber ships which had no return cargo became the usual emigrant carrier. In some of these vessels there were no bunks, and the passengers spread their beds on the lower deck wherever an opportunity offered. A pamphlet published at Quebec observed that

> "thousands of poor Emigrants who are of little value at home are transported by means of these ships to a situation where their exertions largely contribute to the national prosperity; . . . and Canada receives a useful and industrious race who can be rendered faithful citizens by the simple remedy of employment; thus these ships, and the country at large, may be regarded almost as in the light of a safety valve to unhappy Ireland, in relieving her at least from a portion of the pressure which every instant threatens an explosion."

In the regular emigrant ships there was usually a steerage about 75 feet long by 20 or 25 feet wide and 5½ high. On either side of a five-foot aisle were double rows of berths made of rough planks; and each berth, designed to accommodate six adults, was ten feet wide and five feet long. The four rows of thirteen berths might therefore hold 312 people, while the five-foot aisle was congested with their baggage, utensils, and food. Occasionally passengers slept in hammocks which they supplied,—if, indeed, there was any place to sling them. In the semi-darkness dozens of children played, and the confusion and noise may readily be imagined. In the fetid atmosphere the passengers often went days without ventilation. In fact in some ships the dirty bilge water of the hold seeped through the temporary flooring, while the foul-smelling cargo contributed its share to the common misery. The plight of the emigrant under conditions which continued long after the first state regulation was hardly to be avoided, and, as a contemporary points out, "Their trials were so intense that multitudes, who might have reached our shores in good health, came here worn out, impoverished and diseased, and never, in innumerable cases, recovered from the fatal consequences of unexpected impositions."

The Passenger Vessel Act of 1803 limited the number of passengers to one to every two tons of the ship's register. This was no criterion of the vessel's total passenger list, however, for there were not infrequently, in addition, almost half as many small children, those under fourteen being reckoned as half an adult, those under seven merely a third, and infants under one year not counting at all. The passengers who needed most space were denied it by this method of computation, and the large number of deaths among children was the natural result of a condition which encouraged contagious diseases. Among other regulations, the Act of 1803 called for a surgeon on each ship and sufficient provisions for all passengers. The Act brought forth loud protests from shipowners, who immediately raised their rates.

Hostilities with Napoleon greatly restricted the tide of emigration, but immediately after the war the general collapse in wages and prices made a movement of the unemployed increasingly necessary to relieve distress. Several provisions of the Act of 1803 had more or less fallen into the discard, and even in the state-supervised emigration of Scottish Highlanders in 1815 it seems to have been necessary to insist on the inclusion of a surgeon on each vessel, "several of the women being pregnant, some near their confinement, and the children unwell from the difference of the diet." The Passenger Vessel Act of 1817 was much less stringent than that of 1803, the ratio of passengers to tonnage being increased to one to each $1\frac{1}{2}$ tons; and in succeeding years there was still more relaxation in government supervision.

All sorts of frauds were practised by the unscrupulous agents and brokers who frequently bought up the entire steerage accommodation of emigrant ships. As John Campbell wrote to Lord Bathurst in 1815, "What we have chiefly in my humble apprehension to contend with are the wretched and infamous practices that have been followed by those emigration crimps whose unprincipled thirst for gain has led them to such a traffic at times not much less to be dreaded than the slave trade." Ships which had left port with a satisfactory certificate from the government inspector would proceed to some remote spot on the coast to take on many more passengers. Upon arrival they would escape trouble by avoiding the regular ports, dumping the unfortunate immigrants upon some unfrequented shore of New England, Cape Breton, or the lower St. Lawrence. Acts of Parliament might be passed, but masters when well out at sea observed the law perfunctorily, if at all. The Rev. William Bell tells how during his voyage in 1817 on the *Rothiemurchus*, Captain Watson refused to follow the provisions of the Act passed a few weeks prior to sailing, although he had taken plenty of butter, flour, and oatmeal on board to conform with its terms. When he refused to issue these supplies a passenger produced a copy of the Act, and feeling ran high. Finally a week's supply was distributed, and peace was temporarily restored; but on the following day the captain spitefully withheld the usual allowance of soup. At Mr. Bell's intervention a grudging compromise was effected. The master, however, was "a good deal mortified," and during the rest of the passage was "more harsh and unaccommodating than before," causing considerable indignation by ordering the airing of beds and bedding on the Sabbath. This had not been done before, but, "having taken at least his usual allowance of grog," the captain was in no mood to change his orders, and he quoted the legislation giving him such power. So the bedding had to be brought up, and some of the emigrants lost their blankets in a sudden gust of wind. While such experiences were not unusual, there were numerous occasions upon which masters of vessels treated passengers with every consideration, even beyond the requirements of the law.

Following the relaxation in the regulations of 1817, conditions became so bad that there was strict government supervision again in 1823. The pendulum swung to the opposite extreme, and the law restricted the passengers to one to every five tons. Ships were required to carry much better provisions, enough for all passengers, and careful inspection was provided to see that they did so. A general outcry from agents and shipowners was accompanied by an increase of from £2 to £5 in the cost of passage. Conditions were greatly improved, but there was considerable point in a contemporary comment that the Act was valuable "if we wish to keep the pauper population at home, but the most irrational and absurd that can be imagined if we wish to facilitate their egress."

A Select Committee of the House of Commons investigated the results of the Act, and found that the law was generally evaded. A. C. Buchanan, Chief Emigration Agent at Quebec, stated that his experience in conducting emigrations had proved the folly of giving emigrants food of a nature different from that to which they were accustomed. "If you give an Irish peasant beef and biscuit and salt pork and coffee, they will be all over scurvy before they get to North America. The present Act requires the provisions to be found by the ship, but the fact is, it is not so; for the Collector of His Majesty's Customs and the people charged with the clearing out of the ships know that it would be impossible to adhere to that. . . . The emigrants prefer to find themselves." He considered that but few would be able to pay for the provisions required by the Act, which, if rigidly enforced, would raise the price of passage by more than one-half. R. J. Uniacke, Attorney-General of Nova Scotia, gave evidence of a similar nature, describing the voyage in 1824 of some 300 emigrants from the north of Scotland to Cape Breton. They made all the arrangements themselves, and not only was the passage satisfactory in every respect, but also cheaper and speedier than usual. For provisions each person took a pound of oatmeal for each day of the voyage, and all they had besides was a little molasses and butter and a few eggs. Mr. Uniacke was emphatic in maintaining that the provision of better accommodations than they were used to was even more detrimental to the Irish than to the Scotch or English:

> "The Irish emigrant, before he comes out, knows not what it is to lie on a bed; he has not been accustomed to a bed; if you put him in a bed and give him pork and flour, you make the man sick; but when a man comes to Newfoundland he gets no more than his breadth and length upon the deck of the ship, and he has no provisions but a few herrings, and he comes out a hearty man; and he has no doctor."

The Act of 1823 was amended in 1826, when Ireland was exempted from its provisions; and in the following year it was entirely repealed. The belief was general that extensive emigration was essential to provide an outlet for the ever-increasing surplus population. The Passenger Vessel Act of 1828 greatly cut down the food allowance. It was stipulated, however, that ships must carry 50 gallons of pure water and 50 pounds of bread, biscuit, oatmeal, or breadstuff for each passenger. Complaints that many an emigrant had been left at Quebec when he had contracted for a passage to Montreal led to the inclusion of a £20 penalty against masters who landed passengers without their consent at any place other than that originally arranged. The between-decks of passenger ships must be at least 5½ feet in height; but even this space was not entirely clear, for a considerable part of it was often occupied by large beams and other obstructions. Permission to carry three passengers for every four tons resulted in terrible overcrowding. In most vessels this regulation allowed a passenger for every 20½ inches of deck space—a condition hardly paralleled in slave ships. Under this legislation emigration reached a peak. In 1831, 58,000, and in 1832, 66,000 left the British Isles for America; and in the latter year shiploads for Quebec left 36 ports in England, 18 in Scotland, and 21 in Ireland. One vessel was so crowded that, when a passenger attempted to go from one end of the ship to the other, the remaining emigrants had to crowd themselves into a dense mass, often being obliged to clamber on top of chests. Of sixteen vessels reaching Quebec between May 9th and July 15th, 1831, all had more than the law allowed, and half had more than a passenger per ton, the worst offender being the *Ulster*, from Londonderry, a vessel of 334 tons with 505 passengers. Under legislation of an earlier period such a boat would accommodate about 110 passengers, and in order to crowd in several hundred more, triple tiers of berths and false decks were common,

STATE REGULATION OF PASSENGER VESSELS 15

and the miserable practice of alternate sleeping shifts in the berths not unusual; while fraudulent ages of passengers and many another evasion of the law were employed to deceive customs' agents and inspectors. Irish ships were usually the worst offenders, and it is probable that the passage which many a poor Irishman made on a fishing vessel was preferable. Such ships did not fall within the legal interpretation of "passenger vessels," and as they were consequently not subject to regulation, not much accommodation was to be expected. Not infrequently such passengers were never below deck during the entire voyage.

In 1832, in the absence of satisfactory regulations in the United Kingdom, Acts were passed by the legislatures of Lower Canada, Nova Scotia, and New Brunswick to effect improvements in the emigrant trade by an indirect method. All immigrants were taxed 5 shillings on arrival at the port of entrance, but those who had sailed without the consent of the British Government had to pay double. Many persons who had reached America sick and destitute had been a charge upon the port of entry, and this tax was intended to provide funds for their care, as well as to effect better control of immigration. The poorer classes raised an outcry that the added expense would make their emigration impossible, but the Acts went into force and the tax was collected.

In 1835-1836 an Act of the British Parliament reduced the passengers from four to three for every five tons. Otherwise accommodations had not improved. In 1836 two children were killed on one vessel when the crudely-constructed bunks collapsed, and many preferred thereafter to sleep on deck. Captain Levinge crossed the Atlantic in 1835 in a sailing-ship which he describes as "a tub of a vessel, without a sailing point in her composition. . . . Water tanks, heaps of biscuits, barrels of pork and but one of rum; a pennant, an ensign, a skipper, a fat mate, and a superannuated lieutenant of the navy by way of agent, and a most inadequate crew, were put on board, and the transport was reported fit for sea." He refers to another vessel of 800 tons on which were huddled together some 700 men of the Royal or 1st Regiment.

The poor flooring of the decks was frequently a cause of trouble. Rats which swarmed up from the hold were sometimes killed by the hundreds in rat-hunts organized by crew or passengers. Because of temporary flooring, often employed for steerage quarters to facilitate the carriage of freight, washing or cleaning was forbidden, and it was a standing joke that emigrant ships could be recognized by their smell. During the ship-fever year,

1847, when there was but little pretence of passenger limitation on Irish ships bound for Quebec, many disease-infested vessels reached Canada. The *Elizabeth Grimmer* was in such a filthy state after being discharged from quarantine that "persons could not be had to go near her, for the purpose of throwing out the ballast, for three weeks, and then even tempted only by extraordinary wages."

Legislation in 1842[1] had attempted to remedy such conditions by insisting upon 1½-inch floors, but it did not require the use of water in the steerage—merely dry scrubbing, "holy-stoning," or scraping. Bedding was to be aired on deck twice a week, weather permitting, and the ship was to be fumigated with vinegar at the same intervals. Passengers were ordered to clean themselves regularly on the upper deck (whether also by dry scrubbing is not indicated!) and they were urged to bear in mind that their arrival in America in high spirits or in ill-health depended largely upon their attention to these rules. Until the Act of 1847 the only ventilation in the steerage of many ships was obtained through the hatchways, and these, during storms, were sometimes kept closed for a week or more at a time. The combination of darkness, foul air, and illness produced a condition of misery hard to imagine. One family describes that for two weeks the steerage passengers were shut out from the light, with fever raging among them.

Not until the Act of 1847 was there any regulation that "adult passengers of different sexes, unless husband and wife, shall be separately berthed." A man on the *Julius Macgregor* in 1842 noted that "there was no separation for the sexes; yet it is surprising how soon myself and all the other passengers, the females included, became reconciled to it." The matter of segregation appears to have been left to the official emigration agent at the port of embarkation; or failing that, to the master of the ship. Very few agents were as careful as the one at London in 1838, who describes his method as follows:

"All the single women and girls above fourteen are placed in the after berths; . . . adjoining to them, and next to their daughters, I berth (as a kind of safeguard to the whole) the oldest and most respectable married couples. The married people I place in the upper berths, taking great care to put relations, friends, and persons from the same neighbourhood along side of and near each other, which is an advantage also in messing them. Their children are put in the berths immediately under them, observing to separate boys and girls above seven years of age, and avoiding, if possible, putting

[1] By this Act, 5 and 6 Victoria, c. 107, the minimum height of the between-decks was raised from 5½ to 6 feet and it was stated that the bottom of the lower tier of berths must be at least 6 inches from the deck.

more than three children in each berth. . . . The single men and boys above fourteen are berthed in the fore part of the ship in the space partitioned off for the purpose of separating them from the rest of the people."

Delays were frequent in the days of sailing-vessels, and they could obviously not be legislated out of existence; though sometimes the whim of the master had more to do with the postponement than the changing of the wind or the loading of the cargo. Mistakes were often due to dishonesty and misrepresentation on the part of agents. An emigrant sailing from Liverpool was told by a broker to lose no time, as the vessel was already a week behind the date advertised for sailing. He hastened aboard, but the ship "did not leave port for three days after, putting the passengers, many of whom had been on board for a fortnight, to great expense for food, as fires were not allowed on board." During this period he was consequently "obliged to make alternate meals of bread and cheese, and bread and butter"; and he notes that when he got tired of that he "ate both butter and cheese together by way of a change." By the Passengers Act of the 12th and 13th of Victoria the expense incident to delay in leaving port was laid upon the master of the vessel. Passengers were entitled to recover "subsistence money" at the rate of one shilling a day unless the delay was caused by adverse weather only. This enactment came too late to benefit thousands who had suffered financially without any remedy in law.

There was no legislation covering dangers of shipwreck in the early period, and comparatively little even in the last days of the sailing-ship. The Act of 1842 stated that from two to four lifeboats, depending upon the ship's tonnage, must be carried; but such provision was intended for the protection of cabin passengers only.[2] It was hopelessly inadequate to save any appreciable proportion of an emigrant vessel's total passenger list. In 1840 the death rate of passengers to Canada was 1.005 per cent, fairly evenly divided between drowning and disease. Better inspection gradually decreased the number who died from disease, but between 1847 and 1851, forty British emigrant ships were wrecked with a loss of 1,043 lives. In addition to the loss of life, hundreds of the survivors were left in destitute circumstances. In 1852, 1853, and 1855, Acts were passed enabling the payment through government agencies of the full expense of the passage home for shipwrecked emigrants. It was further stipulated that such monies expended

[2] This distinction recalls a newspaper's description of a wreck in which "twenty souls and 240 emigrants" were lost.

were to be recovered from the owners of the vessels. With this legislation the period of the sailing-ship as a passenger carrier drew to a close, and a decade later the steamship had taken over almost the entire traffic.

It is apparent that the regulation of passenger vessels was a matter of great difficulty. Humanitarian standards were not those of today, and a fatalistic attitude suggested that the "lower orders" must survive a great deal of misery—if, indeed, they were to survive at all. Basil Lubbock remarks that the government regulations "might more fitly have been framed for traffic in Hell." This statement might be justified, yet the economic condition of the British Isles and the destitution of those who sought to emigrate were ever-present factors. At the same time those who stood to benefit most by stricter regulation were loudest in their condemnation of attempts to raise the standards and so automatically to restrict emigration. Censure for bad conditions should be laid upon ineffective supervision rather than defective legislation. Regulation of passenger vessels at the port of embarkation was generally perfunctory, and at times almost useless. At Liverpool in 1850 one officer, two assistants, and three medical inspectors comprised the staff which had to superintend the examination of 568 emigrant ships and the departure of 174,188 people. Perhaps it is remarkable that conditions were not much worse.

Only an emigration official on each ship could make possible adequate supervision of regulations at sea, for the steerage passenger seldom experienced kindness, and he was fortunate if his treatment was in accord with his rights. Thousands experienced not only dishonesty and fraud but also the curses and blows of brutal seamen. A rich philanthropist, Mr. Vere Foster, embarked incognito as a passenger on the *Washington* in 1850, with the purpose of learning conditions at first hand. On the first day of the voyage the 900 passengers were mustered on deck for their water, but while it was being pumped into their cans the mates cursed, abused, cuffed, and kicked the people without any provocation, and served only thirty of them. The others had to go without. In spite of the contract, no provisions were served on that or on the following day, and, as many people were almost starving, a letter of complaint was written to the captain. The man who wrote it was knocked down by a blow from the first mate. The next day half rations were served, the supplies being given out raw. To get near the fires many people bribed the sailors, and those too poor to offer money managed to obtain a turn only once in two or three days.

STATE REGULATION OF PASSENGER VESSELS 19

The evidence of Dr. Poole, Inspecting Physician at Grosse Isle, bears out these observations. He stated that while there were plenty of seaworthy vessels, the worst only were generally used in the emigrant trade; and that brokers and ship captains disregarded legislation. The law fixing the height of the between-decks was frequently evaded in small ships by a false deck below the beams. As a result passengers were crowded into the narrowest recesses of the vessel. Misrepresentation of the length of the voyage was another common fraud, most masters of Irish vessels advising emigrants that three weeks or a month would be sufficient. They then extorted as much as 400 per cent on the cost of supplies, knowing that from six to nine weeks would elapse before debarkation. Dr. Poole also found that where provisions were served out daily to the emigrants, short rations, bad quality, or dishonest weight were common frauds. Where the passengers furnished their own supplies the inspecting agent made no effort to see that the law was observed, many men being smuggled aboard with no provisions. These afterwards passed muster on deck through some trick. The surgeon in charge of the average emigrant vessel was usually a mere apprentice or apothecary's assistant, with little or no knowledge of the prevention or cure of disease. Dr. Poole cited instances in which sprains were bound up as fractures, and where the surgeon did not know the bones of the arm from those of the leg; and he considered "ignorance and presumption" the chief characteristic of medical officers. It was entirely impossible to rely upon a surgeon's statement, for upon inspection dozens of cases of typhus were sometimes found in ships certified free from disease.

Many abuses came to an end with the passing of the sailing-ship as an emigrant carrier. In the 1850's most of the unscrupulous operators were squeezed out of business, for fast-sailing clippers and expensive steamships could be constructed and equipped only by large companies. As a consequence the regulation of passenger ships became easy just as the employment of large and speedy vessels was making the Atlantic crossing a very different experience.

CHAPTER III

Assisted Emigration

"According to their own testimony they were removed from misery and want and put into independence and happiness."
Re Conducted Emigration of Irish to
Peterborough County, Upper Canada, 1825

"To throw starving and diseased paupers under the rock at Quebec ought to be punishable as murder."
Lord Sydenham

The line of demarkation between philanthrophy and self-interest is sometimes hardly distinguishable, and never was it less so than in assisted emigration from the United Kingdom. In several instances the state aided the migration of those who were not entirely destitute, but others were transported overseas as the easiest means to be rid of them. Emigrations arranged by parish or landlord were even more objectionable, and in Ireland particularly, every imaginable fraud was perpetrated upon the defenseless tenantry whose eviction and enforced emigration it was the landlord's interest to effect.

In general British emigrants might be classed as those whose expenses were borne in whole or in part by the state, or through the assistance of Emigration Societies or individuals; and those whose voyages were financed by themselves, with the help not infrequently of relatives and friends already established in America. As a rule the latter class provided the better type of settler, and even in years of the largest state-assisted emigration nearly ten times as many negotiated the passage by other means. During the decade 1815-1825 there were 7,090 members of conducted emigrations, but 65,704 arranged their own passage. A large amount of deception has always been connected with emigration, and many a man gave up a certain livelihood in the hope of an illusory paradise in the New World. John M'Donald expressed the opinion that "all the truth which has been written and printed respecting Upper Canada would not cover one-half of the lies that have been told"; while E. A. Talbot facetiously observed that Captain Charles Stuart's *The Emigrant's Guide to Upper Canada* painted conditions so rosily that it might more appropriately have been called

Illustrated London News
EXTERIOR OF A PEASANT'S COTTAGE, ISLE OF SKYE
Thousands in the Western Islands of Scotland existed upon periwinkles and limpets.

Illustrated London News
INTERIOR OF SKYE COTTAGE
Hand-loom weavers and small farmers from Scotland swelled the numbers of emigrants fleeing from poverty.

THE DESERTED VILLAGE OF MOVEEN
Irish destitution was at its height during the mass evictions of 1847.

DISTRIBUTION OF CLOTHING TO THE POOR AT KILRUSH
"Nothing like the misery of the Irish people exists under the sun."

ASSISTED EMIGRATION

The Pilgrim's Guide to the Celestial Regions! Consequently elaborate precautions were sometimes taken to insure the authenticity of reports from the new land.

Apart from the relief of destitution, the underlying argument for government aid to emigration was the establishment of loyal settlements in the British Colonies. Consequently the United States did not receive the state-assisted, although it did accept with considerable protest large numbers of paupers from British parishes. The first state-conducted migration was under way early in 1815, when a proclamation was published in Scotland announcing the provision of ocean transportation and supplies, as well as land, rations, implements, etc., in Upper Canada, to men of good character who could deposit £16 sterling, all monies so advanced being repayable two years later to those settled on their land. It was a special object of this emigration that a patriotic colony, some of whose members were old soldiers, should be formed inland from the St. Lawrence, and produce supplies for armies on duty against the United States if another war should break out. The experiment was in many respects unsatisfactory; there were numerous lengthy delays both in Scotland and the Canadas. Although many reached Glasgow for an April sailing, it was June or July before they could embark, and not until the spring of 1816 were the first of them settled at Perth-on-the-Tay.

In 1818 the Colonial Office announced that, in general, such extensive aid was at an end, but promised land grants of 100 acres to members of conducted groups of ten or more. Each head of a family deposited £10 as security, but other than providing shipping accommodation the government made no contribution to the project. Under this scheme Richard Talbot organized in 1818 a group of fifty-four families of Irish yeomen of from £20 to £300 capital, and after a costly delay of a month in Cork they finally sailed on the *Brunswick*, described as a fine ship of 541 tons, "elegantly fitted up" with cabin accommodation. Twenty-four small children died during the passage, and were either "consigned to a watery grave" or "interred in the different islands of the St. Lawrence." Thirty-one of the immigrants went to Perth to avoid the expense of the longer journey westward, but the balance spent two weeks in the ascent of the St. Lawrence by Durham boat, six days in the schooner *Caledonia* from Prescott to York, and finally by a circuitous land-and-water route reached their destination in the Township of London.

Under the same regulations nineteen English families from

Cumberland proceeded to Upper Canada, settling in remote Smith Township on the upper Otonabee River; and about 100 families of Highland Scotch finally reached Prince Edward Island, or Beckwith Township, Upper Canada, after a vexatious delay in the port of Greenock through their inability to provision themselves in accordance with the Passenger Vessel Act of 1817. Similar arrangements in 1819-1820 enabled destitute Scotch weavers to emigrate to Upper Canada. John M'Donald's *Narrative* reports that the ship *David of London* weighed anchor in Greenock on May 21, 1821, in agreeable weather; but soon heavy storms caused a great deal of misery. The weather was cold during most of the voyage, but became very warm when the ship reached the Gulf of St. Lawrence. Many passengers preferred sleeping on deck to being "nearly suffocated from the smell and heat below." Of four births which occurred during the voyage, only one child lived. On the 25th of June the *David* reached Quebec, and the following morning the steamboat for Montreal came alongside. At eleven at night they set out in the steamer, almost all of the 400 on board having to stand on deck throughout a rainy night. "And," says M'Donald, "we all had to remain, drenched as we were, in our wet clothes till they dried on our backs. We had no alternative, access to our chests being impossible as they were all locked up in the hold." Apparently the Quebec *Mercury's* comment that members of the Lanark emigration had arrived in remarkably good condition did not refer to the *David's* passengers.

In 1823 conditions in the south of Ireland were so bad that the governments of Great Britain and Upper Canada decided to assist the emigration of a small number—more as an experiment than with the expectation that it would relieve distress to any appreciable extent. Only 568 persons benefited by this first effort of the Hon. Peter Robinson, and they were all paupers or other persons whose removal from the country was a blessing to all concerned. For months they had been existing on a starvation diet of one meal a day of dry potatoes and unwholesome weeds, "until their very blood turned yellow." They settled in the midst of "backwoods" life on the Mississippi River, Upper Canada. Supplies were issued to them for twenty-one months, after which period they were able to provide for themselves. Their log houses were far superior to Irish cabins. By 1826 many were selling their surplus crops in Brockville. In 1825, 2024 Irish were similarly removed to Peterborough County, Upper Canada. This was the last North American emigration conducted by the government. There-

ASSISTED EMIGRATION

after state aid to civilians was indirect, and consisted of special terms of settlement. The same type of encouragement was given to half-pay army and navy officers and to pensioners. "Commutation money," consisting of the pension commuted and paid in a lump sum, or in instalments during settlement, aided these immigrants in a new land, but many of them were totally unfit for "backwoods" life and appear to have degenerated in Canada rather than progressed.

One philanthropist alone, Mr. Vere Foster, financed the emigration of 16,000 women to America, and it is said that although they agreed to refund a part of their passage money as soon as they were able, not one ever did. The child emigrations of 1835 and succeeding years were arranged by the Earl of Shaftesbury, Dr. Barnardo, Miss Rye,[1] and other humanitarians. Though not extensive at first, these efforts placed large numbers of apprentices in Canada in later years, and gave a start in life to many "street-urchins" and "girl-arabs." Colonization societies in various parts of the world were active in both the early and later periods. In December, 1825, 260 colonists, largely Scottish, reached Caracas, Venezuela, as a result of the propaganda and assistance of the Columbian Agriculturist Association; while the third shipload of 250 settlers to sail for the Rio de la Plata, Argentina, left Britain on the *Countess of Morley* early in 1826, and settled about 250 miles from Buenos Aires under the direction of the Rio de la Plata Agricultural Society. The former experiment failed, and its members, reduced to destitution, were aided by the British Government a year later to proceed to Galt, Upper Canada, by way of New York.

The experience gained in early assisted emigrations to North America produced general rules for the future. Probably A. C. Buchanan, the Emigration Agent at Quebec, who had made sixteen voyages to America, was best qualified to advise. He wrote in 1828 that those for whom state aid was essential were, in Ireland, "destitute labourers, ejected tenants and poor cotters, who are now found a clog to the consolidating of farms and improvement of estates, and whose better condition at home can never be contemplated"; and some unmarried females suitable for domestic service. In England those in greatest need were parish paupers and "females who may have strayed from the paths of virtue, and are now maintained in the different asylums throughout the kingdom."

[1] Miss Rye conducted over 1,600 young girls to Upper Canada. A short account of her work is given in *The Sunday at Home*, 1882, pp. 28-9.

(The latter were destined for Van Diemen's Land and New South Wales). From Scotland he would draw "poor Highlanders and other struggling labourers with large families."

Allowing two passengers for every three tons of a ship's register, Mr. Buchanan estimated with reference to a proposed Scottish emigration in the spring of 1827, that "in event of twelve hundred families going out this year it will require twelve ships carrying four hundred tons to convey them. . . . It will be necessary to get fast-sailing vessels, and long and roomy between decks, for the greater space in length the more berths you can put up." He also considered that owing to the uncertainty of the passage provisions for three months should be carried. He believed that the captain was better able to advise the sick than a doctor—who would be too sick himself: "The passage to British America is so short and healthy that little beyond cleanliness and purgatives is necessary. A surgeon might be carried where the number of passengers exceeded one hundred, although from personal experience I consider him unnecessary."[2] Concerning one voyage Mr. Buchanan noted that "only one adult died (of old age) and a few infants, although we had the small-pox on board; and I attribute their healthy state entirely to the diet, which was chiefly potatoes, stir-about made from the siftings of oatmeal, sowing or flummery made from the siftings of oatmeal, butter, eggs, and for some few a little bacon."

An English emigrant's rations were calculated at three pence a day higher than those of the Irish and Scotch. Buchanan considered "that £60 would be a satisfactory outlay for the removal of a family of five from the United Kingdom to British North America, providing them with the necessary implements, log house, and fifteen months' provisions." In fact, if the emigrant was not charged with the cost of surveying and other general expenses, £45 would be sufficient—a sum not quite double the cost of a year's maintenance by the parish. Such munificence was apparently anticipated with pleasure by "half-starved Irish paupers," for there was no doubt that "Pat and his wife Bridget will be amazed to have enough to eat, with a log-hut for shelter, his axe in his hand, and his fuel at his elbow." To aid in such a satisfactory consummation he suggested that "a few hundred old military tents, with some artificers' tools, saws, smith's bellows, ironmongery, etc., should accompany the emigrants; . . . and a supply of medicine necessary for forming a dispensary should be pro-

---

[2] Buchanan's reference to the Atlantic passage as "short and healthy" must be accepted in the light of the times, and in comparison with the voyage of from four to six months to Australia.

ASSISTED EMIGRATION

vided, and young doctors will be found who will gladly follow the settlement and look to the individuals for their pay."

The emigrations of 1832-1837 from the estates of the Earl of Egremont in Sussex were among the most successful of the semi-philanthropic type financed by large landowners. Under the Earl's patronage the Petworth Emigration Society was organized, and proceeded to make plans for settlement in Upper Canada. Finding the provisions of the Act of 1828 insufficient for the comfort of the passengers, the conductors planned in 1832 to carry 76 persons less than the legal maximum for the ship. In other respects, too, the *Lord Melville*, of 425 tons, was much better than the average emigrant vessel, for she is described as "A-1 coppered and copper-fastened and sheathed, with 7 feet height between decks and extra ventilating scuttles." The ship sailed from Portsmouth to Montreal direct, and the emigrants were in charge of a superintendent and his wife, who conducted them to York. The outfit of clothing recommended by the Society as a minimum was as follows:

"A fur cap
A warm great coat
A flushing jacket & trowsers
A canvas frock and two pairs of trowsers
A duck frock and trowsers
    Women in the same proportion, especially a warm cloak."

Two Jersey frocks
Four shirts
Four pairs of stockings
Three pairs of shoes
A bible and prayer book

Still less than three-fourths the legal maximum of passengers were carried on later ships sent out by the Petworth Society, and better berthing, more suitable supplies of food, and other improvements were advertised. On April 25, 1833, the *England* sailed with 196 steerage passengers, 6 infants, and 1 cabin passenger. In Petworth there was no small stir as the project got under way, for an effort was made to patronise home industry. Shoemakers who had been doing relief work on the highways were set at their trade to provide at cost the shoes necessary. Shopkeepers sold clothes made by "poor females," and the business of the town was increased generally, for people from nearby parishes also patronised these tradesmen to obtain articles recognized as much better than "shop goods."

Lord Egremont paid the whole of the passage money (£10) for persons in districts where he owned all or most of the land, and other landowners co-operated with him in localities where the proprietorship was divided. The cost of outfitting the emigrants, for which £5 was allowed, was met from the poor rates. Counting two children under 14 as equal to one adult as to cost of passage, and allowing £3 10s. for the outfitting of each, a family of five was set down in York, Upper Canada, at a total cost of £55 10s. A single man could be outfitted and transported to York for £15, or as little as one-fourth more than a year's expense at home—estimated at £12 in the case of highway relief work, or £9 2s. in the poorhouse. It was, therefore, good business on the part of Lord Egremont and the parishes to be so easily rid of large numbers of the poverty-stricken.

Each Petworth emigrant was allowed to select his own equipment to the amount of £5; and if he did not expend it all, the balance was placed to his credit. To such amounts were added gifts and small sums "from the sale of his few goods." The more prudent handed all cash over to the superintendent, who issued the emigrant a bill on the Commissioners of the Canada Company at York. One man had £65 to his credit; but the majority of the bills were for smaller amounts, from £1 upwards. The Society similarly provided transportation from Petworth to Portsmouth.

The provisions supplied to those who sailed on the *England* were comparatively luxurious. The food and water supply was sufficient for 63 days. One gallon of water per day was allowed to each passenger—nearly double the statutory allowance. The weekly issue of food comprised 7 lbs. meat, 7 lbs. flour or bread, 1 lb. oatmeal, 2 oz. tea or ¼ lb. coffee, 1 lb. sugar; and, to those over 14 years of age, ½ pt. brandy diluted with three parts water. Those who chose might reduce the amount of meat and flour by 2 lbs., and receive 10 lbs. potatoes, 1 lb. cheese, ½ lb. butter and ½ lb. raisins. To either selection were added "onions, soap, tobacco, vinegar, etc., in such quantities as may be directed by the superintendent"; while porter and other remedies were dispensed by the surgeon, who had a well-supplied medicine chest. Finding that so many objected to the highly salted Irish beef usually issued to sailors and emigrants, the superintendent substituted some salted the previous week in Portsmouth; and to this was added bacon and pork cured at Petworth, as well as a further supply "of the very best quality that could be procured" from Ireland.

An account of a later Petworth emigration on the *British Tar* in 1834 indicates how much was done to alleviate the inevitable discomforts and sufferings of the ocean passage. Separate sections were allotted to men, women, and couples, and each had a separate means of access, by the fore, main, and after hatchways. A separate water-closet was located near each to obviate the necessity of going on deck in bad weather or during sickness. These arrangements were considered by the superintendent, James M. Brydone, to be "excellent, and such as ought to be adopted on board every ship carrying emigrants." Numerous entries in Mr. Brydone's journal illustrate personal touches usually lacking on emigrant ships:

"Sunday, April 26, 1834—The ship rolling much, the cooking coppers were upset before dinner, without injury than that of dirtying the beef and frightening John Barton, the cook, whose post was immediately filled by Job Hodge.

"May 15th.—A remarkably fine day; the people enjoying themselves dancing on deck to the violin. Mrs. Ditton, who was confined on the 28th ultimo, (seventeen days since), and her husband, the most actively engaged in this exercise."

Among the regulations were those relating to the time of issue of supplies, the detailing of persons "to draw the provisions and water," to assist the cook, to act as heads of messes in the various sections of the ship, to clean the berths and deck of the ship, and to act as inspectors of these duties. A considerable amount of liquor had apparently to be dispensed, largely to the officers and the crew, to promote good feeling:

"I found no difficulty in procuring such services as were required without further extra allowance than a bottle of brandy weekly to Mr. Upton, Gamblin, Greene, and Martin—a bottle of rum weekly to the cook and the men who assisted him, for the days only on which no grog was issued; and a bottle of rum weekly, which I thought it advisable to give to the ship's company in order to promote a good understanding between them and the people—in the latter object I fully succeeded. All were comfortable and contented."

While but little of an unusual nature occurred during the voyage to disturb the superintendent and his emigrants, they were not to reach Quebec without some very annoying experiences. There were a number of light cases of measles when the *British Tar* reached Grosse Isle, and the vessel was detained for more than a week.

"Mortified, however, as I was by these occurrences," writes Mr. Brydone, "I soon found myself placed under circumstances still more vexatious by the sudden changing of wind from fair to foul at Quebec; here I was under the necessity of engaging a steamboat to tow the ship to Montreal; on arriving at which city, a charge of £21:7:6, as half-passage money from Quebec, in addition to £53:7:10 for towage, was preferred against me, which, notwithstanding every remonstrance, I was obliged to pay."

Mr. Brydone used excellent judgment in transporting the immigrants to the interior. Profiting by the misfortunes of previous emigrations, he "engaged of Mr. Cushing a new boat to carry us to Kingston at 12s. 6d. per passage, including one cwt. of provisions. This vessel was different from the Durham boats used on former occasions, of which there has been so much complaint: she was entirely decked over, had a good commodious cabin with fixed bed places, in which were accommodated the principal part of the women, girls, and children."[8]

Instead of such satisfactory management of the last stages of their journey, there were other methods of setting the assisted emigrant down in the new land. In the 1820's, before the movement to America assumed the proportions of an epidemic, numerous laborers from the eastern part of Sussex were given upon landing at Quebec "two pounds in money to the adults, and one pound for each child." Those sent out in 1830 from the Parish of Corsley, Wiltshire, through the aid of the Marquis of Bath, were similarly provided with thirty shillings, with which they were expected to negotiate their passage up the St. Lawrence to Upper Canada. Large numbers of others, however, particularly in later years, were merely dumped off the ship, destitute and ignorant of the means of proceeding further, their plight aggravated by the memory of unredeemed promises. Lord Darnley's agent in Ireland shipped some four or five hundred to Quebec on the *Panope*, with provisions for 23 days; and as if this were not enough fraud, the 50-day passage was fated to end in their dismissal from the ship entirely penniless—though they had been promised £1 each to aid them to push into the interior. Like many another scheme to get rid of the paupers, "it was all a hoax!"

Toward the middle of the century particularly many emigration societies in England and Scotland took the form of associations to relieve tenants or small landowners by assisting in their removal. In the western part of Scotland was the Emigration Union of Ceres, Scoomie, Kennoway, Cults and Largon, which aided many of its members by chartering ships and purchasing supplies. The funds of the Highland and Island Emigration Society were raised by private subscription, a donation of £3 enabling the contributor to experience "the gratification of placing one suffering fellow-Christian beyond the risk of want." This society financed the emigration of several thousand in 1852 and 1853. The appearance of some 800 of them as they embarked upon the *Hercules* and waited for a favorable breeze to carry them away is described by an eye-witness:

[8] This composite account of the Sussex emigrations is based upon three contemporary pamphlets: (1) *Sussex Emigrants for Canada;* (2) *Emigration. A Letter to a Member of Parliament;* and (3) Brydone's *Narrative of a Voyage of a Party of Emigrants Sent out from Sussex by the Petworth Emigration Committee.*

ASSISTED EMIGRATION

"The young women came first—some looking cheerfully around, some sad, and some in tears; but all took pains to adjust their shawls and handkerchiefs, their tresses or their caps, as they made their appearance before strangers. The married women and their children followed, the latter skipping and dancing on the broad deck; the former so completely absorbed by the care of their children, and the fear of losing them in the crowd, that they did not seem to be conscious of where they were, or what had brought them there. The men looked dark and stern, like men about to confront danger and not likely to shrink from the encounter, but relaxed into a smile at the first kind word. Next day they were all cheerful and happy, spoke with gratitude of the pains that had been taken to provide for their comfort, and expressed astonishment at the extent and completeness of the arrangements, which greatly exceeded anything they had imagined to be possible. On the third day they all looked quite at home, some engaged in reading, some in writing to the friends they had left. The young women were working with their needles, or knitting; the children playing together."

In England trade unions extended assistance, many of the largest setting aside a considerable part of their funds to finance the emigration of unemployed members to America or Australia. Some organizations of artisans worked out ingenious, if impractical, schemes. With the seductive announcement, "FARMS! FARMS!! FARMS FOR ALL!!!," the Potters' Emigration Society of Staffordshire inaugurated a peculiar combination of subscription and lottery to enable the settlement of some of its members in Wisconsin. The contributory element consisted of payments of sixpence a week to the funds of the Society, from which the emigration of the lucky was financed within 12 months of their initial payment; or if they were not fortunate in the ballot, single men might claim the benefits of the scheme after having paid in eight years' subscriptions. The Society offered to meet the expenses of the trip for the member and his family, and to provide a 20-acre farm, a log house, 5 acres broken up and fenced, 2 acres sown in Indian corn and 3 in wheat, and two years' credit for provisions sufficient for the first twelve months, the expenses so incurred to be refunded within ten years. The prospectus closed with "Land cleared! soil rich! climate good! A Home in the West! —who'll follow?" A number of similar schemes in which lottery was the most prominent feature were declared illegal, but others died a natural death after effecting the settlement or disappointing the hopes of their members.

In America, too, numerous individuals and societies organized attractive plans of land settlement. One type was the so-called instruction at a high price of one or more "remittance men," who were speedily disillusioned as they became acquainted with the mysteries of backwoods life;[4] while at the other extreme were extensive schemes of colonization by such corporations as the Canada Company. Among smaller efforts was that of Robert Gourlay, prominent Reformer of Upper Canada, whose scheme smacks of the visionary Robert Owen. He offered to settle a maximum of fifty men on his land in the Township of Dereham, Canada West. Contrary to all other advice, he suggested October as the best time to leave Scotland, and enthusiastically described the pleasures of settling on wild land in winter—assuming that those who accepted his offer had saved sufficient money for their maintenance until the next harvest; for if they had not, let them "stay where they are and improve their habits." Thirty of his men were to have land, while the other twenty were initially to be laborers. Mr. Gourlay agreed to have log houses ready, 32 feet by 18, with a cellar beneath. The head of a family paid for his house at the time of occupation and purchased his land three years later. But there were to be several girls, aged 10 to 13 preferably, in each household; and he hoped that all members of his colony would be well educated, carrying Bibles for "the best advice and direction," Shakespeare's Plays for "a knowledge of the world," and the Works of Robert Burns to keep Scotland in warm remembrance. His closing paragraph sums up the advantages of the scheme:

"By my plan, each little community of five men, a wife and four girls, will be strong and efficient from the outset. Should sickness invade the dwelling, there will be abundant aid and sympathy. The girls will have the protection of brothers; be exposed to no risk, to no vice; and by the end of three years will be well trained in all the industrial habits of the country. They may, if they choose, return to Scotland; and if they remain they will be sure of husbands. Huzza for the lassies of Scotland! the best in the world!"

Removing the "redundant population," or "shovelling out the paupers," as it was sometimes less technically expressed, met with the determined opposition of men like William Cobbett, who bluntly observed that unbearable taxation caused poverty, and that for this crime Englishmen were now being transported overseas. He pointed out that high taxes were the result of excessive debt, innumerable pensioners and place-men, and no end of clergy, no-

[4] The life of a "remittance man" of the later period is described in [De la Fosse], *English Bloods*. There were, on the other hand, many young men who were initiated into Canadian life by more capable and sympathetic hands. The *Cobourg Star* of April 25, 1855, describes the "new system of colonization" under which Major Samuel Strickland of Peterborough County brought out from England "young gentlemen of good means whom he instructs in the mysteries of Canadian farming, and who, as soon as they are capable of taking charge for themselves, purchase land and become valuable settlers."

ASSISTED EMIGRATION

bility, landed aristocracy and legislators, who, together with sundry bankers "and other gamblers," were living luxuriously upon the labour of the poorer classes, who were themselves producing (but not receiving) "five or ten times as much food and raiment" as their families required.[5] Arguments of this type made little impression at the time, and pauper emigrations from England reached their peak in 1831-1832, when numerous parishes in some ten counties were raising money for the purpose. A shipload from County Meath, Ireland, in the year of the ship fever plague, 1847, is described as a

"motley crowd—of all ages, from the infant to the feeble grandsire and withered crone.... Many of them appeared to me to be quite unfit to undergo the hardship of a long voyage; but they were inspected and passed by a doctor, although the captain, as he informed me, protested against taking some of them. One old man was so infirm that he seemed to me to be in the last stages of consumption."

These poor people, most of whom had never seen the sea or a ship, were sent out at the expense of their landlord, "without any knowledge of the country to which they were going, or means of livelihood except the labor of the father of each family.... Moreover, they had a settled conviction that the voyage was going to last exactly three weeks." A number of them did not survive the terrifying passage of over two months, but were dropped overboard from time to time as they expired from the ravages of fever; and the others reached America more dead than alive.

Referring to those who arrived a few years earlier, Dr. Poole, Inspecting Physician at Grosse Isle, stated that thousands reached the new land emaciated through lack of food and water, diseased from dirt and bad ventilation; and that, besides many who had died, from twenty to ninety on each vessel had to be admitted to hospital because of contagious fevers. Another authority expresses an opinion which may be taken as representative of the reaction of the countries to which these unfortunate people were shipped:

[5] It is of course quite obvious that such accusations as Cobbett's were much more than Radical "hot air." The Earl of Oxford and Asquith estimated (*Memories and Reflections*, I 295-7) that prior to the Great Reform Bill of 1832, a sum exceeding £1,100,000 annually was distributed among sinecurists and pensioners of one kind and another, not one of whom was an actual worker in the Civil Service. One sinecure in the gift of the judiciary provided the princely return of £9,600 annually, while Charles Greville, the diarist, not only received a high salary as Clerk of the Privy Council, but also held the sinecure of "Secretary and Clerk of Enrolments in Jamaica," which added £3000 a year to his income. The whole system of such emoluments was gradually brought to an end, but not without many protests, and much intensive wire-pulling on the part of those affected. There were in addition all sorts of allowances and pensions for actual service, as well as livings and preferments in the Church Establishment for which, at least from the modern point of view, the incumbent was highly paid for the most nominal of duties. A curious publication of 1831 is *The Extraordinary Black Book*, purporting to be "a complete view of the Expenditure, Patronage, Influences and Abuses of the Government," and containing "Lists of Pluralists, Placemen, Pensioners and Sinecurists."

"Emigrants sent out by parishes are very generally inferior, both morally and physically, to those who have found their way out. The parishes have sent out persons far too old to gain their livelihood by work, and often of drunken and improvident habits. These emigrants have neither benefited themselves or the country; and this is very natural, for, judging from the class sent out, the object must have been the getting rid of them, and not either the benefit of themselves or the colony. An instance occurred very recently which illustrates this subject. A respectable settler in the Eastern Townships lately returned from England in a vessel on board of which there were 136 pauper passengers sent out at the expense of their parishes;'and out of the whole number he could select only two that he was desirous of inducing to settle in the Eastern Townships. The conduct of the others, both male and female, was so bad that he expressed his wish that they might proceed to the Upper Province instead of settling in this district. He alluded principally to gross drunkenness and unchastity."

Even if such charges were sometimes justified, it would seem that the degradation of these people was largely owing to their existence upon the fringe of civilization in the Old Land, and to the miseries of the Atlantic passage which they had barely survived. Such considerations, however, could not be expected to weigh heavily in America where they had to be assimilated. Opposition in the British Provinces and the United States rose from time to time against such immigrants,[6] but the movement died out only when the passing of years brought an amelioration of the conditions which had caused it. At times most of them were directed towards Australia, particularly during and following the years of the rebellions in Upper and Lower Canada. The continued distress among the laboring and agricultural classes of England in the early 'forties led to the emigration at parish and state expense of several thousand persons in 1844. These, while including a considerable number of paupers, were described as mainly small tradesmen and cottagers, and they were quite carefully selected.

Although in this instance they were sent to Australia, the details of the migration may be taken as typical of the later period—always omitting Irish emigrants. The ships were provided with better steerage accommodations than were usual in earlier vessels, and in place of the overcrowded conditions of the early eighteen-thirties the ratio of passengers to tonnage was only about one to three. For each emigrant accepted, a deposit of £1 was to be made either by himself or the parish; and for children the amount was 10 shillings. This was used to provide bedding—a new mattress,

[6] In the "Declaration of the Reformers of the City of Toronto to their Fellow-Reformers in Upper Canada" (1837), for example, one of the complaints is that "a law has been passed enabling magistrates to build and support workhouses for the refuge of the paupers invited by Sir Francis [Bond Head] from the parishes of Great Britain, thus unjustly and wickedly laying the foundation of a system which must result in taxation, pestilence and famine."

ASSISTED EMIGRATION

bolsters, blankets, and coverlids; a small box, fifteen inches square, for clothes; a knife and fork, two spoons, a metal plate, and a drinking mug; all of which became the emigrant's property upon arrival at the destination. They also had the free use of water-beakers and many other necessary culinary articles. Each male had to provide himself with two suits of outside clothing, two pairs of strong boots or shoes, eight shirts, six pairs of worsted stockings, and three towels; while each female, besides other garments, must possess a cloak and a bonnet. The rations served out daily to the emigrants were paid for either by themselves or the parish, and when totalled for a week comprised the following amounts, children receiving one-half: 4 ⅔ lbs. bread, 1 lb. beef, 1½ lbs. pork, 1 lb. preserved meat, 1 ¾ lbs. flour, ½ lb. raisins, 6 ozs. suet, 1 pint peas, ½ lb. rice, ½ lb. preserved potatoes, 1 oz. tea, 1½ ozs. roasted coffee, ¾ lb. sugar, 6 ozs. butter, 5 gallons and 1 quart of water, 1 gill pickled cabbage, ½ gill vinegar, and 2 ozs. salt. From contemporary accounts of this undertaking it would appear that the experience gained in earlier assisted emigrations had borne fruit, and that the arrangements for the four months' passage were not only thorough but exceedingly liberal.

CHAPTER IV

UNASSISTED EMIGRATION—PREPARING FOR A NEW LAND

"All pretty-looking tents, camp-beds, sets of fishing tackle, and articles of hardware of fanciful invention are just so many traps to catch your stray sovereigns, which you will find far ampler use for when you come out."
Rev. A. W. H. Rose

In 1850, when 257,663 persons left the United Kingdom for America, it was estimated that four-fifths were Irish, chiefly peasants and laborers. Many of them, a contemporary publication suggests, had been "hoarding and saving for years, and living in rags and squalor, in order to amass sufficient money to carry themselves and families across the Atlantic, and to beg their way to the Western States, where they may 'squat' or purchase lands"; but large numbers were still more destitute, and were able to emigrate only because of the generosity of compatriots in the United States and in Canada. Through Liverpool houses alone, almost a million sterling, in drafts varying from £2 to £10 each, was annually sent to enable poor persons in Ireland to emigrate. Similar aid was provided by English and Scottish settlers for their friends in the Old Land. A short item in the *Illustrated London News* tells a story of Scottish emigration through such assistance:

"The spring fleet has just sailed for Canada from the north-east coast of Scotland, carrying about 1,500 passengers. They are chiefly agricultural labourers, and for the most part young and newly-married people. Large sums of money continue to be received from settlers in Upper Canada, who had previously gone out, chiefly from Aberdeenshire; and there is every prospect that, before many years, few agricultural labourers will be left at home; but, when we state that the highest rates do not exceed £20 a year, it will not be thought surprising."

It is estimated that well over one-half of the emigrants to America in some years had their passage paid in whole or in part by friends. The peak year for such assistance was 1854, when a total of £1,730,000 was received in the United Kingdom; and in addition to this, the passage of many thousands was paid in New York. A despicable trade was carried on by some of the more unscrupulous captains and their confederates on the American side. Very poor people frequently mortgaged themselves to captain or ship-

PREPARING FOR A NEW LAND   35

owner for the amount of their passage and that of their families, and then worked off their indebtedness in America, and possibly on board ship as well. An early guidebook, in referring to this iniquitous system of slavery, states that "immense numbers (from Ireland particularly) emigrate on these conditions. When the ship in which he sails arrives at her destined port, the captain turns him over to someone who requires his services, who redeems him, paying the captain his demand, and paying himself out of the labour of the poor emigrant who is bound to work for the man who redeemed him until he cancels the debt." While a superficial glance at this system might suggest that it facilitated the emigration of the poverty-stricken, deeper consideration shows its abuses, thousands of men being virtually slaves for a period often five times as long as it would have taken to earn the passage money anywhere else in the labor market. One of them compared himself to "Joseph the Israelite; for he had been entrapped, and indented to work several years for his passage; and he considered himself little better than a slave till his term was expired."

The preparations of emigrants who arranged their own voyage were naturally much greater than those necessary for assisted or conducted passages; and the emigration literature of the day contains directions and warnings of every imaginable kind. To leave home was not a matter of great difficulty to many people; they had little or no property to dispose of—a cow, a pig, a few tools and furnishings, perhaps. But, though most of them had very little money, careful plans were necessary if misfortune and extreme misery were to be avoided.

The unmarried emigrant found the undertaking much less complicated than the family man; though, since there were many more males than females in America, it was a distinct asset for a man to control the labor of one, and A. C. Buchanan advises "every young farmer or labourer going out (who can pay for the passage of two) to take an active young wife with him"; or, as another writer puts it,

"Unmarried Women, who have no fortunes, and are *active, and industrious, without much pride or vanity,* and who can relish a *quiet* and *retired* life, should emigrate to the Canadas, in any of the country parts of which they will not reside long before they can have an opportunity of being well married, such being very scarce, and considered in that country a fortune in themselves."

Another emigration tract advises men how to manage refractory women, suggesting that, if no other argument would induce one's wife to undertake the great adventure, "the ultimate, 'I'll go without you', if persevered in without any wavering, seldom fails."

Thousands took with them nothing but the rags on their backs. At the other extreme were many who not only took to America their personal possessions but even invested all their savings in woolen cloth and other goods which they planned to sell—a practice which drew from a guidebook the statement that "no better evidence can be adduced as to the prevailing ignorance in the minds of many in Great Britain regarding this country." Even if the goods were smuggled in duty free, the chances of selling to advantage any of them, except books, would be almost negligible. Books, this writer maintained, "will always sell for double what they cost in the mother country, while the purchaser has had the use of them into the bargain." In many instances baggage proved no end of trouble and worry and never reached its destination. Probably S. S. Hill's directions on this point were the most sensible:

"Some books recommend you to take a great variety of articles; but if the emigrant go to Upper Canada he will find the difficulties of transport after landing so tedious that, in general, it would be better to turn into money everything at all cumbersome that belongs to him, even at a considerable loss; but should he have made choice of either of the lower Provinces, he had better make no sacrifice, nor sell any useful article, unless the carriage to the port of embarkation should be an object. Cumbersome articles of mere ornament should, however, be always disposed."

Those with money had to be very careful, for there was no place of safety on board ship in which it might be deposited. Emigrants to the United States frequently changed their cash into American dollars—often losing a good deal by the exchange. Those going to Canada might take English guineas or sovereigns, Spanish dollars, or bills upon some house in Quebec or Montreal. Francis Thomas describes in his diary that on the *Hebe* there were robberies "almost every night in a sort of a wholesale way," and several members of the crew were in this instance suspected to be the culprits. Even if he arrived safely in America with his sovereigns, the emigrant had still to run the gauntlet of dishonest brokers, for one of the "rackets" of the day was money-changing:

"Anyone intending to emigrate, tell them to bring with them new sovereigns, as the exchange brokers weigh them. Sell them at New York. I got 4 dollars 84 cents, the rate of exchange being there high. Tell them to try several brokers, and find out the highest price, and haggle with them; keep a sharp lookout, for the one I dealt with was the greatest rogue I ever met with; it was with difficulty I could keep him from cheating me."

Illustrated London News

THE PRIEST'S BLESSING

Irish emigrants receive their last religious consolation in the homeland.

ON THE WAY TO THE SEAPORT

Emigrants from Buckinghamshire and Northampton proceeding to London.

PREPARING FOR A NEW LAND

In general, emigrants of the early period carried more funds than those of later days. In 1802 four vessels sailed from the west coast of Scotland with 1400 emigrants, who had with them a total of no less than £100,000 sterling. But even in the years when thousands were destitute, numerous colonists were in affluent circumstances. On the *Westmoreland* in 1834 were four English families with from 700 to 1000 sovereigns each, and "scarcely one that had not 100"; while among some 250 Irish emigrants who were drowned when the brig *James* was wrecked in the same year were several well-to-do passengers who carried with them from £2000 to £3000 in gold.

Many writers, however, suggested a large assortment of household goods and many other articles which might be taken along with advantage. These included such heavy furnishings as beds and tables, and also tools and implements, rifles, and fishing tackle. One authority suggests a particularly formidable array of heavy farm implements:

"Farmers or laborers going to America should carry with them, if their means will admit, as much clothing, bedding and linen as may be necessary for four or five years; some leather, one or two sets of light cart harness, two or three spades or shovels, scythes, sickles, hoes, ploughs, traces, the ironwork of a plough and harrow of the common kind used in Scotland; the cast machinery for a corn fan, cooking utensils, a few door hinges, and a small assortment of nails."

The cost of carrying such a collection of hardware from Quebec or New York was staggering, even if there was no thievery by the bateaumen of the St. Lawrence—if the settler were unfortunate enough to have come by that laborious route. Heavy articles of furniture such as bedsteads and tables could be bought in the settled parts of the United States for about one-half what they cost in Britain; while in the "backwoods" of America a settler usually contrived to make his own. Most authorities pointed out the futility of transporting them to the new land. Martin Doyle's *Hints on Emigration to Upper Canada*, described by a contemporary reviewer as "the best manual on the subject," suggests, with reference to a settler's bed, that "the bark of a bass tree, woven or laced across his bedstead, will support his mattress, and that mattrass need consist of nothing more expensive than the boughs of the spruce fir, or dry beach leaves; a buffalo skin will answer for quilts and blankets." To construct such beds, says Doyle, "a man need not serve a seven years' apprenticeship." The same writer knew of an immigrant near York, whose three sons had learned to use the lathe in Ireland. In a very short time,

"They made all the wooden furniture of his new frame house—sofas, and tables of every kind—from a lady's work table (with roped pillars of black walnut), to the kitchen table; chimney pieces, painted, polished and varnished; bedsteads, carts, waggons and wheelbarrows. . . . They had taken out a good box of tools with them, the use of which saved them large sums of money; and when I last heard from them they were putting up a frame barn 65 feet in length, 35 in breadth, and 20 feet in height, with an ice-house under it, and a store-house for roots, to preserve them from frost."

Artisans bound for the United States did not need to take tools, but in the earlier period they were frequently expensive, if not unobtainable, in the British Provinces. Many settlers considered English spades and other implements superior to those in America. On the other hand, axes from the Old Land were described by a backwoodsman as "useless for chopping down trees"; and he adds that "they serve when brought here for chopping up meat, and are therefore useful in the kitchen." J. Hunt of Nelson Township, Upper Canada, suggested in 1830 that "hooks, hatchets, scythes, reaping-hooks and fire-irons" be brought out. A bricklayer wrote his father that he might have earned many dollars more if he had had a "plaistering trowel," while another workman asks his brother to bring "a good set of carpenter's tools, picks, prongs, door hinges, hooks, a good hayknife, rings, wedges. Tell Rhoda and Tabitha to bring me a good hay-cutting knife, and tell brother Nathan or Noah to send me the iron of the lathe." Timothy Trussler requested that "if Thomas West comes I wish he would bring me ½ doz. sacks, ½ doz. Birmingham reap hooks, a prong that will answer for a pitch prong or barn & a hog killing knife & I will pay him."

Fifteen or twenty years later manufacturing had advanced considerably in the Canadas, and it was unnecessary to bring out agricultural implements, furniture, and most other heavy articles. The Rev. A. W. H. Rose, in the late 1840's, advised farmers to bring along a "Cleveland bay stallion and brood mares," or "a good Durham bull and cows"; but that unless they were of the best breeds they might better be left at home, for there was "an abundance of mixed blood in the country already." Even more impracticable was the advice of a resident of Prince Edward Island, that "an entire Horse of the Suffolk Punch Breed, with lively action, would prove a great acquisition, and pay the Importer well. . . . As the Prince Edward Islanders may find it possible to breed for exportation, and as mules sell at considerable prices in the West Indies, any person importing one or more Spanish or Italian male asses, not less than fourteen hands high, would render the Colony a great benefit." The few who found it possible to take out stock with them were well advised, of course, to have all animals fully insured.

Among miscellaneous heavy articles which Cattermole recommended emigrants to take with them were books and clocks. The days of Sam Slick, the Yankee clockmaker, are called to mind as we read his advice to take "an eight-day clock without case or dials, for the mere movement would cost £10 in any part of Canada, the whole country being over-run with wooden clocks which sell as high as £5." Some requests were for personal requirements—a bonnet, a muslin dress, "a few ballads for the boys, as they wish to learn to sing." William Cooper wrote: "Dear Father, I should like to have a malt mill and a few pounds of thread, and above all things a Newfoundland Dog for myself, and take this letter to Merston to Philips father and tell him to be sure to bring him a dog to catch the Dear." George Scott was not nearly so modest, suggesting to his parents that "if Steadman should come out I wish he would be so kind as to fetch me a wife out with him."

Concerning clothes, advice varied from the inclusion of furs to the optimistic suggestion that shoes and stockings might almost be dispensed with, since most of the rural inhabitants went barefoot in the summer months *by choice*! When the Rev. Mr. Rose left for America he thought it was "carrying coals to Newcastle to bring fur robes to a fur country"; but he learned on arrival that the best furs were exported to London, from which they had to be reimported into Canada. Heavy clothes were generally commended as among the most useful things that an emigrant could bring with him. Robert Mudie observed that

"as the settlers must scramble about in all weathers, hot and cold, wet and dry, stout flannels and coarse cloths of the twilled kinds with thick threads which are not easily torn are by far the best. Emigrants must not mind fashion; the best coat and breeches are those that can come farthest through the brush with fewest holes in them; and probably there is not a better article for the purpose than Scotch blanket, or what is in that country called plaiding."

Martin Doyle advised the inclusion of "good warm frieze coats and jackets and worsted stockings and mittens for the winter; linen trowsers and jacket for the summer, as many linen shirts as you can afford to take out (linen being dear in Canada), and a short flannel shirt to be worn next to the skin both in summer and winter,"—to prevent ague in summer by absorbing perspiration. A. C. Buchanan reported that but few clothes were needed in America during six months of the year—"only a coarse shirt and linen trowsers," and the usual straw hat; while for winter, in addition to linen shirts and woolen stockings, moccasins and a fur or Scotch woolen cap could be purchased cheaply. Another writer suggested that "gentlemen" emigrants would do well to take out "boots and shoes cut out but not sewn," for English leather was the best; but owing to the quickness with which thread rots, it was customary in Canada to use pegs in making boots.

Evans' *Guide*, after naming the usual necessities, lists fowling-pieces and fishing tackle; and, according to another writer, gentlemen might carry out "a favourite pianoforte" for the ladies; while it would be "a positive advantage" to bring along "curtains, carpets, plate, glass and crockery, and especially bed and table linen and blanketing," for such things were frequently dear and of poor quality in Canada. Some of the more cultured colonists might heed his advice that, "if you are musical, a little good music is always desirable, especially sacred music well set"; and the same writer, a Church of England clergyman, piously hoped many would bring out

"religious and loyal prints—coloured Scriptural subjects with texts attached, home scenery of school and village churches. Portraits of Her Majesty, Prince Albert and the royal children, Wellington and Nelson, views of Windsor Castle, the House of Parliament, our cathedrals, our wooden walls, and such like, are greatly wanted to be largely disseminated in Canada, to supplant, as far as possible, the influx of tawdry sheets pourtraying 'The Signing of the Declaration of Independence,' portraits of Washington and General Taylor, the Capitol, the Mexican battles,"—

and others of the kind, which he considered "anything but calculated to instil sentiments of either religion or loyalty into the minds of the rising youth and backwoods population of Canada." In general, however, Mr. Rose advised emigrants to beware of advertisers of all sorts of settlers' supplies.

One homesick settler wrote:

"NO IDLE MEN ARE WANTED. They are a nuisance and a curse everywhere, and especially in a new community. Take out garden seeds, bulbs, suckers of filberts, nuts, etc. . . . I think goats would answer well, and our common tame rabbits (not those lop-eared enormities) would soon be acclimatized. No ponderous implements should be taken. Guns and fishing-rods may. Persons who have setters, spaniels and terriers would do well to take them. There are lots of vermin whose skins are valuable. Some, I hope, will take out ferrets, and many our old-country song-birds, to recall the memories of home. I cannot tell you how deeply I was moved by, and how long I listened to the incessant song of English skylarks[1] hung out in a sunny spot, weeks before ice and snow had disappeared."

[1] A pleasing story, "The Emigrant's Lark," recounts the affection which Henry Patterson and his wife, immigrants of 1834, lavished upon the skylark which they had brought out with them from the Old Land. See Sir Francis Bond Head's *The Emigrant*, Chapter V.

PREPARING FOR A NEW LAND

Another lonesome settler suggested that emigrants bring out "a few thousands of quickwood, or a bushel or two of haws; for nothing, in my belief, is so much wanting as good and neat thorn hedges. . . . I am tired of these snake fences."

Perhaps "Tiger" Dunlop's *Statistical Sketches of Upper Canada* was intended especially for the information of colonists rather than emigrants, for he filled twenty-one pages in describing the rare hunting, gaming, hawking, and fishing available in America. The best take-off on such advice for emigrants is that of James Inches:

"Bring out a great many things to be useful to you when there; among others a good bull, a good stallion, dogs for household use, as one-half of the day is often spent in hunting up and driving home the oxen; taking care, also, not to forget fishing and shooting tackle. . . . He then gives you 22 pages upon 'field sports,' and five upon comfort in travelling and recipes for 'cookery,'—thus occupying 27 out the whole 120 pages with these subjects so very important to the stranger! . . . With these little accompaniments—plenty of all kinds of clothing (not forgetting shooting jackets)—cooking utensils—implements of husbandry—barrels of books—a sufficient quantity of Anderson's pills—Epsom salts—and, though last not least, good Jamaica or Cogniac—he recommends to you the Canada Company's Huron Tract, and sets you down altogether with very little trouble, about 700 miles to the westward of Quebec. . . . This book, although written with much ingenuity, and in some instances very amusing, is evidently a piece of as complete quackery as any of the 'puffs' which have been written upon Upper Canada."

Well-to-do colonists were usually advised to take out servants with them, those available in democratic North America being noted for an objectionable spirit of independence. William Cobbett was of the opposite opinion; though, after all, his advice that one's servants should be left at home was certainly not a source of worry to many emigrants. His precepts on liquor-drinking were, on the other hand, worth following:

"Above all things do not take your decanters or your cork-screw. . . . You are going to a country where you may literally swim in whiskey or gin, and pretty nearly in brandy or rum. But resolve never to taste either. Drinking is the great vice of the country."

Besides a few ordinary drugs as remedies for seasickness or other common ailments, others recommended for use after settlement included "Epsom salts, calcined magnesia, castor oil, cream of tartar, ipecacuanha (commonly called hippo), and tartarised antimony (called tartar emetic)." Another item of advice of which the utility would one day be apparent was that emigrants take "copies of marriage or baptismal registers or any other certificates or papers likely to be useful, the whole to be inclosed in a small tin case." To this was added the somewhat gratuitous suggestion that "it is also a matter of great importance that emigrants should take with them a good character (if they should have the happiness to possess one), fairly written and well attested."

There were thousands, of course, to whom these recommendations meant nothing—even assuming that they could read and were in contact with advice. Contemporary descriptions of actual starvation and of the destitute appearance of many show that their worldly possessions comprised no more than a mind warped and embittered, in a body diseased and debased by unparalleled suffering.

CHAPTER V

Proceeding to the Seaport

"Oh, it is a sore and a heart-sinking thing to lose sight of the farm where we were born—the village at which we went to school—the woods and glens in which we played—the kirk in which we were christened and where we first heard in public the Word of God, and under whose shadow is the turf that covers the mouldering bones of our parents—blessed be their memory. But for their pious instruction I should have sunk in despair."

Robert Stevenson

In 1773 when James Boswell visited the Hebrides, he was asked to participate in a dance the *motif* of which was the infectious nature of emigration. He was informed that, while the emotional inhabitants of these isles had formerly been greatly agitated at the departure of their friends, they had come to consider the occasion no time for tears. Boswell describes as follows the dance and its interpretation:

"We performed, with much activity, a dance which, I suppose, the emigration from Skye has occasioned. They call it 'America.' Each of the couples, after the common involutions and evolutions, successively whirls around in a circle till all are in motion; and the dance seems intended to show how emigration catches, till a whole neighbourhood is set afloat. Mrs. M'Kinnon told me that last year, when a ship sailed from Portree for America, the people on shore were almost distracted when they saw their relations go off; they lay down on the ground, tumbled, and tore the grass with their teeth. This year there was not a tear shed. The people on the shore seemed to think that they would soon follow. This indifference is a mortal sign for the country."

The emigrant who dwelt by the sea had neither the fear of an ocean voyage nor the difficulties of arrangement which beset the inlander, who, particularly in the days prior to railways, had no little trouble in transporting his family and goods to the seaport. A more distant port on the west coast might provide a much speedier passage than could be obtained from Hull or Leith, for a voyage by way of the north of Scotland was usually slow as well as stormy. Spring was the best season in which to set out, for the weather on the ocean was much better, and it was, besides, a distinct advantage to reach America early in the summer, while there still remained several months of good weather to facilitate settlement. The stage or a wagon—if there was money to pay for it—

might carry them to the nearest seaport, but most emigrants had to conserve their slight means in every possible way. A London newspaper in 1844 printed the following account of a group bound for their port:

> "There were two covered or tilted farmer's hay-waggons—one from a parish in Buckinghamshire, and the other from the neighborhood of Northampton: they had joined company on the road. The women and children, with but few exceptions, occupied the conveyances, which were loaded with packages, bundles and boxes; a few of the more elderly females walked on the pathway by the side of their husbands and sons; the younger men trudging it with seeming glee, and carrying various articles we conjecture for immediate use.... The leafless trees and hedges—the miry road, with its long serpentine wheel tracks; the yellow waggons, with their inanimate and living freight, covered with light canvass; the women habited in blue or red cloaks; the men in their frocks blending in colour with the many hues of the bundles; and above all, the object of their journey was well calculated to excite human sympathy. Yet no one appeared sad or sorrowful—on the contrary all seemed to be cheerful; and their clean and decent appearance bore witness of the propriety of their general habits; the whole looked remarkably healthy, especially the children."

Among the saddest episodes in Irish history is the great exodus of the late 'forties and early 'fifties. In the spring of 1851 some 5,000 emigrants were leaving Cork, Limerick, Dublin, Waterford, and Belfast every week for America. An eye-witness of the great migration wrote that "in England you can have but little conception of the sufferings of the poor Irish emigrant from the time he first announces his intention of leaving home to his final departure." As he passed through many southern counties he saw heartless evictions in full swing. Ejections applied for in court were seldom defended, and the cases "were disposed of at the rate of one each minute . . . 5 souls to each family . . . 300 per hour cast upon the poor-house relief, and remaining in the union workhouse until remittances arrive from their friends in America."

The Roman Catholic clergy took an active part in seeing their parishioners safely out of Ireland, and in company with one of these "humble but exemplary men," our informant came upon

> "the packing and making ready of an entire village—for there were not more than half a dozen houses on the spot, and all their former inmates were preparing to leave. Immediately that my reverend friend was recognized, the people gathered about him in the most affectionate manner. He had a word of advice to Pat, a caution to Nelly, a suggestion to Mick; and he made a promise to Dan to take care of the 'old woman' until the five pounds came in the spring to his 'Reverence' to send her over to America. Then ensued a scene of tears and lamentations, such as might have softened a much harder heart than mine or that of the priest. He stood for a while surrounded by the old and the young, the strong and infirm on bended knees, and he turned his moistened eyes towards heaven and asked the blessing of the

PROCEEDING TO THE SEAPORT

Almighty upon the wanderers during their long and weary journey. Many were the tears brushed quietly away from the sunburnt cheeks of those who there knelt and had implicit faith that the benediction so fervently and piously asked would be vouchsafed to them."

Glad to leave such a scene, they passed on along the road to Kenmare, coming upon from two to three hundred more emigrants, who looked "most picturesque in their gay plaid shawls and straw bonnets." This group was one of a large number sent out at the expense of the ratepayers. They were from ten to thirty years of age, and, although the only alternative appeared to be starvation, "It is sad to see so much young blood sent from amongst us; . . . at present it is the bone and sinew of the land that appear to go out."

Arriving at the quay in Cork after a journey of nearly 100 miles, the emigrants "stretched and tumbled about upon boxes and straw to seek some few moments' repose." Here and at the emigration office they were pounced upon by all manner of ruffianly man-catchers, crimps, and touters. The "lodging-houses for emigrants," where many had to wait a week or more, were dens of abject misery. It was not unusual

"to thrust from twenty to forty persons, of all ages and both sexes, into rooms not more than four yards by five or six yards square, with no other accommodation than a mass of filthy straw placed around the room, upon which the weary traveller is expected to find repose. In the event of his being provided by the proprietor with some sort of covering he is charged threepence a night; should they bring their own bed-clothes they pay twopence; and those who are content to sleep on the straw, without divesting themselves of their rags, pay one penny."

Standing room for meals was charged for upon a similar scale, and the overcrowding, misery, and filth of such houses frequently endangered the health of entire communities. Many families, too, who had formerly avoided liquor, lost their money in these lodging-houses by being persuaded that the "pledge" they had taken was no longer binding, since whisky was the very best preventive of seasickness.

Many emigrants had been fraudulently induced to undertake the voyage by being assured that they would be abundantly provided for during the passage, and receive immediate employment at a dollar a day upon reaching America. Some, too, thought they were embarking from an Irish port, but were introduced to the miseries of emigration by a preliminary voyage eastward, for they were crowded to suffocation in steam packets plying across the Irish Sea to Liverpool, the great port of embarkation. The quays in

Cork leading to the packet offices were, from dawn to sunset—and often far into the night—packed with a continual stream of carts, trucks and porters, all heavily laden with feather-beds, furnishings, and the inevitable sacks of potatoes. When the packet was ready to sail, the emigrants and their goods occupied every inch of the deck, "standing room only" being the usual accommodation. Fortunate indeed were the travellers if the weather was fine during the voyage across the Irish Sea.

CHAPTER VI

Arranging for the Voyage

"The first care of the emigrants, if their passage have not been previously paid for them by their kind friends in New York, is to make the best bargain they can with the passenger-brokers. The competition in this trade is very great, and fares, accordingly, vary from day to day, and even from hour to hour."
"Emigration from Liverpool," *Illustrated London News*, July 6, 1850

The difference between leisurely emigration in 1815 and the mass exodus of the 1840's and '50's was more than one of numbers. The attitude of mind—both of emigrants and captains—was not the same, the ships and the mechanical details of embarkation were dissimilar, and the preparations for the voyage varied considerably. But there were some respects in which conditions at the seaport changed but little, and of these the suspicion with which almost everyone should be regarded was the most unfortunate. An agreeable captain might allow his passengers to come aboard ahead of sailing time. "We were ten days on board before we sailed," wrote one lady; but such courtesies were not general. A pamphlet suggests that, "as emigrants may have occasion to continue a week or ten days at Liverpool," they should obtain lodgings in which they might board themselves. In this way they might live more agreeably, avoid unnecessary expense, and be able "to equip themselves with greater privacy and with less molestation" than at an inn.

On such matters as the custom-house examination the emigrant was advised that the captain would

"give him the necessary directions how to proceed, and assist him through it. He will also have to take an affidavit at the custom-house. He may take his sea-stores of provisions, etc., on board his vessel at any time, placing them under the charge of the mate as they are never examined by the custom-house officer. When his baggage is to be examined, he may hire a cart and take it to the custom-house accompanied by the captain of the vessel. After having finished his business there, he can have it conveyed in the same cart to the dock in which the ship lies, and from thence immediately taken on board; one journey and one expense will thereby answer both purposes."

In the days of the great rush for the new land, the pitfalls increased and no aid could be expected from captains or crews. His dress, bundles, and confused appearance advertised the emigrant, and man-catchers of every variety pounced upon him. One sufferer notes that the goods sold "are merely made to sell. It is ten chances to one that your water-can will leak out half your allowance, and your sauce-pan go to pieces the first time you use it." Similarly, old tea was sold; cheese so tough that it was "eminently well adapted for boot soles"; and sugar composed of "a very curious compound of sand and timber, with but a few traces of saccharine matter."

Almost every guidebook contained warnings, of which that of A. C. Buchanan is typical:

"Make your bargain for your passage with the *owner* of the ship, or some well-known respectable broker or ship-master; avoid, by all means, those crimps that are generally found about the docks and quays near where ships are taking in passengers. Be sure the ship is going to the port you contract for, as much deception has been practised in this respect. It is important to select a well-known captain and a fast sailing ship, even at a higher rate."

A publication of the Colonial Office similarly sounded the warning that "sometimes agents take payment from the emigrant for his passage, and then recommend him to some tavern, where he is detained from day to day, under false pretences for delay, until, before the departure of the ship, the whole of his money is extracted from him."

In 1850, when the emigrant trade reached the peak of corruption, there were twenty-one brokers in Liverpool, and the list is given in a contemporary publication with the warning that while some were known to be men "of high honour and strict integrity," others had no such reputation, and the official agent was consequently kept "in a state of constant combativeness." But the government was very lax in its supervision of these brokers, for while they had to obtain a license and deposit sureties to the amount of £200, yet even in the most flagrant cases there is no record of the forfeiture of a bond, though occasional instances of the withdrawal of a license. Following is a complaint made to the Emigration Agent in Liverpool in 1831:

"June 25th, Michael Donnolly and wife paid £8 for their passage in the ship *Florence* to a person of the name of Yonge, who gave him a receipt without any date or ship's name filled into it, and he, not being able to read, did not find out the imposition until this morning, when Yonge told him that he was to go to St. John. He complains of this alteration as he has some friends on board the *Florence*, and paid his money on the express condition that he was to go with them on that vessel. Michael McCormick was a witness to this transaction and certifies the truth of this statement.

"I consulted the Mayor about this case, but he regretted that he had no power either to compel him to come before him or to pay back the money. Under these circumstances I thought it best for the interest of these poor people to try my influence and remonstrances with them, and Yonge agreed to pay £7 and Donnolly and family not having the means of proceeding returned to Ireland."

The Liverpool docks presented an animated and confusing scene to the thousands of emigrants who thronged the waterfront. It was usual to bargain with brokers who controlled the accommodation of numerous vessels, and at times, as *The Emigrant's Informant* states, a shrewd traveller could secure his passage for two-thirds or even one-half of what was originally demanded. Among the steerage passengers on the *John Dennison*, from Greenock, in 1833, were many who had paid the full price of £4, but some had negotiated their passage for as low as £2 10s.

At most ports the choice of vessels was generally wide enough, and the walls of warehouses and offices were thoroughly placarded with advertisements and notices of sailing dates of such well-known packets as the *Yorkshire*, the *New World*, the *Isaac Webb*, the *West Point*, the *Constitution*, the *Isaac Wright*, the *London*, the *Star of the West*, the *Queen of the West*, and scores of others. Less biased information on ships and captains might be obtained from the port's official emigration agent, but many did not take advantage of this service. William Cobbett, who bore no love for the government which had persecuted him, was most emphatic in his preference for all things American. A journey by stage-coach from London to Exeter was, he believed, "far more perilous than a voyage across the Atlantic in *American* ships commanded by an *American* captain." He also considered that American packets were faster, carried more sail, and were better navigated than British vessels. The captains were more vigilant; took in their sails before a squall reached the ship, but let them out immediately after to gain the advantage of the strong wind; made eight or ten miles per hour at night as compared with the slow progress of ships which took in most of their sails at sunset; in fact, says Cobbett, "I never knew an American captain take off his clothes to go to bed, during the whole voyage; and I never knew any other who did not do it." He, like other writers, warned emigrants to avoid small ships, which were tossed about by the wind and seldom had any conveniences. He advised having a written memorandum of the agreement with the captain, and that when this had been obtained it was preferable to keep out of his way and not pester him with senseless questions and incessant wailings: "A captain of a ship is *one* man on shore and *another* man on board; and perhaps the rougher he is in the former state, the smoother he is in the latter."[1]

Before 1835 emigrants were officially advised to make preparations for a voyage of twelve weeks, but in that year the period was reduced to ten, and ships and travellers could decrease their provisions accordingly. Some emigrants were fortunate enough to make a voyage of twenty-five days, while others were driven by contrary winds to the Azores or Greenland, and barely survived a terrifying experience of four months. The average passage to Quebec was around forty-five days; and in the late 1820's that from Liverpool to New York averaged forty days, requiring only thirty-one in the early spring. Ships and weather varied so greatly that averages meant but little to the individual. It was always advisable to take passage to Montreal rather than Quebec, since captains frequently charged no more for the additional 180 miles, and a part of the St. Lawrence trip by bateau or steamship was thus avoided; for the same reason many entered Canada by the more expensive New York and Erie Canal route and made better time than those who had to ascend the St. Lawrence.

Because of the competition and varied accommodations of ships, there was little attempt at standardization of rates. The cheapest appears to be the 10-shilling rate which numerous Irishmen paid to cross to Newfoundland by fishing vessel, their food supply consisting of a few dried herrings. Timber ships charged as low as 20 shillings. Provisions—for Scotchmen, sixty pounds of oatmeal and possibly a small quantity of butter and eggs—added from 10 to 20 shillings more. Some vessels from Irish ports charged 40s. to 50s., and the emigrant carried a sack of potatoes as his provisions. Accommodations consisted of a place in the hold to throw his chest and stretch himself out at night, and an allowance of water, usually filthy. From English ports, especially on the east coast, steerage rates were generally much higher, sometimes from £10 to £15 in the better ships, including provisions. John Palmer paid £14 in 1817 on the *Importer*, "including beef, biscuit, soup, flour once a week, cooking and water," and he laid in a supply of tea, sugar, etc., himself. If no provisions were supplied, passages could usually be arranged from London at £3, and from western ports, such as Bristol, Liverpool, Glasgow, and Greenock, for

---

[1] Among other writers who preferred American ships was James B. Brown, who considered them "good sailers and very well managed"; some, too, were on "temperance principles," which could seldom be said of British vessels. (*Views of Canada and the Colonists*, 254.)

ARRANGING FOR THE VOYAGE

£3 10s. In the 1840's and '50's the steerage fare from Liverpool, including rations, varied from £3 10s. to £5.

There were three types of regular emigrant vessels—those carrying cabin passengers only, others which had also intermediate and steerage accommodations, and exclusively steerage ships. In the late 'forties the cabin ships charged from £12 to £20, including provisions and, at the latter price, liquors. But there were the regular Liverpool-New York packets upon which more luxurious accommodation might be obtained for from 30 to 40 guineas. Intermediate or second-class accommodation usually consisted merely of a part of the steerage separate from the rest, and differing from it only in the imagination of the ship broker. Sometimes, however, there were certain improvements which made life less unbearable. One traveller observed that on his ship, which was a transient or merchant vessel, the second cabin was the after part of the steerage, and separated from it by a partition of inch boards. Such accommodations cost £1 more than the steerage rate; while "families of four persons may have a separate room erected, with a door to lock, for their exclusive use, by paying about £2 additional, or 10s. each, to defray the expense of putting it up, which is often done by those who wish to keep themselves separate from the other steerage passengers." Another writer notes that he knew "a very respectable family in which there were several agreeable young ladies," who crossed the Atlantic in this fashion for £6 each; and their food, which they provided, averaged £3 additional. The *Isaac Webb*, a large emigrant vessel of 1850, charged £4 for steerage passengers and from £6 to £7 for second-class accommodations, including provisions.

The chief advantages in steerage on the Liverpool packets, according to a citizen of Edinburgh, were a comparatively short passage, "a gentleman for a captain," a small number of fellow-passengers, and the avoidance of "mixing with the Irish emigrants, who generally go in the steerage of transient vessels." These things he considered worth the higher rates. In merchant ships the type and disposition of the cargo was a matter of importance to the steerage passenger, who was often close to it. The smell from hides was exceedingly objectionable, while a heavy load of pig-iron, though exerting a steadying influence in light weather, tended to make the ship roll much more during storms, and caused serious damage when it broke loose.

In earlier years when the trade was less organized, it was usual for a family to make a bargain "for the whole in a lump." When a considerable number were leaving one neighborhood, they formed into groups or societies to simplify arrangements and save money. "By doing so," an early writer observed, "they will be able to charter a ship for themselves, and provision themselves. In this way they will obtain their passage for one-half, or perhaps one-third what it would cost them were they to take their passages by single families from masters of ships and be provisioned by them."[2] Most emigrants could not afford a higher rate than that in the steerage; and the attitude of many was that of the writer who said that when emigrants had reached America, "No one will think the better or worse of them on account of the part of the ship in which they chanced to come. Indeed, with the really worthy and discerning they will be the higher esteemed for their economy."

Cobbett, who had little respect for anything or anybody higher than middle class, based his preference for the steerage on the food. There he might arrange his own supply of "neat's tongues, recently salted, little cakes of bread baked by the cook, now and then an egg, washed down by water or by tea or coffee"; while in the cabin the so-called fresh meat might be found to consist "of pork fed in the long boat; of mutton from sea-sick sheep with eyes as white as those of whitings; of turkeys and fowls that are never killed until at the point of death; and of ducks and geese that would not die, but that will be poor as a dog-horse." He is corroborated by John Palmer, a fellow cabin passenger on the *Importer* in 1817, who said of the ducks and hens that if he "had met with them in the States, I must confess I should have been tempted to suppose they were brought over by some of the first settlers!" Another contemporary, however, wondered whether Cobbett "means what he writes," or intended his advice as "a premeditated *hoax* upon the public."

In spite of the danger of travel by sailing-ship, but very few emigrants carried insurance. Lives could be insured for 3 pence and baggage for 3 ¾ pence for every pound sterling of value. The following paragraph from William Cattermole's advice to emigrants indicates other precautions for minimizing risks:

"Parties going together in the steerage, or half deck, would do right in closely examining into the exact accommodations they are to receive—such as water-closets; if they are allowed the use of the quarter-deck; at what time the lights are expected to be out; these cautions may prevent bad

[2] A. Bell, in appendix to W. Bell, *Hints to Emigrants*, 210. Having made all their arrangements, they set off on their voyage, as Robert Gourlay said, "like swallows in autumn, never again perhaps to be identified in union." (*Emigration and Settlement on Wild Land*, 17.)

Illustrated London News

LIVERPOOL PACKETS LEAVING CORK
Many Irish emigrants to America first crossed the Irish Sea.

THE EMIGRATION AGENT'S OFFICE

In the years of mass migration both information and the physical examination were given in a perfunctory manner.

ARRANGING FOR THE VOYAGE

feelings on the passage; and cabin passengers, particularly those with families, should do the same, ascertaining what wine, spirits and porter is allowed, to prevent misunderstanding when out."[8]

To know what their rights were, even if they could not always enforce them, was advice that was particularly necessary for steerage passengers. On one ship, for example, the captain "thought nothing of kicking them should they trespass on the after part of the deck, where they would sometimes lie down to get away from the surroundings of the forecastle." Some vessels, too, supplied nothing but a rough bunk, while others provided at least the straw or mattresses which were essential. The issue of the food and water and the use of grates or stoves were other matters which frequently caused disputes during the passage.

A second-cabin passenger on the *Julius Macgregor* in June, 1842, found that things had been misrepresented, his accommodation being "merely one end of the steerage—an excellent practical joke on the part of the captain." "Besides sharpers on shore at both ends, beware of sharpers among your fellow passengers," warned Sidney Smith. For carrying supplies A. C. Buchanan advised "a strong deal chest in the shape of a sailor's box"—broader at the bottom than at the top, in order to increase its steadiness on board ship. Strong linen or sacking bags or baskets were very useful for potatoes, but oatmeal and flour should be packed in a strong barrel or flax-seed cask, and, in addition to the usual hoops, "two of iron," as well as "a strong lid and a padlock," should be used. Another writer emphasizes the care needed to prevent loss:

"The tin articles required are: a water-can to hold the supply of water, ... a wash basin, baking dish, a tin pot to fit into the ship's stove for broth, etc., a can for drinking from, a pot to hang on the stove for heating water, tin plates for meals, small tin dishes for tea or coffee, table- and teaspoons, and knives and forks for each individual. All should be marked, and all packages should not only have locks but be kept locked, and the keys taken out. This cannot be too carefully attended to, as loss of articles on shipboard are not infrequent, and such losses unfortunately cannot be supplied."

But few people provided special clothing for the voyage. One man, however, wrote that "the kind of apparel I would recommend to male passengers would be short jackets or waistcoats with sleeves, a dark handkerchief for the neck, and coarse trowsers:—for women, a long bed gown, or wrappers with dark shawls or handkerchiefs, as cleanliness cannot be observed with any degree of precision."

[8] He wrote from experience, for the *Cobourg Star* of June 6, 1832, refers to the arrival there of 100 immigrants who "came out in the *Caroline* with Mr. Cattermole."

The cost of provisions bulked large unless the emigrant was used to a very meager diet. Extensive references to the subject are found, for even those who relied largely on the steward's rations commonly took along many extras and luxuries. Commenting upon the usual recommendation of fifty days' provisions, Samuel Butler observed that, "as the emigrant on arrival can sell whatever he may have over, we urgently advise that a safer provision than this be made. Of the vessels sailing from British ports in April, 1841, although there were instances of some making the voyage within 30 days, the longest passage was 78 days. The misery and loss of health to the emigrant being on short allowance under such circumstances, where he is in want of funds, and the expense incurred by those who have, in purchasing at an extravagant rate from the captain, may well be conceived. We would urgently recommend, therefore, emigrants sailing with the ordinary ships advertised not to victual for less than 10 weeks."[4] That such advice was worth following is apparent from the experience of numerous emigrants, as reported by A. C. Buchanan:

"In the brig *Lady Hood* from Stornoway were 14 families, 78 in number, all very poor; and landed here, after a passage of 70 days, in great distress from want of provisions. They had expended all their money in purchasing supplies from the master during the passage. . . . 139 passengers in the *Cumberland Lass* from Belfast were 66 days on the voyage. Many of them landed in great distress from want of provisions. They purchased from Captain Smith as long as their money lasted, and he had to support from 40 to 50 of the poorest for the last three weeks. When he arrived here all his ship's stores were exhausted, besides supplies which he obtained from different places in the Gulf."

Among the most suitable foods were oatmeal, beef, eggs packed in salt, ship-biscuit or half-baked bread, and preserved milk, "boiled with loaf sugar, a pound to a quart, and bottled." Those who could afford luxuries were advised that ale and porter were useful, while rice and sago for puddings, and dried herrings or other fish supplied variety. A suggestion advanced in the earlier period was that an emigrant might add to his food supply by taking along fishing tackle to be used off the Grand Banks, where it was customary for sailing-ships to stop a few hours. J. Abbott, for example, caught three codfish on his voyage out (one weighing 39 pounds), though the vessel lay to for only seventeen minutes; but such sporting interludes disappeared as the tide of emigration increased and the trade became better organized.

[4] Based upon 616 emigrant vessels entering at Quebec, the average in 1841 was 45 days; in 1842, 46 days.

ARRANGING FOR THE VOYAGE

One family brought along "a quantity of fowl in pickle, which when watered eat very delicious." "Beggars' dish,—peeled potatoes, and either beef or bacon cut in thin slices and mixed through them,"—was recommended by an emigrant who found that pickled cabbage was the only thing he could eat during seasickness. Another advised bringing "a few pieces of buttocks of beef well cured, which you can hang up in the rigging of the ship, where it will keep well the whole passage." Andrew Picken writes that "when emigrants go in parties they may arrange to take a pig or two with them, which stock are easily supported on board ship; and, when killed on the passage at proper intervals, form most agreeable fresh food. Ducks also do well at sea."

A Canadian settler advised a group of four steerage passengers to provide themselves with

"16 or 18 pecks of potatoes in a barrel with a lock on it; 40 lbs. of good beef well salted in brine; 15 lbs. of butter; 3 lbs. of coffee; 3 or 4 dozen old bottled beer, which has less chance of flying than if new; some dozens of eggs packed in salt, half a dozen codfish, cut dried for keeping. Milk does not keep well; no sweetmeats are relished at sea; a few oranges, which at times taste very pleasant to the parched palate; some cheese; 8 lbs. of treacle in a flagon; 1 stone of barley; a good deal of pepper and mustard; plenty of carrots, turnips, and onions for broth—they will keep all the voyage; 28 lbs. of fine ship bread, 8 or 10 quartern loaves, baked hard; 1 boll of oatmeal, 6 packs baked into bannocks and cakes, very well fired, and flat for packing; some white puddings; some suet for dumplings. A few candles, and a white-iron lantern with horn; 1 bottle vinegar, to use in water on ship-board; 1 bottle of castor oil; two or three dozens of colocynth and rhubarb pills; 6 lbs. of epsom salts and one lb. of senna—these medicines are very dear here; tin pan to fit the stove of the ship, and it is convenient to have one for hooking on the ribs of the grate when the top of the fire is occupied; kettle for making coffee, etc. Use no crockery, but instead jugs and bowls of tin; broth pot, frying-pan, and tin kettle."

The suggested use of vinegar in water was for the purpose of smothering as much as possible its taste and smell.

A somewhat similar list of foods, with variations due to nationality, is contained in a letter uniquely addressed to "Mr. James Parks, to be left at Mr. Benjamin Boot's, Wheelwright, Staple Cross, in the Parish of Ewhurst, near Northiam, in the County of Sussex, Old England, Great Britain":

"Don't bring a great deal of beef; and what you do, get a cask and salt it down yourself; for we had beef two years old, not fit for a dog. Our tea was not half tea; our oatmeal was half ground pease; our split pease, gray pease; our biscuits was the worst that could be got. Be sure to bring plenty of flour, some dried ham and other bacon, plenty of potatoes, plenty of butter, sugar, tea, coffee, oatmeal, patent groats, rice, salt, pepper, vinegar, a few bottles of port wine to make sap if you are ill. Take care your biscuits are good; be sure to bring plenty of flour and rice; don't be afraid of bringing too much, nor few. But you can sell what you don't want, but don't sell too soon. Great many in our vessel would give three times the value of a thing before they got over. Take ginger with you for sap; plenty of rush candles—we had not near enough."

The warning was frequently given that too great a dependence upon potatoes—which Cobbett called "Ireland's lazy root"—sometimes led to disaster. In one of his weekly reports A. C. Buchanan wrote from Quebec:

"The passengers per *China*, from Limerick, were ten weeks on the voyage; their supply of provisions falling short, they were obliged to purchase from the captain at higher rates. They stated that their supply of provisions was sufficient, when they left, for three months, but that their potatoes, which constituted their chief stock,[5] owing to the wet and heat in the vessel's hold, soon rotted and became unfit to use. . . . Several cases have occurred this season in which this most essential and, I may say, principal food of the Irish emigrants has been destroyed from neglect and improper stowage. I should recommend, if considered practicable, that this article of provisions should be placed in charge of the master of the vessel, and be issued by him to each individual twice a week, or oftener if he thought proper. At present they are brought on board in sacks, and thrown into the hold on the wet ballast, or on the water casks, and in the course of a few days, owing to the thoroughfare made over them by the crew and passengers going for water and other provisions or baggage, they soon become so trampled on and bruised as to be unfit for use."

Oatmeal had much to commend it, for hard bread or biscuit of most types became rather repulsive when continually eaten without other foods to vary the diet. A good method of preparing loaf-bread as a substitute was advanced by *The Mechanic and Labourer's Guide to America*:

"For immediate use a few stale loaves may be rebaked, that is, put a second time in the oven in order to take out all the moisture from them and in this state they will keep good for at least a fortnight; but to last well for a longer period the loaf must be cut up into thin slices and toasted slowly on both sides until they become perfectly dry—on a gridiron over a slow fire, perhaps, is the best way of preparing them—and then let them stand separately on end until perfectly cold. If these be kept in a dry place they will continue in a good state for months, and all that is necessary previous to use is to moisten them with a little water and hold them a short time before the fire, or else immerse them in any hot liquid, as tea, soup, etc. If bread thus prepared be put up in a tin box with a tight-fitting lid or cover, and when used treated as directed, it will be almost impossible to distinguish any difference between a toast of this description and one from a loaf only a day old."

An Irishman advanced the following recipe for preserving milk, and stated that one family who took a supply found it just as good when they landed in America as when they left home: "Take

---

[5] By the late 1840's the potato had become too expensive for general use, and oatmeal and biscuit replaced the Irishman's favorite food.

ARRANGING FOR THE VOYAGE

a large or small jar or jars and clean them remarkably well, and when done put the milk therein, and after securing it well by corking it close, put the jar or jars into a large pot of water and boil them over a good fire, and when done pack them in a hamper or some other place and it will keep sweet the whole of the passage." The value of "portable soup" and preserved meat, as well as fruits and vegetables and acid foods, the lack of which rendered the diet of many emigrants deficient and monotonous, is outlined in another publication:

"Acids of all descriptions—that is, those used at table—are not only serviceable at sea, but particularly grateful to the palate. Of vinegar, therefore, as the most common, there should be ample store; pickles likewise of various descriptions; but above all, lemons or the juice of them. For this kind of acid there can be no proper substitute; it counteracts the effects of salt diet, allays sea-sickness, and forms occasionally a very refreshing and invigorating beverage. About two or three pounds of figs also should be taken to be used medicinally, and a box or two of soda-water powders. A small hamper of porter likewise, and a bottle or two of spirits, not omitting a little brandy. A few good keeping apples and some oranges also, managed in the same manner as directed for the lemons, may be provided."

Even teetotalers usually took along a gallon or so of brandy "to be judiciously administered in bribes to the black cook." On many vessels only those who could bribe were accorded their fair share of food and water or the use of fire-grates and other conveniences.

A. C. Buchanan recommended that the following supplies, costing about £5 in Ireland and from £6 to £7 in England, (or roughly from a third to two-fifths the amount per person that more prosperous travellers expended), be taken as the food of five persons during a voyage of from 60 to 70 days:

48 stone of potatoes
2½ cwt. of oatmeal or flour
½ cwt. biscuits
20 lbs. butter
20 lbs. bacon

50 lbs. fish (herrings) in small keg
1 gal. spirits
1 gal. molasses
a little vinegar

By way of luxury, Buchanan suggested that a pound of tea and fourteen pounds of sugar might be taken. While such a diet was obviously deficient in both vitamins and variety, thousands existed on much less. In the later period of the sailing-ship particularly, almost all passengers relied upon the vessel's stores; but reports were not infrequent of miserable treatment at the hands of the ship's steward, and of rotten food distributed to starving steerage passengers. As the Rev. William Bell observed, "In some ships you may find abundance of good and wholesome food for the passengers, but in others it is scarcely fit for hogs."

CHAPTER VII

FAREWELL TO THE OLD LAND

"The bark is o'er the lonely seas,
   Which bears me from the land I love;
Her sails swell gently to the breeze,
   And all is calm, around, above.

Not so this restless heart of mine—
   Its hopes are clouded still by fate;
Its morning sun hath ceased to shine,
   And left it dark and desolate."

"An Adieu to Scotland" by J. F. E., *Cobourg Star*, January 2, 1833

"Nothing," wrote Robert Louis Stevenson upon emigration, "is more agreeable to picture and more pathetic to behold. The abstract idea, as conceived at home, is hopeful and adventurous. . . . This picture is found on trial to consist mostly of embellishments. The more I saw of my fellow-passengers, the less I was tempted to the lyric note. Comparatively few of the men were below thirty; many were married, and encumbered with families; not a few were already up in years; and this itself was out of tune with my imaginations, for the ideal emigrant should certainly be young. Again, I thought he should offer to the eye some bold type of humanity, with bluff or hawk-like features, and the stamp of an eager and pushing disposition. Now those around me were for the most part quiet, orderly, obedient citizens, family men broken by adversity, elderly youths who had failed to place themselves in life, and people who had seen better days. Mildness was the prevailing character; mild mirth and mild endurance. In a word, I was not taking part in an impetuous and conquering sally, such as swept over Mexico or Siberia, but found myself, like Marmion, 'In the lost battle, borne down by the flying.'"

"The prospect of happiness and independence," wrote a cabin passenger, Mrs. William Radcliff, upon setting sail, "qualified every sentiment of regret, and reconciled me to the painful alternative we had chosen." Another writer asserted that the steerage of many a vessel consisted almost entirely of "tall, pale, lean fellows, with ignorance strongly expressed on their vacant countenances, which betrayed no regret at leaving their native country." The Rev. William Bell observed that as Scotland faded from view, "some appeared lively and cheerful—some thoughtful and serious—while a few, by the tears which they shed, showed that they were not leaving their country and their friends without a struggle." Similar feelings are expressed in the diary of a member of the Tripp family, who left London on the *John Stamp* for Fitz-

FAREWELL TO THE OLD LAND 59

roy Township, Upper Canada, in 1835. Relatives and friends accompanied them to the docks, and the diarist recorded that "when we came opposite Woolwich we went on deck to take a last farewell of our deserted home and the friends we had left behind."

Sometimes, too, these "sorrowing friends left behind, as they sobbed a last farewell, would rather have seen the departing ones going to their graves." On at least one occasion a shipload of evicted Scottish crofters set sail "to the wail of the bagpipes and the singing of McCrimmon's Lament."[1] They were in a very real sense "outcasts," but their finer feelings had not yet been blunted by destitution, and the final wrench from the associations of home was a heart-rending struggle.

"Many and deep," wrote a cultured Irishman as he left his home in the great "ship fever" year, "are the wounds that the sensitive heart inflicts upon its possessor as he journeys through life's pilgrimage; but on few occasions are they so acutely felt as when one is about to part from those who formed a portion of his existence. . . . But as the skilful surgeon tears off the bandage which the hand of affection gently withdraws from the wound,— thereby unconsciously inflicting greater pain; so it is better not to linger upon the affecting scene, but rush suddenly away." . . . "I think it was inconsiderate in our worthy sea-captain," wrote another, "to direct his course so near the pleasant coasts of Hampshire, Dorset and Devon, that, as we left our native isle, we could see the slow wain and the gay chariot journeying on the high-roads—the country-seats and farmsteads surrounded by luxuriant crops in large chequers of yellow, green and white. Lovely did they look, and hard to leave. A wistful, regretful expression was strong in every face on board; and when the night closed in, dark, raw and showery, a young emigrant leaped into the sea and was lost."

Until the 1820's vessels usually rode at anchor—sometimes five miles from shore, where the sails would quickly fill out in the breeze. Emigrants came on board in the ship's boats, or in hired harbor craft. With the development of steam navigation, however, tugs were used to tow sailing-vessels out to sea into the wind. At Liverpool cabin passengers frequently remained on shore until the vessel had been towed down the Mersey, and then went aboard by

---

[1] These emigrants sailed from Loch Broom for Pictou, Nova Scotia, on the barque *Frances Ann* in 1817, reaching port after a very rough trip. Their minister and leader, the Rev. Norman McLeod, decided to remove to the Ohio region, *via* the Gulf of Mexico and the Mississippi, and with some 200 followers set sail in 1820; but the ship ran into a storm at the start and was driven into the harbor of St. Ann's, Nova Scotia, where its Scottish passengers decided to commence pioneer life anew. About 1847 the eyes of Mr. McLeod and many of his colony were turned towards Australia, but it was 1851 before two vessels had been constructed and provisioned; whereupon one ship set out, reaching Adelaide, South Australia, after "a delightful voyage" of 164 days. Not satisfied with Adelaide, they proceeded to Melbourne; and still in search of the ideal they sent scouts by a whaler to Auckland, New Zealand, whither the whole shipload— and the other which had meanwhile come from Nova Scotia—arrived early in 1853, settling on the Waipu tract. Reinforced by several additional emigrations, including 66 persons on the diminutive brigantine *Spray*, of 99 tons, the "Waipu Highlanders," as they are still called, formed a distinctive settlement. This epic of colonization is described by A. J. Clark in *The Scottish-Canadian Pilgrims of the Fifties*, Ontario Historical Society *Papers and Records*, XXVI, 5-15.

a steam tug. If there were a large number the cost might be as low as sixpence a head; but small boats often extorted exorbitant amounts from passengers who were caught unprepared and were afraid of losing their passage. Prices ranging from 7s. 6d. to £1 are recorded.

The departure of the *St. Vincent* from London in 1844 was reported in considerable detail by a contemporary writer:

"On Monday the *St. Vincent* received her living freight on board.... Many had travelled a long distance to the depot, and most of them had never before seen a ship; yet there was a display of cheerfulness that was remarkable—as if their minds were made up for whatever might betide, or that the novelty of their situation had produced an excitement which cheered them in the hour of parting from their own home, shores, and the friends they loved. Mothers were sitting giving nourishment to their infants—but they had their husbands with them; children were eating or playing, but they were not separated from their parents;[2] and in no instance was a saddened countenance to be seen amongst them."

He stated that "perhaps a more healthy and robust set of boys and girls could not well be found"; while "the principal portion of the single men and youths were also fine athletic fellows, generally well dressed, for their station, and apparently full of spirits for the enterprise." As for the "unmarried females," there were "several really handsome countenances and good figures, particularly four or five, whose departure from Old England seemed to cast a reflection upon the bachelors they left behind—only one seemed to be sorrowful, and she was in mourning.... There was not the remotest indication of want or pauperism amongst the whole.... In several instances, both male and female, there were indications of gentility in dress and manners that caused surprise." The married people were described as "very decently attired, though not so much so as the single."

Further interesting details are found in an account of the departure of the *Artemisia* in 1848. Included among laborers and artisans from various parts of England and Scotland were a few children from the Ragged Schools,[3] an educational association aiming to give "a plain education" to destitute boys and girls from the streets of London. Lord Ashley, the famous philanthropist, a foremost worker in humanitarian movements, made a tour of inspection of the vessel just prior to her departure. A reporter on

---

[2] This reference is to the division of families which usually accompanied incarceration in the workhouse.

[3] The Ragged School Union, which still exists, was established in 1844 through the efforts of John Pounds, a shoemaker of Portsmouth who brought poor children into his workshop and taught them while he worked at his trade.

FAREWELL TO THE OLD LAND

the *Illustrated London News* who accompanied him gave this account of the occasion:

"We now inspected the accommodation between decks, where a number of the passengers were seated—some playing with their children, others reading, and here and there might be seen one whose thoughtful air rather denoted sorrow for the past than fitting spirits for the future. We were glad to find so many books in hand; what a friend must a huge entertaining volume be upon a long voyage! We were happy also to see the officers of the Prayer-book and Homily Society distributing their publications; what hopes must they nourish in time of peril upon the waters! Bye-and-bye came the dinner—the meat well cooked and of good quality; though, of course, the table had not all the snugness of the cottage meal. The parties were in 'messes' of six or eight individuals; and the comfort of the voyage is much studied by berthing near each other those who come from the same part of the country, and messing as nearly as possible those who are friends. The great order maintained on board is also indicated by the 'Regulations' and 'Dietary Scales' hung up in conspicuous places between decks.

"The time had now arrived for Lord Ashley quitting the ship; before which his Lordship took leave of each of the 'Ragged' Scholars, receiving from each a promise to write to his Lordship, and acquaint him of their fortunes. As the boat conveyed the benevolent nobleman from the ship, there was a warmth of cheering which it was delightful to hear, and an earnest expression of gratitude upon many faces which it was delightful to witness. We should add that his Lordship declared himself highly gratified with his visit, a feeling in which all around him fully participated."

The emigration expenses of the passengers of the *St. Vincent* and the *Artemisia* were paid by the government, so they were relieved of those details which made the average departure such a scene of confusion. The emigrant's experiences as he awaited the raising of the anchor are described by Richard Weston, who went to America in 1833. Having seen numerous advertisements of the departure from Greenock of a large number of first-class vessels on a certain day, he went to the port, but on visiting several ships he found they had no intention of leaving. Deciding not to take passage until he saw some signs of sailing, he walked about the town and the quays to see how the emigrants were faring. Lodging-house keepers and storekeepers were reaping a harvest at the prevailing high prices; while numerous fire-grates, surrounded by people cooking their meals, were scattered along the waterfront, the ships being bound to furnish fuel from the time the emigrants took their berths.

Finally, more than a week later, the *John Dennison* seemed in readiness to sail, and Mr. Weston took passage in her. But little notice of the time of departure was given, and even though the passengers had had ten days to prepare, many were taken by surprise:

"Some were running with trusses of straw to lie on, some with crockery, and some with old butter casks to hold water in. They had to employ watermen to bring them and their luggage on board, which occasioned another drain on the finances of the emigrant, who began to find his little stock of money gradually melting away. . . . Some of the emigrants might be seen gazing on the nimble sailors running up the shrouds, creeping along the stays, and lying out on the yardarms. Some were lingering on the shore, to drink a farewell glass with their friends; and others were making merry on board, at the near prospect of leaving Britain and its oppressions, their griefs and sorrows behind them, and entering upon a land where sighing and suffering, want and misery, were believed to be unknown."

Very shortly a stirring scene was in progress on the *John Dennison*:

"A warp was sent out and made fast to a buoy in the stream. It was stretched along the deck, and manned by the seamen. The captain, whose name was M'Kissock, desired some of the passengers to lend a hand, . . . and when every thing was got ready, a sailor sung the following words to a lively air, and keeping time to the music as they all pulled:

"'Pull away, my hearty boys—pull away so cheerily,
She moves along, my boys—pull away so heartily!
We are for America; the wind is whistling cheerily,
Then bouse away together, boys, and see you do it merrily!'

"The cheerfulness of the song revived the spirits of the emigrants; all of them were filled more or less with joyful anticipations of the country they were about to visit. When the ship was brought into the current, the foresail was set, and the warp cast off from the buoy; and we moved a little further out. The quay was crowded with spectators, who cheered us as we moved along, to which we cordially responded. The day was fine, and the spectacle must have been imposing."

Soon afterwards, however, the ship anchored again; and a few hours later a steam tug towed her down the river. More emigrants came aboard, some officers from the town captured a runaway bankrupt—there was also a deserter from the army, a farmer fleeing from debtors, and a master baker who was escaping a £25 fine for having been in company with one who had shot a hare in an enclosure—and finally at 3 a.m. all hands, emigrants included, were loosening the sails and manning the halyards to the tune of

"Sally is a pretty girl—sing Sally-ho!
Sally she is fond of me—sing Sally-ho!
We are for America, so cheerily we'll go;
Then pull away strongly, boys, and sing Sally-ho!"[4]

The *Morning Chronicle* reported in 1850 the departure of several ships from Waterloo Docks, Liverpool, among them the *Isaac Webb* and the *Star of the West*, a new ship of 1,200 tons. On her maiden voyage, the latter carried 385 passengers, of whom 360

"Being the Sabbath," wrote a passenger in describing the departure of an Irish ship, "they did not accompany the action with the usual chant." (*The Ocean Plague*, 20.)

were Irish. Though certified fit by a medical practitioner, most of them were emaciated by disease or destitution, and their faces bore a prematurely aged expression. People arrived in twos and threes up until the moment of departure, carrying chests, barrels, and cooking utensils. Fifty or sixty were still missing when the ship began to be towed through the dock gates, and "many of them had to toss their luggage on board from the quay, and to clamber on to the ship by the rigging. The men contrived to jump on board with comparative ease; but by the belated women, of whom there were nearly a score, the feat was not accomplished without much screaming and hesitation." One drunken man fell into the water in the process, and was hauled on deck considerably sobered.

"Thick as flies upon a honey pot, they might be seen clambering over the side of the vessel, threading their difficult way among ropes and cordage. Here and there a woman becoming entangled, with her drapery sadly discomposed, and her legs still more sadly exposed to the loiterers on shore, might be heard imploring aid from the sailors or passengers above. . . . Many a package missed its mark and fell into the dock, where it was rescued and handed up by a man in a small boat who followed in the wake of the mighty ship. . . .

"When at last the ship cleared the gate and floated right out into the Mersey, her full proportions became disentangled from the maze of shipping in which she had been formerly involved, and she seemed indeed to be a Leviathan. The spectators on shore took off their hats and cheered lustily, and the cheer was repeated by the whole body of emigrants on deck, who raised a shout that I suppose must have been heard at the distance of a mile even in the noisy and busy thoroughfares of Liverpool."

As the *Isaac Webb* left port all the berths were already occupied, some of the passengers eating breakfast, while others tried to sleep, to shave, or to sort out their goods. The women talked, the children cried, sang, and shouted, and there was no sorrow evident at leaving. A few of the passengers had fiddle, flute, or bagpipe, and vigorous joyousness was demonstrated in the four-handed jigs and reels in progress in various parts of the double steerage which was carrying 780 emigrants to the new land. It was quite apparent that "hope was before them, and nothing was behind them but the remembrance of misery."

At last the steam tug came alongside and took on board some forty merchants, orange girls, and "dealers in Everton-toffy, ribbons, laces, pocket mirrors, gingerbread nuts, sweetmeats, etc.," who had done their best to extract from the emigrants their remaining cash. Passengers and their tickets were then checked, and stowaways searched for. These ceremonies were usually performed while the tug was towing the vessel down the Mersey. So great was their misery at home that many a person was willing to hide, suffocating and half-starved, packed to the chin in barrels of salt or biscuits, with only the smallest of airholes. Sometimes they were aided by other emigrants. Ten stowaways, both men and women, appeared before Captain Lowber of the *Montezuma* when she was far out to sea. Such unfortunates could neither be thrown overboard nor starved, and, although cases are known of death from suffocation, their worst fate was generally—as it is today— to be assigned the dirtiest work on board during the rest of the passage.[5] An occasional vindictive captain might sentence them to walk on deck in the bitter cold for several hours, or inflict some other punishment, such as tar and feathers. Sometimes a barrel was suspected of being the hiding-place, and rather than break it open it was stood on end so that its occupant, standing upon his head, was soon forced to cry for mercy. On the *Star of the West* the passengers were roped off on deck, while the crew, armed with long pronged sticks and masked lanterns or candles, penetrated into every hole and corner, lifting, hammering, and testing all baggage, barrels, and bedding.

The roll-call, from which only cabin passengers were exempt, followed. Plenty of Hollaghans and six families of Smiths were gradually sorted out and checked off. The clerk apparently considered himself a wit, and his shout for Patrick Boyle—

"Paddy Bile
Come here awhile,"

was followed by an order for William Jones to "show his bones." After an hour and a half, the only fraud uncovered was that of an Irish couple who had represented their 18-year-old son as "under 12." The threat to put him ashore brought forth only tears, for they had neither money nor baggage to make up the difference; but some kind-hearted fellow-passengers raised 10 shillings, and the youth was permitted to remain on board, several persons offering to provide security that another son in New York would make up the balance of the money. Occasionally the roll-call would uncover an attempt to pass off an eight-year-old as an infant at the breast; while there were instances of a whole family coming on board without tickets, hoping to escape notice in the confusion of departure.

[5] Robert Louis Stevenson devotes a chapter to stowaways in *The Amateur Emigrant*, 69—87. See also *The Ocean Plague*, 24-5. On the ship *John Dennison* there were two very careful roll-calls and searches for stowaways or fleeing bankrupts. (Weston, *A Visit to the United States and Canada*, 8-11.)

In addition to the clerk of the passenger-broker, the ship's surgeon was present during roll-call to see that helpless or deformed passengers had not slipped past the official medical examiner. Any such emigrants who might become a public charge would cost the owner of the vessel $75 upon reaching the United States. After the roll-call, a tug came alongside to take the unsatisfactory to shore. At that time some who had pleaded inability to pay the full rate would produce sovereigns which had been stitched "amid the rags of petticoats, coats and unmentionable garments"; and these, amid the execrations of the crew, would be allowed to remain aboard. The arrival alongside of a prisoner in a small boat,—the Negro steward who had earlier deserted by jumping overboard—now created a stir; but when it became apparent that he would remain only under guard he was allowed to return to Liverpool. All that now delayed the hoisting of the sails was the arrival of the captain with a new cook and steward, for the confusion of departure had been intensified by their sudden desertion. The Old Land was soon to be but a memory.

CHAPTER VIII

Daily Life in the Steerage

"We have dancing on the main deck,
And preaching down below,
We have swearing in the foretop,
As through the waves we go."
            A sailors' jingle

It is recorded that the members of one of Lord Selkirk's emigrations stood sorrowfully on deck as long as it was possible to see their native land, but as Scotland faded from view they held a solemn conclave for the purpose of organizing the elements of life so dear to them in the Old Land—the home, the school, and the church; and so were transplanted on board ship, and eventually perpetuated in the wilderness of America, the traditions of generations of their ancestors.

The beginning of an ocean voyage is usually pleasing, and in the days of sail as the fresh sea breeze filled the sheets the passengers often felt quite jaunty for a short time. But as the land passed from view the wind increased, and the vessel tossed and rolled to the discomfiture of all but the most hardened voyagers. "After embarking," wrote William Wright, "we had a fair wind for three days, in which we sailed off in high glee; but after that we had a rough passage." When seasickness descended upon them, some were "bitterly cursing Columbus for having discovered America"; and, one writer observed, "While it lasts you will hardly have any reflections at all; you will think, if you do think, that the world ought never to have been made, particularly the watery part of it."

Numerous arrangements had to be effected before the evening of the first day at sea. On the *Rothiemurchus*, for example, the berths were still to be allotted. The Rev. William Bell considered that "the crying of the children, the swearing of the sailors, and the scolding of the women who had not got the beds they wanted, produced a concert in which it was difficult to discover any harmony. Its disagreeable effect was heightened by the darkness of the night and the rolling of the ship. . . .

DAILY LIFE IN THE STEERAGE

"The morning was fine, and the ebbing tide in a few hours carried us out of the river. During the day the wind, though light, continued favorable, and we had, literally speaking, a pleasure sail. Every heart was light and every face wore a smile. Some were reading the books they had the precaution to take along with them; some conversing about their prospects in America, or the friends they were leaving behind; and between decks a party of young people were dancing a good part of the day. . . . On the following morning I was awakened at an early hour by the violent motion of the ship and an unusual bustle on deck. On getting up I found that we were likely to have dancing enough against our will. A gale blew from the north-west. The sea roared and foamed around us, the passengers became sick, and everything began to wear a discouraging aspect. As we entered the Murray Firth things began to grow worse and worse. . . . Consternation and alarm were soon visible in every countenance; children were crying, and women wringing their hands and wishing they had remained at home."

The typical emigrant packet, writes Basil Lubbock, was "little better than a hermetically sealed box; as deep as it was long, with clumsy square bows and stern, with ill-cut, ill-set sails—its standing rigging of hemp a mass of long splices; and with a promenade deck no longer than the traditional two steps and overboard." As for the crews, they were commonly composed of "rum-soaked, illiterate, bear-like officers, who could not work out the ordinary meridian observation with any degree of accuracy, and either trusted to dead reckoning or a blackboard held up by a passing ship for their longitude; whilst they were worked by the typically slow-footed, ever-grousing Merchant Jack of the past two centuries." The poorest of such vessels were—like John Cabot's *Matthew*—so small that passengers could reach the water from the deck; and they carried so little sail that the passage was inevitably slow, even during favorable weather.

Upon the most overcrowded vessels the life of the steerage passenger was a continuous nightmare of suffering. To substantiate the statement "frequently heard" that the character of emigrant ships from Ireland was worse than those engaged in the African slave trade, the *Montreal Advertiser* cites the case of the *Thomas Gelston*, from Londonderry. This vessel carried a somewhat uncertain quota of passengers, estimated at from 450 to 517. "Upon the concurrent testimony of several of the passengers" it is stated that during the entire passage of nine weeks they were confined to the between-decks, where they suffered considerably from a shortage of food and water. The berthing arrangements alone were enough to demoralize them, for we learn that,

"besides two tiers of berths on the sides, the vessel was filled with a row of berths down the centre, between which and the side berths there was only a passage of about three feet. The passengers were thus obliged to eat in their berths. In one were a man, his wife, his sister, and five children; in another were six full-grown young women, whilst that above them contained five men, and the next one eight men."

These poor emigrants were fortunate in one respect only, for the weather was fine, enabling the hatches to be kept open; otherwise they must all have been smothered, or ravaged by disease. As it was, a dozen of them had to be taken to the cholera hospital immediately upon arrival at Montreal.

Some of the features of the 628-ton emigrant ship *St. Vincent* in 1844 were to be found in the better contemporary vessels. She accommodated about 240 passengers, and her length between decks was 124 feet, the height 6 feet 4 inches, and the breadth of the main hatchway 25 feet 3 inches. Stationary tables and benches were located midway between the rows of berths throughout the length of the ship, and beneath the tables were plate-racks and battens to hold the water casks. Hanging shelves were secured between beams. Double berths were six feet by three, single six feet by two, and each was separated from the next by a partition extending from top to bottom. Seats were fixed at the outer extremity of each bed-place. Water-closets for females were located on either side of this deck, but those for the male passengers were on the upper deck. Both ventilation and lighting were dependent upon scuttles, and the bulkheads were constructed to allow a free circulation of air. The officers and crew were berthed separately, handy to the upper deck. Hospital facilities included a six-bed room for women and one of four beds for men. These accommodations were undoubtedly superior to those of the average emigrant ship, for the expense was being borne almost entirely by the government, aided to some extent by the emigrants themselves or the parishes which sent them.

In most vessels there were rules of conduct, at least elementary, which steerage passengers particularly were forced to obey. Usually all lights had to be put out at 9 or 10 p.m. Married women were frequently asked to superintend the conduct of single females, a pretence at supervision which would not have been necessary if the Passenger Vessel Acts and instructions to emigration agents had been enforced. Male passengers were sometimes required to act as night watchmen, being appointed in rotation for three or four hours' duty. They were not only to prevent irregularities but, in the more primitive ships, to regulate ventilation by opening and closing the hatches according to the weather. In general, the passengers were advised that they should "do all in their power to assist the officers in the maintenance of order and clean-

Illustrated London News

LOADING THE BAGGAGE ABOARD

Many emigrants carried nothing but the rags on their backs, but others took all manner of goods to the New World.

Illustrated London News
DEPARTURE FROM WATERLOO DOCKS, LIVERPOOL

"The spectators on shore took off their hats and cheered lustily, and the emigrants raised a shout that must have been heard in Liverpool."

Illustrated London News
TOWING OUT

In the later period of the sailing-ship, vessels were usually towed out into the wind by steam tugs.

liness on board, as these are necessary to secure the safety and health of all. Any smoking in the between-decks, the lighting of lucifer matches or other unprotected lights, immoderate use of spirits, and, most dangerous of all, the giving of spirits to the crew, should at once be put a stop to, as calculated in a very great degree to endanger the safety of the ship and the lives of the passengers."

In the later period of the sailing-ship as an emigrant-carrier the regulations were not only more extensive but also more generally enforced—except during the great Irish exodus of 1847-1854. The improvements were a result of greater restrictions by American authorities. It was usually greatly to the disadvantage of a ship's master to arrive with an undue amount of disease among his passengers or an exceptionally filthy and ill-managed ship. A report of 1848 lists twenty-two regulations "for preserving order and cleanliness" on board ship, and from them it is possible to visualize the daily life of steerage passengers. Unless excused by the ship's doctor or the master, all were to rise by 7 a.m., and before breakfast they were to roll up their beds and arrange their effects. The daily cleaning of the passenger decks was done by sweepers appointed in rotation from all males over fourteen years of age, five for each one hundred passengers, their duties including scraping the deck and throwing overboard all accumulations of dirt and refuse. Two days each week were to be set apart as washdays, the deck only to be used for the purpose. Rules frequently disobeyed were those which prohibited the taking of spirits on board and "all fighting, gambling, riotous or quarrelsome behavior, swearing and violent language." No gunpowder was to be taken aboard, and swords or other offensive weapons were, like spirits, to be placed in the custody of the master until the close of the voyage. Owing to the danger of fire, the use of lights was greatly restricted. No naked lights were allowed at any time, while at night there were usually three safety lanterns, of which the one at the main hatchway burned all night, while the other two were extinguished, sometimes at 10 p.m. Cabin passengers were usually allowed to ignore the no-smoking regulations. On most ships three or four men were elected from the steerage to enforce the vessel's regulations, and to represent the group in any complaints to the captain, such representatives on one ship receiving a glass of rum as a fee—and to interview some captains was well worth it! Assisted or conducted emigrations were usually quite highly developed in the matter of self government, for there was frequently a superintendent in charge of the vessel, and he detailed persons to issue provisions and water, to act as cooks or take charge of the messes, or to inspect the performance of these various duties.

Some vessels required each passenger to appear on Sundays at 10 a.m. "in clean and decent apparel," and the day was observed "as religiously as circumstances will permit." In general, however, religious observances depended almost entirely upon the inclination of the individual. On most ships no encouragement or hostility was shown by the master or his crew. Some captains thought "that religion was all right in its place," and might be of some advantage in the general discipline of the passengers. Occasionally an officer would officiate at Sunday services for the cabin passengers only; and sometimes, when a clergyman happened to be on board, regular services were also held in the steerage—though more commonly a few worshipers gathered together for singing and prayer without clerical leadership, or would spend most of each Sunday, and frequently other days as well, in the study of the Bible. Many an emigrant was particularly homesick on the Sabbath. James Hopkirk of Glasgow wrote in his diary on the first Sunday at sea:

"I never shall nor can forget the happy days—particularly Sunday evenings—the western sun shining sweetly in—over the tops of laurel and acacia trees—the blackbirds and thrushes singing sweetly—ah, never, never shall I be so happy again, go wherever I may, I shall never see the place so beautiful in my eyes."

For the state-aided emigrants on the *Hope* two religious services were held every day after tea, the Roman Catholics selecting one of their number to recite prayers, while the ship's surgeon read to the rest the service of the day as set forth in the Book of Common Prayer. On the *Lord Wellington,* in addition to two Sunday services of the same nature, there was a third at which "the Captain prayed and read for an hour." The presence of a zealous clergyman sometimes resulted in several religious services daily. On the *Rothiemurchus* in 1817 were the Rev. Messrs. Bell and Taylor, who alternated in conducting the Presbyterian form of worship morning and evening. On the other hand there were many vessels upon which the unfortunate steerage passengers were too miserable even to know when Sunday came: "The poor emigrants," wrote a cabin passenger of a ship ravaged by fever, "were in their usual squalid attire; neither did the crew rig themselves out as on former Sundays." On some Scottish vessels the service was conducted in Gaelic, while on Irish ships the passengers were sometimes "divided into two parties,—those who spoke Irish, and those who did not; each section having a leader, who gabbled in his respective language a number of 'Paters and Aves,' as quickly as the devotees could count their beads." On one vessel a Protestant clergyman performed family worship every evening for all who cared to attend, "but the Irish Roman Catholics take great pleasure in dancing Irish jigs over his head during the service"; while on another a rather unorthodox service came to an informal end when the speaker, who stood on a flour barrel, was hurled headlong down the main hatchway by a sudden lurch of the ship. The barrel followed him, and his radical message was, in the opinion of his auditors, quite justly rewarded when his appearance was vastly changed by the flour!

Among the difficulties aboard ship, that of keeping clean was prominent. An agreeable captain sometimes allowed clothes-lines to be erected between the masts, but there were more vessels upon which no such privilege was conferred. It was easy enough for guidebooks and official circulars to advise emigrants that personal cleanliness was one of the primary essentials of a satisfactory passage, but it was another matter to clean either oneself or one's clothes when the use of water for such purposes was greatly restricted—if not prohibited; and it was usual, in addition, to insist that even personal cleaning be carried out upon the deck. Vermin frequently infested the steerage, and sometimes the cabin quarters as well. Those in the steerage of the *Tennessee*, for example, are described by a cabin passenger as "except one or two decent-looking Welsh, the most filthy and abominable wretches I ever saw, all of the very worst and lowest class of Irish, covered with the Itch and Lice to a most inconceivable degree." One guidebook, in emphasizing the importance of personal cleanliness, observes that "if fresh water is not allowed, use salt water with oatmeal"; and adds the advice that "keeping as much as possible on deck in the air, even in blowing weather, will contribute very much to preserve health, and prevent or relieve sea-sickness."[1] Evidence before a parliamentary committee indicates the state of affairs on some emigrant ships even in ordinary years:

"It was scarcely possible to induce the passengers to sweep the decks after their meals or to be decent in respect to the common wants of nature; in many cases, in bad weather, they would not go on deck; their health suf-

[1] *A Few Plain Directions*, 14-15. A. C. Buchanan assured emigrants that if they kept themselves and their possessions clean, remained on deck as much as possible, got up at five o'clock and retired at eight, and took a mug of salt water occasionally in the morning, they would land in America "in good health and better-looking than when you embarked." (*Emigration Practically Considered*, 88-9.)

fered so much that their strength was gone, and they had not the power to help themselves. Hence the between-decks were like a loathsome dungeon. When the hatchways were opened under which the people were stowed, the steam rose and the stench was like that from a pen of pigs. The few beds they had were in a dreadful state, for the straw, once wet with sea water, soon rotted, besides which they used the between-decks for all sorts of filthy purposes."

Throughout the sailing-ship period many emigrants provided their own supplies. The procedure when the vessel supplied the food was that the cook, steward or mate dealt out the rations daily, or at less frequent intervals, from barrels which had been brought on deck or into the steerage by the crew. By the late eighteen-twenties stoves were coming into general use in place of open grates,—at least on the better vessels in the emigrant trade. The ship's cook was frequently a disagreeable character—one man found him "as complete a blackguard as I ever saw,"—but his importance made it necessary to curry his favor by bribery or any other possible means. Sometimes passengers were so sick that they were unable to prepare their food—others, for the same reason did not receive their allowance. It was reported in 1844 that such conditions led to starvation amid plenty, as well as to a condition of lawlessness and tyranny in the steerage: "The strongest maintained the upper hand over the weakest, and it was even said there were some women who died of starvation." On a typical vessel in 1847 each adult received a pound of meal or bread daily, children under fourteen half that quantity, and those under seven, one-third. The meal, which was "of very bad quality," was distributed five days a week, and biscuit, which was good, was given out the other two. On either side of the foredeck were the fire-places, and at these were continually to be found a rabble of people.

"The fire was contained in a large wooden case, lined with bricks and shaped something like an old-fashioned settee, the coals being confined by two or three iron bars in front. From morning till evening they were surrounded by groups of men, women and children; some making stirabout in all kinds of vessels, and others baking cakes upon extemporary griddles. These cakes were generally about two inches thick, and when baked were encased in a burnt crust coated with smoke, being actually raw in the centre. Such was the unvaried food of the greater number of these poor creatures. A few of them who seemed to be better off had herrings or bacon. . . .

"The fire-places were the scenes of endless contentions. The sufferings they endured appeared to embitter the wretched emigrants one against the other. Their quarrels were usually only ended when the fires were extinguished, at 7 o'clock p.m., at which time they were surrounded by squabbling groups, preparing their miserable evening meal. They would not leave until Jack mounted the shrouds of the fore-mast and precipitated a bucket full of water on each fire; when they snatched up their pots and pans and,

DAILY LIFE IN THE STEERAGE

half-blinded by the steam, descended into the hold with their half-cooked suppers."

In general the rations were supposed to depend upon the terms of the various Passenger Vessel Acts in force from time to time, but lax inspection and enforcement, or mere fraud, varied the issue in such a way that the laws bear but little relation to actual conditions. On one voyage in 1821 casks of beef and flour were brought on deck each morning, and the mate weighed out the rations of each passenger, the quality in this instance being satisfactory even if the variety was not great. The bread given out by the captain of the *Rothiemurchus* in 1817 was, on the other hand, more than a year old, and the beef much older. "Indeed," says the Rev. William Bell, "I have never seen anything like the latter presented to human beings." The soup issued from time to time was "merely stinking water in which stinking beef had been boiled, which no dog would taste unless he was starving." On another occasion, during a storm, the only food served out was "rotten Dutch cheese, as bitter as soot, and bread partly alive." "Many of our passengers," wrote Mr. Bell, "were seized with a dysentery in consequence of eating putrid fresh beef; I mean some that was fresh when we left Leith, five weeks ago. They were not allowed to taste it till it was unfit for use, and then they were made welcome to use it. Three or four seemed almost in a dying condition, and were placed under the doctor's care." No wonder he advised prospective emigrants that "if passengers find their own provisions they will then have what is fit to eat."

But those who carried their own food were not always fortunate. John and Hester Parks wrote that they had "salt beef 3 years old, and sea-biscuits not fit for hogs," and the blame in this instance was laid at the door of a dishonest merchant; while many a passenger had to throw overboard supplies which had become rotten or mouldy. Plenty of travellers, of course, had satisfactory food throughout the voyage. Irish emigrants of the early period, we are told, lived "on oatmeal porridge, sometimes sweetened with molasses, a wholesome diet, but not common among Englishmen; and for dinner, herrings and potatoes." Nets were employed to keep each family's potatoes separate. This vegetable, frequently the Irishman's sole diet, and described by a clergyman as "the perfect luxury upon the ocean," became too expensive in the late eighteen-forties, and small quantities of oatmeal and sea-biscuit, often mouldy and of the poorest quality, were the poor man's food; while on the same vessels the crew's rations were much greater and very noticeably superior—beef, pork, biscuit, coffee, and lime juice. The effects of seasickness on the appetite varied greatly, some being unable to enjoy meals throughout the voyage, while others were cooking continually—"having had their stomachs completely emptied, they set about replenishing them with great industry."

Legislative enactments were more effective in increasing the cost of passage than in raising the standard of food. Barrelled beef and pork, bread-stuffs and potatoes always remained the staples, but other foods were frequently included. The first meal served to emigrants whose passage was being financed by the government in 1844 consisted of "good mutton, beef, potatoes and soup"; and the rations issued to them during the rest of the voyage included small quantities of rice, raisins, tea, coffee and sugar, which many an unassisted emigrant could neither afford to take with him nor expect the ship's master to issue. On vessels of the best class, where an attempt was made to serve passengers in an expeditious and satisfactory manner, the scene of activity which the deck presented at mealtime was no doubt similar to the impressions recorded in the diary of T. Skinner Prout:

> "Dinner is now announced, and the hatchways fore and aft are pouring a stream of hungry mortals. It is pea-soup day, and the cook, almost lost in the dense and savoury atmosphere of steam which rises from the coppers, is ministering to the creature wants of the attendant crowd, who, with hook-pot or pannikin in hand, are patiently waiting their turn. . . . Sometimes the forecastle (or fox'cle, as it is always called), an elevated platform in the bows of the vessel, is chosen for a select dinner-party, who, in the fresh open air, enjoy their meal in true pic-nic style. Tobacco is now the order of the day—the silent indulging in a pipe, the talkative enjoying a cigar—whilst all are happy. . . . The pipe finished, the afternoon's nap is a retreat to which emigrants on the passage out generally retire near tea-time, or near six-bells, when the cook is again at his post—the cry of 'Tea-water!' penetrates the depths below, and soon, in noisy response, clattering hook-pans, pannikins and pans are again rushing up the hatchways and crowding around the galley."

Legislation in 1850 further improved the rations—at least in theory. Supplies of food were to be issued at least twice weekly, and a week's supply as stipulated in the Act comprised 2½ lbs. bread or biscuit, 1 lb. wheaten flour, 5 lbs. oatmeal, 2 lbs. rice, 2 oz. tea, ½ lb. sugar and ½ lb. molasses; and it was legal for the ship's master to substitute 5 lbs. potatoes for 1 lb. of oatmeal or rice.

One of the most important considerations in the days of sailing-vessels was the water supply. The Passenger Vessel Acts regulated the minimum to be provided, but in early years the amount

DAILY LIFE IN THE STEERAGE 75

of water doled out more or less regularly to each passenger depended more frequently upon the agreement he arranged with the master before the voyage started; though when the ship was well out to sea the captain or his steward would frequently refuse on one pretext or another to live up to the contract. Similar treatment was usual even in the later period of emigration.

The amount of water to be supplied to each passenger varied slightly from time to time, but under the Act of 1842 it was required to be at least three quarts per day for each adult passenger. In the same Act it is stated that the water supply was to be stored in tanks or "sweet casks" of a capacity not exceeding 300 gallons; and the better vessels had small kegs or breakers in which was placed daily each family's allowance. In many ships, however, the water was never good, for the casks were filled from the river in which they happened to be anchored, and if enough was left for a second voyage they did not take the trouble to renew the supply; while even if the water was pure at the start it was often quite filthy before the voyage was half over, and it was usual to attempt by one means or another to smother the taste and odor. The Rev. William Bell writes as follows concerning his experiences with respect to the water supply:

"Our water for some time past has been very bad. When it was drawn out of the casks it was no clearer than that of a dirty kennel after a heavy shower of rain; so that its appearance alone was sufficient to sicken one. But its dirty appearance was not its worst quality. It had such a rancid smell that to be in the same neighborhood was enough to turn one's stomach; judge then what its taste must have been. . . . The stink it emitted was intolerable."

The innumerable references to impure water suggest that on only the best packets was it satisfactory. On one vessel in 1817 the passengers received three quarts per day at the start, but long before the two months' passage was over it had to be cut to the government minimum of five pints. It was at the same time very bad, and the lack in both quantity and quality led a Methodist preacher to reflect that "never did the children of God pant and long more eagerly for the water of life than the people do here for the clear spring water; but when will they long for the fountain of living waters? I fear some never; I hope others in due time." An entry in the diary kept by a traveller in 1847 represents the unrecorded experiences of millions of emigrants:

"The Head Committee brought a can of water to show it to the captain: it was quite foul, muddy, and bitter from having been in a wine cask. When allowed to settle it became clear, leaving considerable sediment in the bottom of the vessel; but it retained its bad taste. The mate endeavoured to improve it by trying the effect of charcoal and of alum; but some of the casks were beyond remedy, and the contents, when pumped out, resembled nauseous ditch water."

Towards the close of this voyage the water became entirely useless, and the steerage passengers had to employ salt water. Of that reserved for the crew and the one cabin passenger there was half a cask left, and this was all that the ship contained. So great was the suffering of those in the steerage that the cabin passenger gave "one or two of them a mouthful from the cask upon the quarterdeck. . . . They asked for it so pitifully and were so thankful; but I could not satisfy all, and regretted the disappointment of many."

In general the best that could be expected was that the ship's water could be made usable, even if still repulsive, by the addition of vinegar or some other more pleasing liquid. Like the other conditions of the passage, it was something that had to be endured with the best grace possible, and by people many of whom had no moral or physical reserve to enable them to bear hardships the most intense of which were entirely unnecessary.

Apart from the defective water supply, there were, however, numerous ships upon which the greatest inconveniences suffered by many emigrants were seasickness, monotony, and lack of privacy. Lavatories, except of the most primitive nature, were never available, and, as William Cobbett says, "A married man will easily conceive the many awkward, ludicrous and painful circumstances that must here occur." In some cases the men went on deck while the women were dressing, but conditions were most oppressive when everyone was seasick and incapable of moving about. Refined women often hesitated to use the primitive public conveniences, and so permanently injured their health while in some degree preserving their modesty.

It was the general experience that children were "never troubled with seasickness the whole voyage," or recovered very quickly. Many adults, on the other hand, were ill for a month or more. Robert Mudie observed that "females, though a little more inclined to be sick than men, are still very hardy at sea, and probably accommodate themselves more speedily and completely to the circumstances than the other sex. Generally speaking, they can be managed by a little attention, and a few words bordering upon flattery." Another guidebook, offering "practical advice to emi-

DAILY LIFE IN THE STEERAGE 77

grants," suggests that "there is much unoccupied time on shipboard, and women should take with them some linen to make up, or materials for knitting, and a few books if they possess any, by no means forgetting that book of books, the Bible." James Brown adds other works of a miscellaneous character, "such as *Chambers' Journal*, and *Information for the People*, the *Penny* and *Saturday* magazines"; and he suggests that "even a few odd numbers of *Punch*, the *Illustrated London News*, or it may be, one or two old newspapers, will be generally found very acceptable antidotes to the ennui usually attending a voyage across the Atlantic."

Many passengers spent much of their time in the care of their families; and when this was impossible because of the illness of the parents the children not infrequently died. In fine weather and under favorable conditions it was no doubt amusing, as one cabin passenger pointed out, to observe how quickly the small sons and daughters copied the characteristic rolling gait of the sailor, and balanced themselves in capital fashion as the ship was tossed about by the waves. On typical emigrant ships, however, the unfortunate children were so confined that they spent most of their time in the vitiated air and cramped quarters of their bunks, and it is hardly necessary to add that neither for them nor their parents was there any attempt at organized entertainment, and certainly no aid in that direction from the ship's crew. On one vessel it was the duty of the Head Committee to administer the "cat" to such little boys as became too uproarious. The steerage passengers of the best packets might rarely be permitted to derive some amusement from the more highly developed activities in the cabin, where sometimes a band played, and concerts, plays and organized sports were arranged. On the *Julius Macgregor* there was "a melancholy attempt to get up a debating club," but the only persons who seemed to enjoy the voyage were "a young farmer and a rather pretty girl," who were never at a loss for a subject of conversation.[2]

Conduct aboard ship varied, as on land, with the initiative and habits of individuals. On some vessels tradesmen made money repairing shoes and clothes, while other passengers were frittering away their time and cash gambling or drinking rum. Whether or not anyone ever acted upon the unique suggestion of the author of

---

[2] "Voyage in an Emigrant Ship," *Chambers' Edinburgh Journal*, April 13, 1844, p. 230. In listing activities in the steerage, William Hancock emphasizes lovemaking. "Of this," he says, "there is plenty—of its kind—and at all times; most of the arrangements, or lack of such, being such as to permit of the most unrestricted intercourse between the sexes; to promote immorality and place modesty and decency at a discount." (*An Emigrant's Five Years in the Free States of America*, 9-10.)

The Emigrant's Pocket Companion, it is at least commendable enough to record:

> "Another very useful preparation is the materials of a mimic log house. A bundle of sticks may be had for a few pence. When the emigrants are on board, the men, and especially the boys, will find something more than amusement in cutting them off the proper lengths for sides and ends, notching them when they cross the corners, piling them up, making a roof, and so finishing a miniature habitation. Plain models of houses, and of the more necessary implements used in the settlements, would make excellent additions in every emigrant's ship, because by the assistance of them a clever emigrant might have all his new trades half learned before he landed; and time which otherwise is absolutely lost would thus be applied to the most useful of all purposes. Even a gnarly piece of wood, to exercise the axe upon, is good for keeping the hand employed; and the notion of a Scotchman having always a knife and a stick in his fingers, which is ridiculed in English company, is far from a bad one among emigrants."

The damage which might result when a hundred strong-armed Irishmen were wielding axes at one time, supposedly upon blocks of wood but more frequently against the hull of the vessel, is quite apparent; and that the temptation to use them upon one another might be hard to resist is seen from the following description:

> "When seasickness had done its work amongst the steerage passengers the natural passion for a fight soon showed itself amongst our Hibernian friends. The Munster and Connaught men got up a good old-fashioned faction fight, perhaps to illustrate the beauties of 'Home Rule' on the 'rolling deep.' So at it they went, hammer, tongs, and shillalahs, pitching each other down the hatchways head over heels. Matters having become serious the sailors thought it time to spoil the sport. Handspikes, from 'heaving' the capstan, were heaved to some purpose, and the Irishmen soon beat a retreat."

The Irish very frequently aroused apprehension on board ship. William Brown, who travelled second cabin on the *Oxford*, states that the greatest concern was felt that the vessel would be "set on fire by the thoughtless Irish." Three hundred of them were huddled together in the steerage, and some would,

> "through the whole night, stick a candle against the side of the ship or against the berths as they played at cards or smoked tobacco; and if there should be any appearance of the ship's officers, the lighted candle or the pipe was thrust under the bedstraw, or into any place at hand. . . . If there had not been one or two steady Englishmen among the wild Irish, the ship would have been set on fire, and perhaps hundreds of lives sacrificed."

Dancing was a common pastime on shipboard, if the passengers were not too miserable to think of amusement. Much depended, of course, on whether they were congenial companions, or preferred to keep out of one another's way. On the *John Dennison* there was a dance almost daily, and plenty of rum from the captain's grog-shop to sustain the enthusiasm of the participants:

DAILY LIFE IN THE STEERAGE 79

"My acquaintance the surgeon could play the fiddle well and also take his glass of grog. The captain having given his consent, a gallon of rum was purchased from the ship's steward; and at six p.m. the quarter-deck being cleared, the surgeon playing the fiddle and the master baker acting as master of the ceremonies, the dance and merriment were kept up with great spirit until four bells, or 10 p.m. Many more bottles besides the gallon were drunk."

Even on a plague-ridden ship of "the black year of emigration" (1847) the young people got up a dance; though the remonstrance of the mate altered their diversion to singing, and their "monotonous howling was quite in unison with the scene of desolation." On the good ship *Hope*, after eight bells, it was usual to make ready for a dance in the forward part of the vessel:

"A musical Jack is soon found, who, seated on a coil of rope or perched on a spar, in a very short time is plying most vigorously the fun-inspiring fiddle. In the confined space of a ship's deck polkas and quadrilles are out of the question, though at first much affectedly fastidious disinclination is expressed against the reel and jig. But it is not long before these last reign triumphant, and delicate forms and choice spirits foot the monotonous but merry-going measure with as much enjoyment as if they moved in a minuet before hundreds of observant eyes."

Dancing was not the only amusement on the *Hope*: "On the poop, children are gambolling; whilst those in converse sweet, or in gossip most intent, keep up a continued promenade on the deck." Some wide-eyed passengers were always to be seen watching the ship's officers adjust their instruments to take the sun's altitude in order to determine the vessel's latitude. Below deck, various activities passed the evenings away. In one place

"a little group surrounds some learned friend, who has industriously worked the ship's course for the last day, and is now giving a detailed report to his companions, who all busily examine the amateur's well-thumbed chart, as if they knew a great deal about it. A little beyond, perhaps, the boatswain, from his cabin door, spins one of his long, marvellous yarns to his credulous open-mouthed neighbor on the opposite side. Further on, again, is the emigrants' quarters, the interior of which can be seen through an opening in the bulkhead. Good wives are now displaying their matronly qualities, but in most cases vainly endeavouring to calm the *Baby-Ionish* confusion of tongues and screaming squall that, for at least one hour, prevails in the family compartment of the ship. To add to the quiet enjoyment of compelled but resigned spectators, sundry night-capped heads of disturbed damsels, retired for the night, appear from their berths, but produce little effect by their complaining, whilst the unblanketed lower extremities of others, more calm and philosophic, may be also seen projecting from the narrow confines of their beds. But hark! Four bells is striking; 'Lights out' is heard in various quarters; and in a few minutes, save the measured tread of the watch on deck, the rustling sails, and rippling waters on the vessel's way, not a sound is heard."

Although the modern liner's luxurious swimming pool had not even been thought of, there were sometimes substitutes. A number of the emigrants on one ship had a swim in the ocean one fine calm day; while a passenger of another was nearly drowned when he found it much harder to climb up the side of the moving ship than to lower himself into the ocean. An occasional agreeable captain made it possible for his passengers to enjoy the luxury of a bath on deck. On the *John Dennison* in 1833 the master ordered an empty puncheon with its head stove in to be filled with sea water, and "men and women availed themselves of it as if they were so many ducks." . . . "There is," wrote John Weston, "little ceremony in such matters on board an emigrant ship."

There were, of course, other diversions available on all but the worst of Atlantic vessels. "Pitch and toss" and "bowling at sea" were among the games played on deck when the ship was not rolling too much. "The great American game of Eukre" was often popular below deck, and "numerous parties were busy playing cards at the rate of one penny per game, which was spent in rum," for the captain ran a lucrative grog-shop on this vessel. A special celebration took place on most American packets on Independence Day, since "wherever an American happens to be on that day, whether in the midst of the ocean or in the forests of the Western Country, the 4th of July must be observed."[3] On the ship *Magnet* in 1819 "the natal day of a female on board was celebrated by a general tea-party on deck; hyson and bohea, Yorkshire cakes, biscuits, pickled tripe, and salt beef abundantly furnished the sumptuous *gala*, interspersed with a profusion of chat and some scandal, usual in such *converzationes*." The weather suddenly changed, however, and a sharp wind caused considerable derangement and confusion, accompanied by

"'Hawl in the main sheet! . . . Down topsails! . . . Reef the foresail! . . . Cheerly, my hearts, now she rights again! . . . My timbers, what a squall was there!' . . . In ten minutes all was calm and the violin reassembled the company, dancing commenced, and all the variety of the capering *melange* was exhibited—from the graceful attitudes of the *catabaws* to the spread-eagle monotony of the *minuet de la coeur.*"

[3] Arfwedson, *The United States and Canada*, I, 7. Captain Lines of the French-American packet *New York* ordered champagne for his cabin passengers to drink the health of the United States on July 4th, 1847. (Playfair, *Recollections of a Visit*, 7.)

CHAPTER IX

STORM AND MISERY

"We were very sick for three weeks coming over. We had the misfortune to lose both our little boys. We were very much hurt to have them buried in a watery grave."

Harriot Veness

A storm at sea! What a vision these words call up before the imagination! The adventures of Robinson Crusoe, Richard Henry Dana's *Two Years before the Mast*, Captain Marryat's tales of the sailor's life in the days of the wind-ship! But if those accustomed to the sea endured hardships, how much greater were the sufferings of emigrants in the hold, many of whom had never seen a ship before, and who were, besides, shut down in the dark amid indescribable sickness and misery. The waves broke upon the deck, the wind tore through the rigging, and the ship creaked and groaned as if about to break up. In the pitch black of midnight all hands had been called on deck, and the captain's orders, shouted through his trumpet, were answered by the wails and chants of the sailors in the shrouds. The tramping above and the confusion all around frightened those in the steerage out of their wits. The air was foul, for the hatches had been battened down for a week. With each roll of the ship the people in the crowded berths were bumped and bruised as they were hurled from side to side against the rough partitions, and there was real danger of crushing the children to death. Water leaked through from the deck in such quantities that the beds were soaked and the floor ankle deep, so that many thought the vessel was sinking. Candle lanterns could not be lighted, nor had there been any cooking for days—not even the preparation of a warm drink. The crashing of casks, tinware, and dishes as the ship pitched and heaved, the shrieking and crying of women and children, and the wild noise of the storm combined with the weakened and impoverished condition of the steerage passengers to create a time of horror which could never be effaced from memory.

The Atlantic passage westward has been noted for its roughness since the days of Columbus, and the strength of the prevailing westerly winds is best shown by the addition of ten to fifteen days to the average eastward voyages of the best ships. The vessel which escaped storms was most fortunate. When the forerunner of the great modern liners—the *Great Eastern*—was constructed in the late 1850's it was confidently hoped "that her vast weight will effectually resist the attacks of storm and wind, and that seasickness will be a thing unknown in her experience." But, like many another prophecy, this optimistic suggestion did not prove correct, and even the best of the steel liners of the present day have frequently to survive a battering of sustained intensity.

There was a saying among seamen, "Never be alarmed until the captain is"; but it was very hard for steerage passengers, shut up as they were in darkness, to avoid imagining the worst. "A sudden heave of the ship," wrote one traveller, "often dislodged whole families from their berths, and hurled them headlong among their companions who lay on the opposite side. . . . Ejaculations, shrieks, and screams burst from the mouths of men, women and children." . . . "No tongue," wrote another, "can express, or mind conceive the state we were in—all, I may say, expected every moment to be swallowed in the great deep." . . . A cabin passenger describes the situation on a vessel where 180 people were confined in the dark in a space "not larger than a large drawing-room": "I popped my head down for a minute or two, but the smell was too powerful for my olfactory nerves—children crying, women screaming; butter, biscuit, treacle, herrings, beef and potatoes, . . . all rolling from side to side, made up a scene of misery and confusion such as I never saw before." But in the cabin it was not so bad—perhaps the worst was when "one of the passengers received a plateful of pease-soup into his breast which he intended to have gone down by his mouth into his stomach."

Richard Weston gives a vivid description of one of the stormiest passages any vessel ever survived. Almost from its commencement, until, battered and crippled, the *Camillus* approached her destination, there had been but little expectation that she would ever reach land: "Ship quivering, masts creaking, pumps going. . . . The ship now seemed perfectly unmanageable. . . . The water poured down in torrents. . . . The condition of the women especially was deplorable; one told me she had not been in bed for four nights, and had remained all that time in her wet clothes. . . . The women were screaming at a dreadful rate. . . . Death appeared now certain." Sometimes people were killed by lightning during a storm, or the ship was disabled by having its mainmast splintered. On one vessel two waterspouts followed a disaster of

STORM AND MISERY

this kind, and so terrified were the passengers that all sense of delicacy was temporarily abandoned—"delicate females were seen, half frantic, staggering about in their chemises."

When at length the storm subsided, many a vessel was, both internally and externally, little better than a wreck: "On getting up after a sleepless night, in which we received many a bruise and uttered many a groan, I was informed that we were on our way back to Leith to refit." In most cases, however, the crew contrived to repair the vessel at sea. "At one period," writes George Philips, "her top-masts, yards, and different parts of the rigging were carried away, her sails were split, her quarter boards stove in; everything that was loose on deck washed away; yet in an incredibly short time the hardy sailors had repaired the damage." But while the injury to the ship could speedily be estimated and repaired, it was very different in the case of the passengers and their effects: "What a sight was now presented between decks! Clothes and vessels of all descriptions; spoons, knives, broken bottles, basins and jugs, shoes and hats, with provisions of all sorts, were strewed over the decks or lying in promiscuous heaps." On the *John Dennison* several passengers were badly cut up, and many quarrels arose as each person tried to collect his smashed and scattered possessions. On a fever-ridden ship "the poor passengers were greatly terrified by the storm and suffered exceedingly. They were so buffeted about that the sick could not be tended; and after calm was restored a woman was found dead in her berth." Instances of excessive damage in the steerage were not uncommon, as is shown by the following note from a woman to her father:

"I write these few lines to you, hoping to find you in good health, as, thank God, it leaves us at present. We had a very long voyage over. We were 9 weeks on the seas. We landed the 7th of June. We were tossed about very much indeed. The 3rd of May we all thought of being lost; the berths all fell down, from one end of the ship to the other; and I was not well after that, till I was confined, and that was on the 3rd of June. I got about again quite as soon as I could expect."

Births during the voyage were quite a usual occurrence. One woman wrote home: "I should think it a great mercy that near 400 people came over in one ship and only one little infant died of them, and there was four births before we got there." William Bell, in his exhaustive narrative, records a birth on his ship:

"About midnight a woman lately married was taken with premature labour, and added much to the horror of the scene by her dismal cries. But before morning she was safely delivered of a male child, and in a few days was as well as before. The surgeon's situation, during her labour, was scarcely less embarrassing than her own. He was several times thrown down by the violent motion of the ship, and at one time the berth in which she lay went to pieces with a crash, which made some people think that the good *Rothiemurchus* herself had uttered her last groan."

When overcrowded conditions led to disease and death, the agony of parents who saw their loved ones sink to a watery grave was enough to drive them to madness. A letter records the suffering of a mother and father who lost both their sons during the voyage:

"We had the misfortune to lose both our little boys; Edward died 29th April, and William 5th May; the younger died with bowel complaint, the other with rash fever and sore throat. We were very much hurt to have them buried in a watery grave: we mourned their loss; night and day they were not out of our minds. We had a minister on board, who prayed with us twice a day: he was a great comfort to us, on account of losing our poor little children. . . . There were six children and one woman died in the vessel."[1]

The entire passage of some vessels in the plague years was a time of horror in which hundreds were ill and sea-burials a daily occurrence. On three vessels alone in 1847 there were 313 burials at sea, apart altogether from subsequent deaths among the 322 who were sick on arrival, and it may be assumed that sea-burials in such numbers were marked by no ceremonies whatever. In ordinary times it was an impressive occasion—"No outward symbols of woe, no crape, no weepers, but the hearts of all were affected." On the better vessels, upon which a death was unusual, there was a ceremony that was often quite elaborate:

"The scene on board the little vessel in mid-ocean, when the body was committed to the deep, was most impressive. . . . On the morning preceding the burial, notices were posted here and there on the ship, setting forth that the body would be committed to the sea at a certain hour. It was a beautiful day, and a cloudless sky was mirrored in the great ocean that lay beneath it like a sheet of glass. On the deck the passengers moved around as if afraid to disturb the quiet repose that seemed everywhere. . . . At length the ship's bell began to toll slowly in the solemn tones of a funeral knell. At one of the hatchways on the upper deck two stout sailors were seen to emerge, followed by two more with heads uncovered, and moving with that measured and solemn tread that seemed to keep time to the tolling of the death bell. They bore between them the dead body, which had been tied up in a piece of sail-cloth, with a great weight fastened to the feet. The mournful cortege moved round the ship till it came to a part where a board was laid to receive the remains. On this they were placed, when the captain took

[1] Letter of John and Harriot Veness, in Cobbett, *The Emigrant's Guide*, 73. The following obituary notice appeared in the *Cobourg Star* of June 6, 1832:
"At sea, on their passage out to Quebec, the three younger children of John Mewburn, Esquire, late of Whitby, in Yorkshire, Surgeon.—Rebecca Elennor, Margaret and Arthur. Their remains were interred in one grave, in the Protestant Burial Ground, on Friday morning, the 25th May, 1832. The funeral service was performed by the Venerable the Archdeacon of Quebec. 'They were lovely in their lives, and in death they were not divided.'"

Illustrated London News

THE ROLL-CALL

Before the ship put to sea it was necessary to eliminate the helpless or deformed and those who could not produce tickets.

Illustrated London News

THE SEARCH FOR STOWAWAYS

Many destitute men passed days or weeks hidden in barrels or chests and were more dead than alive when discovered.

Illustrated London News

EMIGRANTS IN THE STEERAGE

In many instances the passengers were never out of the overcrowded steerage quarters during the voyage.

his place and read the beautiful service of the Church of England. As he reached 'O death, where is thy sting? O grave, where is thy victory? With the full hope of a glorious resurrection we commit this body to the deep,' one end of the board was raised, and all that was mortal of the poor emigrant shot down into the dark sea with a weird-like splash that seemed to strike every person on board with horror. All looked eagerly over the side of the ship, but nothing was to be seen but a slight ripple on the face of the deep water. Orders were now given to the men to man the yards, the boatswain piped for wind, which slowly arose, filling the sails, and the good ship bore away to the distant west."

Low and vulgar fellow-passengers increased the miseries of many a voyage, and, as one man records, the "floating hell" would have been unbearable had there not been "the hope of being speedily out of it." Charlotte Willard wrote home: "We had a very uncomfortable set to come with; there was not a day went over our heads but what there was a quarrelling or a fighting." On one vessel there were "robberies almost every night," the blame in this instance being laid upon the crew. "I was deprived of my new blankets," wrote one woman, in a letter describing her experiences. "They was stolen out of my berth and one old one placed in the room, and many more things, James' best hat, Charlotte's bonnet, Maria's shawl and caps besides; I know where they went to, some had them."

The success or failure of individuals has often a remarkable reaction upon those with whom they are in personal contact, and the old proverb, "Misery loves company," was well exemplified on board an emigrant ship. On the worst vessels those in the overcrowded steerage frequently degenerated—mentally and physically. Very few passengers were comfortable, and there was sometimes a distinct tendency to be jealous of a fellow-emigrant's good luck and to rejoice at his misfortune. Perhaps the humor of a disagreeable situation was more apparent at sea than elsewhere, or it may be that the joyful prospect of the promised land weakened one's sense of balance,—whatever the reason, "Everyone bound for America," writes one man, "laughs at his comrade's misfortunes, let them be ever so serious." On the *John Dennison* a water cask broke loose, careened drunkenly along the deck, and overturned upon a poor woman asleep in her berth—and everyone laughed; he who laughed loudest was soon afterwards thrown from his position by a sudden lurch of the ship, smashing an expensive jar of highly-prized snuff in the process—and everyone laughed again, including the water-soaked lady; irreplaceable food was destroyed, people were painfully injured—but it was all a good joke: "Every misfortune that befell any one in our ship was a source of amusement to the rest."

The characteristics of ship captains and their crews were almost as variable as the vessels themselves or the weather. But the hardship of the life was conducive to the development of a rough and vulgar set of men, among whom the milk of human kindness was not a prominent feature. In some vessels there appears to have been no discipline among either passengers or crew. "We don't wish you to come with such company as we did," wrote Stephen Turner in 1828. "From the captain to the lowest sailor they were abominable wicked; and there was no order, but swearing, cursing and drinking." Similarly Francis Thomas, who crossed on the *Hebe* in 1833, observed in his diary that the crew were "a set of the most vile abandoned wretches I ever met with." On the worst vessels women were subjected to molestation and assault, and one guidebook observed with some heat that it was high time a determined effort was made "to prevent the violation of innocent and unprotected females by the brutes who are to be found sailing as officers or crews."

Drunkenness was a cause of much misery on board ship. Many captains had a grog-shop, and were not only frequently drunk themselves, but allowed the crew and passengers to purchase it, "whereby many have been known to have passed from England to America in a continued state of drunkenness." On the *John Dennison* the decent passengers were kept awake all night by the carousals of the drunken; and the captain found his grog-shop so popular that he tried to raise the price of rum, but a threat of refusal to purchase brought him around. The only excitement in the voyage of Walter Riddell on the *Lancaster* in 1833 was occasioned by the drunkenness of the captain during the ship's passage through an ice field, but it was almost enough to put a sudden and disastrous end to the voyage:

"Last night about ten o'clock got among a field of ice; it was that thick we could see no way through it: about 6 the Captain appeared to be drunk, and the seamen would not obey his orders; at the same time Edgar Mitchell, one of the seamen, got his thigh broken between the yard and the mast; the Captain having hold of the helm, run the ship betwixt two pieces of ice, and some of the seamen cried we were all gone. John Fairgrieve ran and took the Captain from the helm; they struggled together till some of the men interposed; the Captain threatened dreadfully what he would do when he reached Quebec."

Foreigners who could not speak English were sometimes subjected to exceptional brutality. Details are on record of a voyage towards the close of the sailing-ship period in which Germans, Swedes, and Dutch formed a large proportion of the passengers, the remainder being Irish. The passage from Liverpool to Quebec occupied nine weeks, and it was a time of unmitigated terror. The Irish were let alone, but the others were treated like slaves. The sailors drove them to work with rope's ends, forcing them to man the pumps, and pouring cold water on any who could not keep pace with the demands. Only those who could pay handsomely received the proper allowance of food; and women, children, and the aged and infirm found the hardships unbearable. One man was actually murdered, and though there was no disease aboard, twenty-six others wilted under the harsh treatment and were thrown into the sea. "It's a wonder we didn't all die," commented one passenger. A complaint was entered upon arrival at Quebec, and the unfortunate immigrants were told that the captain was imprisoned and it would go hard with him—but the wise ones doubted the truth of the assertion.[2]

Experiences of individual passengers on merchant ships were very different from those of emigrants closely packed in vessels engaged solely in the trade. "A Young Emigrant," who was the only passenger aboard an American vessel of 850 tons bound from Liverpool to Boston, experienced a passage in the summer of 1851 that was quite unique in many respects. Although they differed in kind, there were plenty of anxieties and misfortunes on this vessel. She was new, but had been badly caulked, and the pumps had to be worked most of the way. Worse still, the crew was frequently mutinous, among its members being a first mate who had formerly sailed on a slaver, a "black nigger for a steward," who during the crossing was almost murdered in a fight with the cook, and numerous other undesirable characters whom the captain, "a humane, reasonable man," found it almost impossible to control. As a result of the stabbing affray the deck was "stained with splashes of blood," and the cabin "slippery as glass with the same abomination in spite of all the washing." As if such conditions were not enough, the weather, too, was unfavorable. Two weeks after setting sail the vessel had merely been driven southward towards the Azores, the weather throughout that period being a mixture of fogs, rains,

[2] Kohl, *Travels in Canada and through the States of New York and Pennsylvania,* I 327-9. While it was illegal for a master to inflict corporal punishment on his passengers, Richard Weston reports the case of a steerage emigrant put in irons and severely ruptured in the process. He was very ill during the rest of the passage, but upon reaching New York he laid a charge against the captain and the mate and recovered $150 damages. (Weston, *A Visit to the United States,* 12 fn.)

calms, and squalls. On August 6th the passenger wrote as follows in his diary:

"Since yesterday a strong south breeze, with a wild electric sky and constantly falling barometer, made us expect a gale, and from royals we came down to single-reefed topsails, and then at 9 p.m. appearances were such that the Captain furled everything but the three close-reefed topsails and foretop staysails. Lightning flashed incessantly, gusts of wind wandered over the sea as though they knew not where to go. We expected a heavy gale but have since had calms and squalls, lying to under a mere nothing of canvas, still in the same wearying uncertainty of what is in store for us. . . . A huge rolling sea flings us helplessly about and astonishes everybody."

A week later the storm broke, and a very different picture is presented:

"The storm was rushing and howling over us like legions of insane lions, or rather it was as though a Niagara of wind was dashing against us. The gusts seemed too solid for air; they came with the resistless weight of a torrent of water, bearing the poor ship down before its mighty onset till she looked like a helpless woman cowering beneath the rage of her drunken husband. As long as she could be kept right before the wind there was not much to fear, but with such a press of canvas, main-topgallant sail over single-reefed topsails, it was no easy matter to steer her steadily. At last a sweep to windward—a sickening lurch as the blast caught her beam, soon brought our captain out from his lair, when, instead of adding to the already scarce endurable strain on the spars, as he had before been promising himself to do, he had only time to get in his topgallant sail, and two more reefs in his topsails, before the gale seemed suddenly to wake up to its work with a fury I had not before seen equalled, horrible in its grandeur—a storm run mad—a delirious tempest—such it seemed to me. I used to imagine I had had experience in the wrath of the wind, but this was an exhibition of its frenzy quite novel to me. I could not stand without holding on by the rigging before blasts which came down on us with a vengeful violence—a crushing weight as though they would grind the ship to powder. The yelling of the gale through the blocks, the hoarse roaring in the shrouds and rigging, might be compared to the war-whoop of a whole nation of Red Indians among their own stormtost forests. It was very dark, but through the darkness gleamed the snowy manes of the huge waves as they came toppling after us like mountains torn up from their roots. . . . I felt the poor ship fairly quiver in the mighty grasp of the tempest."

Although the writer of this description was no novice at sea, having made the round trip to Australia, he found but little to relish on the Atlantic crossing. There were annoyances like "the incessant shower of tobacco juice which rains on the deck in a way which would not be permitted in an English ship," and the miserable oil lantern by which one read and wrote at night. These, however, were minor inconveniences on a leaky ship in bad weather with a mutinous and murderous crew. It is not surprising that, like many another emigrant, he was inclined to "wish myself out of the ship as soon as may be."

CHAPTER X

Cholera and Ship Fever

"The wretched husband was a very picture of desperation and misery. After the grave was filled up he took the shovels and, placing them crosswise upon it, calling heaven to witness, said, 'By that cross, Mary, I swear to revenge your death. As soon as I earn the price of my passage home I'll go back and shoot the man that murdered you, and that's the landlord.'"

"Untutored, degraded, famished and plague-stricken as they were, I assert that there was more true heroism, more faith, more forgiveness to their enemies and submission to the Divine Will exemplified in these victims than could be found in ten times the number of their oppressors."

"A Cabin Passenger": *The Ocean Plague*

The overcrowding on emigrant vessels, together with defective diet and the lack of medical supervision, provided the best of soil for the spread of contagious diseases among those whose power of resistance had been greatly lessened by poverty and destitution. In 1831 a plague of Asiatic cholera devastated the north of England, and continued in the spring and summer of 1832 on board vessels bound for America; but even in ordinary years there was frequently an excessive amount of disease. In 1827, of 160 who set sail from Ireland on the brig *James*, five died during the passage, 35 were left at Newfoundland as they were too ill to proceed, and the remaining 120 were suffering from the disease when the infected ship finally reached America. Nor did such a record call forth more than passing comment.

In 1837 James Stuart, Colonial Assistant Surgeon, examined the *Lady Macnaughton* and *Minerva* as they reached Grosse Isle —before approaching which it was usual for ships to clean house thoroughly. He found the steerage quarters filled from stem to stern with boxes, leaving only a narrow passage to afford access to berths. Bulkheads to separate males from females added to the obstructions, and wherever any spaces remained, as underneath the lower berths, they were "filled with every sort of filth, broken biscuit, bones, rags, and refuse of every description, putrefying and filled with maggots." Toilets were in the immediate vicinity of the berths and "horribly offensive." In fact the atmosphere throughout the entire steerage quarters was "almost insufferable to those who came into it from the fresh air." On the *Lady Macnaughton* over fifty deaths had occurred during the voyage, but even though the living pushed into the former quarters of the dead, the vessel was still "very overcrowded."

In 1831-1832 emigration to America had reached a peak for the early period, and the English cholera epidemic quickly spread to the unsanitary ships. Many vessels had experiences similar to that of the *Brutus*, which left Liverpool on May 18, 1832, with 330 emigrants:

> "On the 27th, the ninth day out from Liverpool, a healthy man about thirty years of age was seized with malignant cholera. The usual remedies were used and he recovered. The next case was that of an old woman, 60 years of age, who died 10 hours after the attack. The ravages of the pestilence then rapidly increased, the deaths becoming numerous in proportion to the cases. The greatest number of deaths was 24 in one day. The captain had not, it seems, any intention of returning to port, until the disease began to attack the crew. He then saw that to continue the voyage was to risk the lives of himself and the survivors, as well as the property entrusted to his care. Under these circumstances, his vessel a lazarhouse, and men, women, and children dying about him, he resolved to put back to Liverpool. The resolution was formed on the 3rd instant and the *Brutus* reached port on Wednesday morning. Up to that day the cases had been 117, the deaths 81, and the recoveries 36."

Perhaps the reaction of the passengers under such conditions is best expressed by one Sholto, a Scotchman who saw 53 emigrants, including his mother and sister, thrown into the sea "one after t'other."

> "One got used to it—it was nothing but splash, splash, all day long—first one, then another. There was one Martin on board, I remember, with a wife and nine children—one of those as sold his pension: he had fought in Spain with the Duke of Wellington. Well, first his wife died, and they threw *her* into the sea and then *he* died, and they threw *him* into the sea, and then the children, one after t'other, till only two were left alive; the eldest, a girl about thirteen who had nursed them all, one after another, and seen them die—well, *she* died, and then there was only the little fellow left. . . . He went back, as I heard, in the same ship with the captain."

Over 1,500 died at the port of Quebec during a few days while this epidemic was at its height. In 1834 there was a serious recurrence of typhus fever, cholera, and measles. The barque *Mary*, from Cork with 300 emigrants, reached Grosse Isle with forty cases of measles or fever, and seven deaths had occurred during the passage, while nine other vessels were being detained at the Quarantine Station at the same time.[1]

---

[1] *Quebec Gazette*, May 19, 26, and June 13, 1834. In addition to the epidemics of Asiatic cholera described in this chapter there were recurrences of the disease in 1835-36 at Quebec and New York, in 1848 and 1849 at New Orleans, and in 1854, 1866, and 1867 at New York. The plague spread through parts of America with varying intensity.

CHOLERA AND SHIP FEVER

Two references to ships entering at New Orleans are among the most terrible examples of the ravages of disease. On one of them, out of 108 passengers and 17 seamen, yellow fever or ague carried off a total of 107, leaving but 18 demoralized and hardly human beings to sail the vessel into port; while the other landed 97 Irish from Belfast "in good health," but fever broke out among them and "in five days the whole were consigned to 'that bourne from whence no traveller returns.' "[2]

Although these were extreme cases, the worst plague years were still to come. Crop failure, disease, and famine in Ireland in 1846-47 led to mass migration of the destitute in such numbers that almost all restrictions on ships bound for Canadian ports were withdrawn. An observer wrote, "It would in my opinion have been more humane to have deprived them at once of life."[3] A particularly virulent form of dysentery, together with smallpox, measles, and "ship fever"—similar to that induced by overcrowding in jails —broke out on most of these vessels, bringing death to some 30,000 people, and the most intense suffering to the survivors. Of slightly more than 100,000 persons who left the British Isles for America in 1847 a total of 17,445, or 16.33%, died during the passage, in quarantine, or in hospital.

On May 30th, 1847, a small vessel left an Irish port with 110 steerage passengers and one in the cabin. The emigrants were chiefly from County Meath, and in appearance typical of those hard times—ragged, undernourished, "quite unfit to undergo the hardship of a long voyage." But they had all been passed by a doctor.

On the tenth day out two women were reported ill, and were sent drugs by the captain's wife, whose knowledge of medicine— such as it was—provided the only treatment available. The captain, however, refused to allow her to enter the hold to see the patients, apparently in the belief that the disease was contagious. Two days later several more were ill, "and the mistress was kept busy mixing medicine and making drinks, hoping that by early attention the sickness might be prevented from spreading." On June 12th it was apparent that at least two of the women had severe attacks of fever, but their pleas for an extra allowance of water could not be

---

[2] Cited in Wilson, *The Wanderer in America*, 102-3. There were many epidemics of yellow fever in the United States in the closing years of the 18th and the early years of the 19th century. The Southern States particularly were ravaged by the disease in 1853, when 8,000 died in New Orleans alone, and there were less severe epidemics in 1867, 1873, and 1878.
[3] Letter of Adam Ferrie in *Papers Relative to Emigration to the British Provinces in North America* (1848), pp. 36-7. A notable result of the plague of 1847 was that Irish immigration was largely diverted to the United States in subsequent years.

granted, "as the supply was very scanty, two casks having leaked." By the 14th there were six cases of fever and two of dysentery, the former seeming to be "of a peculiar character, and very alarming." The attentions of the captain's wife greatly alleviated the suffering of the sick, and the captain, too, "desired the mistress to give them everything out of his own stores that she considered would be of service to any of them."

The night of June 16th was very rough, which greatly aggravated the misery of those in the steerage. There were signs of insubordination among the passengers, who bitterly complained of the lack of water to make drinks for their sick wives and children, and stated that their food was insufficient. A deputation to the captain and mate received scant consideration, however, and were given to understand that cutlasses and firearms might come into use to enforce discipline. The cabin passenger wrote in this connection: "If they were resolute they might easily have seized upon the provisions. In fact I was surprised how famished men could so patiently bear with their own and their starved children's sufferings." But he adds that the captain would gladly have relieved their distress if it had been in his power to do so.

Two new cases of fever were announced on June 17th, and conditions in the steerage were "in a shocking state." Flour porridge, with a few drops of laudanum, "the mistress's prescription," relieved the cases of dysentery; but many of the fever patients were delirious, and their relatives were demanding beef, wine, and other luxuries for the sick, and laudanum for the well, so that they might put themselves into a deep sleep and become oblivious to their terrible surroundings. Such demands were preposterous or dangerous, and had to be refused. The ship was making but little headway, and as only 50 days' provisions had been taken aboard it was considered necessary to reduce the already meager allowance of water, and urge the passengers to use sea water for cooking purposes.

On June 19th a shark—a certain forerunner of death, the mate said,—was observed following the boat, and it had not long to wait for its prey. The captain, the mate, and the cabin passenger alleviated the suffering in the steerage in every way possible, and the mistress was "a perfect slave" in tending the sick. Sunday passed without any observance. One of the female fever patients became worse, "her feet swollen to double their natural size, and covered with black putrid spots," and the following day she died and was dropped into the sea without ceremony. Twenty were

CHOLERA AND SHIP FEVER 93

now sick, and most of the rest absorbed in grief for their relatives; though some had experienced too much misery to have any feelings left, "either for their fellow creatures' woe, or in the contemplation of being themselves overtaken by the dreadful disease."

The fever attacked its victims with the suddenness of the Black Death of 1665, so ably described by Defoe. On June 25th

"a little child who was playing with his companions suddenly fell down, and for some time was sunk in a death-life torpor, from which, when she awoke, she commenced to scream violently and writhed in convulsive agony. A poor woman who was warming a drink at the fire for her husband, also dropped down quite senseless and was borne to her berth. . . . The first symptom was generally a reeling in the head, followed by a swelling pain, as if the head were going to burst. Next came excruciating pains in the bones, and then a swelling of the limbs, commencing with the feet, in some cases ascending the body and again descending before it reaches the head, stopping at the throat. The period of each stage varied in different patients; some of whom were covered with yellow, watery pimples, and others with red and purple spots, that turned into putrid sores. . . . The moaning and raving of the patients kept me awake nearly all night; and I could hear the mistress stirring about until a late hour. It made my heart bleed to listen to the cries of 'Water, for God's sake some water!'"

By June 28th there were thirty cases of fever, and "the effluvium of the hold was shocking." Revolting scenes, too disgusting to be described, were of common occurrence. Death literally stared one in the face:

"Passing the main hatch, I got a glimpse of one of the most awful sights I ever beheld. A poor female patient was lying in one of the upper berths—dying. Her head and face were swollen to a most unnatural size, the latter being hideously deformed. . . . She had been nearly three weeks ill, and suffered exceedingly. . . . Her afflicted husband stood by her holding a 'blessed candle' in his hand and awaiting the departure of her spirit. . . . As the sun was setting, the bereaved husband muttered a prayer over her enshrouded corpse, which, as he said 'Amen,' was lowered into the ocean."

Early in July the dense fog which enveloped the ship showed that she was off the Grand Banks of Newfoundland. Her foghorn was sounded continually to avoid collision with fishing-boats, the tolling of whose bells could occasionally be heard; and in between these dismal sounds were the horrible wails and ravings of the thirty-seven delirious fever patients. On the 6th two brothers died of dysentery and were consigned to the deep covered by an old sail; by the 9th fifty were sick, and the third brother, his death hastened by grief, was placed in two meal-sacks, a weight fastened to each foot, and the remains lowered into the sea. He left two small orphan boys, one of whom might be seen wearing his late father's coat, "quite unconscious of his loss, and proud of the accession to his scanty covering." The remainder of the dead man's clothes were sold by auction: "There was great competition, and the 'Cant,' as they called it, occasioned jibing and jesting, which it was painful to listen to, surrounded as the actors were by famine, pestilence and death."

On July 15th a child was born, and several deaths were momentarily expected. Conditions had become so bad that "it required the greatest coercion to enforce anything like cleanliness or decency." On the 19th there was another burial; and a pilot boarded the ship, bringing with him a copy of the quarantine regulations. Three days later one of the orphan boys died, "no friend being by to see the frail body committed to its watery grave." No water was available for the steerage passengers, and they were forced to use salt water as it came from the Gulf. Several of the fever patients who had appeared to be recovering relapsed into a serious state, and three new and most virulent cases broke out. On July 27th fresh water was at last reached, and the wretched emigrants relieved in at least one respect. Many immediately set to work washing themselves and their clothes and scrubbing their bunks to make a favorable impression. On the following day, after more than eight weeks at sea, the vessel dropped anchor off Grosse Isle and awaited the arrival of an inspecting physician.

After a five-minute visit from a doctor, who left official forms to be filled out by the captain, two entire days passed before any further attention was given. Assuming that they would be inspected at once, the emigrants "were dressed in their best clothes and were clean, though haggard and weak." But the sick were not taken to the hospital, nor the well transported to Quebec by steamer, as stated in the quarantine regulations; on the contrary they remained "enveloped by reeking pestilence, the sick without medicine, medical skill, nourishment, or so much as a drop of pure water; for the river, although not saline here, was polluted by the most disgusting objects, . . . a floating mass of filthy straw, the refuse of foul beds, barrels containing the vilest matter, old rags and tattered clothes." Two French-Canadian priests came aboard on the 29th and spent a few minutes with each of the sick, administered the last rites to a dying woman and a feeble old man, and baptized the recently-born infant. These worthy men told the passengers how much worse was the condition of many other ships. Their visit was the only bright spot in a miserable reception.

At last on July 30th a doctor came aboard and stated that one-half the sick would be admitted to the hospital, and the rest when there was room. The former, with a written order from the doctor, were then lowered into one of the ship's boats, amid a scene of indescribable sorrow:

"The husband—the only support of an emaciated wife and helpless family—torn away forcibly from them, in a strange land; the mother dragged from her orphan children, that clung to her until she was lifted over the bulwarks, rending the air with their shrieks; children snatched from their bereaved parents, who were perhaps ever to remain ignorant of their recovery, or death. The screams pierced my brain; and the excessive agony so rent my heart that I was obliged to retire to the cabin, where the mistress sat weeping bitterly. . . . O God! may I never again witness such a scene."

No steamer came that day to take away the healthy—if any could be so called; but having been assured that one would arrive on the day following, the captain ordered all the bunks broken up and the hold whitewashed. Again the wretched emigrants were disappointed, and lay all night huddled in the hold without space to stretch their limbs. On August 1st a doctor once again inspected the passengers, stating he would have the remaining sick conveyed to the hospital, and that a steamer would come for the others. An hour or so later a steamship transferred the steerage passengers to its decks. Each of them shook hands with the mistress, and all heaped blessings upon her head. As for the captain, one of them remarked that "though he was a divil, he was a gintleman." But the cup of disappointment was not yet full, for the steamship went direct to Montreal, and some of those who had left relatives in the hospital at Grosse Isle were fated never to see them again. As the ship steamed away amid the cheers of her passengers, the mistress, who had been so exceptionally kind and considerate, "was quite overcome by the expressions of the poor creatures' gratitude for her unceasing, and otherwise unrequited attention and benevolence."[4]

The sufferings of these passengers were mild when compared with the horrors endured on many other vessels. There were but few ships upon which anyone made such self-sacrificing attempts to alleviate suffering; nor was the overcrowding as intense, or the weather as bad during the passage. A death list of six out of 110 was not comparable to the mortality experienced on many other emigrant ships in the same year. The brig *Lorch* from Sligo with 440 passengers buried 108 at sea—more than four times the proportionate death rate on the former vessel—and there were 150 sick when she reached the Quarantine Station. The *Lord Ash-*

[4] The narrative of this voyage is *The Ocean Plague: or a Voyage to Quebec in an Irish Emigrant Vessel, Embracing a Quarantine at Grosse Isle in 1847, with Notes Illustrative of the Ship-Pestilence of that Fatal Year*. By a Cabin Passenger. Boston, Coolidge & Wiley. 1848.

burton, from Liverpool with 475 steerage passengers, had a death list of 107, and 60 were still sick with fever or dysentery on arrival at Grosse Isle; the *Sir Henry Pottinger*, of Cork, reported 98 deaths and 112 still sick, out of 399 passengers; and the *Virginius*, which set sail with 596, buried 158 during the passage, 186 more were very sick, and "the remainder landed feeble and tottering; the captain, mates and crew were all sick." As the London *Times* commented, "The Blackhole of Calcutta was a mercy compared to the holds of these vessels."

Stephen E. De Vere, a public-spirited Irish landlord, performed a notable act of disinterested philanthropy when he travelled steerage in an overcrowded emigrant vessel in April, 1847, to learn the actual conditions at first hand. His description of his experiences, which eventually came to the notice of a Select Committee of the House of Lords, must be taken not only as characteristic of conditions existent during the ship fever and cholera years but also as typical of the terrifying and degrading experiences through which hundreds of thousands passed even in ordinary times.[5] It presents an outstanding example of man's inhumanity to man:

"Before the emigrant has been a week at sea he is an altered man. How can it be otherwise? Hundreds of poor people, men, women, and children of all ages, from the drivelling idiot of ninety to the babe just born, huddled together without light, without air, wallowing in filth and breathing a fetid atmosphere, sick in body, dispirited in heart, the fever patients lying between the sound, in sleeping places so narrow as almost to deny them the power of indulging, by a change of position, the natural restlessness of the disease; by their ravings disturbing those around, and predisposing them, through the effects of the imagination, to imbibe the contagion; living without food or medicine, except as administered by the hand of casual charity, dying without the voice of spiritual consolation, and buried in the deep without the rites of the Church.

"The food is generally ill-selected and seldom sufficiently cooked, in consequence of the insufficiency and bad construction of the cooking places. The supply of water, hardly enough for cooking and drinking, does not allow washing. In many ships the filthy beds, teeming with all abominations, are never required to be brought on deck and aired; the narrow space between the sleeping berths and the piles of boxes is never washed or scraped, but breathes up a damp and fetid stench, until the day before the arrival at quarantine, when all hands are required to 'scrub up,' and put on a fair face for the doctor and Government inspector. No moral restraint is attempted, the voice of prayer is never heard; drunkenness, with its consequent train of ruffianly debasement, is not discouraged, because it is profitable to the captain, who traffics in the grog. . . .

[5] William Huskisson stated in the House of Commons that a captain of the navy who had been engaged in suppressing the slave trade off Africa declared that "the condition of many vessels which he had seen arrive at Newfoundland with emigrants beggared all descriptions of the state of the captured slave ships." (Hansard, 2nd Series, XVIII, 1828, p. 1212.)

CHOLERA AND SHIP FEVER

"The meat was of the worst quality. The supply of water shipped on board was abundant, but the quantity served out to the passengers was so scanty that they were frequently obliged to throw overboard their salt provisions and rice (a most important article of their food) because they had not water enough both for the necessary cooking and the satisfying of their raging thirst afterwards. They could only afford water for washing by withdrawing it from the cooking of their food. I have known persons to remain for days together in their dark, close berths because they thus suffered less from hunger. . . .

"No cleanliness was enforced, and the beds were never aired. The master during the whole voyage never entered the steerage, and would listen to no complaints; the dietary contracted for was, with some exceptions, nominally supplied, though at irregular periods; but false measures were used (in which the water and several articles of dry food were served), the gallon measure containing but three quarts, which fact I proved in Quebec and had the captain fined for. Once or twice a week ardent spirits were sold indiscriminately to the passengers, producing scenes of unchecked blackguardism beyond description; and lights were prohibited because the ship—with her open fire-grates upon deck—with lucifer matches and lighted pipes used secretly in the sleeping berths—was freighted with Government powder for the garrison at Quebec."[6]

The horrors of the passage may also be estimated by the condition of vessels upon arrival at the Quarantine Station. The priests who went from ship to ship to comfort those who remained alive found the holds of some of them "up to their ancles in filth; the wretched emigrants crowded together like cattle, and corpses remaining long unburied, the sailors being ill and the passengers unwilling to touch them." Some conception of the blasted hopes of the destitute Irish emigrants may be obtained from one sufferer's comment:

"Ah! Sir, we thought we couldn't be worse off than we war; but now to our sorrow we know the differ; for sure supposin we were dyin of starvation, or if the sickness overtuk us. We had a chance of a doctor, and if he could do no good for our bodies, sure the priest could for our souls; and then we'd be buried along wid our people, in the ould church-yard, with the green sod over us, instead of dyin like rotten sheep thrown into a pit, and the minit the breath is out of our bodies, flung into the sea to be eaten up by them horrid sharks."

The London *Times* summed up the tragedy of "the black year of emigration" in a contemporary editorial. Commenting in no uncertain terms on official negligence in allowing the emigrant fleet to be crowded "with wretches already at death's door," transported across the Atlantic under the worst possible conditions, with "ridiculously insufficient" accommodations at the Grosse Isle

---

[6] Stephen E. De Vere to T. F. Elliot, in *Evidence before the Select Committee of the House of Lords on Colonisation from Ireland, 1847*, pp. 45-8. Instead of exporting his tenants like so many cattle, Mr. De Vere took a dozen volunteers with him; and when his companions were stricken with fever he personally attended them. His beneficence merited the approbation of the author of *The Ocean Plague*, who felt "extreme gratification" to be able to refer to him as "a most honorable exception" among Irish landlords.

Quarantine Station and no other preparations for their reception or transportation inland—much less their employment or settlement—the *Times* concluded: "Nor do we see any way to escape the opprobrium of a national inhumanity except by taking the earliest and most effectual means to rectify past errors and prevent their recurrence." But even this was not accomplished, and the ship fever year, with its less virulent successor, 1848, passed into history to rank among the most tragic episodes in the annals of the sea.

CHAPTER XI

THE TANG OF THE SEA

> "Sailors are never so happy as when all the sails and yards are taken down and stowed away, and when the masts are lowered to the lowest possible point. Tied by ropes to the bulwarks for fear of being washed overboard, they sing like birds in a shrubbery."
>
> William Cobbett

On the more auspicious voyages the amazed landsman found plenty to marvel at:

> "The rising and setting sun; the brilliancy of the night; falling-stars; the sporting of schools of bonitos; the occasional falling on board of a flying fish; land birds settling on the rigging so fatigued as to be caught by the sailors; dolphins racing, as it were, with the vessel, leaving their long blue tracks behind them; the brilliant and beautiful but yet unexplained phosphoric phenomena of the waves; the various curious and minute animals found in the gulf-weed, when fished up and shaken into a basin of water;— all these afford pleasure to the inquiring mind."

Allowing for a little propaganda to aid Captain Martin in filling his brig with Scottish emigrants on the next voyage, we may still admit that Walter Johnstone had an agreeable passage on the *Diana*, from Dumfries, in April-May, 1820; for the crew were obliging, the water supply good and abundant, the beds dry, open hatches, and no vermin. "Except two or three married women who were pregnant and a few sucking children who were unwell with colds and who also suffered from a want of dry clothes, we were rather improved in health than otherwise. . . . I may say with truth that a more comfortable passage was never made across the Atlantic." The *Diana* reached Cape Breton on the 28th day, but cold and fog necessitated an eight-day delay in the Gulf of St. Lawrence, "the most unpleasant part of the whole passage"; following which the ship entered the harbor of Three Rivers, Prince Edward Island.

Those who manned Atlantic sailing-ships were obviously not all villains, despite the existence of no small number of disreputable characters. On some ships, of course, they were like those who manned the *Camillus*—"Falstaff's recruits over again. . . . A Frenchman, two Portuguese, three Americans and a man of colour, all so drunk that they had difficulty in getting up the ship's side."

But these same sailors successfully navigated their vessel through a series of the worst storms any boat ever survived. Patrick Shirreff found Captain Smith of the *Napoleon* "indefatigable, attentive and forbearing," and "courteous and gentlemanly in a high degree," but of course he was a cabin passenger on a packet of the better class, and to such the captain and crew were more obsequious than to the poverty-stricken emigrant, from whom but little passage money was collected. But even steerage passengers were well treated upon innumerable occasions. On the *John Dennison* the captain, although he kept a lucrative grog-shop and overcharged his passengers in the matter of the American "hospital tax," was found to be "always attentive to our comfort, and indulged us in every amusement." It is recorded similarly with reference to Captain Blake of the *Brunswick*, that,

"from the moment of our embarkation at Cork to the night of our departure from his ship, his attention, not only to the cabin passengers, but also to the humblest individual in the steerage, evinced a disposition highly creditable to himself and honourable to his profession. . . . He was to all a friend, an attendant, and a physician; and constantly solicitous for our health and comfort. To the inferior officers and crew of the *Brunswick* we are also very much indebted. . . . We parted from the whole of them with regret, and hope they are fully aware how sensible we are of their praiseworthy conduct."

Many passengers were greatly interested in the varied activities of the sailors, who were always busy. In a brisk wind they were often in the shrouds, and their agility in climbing into the rigging was a source of amazement. Even when becalmed there was plenty to occupy their attention, for the deck had to be swabbed, ropes tarred, and sails mended. There were salt-water customs among these men which were crude, doubtless, but they liked nothing better than to demonstrate them to the astonished landlubber. A passenger on the *Hebe* in 1833 records one of the traditions:

"June 13—A fine day with but little wind, when, to gratify the whims of a few young men, cabin passengers, the Captain allowed the ludicrous ceremony of Neptune shaving the green horns on board to take place, and a most certainly laughable scene it was—the boatswain dressed in a large wig made of Jaid Twine, a white jacket and a red sash, no shoes and stockings, face painted red, two old fish spears in his hand for a trident, represented the grim old sea dog—his wife was a man dressed in woman's clothes in a most grotesque style, leaned on his arm, and 7 stout fellows with their faces painted, holding rusty swords in hands, were his attendants. After a glass or two of Rum his Majesty demanded who there were on board that presumed to come upon his domain without his permission. He then ordered his attendants to seize the offenders one at a time, and take them to the fore part of the ship to be shaved, which was performed with tar for soap and an old iron hoop for a razor. Afterwards a pail of water was thrown at the offender and he was then suffered to go about his business. About 40 others

Illustrated London News

EMIGRANTS AT DINNER

Only in the better vessels was it possible to have mess tables in the passageway between the rows of steerage bunks.

Illustrated London News

DANCING IN THE STEERAGE

"The surgeon playing the fiddle, the dance and merriment was kept up with great spirit until four bells."

Illustrated London News

TRACING THE VESSEL'S PROGRESS

"A little group surrounds some learned friend, who has industriously worked the ship's course."

underwent the same kind of ceremony, and the afternoon and evening was spent in drinking, noise and merriment."

Another traveller describes how he first became acquainted with the custom of "paying your footing." Having occupied a vantage point in the forecastle "to watch the figure-head of the gallant ship as she alternately rose high on the crest of a wave and then plunged into the deep abyss," he shortly found that a sailor had quietly made a ring with chalk around his feet, "and out of this we were expected not to move till we had 'paid our footing,' and of course we could not refuse the jolly tars their usual *douceur*."

Somewhat similar was the payment of a bottle of rum demanded of anyone who ventured into the rigging. Unaware of the price of their temerity, several passengers on one ship climbed aloft, and upon attempting to descend they were met by a blockade of members of the crew. Quite indignant at the proceedings, they sought to evade the issue by remaining in the shrouds; but much to the amusement of the onlookers the wind suddenly arose, and they were glad to get their feet on deck again at any price.

A "christening" occurred on one vessel when the captain's kindly wife brought into the cabin a baby recently born in the steerage. The master took from his locker an egg, which he held up to the light and looked through, to see if it were good.

"Not being satisfied on that point, he tried another, and then another, until he got one to please him. He next got some salt, and opening the infant's little hand, placed it upon the palm and gently closed the tiny fingers upon it. He then performed a similar operation upon the other, enclosing a shilling in lieu of salt. The egg he handed to the mistress to send to the mother and acquaint her that he wished the child to be called 'Ellen' after her."

On another vessel the sand from the first soundings off the Grand Banks was placed under a baby's feet "so that she might be the first who stepped on American soil."

It was a popular diversion on deck to watch the waves and the spray as the vessel dashed along in a brisk wind; but the sea proved treacherous at times, as Richard Weston, who avoided many a pitfall, relates with some gusto:

"A number of passengers were standing on the weather-gangway and quarter-deck admiring the sight, and watching the sea-fowl called the stormy petrel as it rose up on a pinnacle and again seemed to sink into a gulf, though in perfect security and at its ease. A lady neatly dressed in white, and a gentleman, were standing beside the companion. I happened to be on the forecastle, which was raised. A sea, one of the above-mentioned undulating cups or surges, rose at the weather fore-chains and broke over the ship. Many of the passengers were rolled along with the waves into the leescuppers. The lady and gentleman were both upset, and they rolled to leeward along with the rest. The lady got a complete ducking; her dress was completely deranged, and she was carried into the cabin. Even the captain was taken by surprise on this occasion. . . . This cleared the deck of idlers for the present."

In this connection the difference between the modern liner and the typical packet of other days is particularly apparent from advice to passengers in guidebooks: "All passengers ought to avoid sitting on the side rails of the vessel, as they may be pitched overboard before they are aware. Sometimes experienced men lose their lives in that way."

There is something about the sea which encourages gambling. On sailing-vessels, as on modern liners, the element of chance entered into one's diversions as well as affecting the ship's progress, and many passengers who would never have considered gambling on land entered with great zest into "the daily stock exchange," as one man aptly calls it. There was betting on the progress of the vessel during the day—often little enough, or even a retrograde movement; on the first appearance of another ship or the first sight of land; on the day upon which the pilot would board the vessel at Sandy Hook or in the Gulf; and in some cases tickets bearing a possible date were issued to each cabin passenger early in the voyage, a considerable part of every day being consumed in buying and selling. Wagers on the day's mileage have remained a favorite down to modern times, but in the days of the sailing-ship it was harder to estimate distances. The speed of a vessel's progress was ascertained by "heaving the log," which was done at frequent intervals throughout the day. From the number of miles per hour she was making could then be roughly calculated the mileage for 24 hours, and the bets on the result which would be posted up in the cabin were paid in cash, rum, lemonade, or other commodities.

Establishing contact with other ships was always of interest to both crew and passengers. Occasionally some of the passengers were allowed—during a calm, no doubt,—to pay a visit to a near-by ship. But in general an exchange of greetings, a request to report their safety, or a comparison of estimates of the longitude was the extent of the contact. Flags or other signs—rockets at night—were the usual means of communication. Sometimes, however, the captain put off in a small boat to get fish from a smack off the Grand Banks; and great was his delight on one occasion to learn that an extensive conversation which he was carrying on by speaking-trumpet with a neighboring ship was with an old friend. There were occasions, however, when feelings of a very different nature were aroused by contact with vessels in distress. One writer recalled that his ship came in touch with a vessel one hundred days out from Ireland and short of provisions, which were liberally supplied her; while another wrote that in mid-ocean they were hailed by a ship whose crew "had a harrowing tale to tell. They had been out of food and were starving. Their captain had died a week previously, and they were casting lots to see who would first fall a sacrifice for the benefit of the others. Our captain was grateful to be in a position to help them." Of a similar nature were the feelings of all but the most callous when a poor, emaciated, half-crazed stowaway was discovered in the hold.

The thrilling adventure of chase and attack by French privateers was reserved for the few travellers who were on the high seas during the Napoleonic wars. Between the 24th of August and the 4th of October, 1800, a group of missionaries made a voyage from Liverpool to Halifax in the *Snow Sparrow*, a small vessel armed with 12 guns. The Rev. Joshua Marsden's impressions of the passage are of considerable interest owing to the peculiar circumstances existing at that time:

"Our vessel was small and very leaky, than which no circumstance is more unpleasant at sea; and the ominous sound of the pump, combined with the whistling of the wind, the dash of the waves, and often the stentorian voice of the captain, created a chilliness of soul that nothing but the warmth of faith and devotion could beguile. Our crew was a mixture of all nations; we had also several passengers on board; but as they did not fear God, they added little to our stock of comfort. We all united to reprove and discountenance open sin, and doubted not of proceeding with innocence and comfort through the whole of our voyage.... The sailors were always at the pumps; and as the cargo chiefly consisted of salt, more than thirty tons were dissolved in the forty days we were upon the ocean.

"After the seasickness had subsided, we spent many truly profitable seasons either in singing, reading, prayer, or religious conversation. If at any time the trifling conduct of the other passengers made the large cabin disagreeable, we had an asylum in the state room.... Sometimes the rolling of the ship prevented us from either standing or kneeling; at other times in the midst of our stated daily prayers, the captain or mate was loudly called for upon deck; then a lurch of the vessel put the gravity of our passengers into something more than a smile; in a word, the shouting of the sailors, the roaring of the waves, and the tossing of the ship all seemed to conspire against the calmness of recollection and fixedness of the soul in prayer.

"As we did not know but any hour might present the appearance of an enemy's vessel, either privateer or national ship, our captain was anxious that all the passengers, in the event of such an encounter, should have their stations assigned for the defence of the ship, and as the twelve guns we carried demanded all the forty hands composing the crew, the missionaries were equipped as marines, with our worthy Mr. Black to act as captain. This, however, I could by no means reconcile to my own views of the unlawfulness of war. . . .

"Our voyage was very rough and stormy, which, with the water continually pouring in and running down the sides, made my berth very uncomfortable. . . . My bed-quilt and blankets were seldom dry, and probably nothing but the blessing of God on a good constitution prevented the most serious indisposition. Once, indeed, I was seized in the middle of the night with a cramp in my stomach, so severe and alarming that for some time it appeared that both my marine and mortal voyage were almost ended. . . . In this distress, after several things had been applied in vain, one of the missionaries brought me some brandy, requesting I would drink it off, which, as my case appeared desperate, I consented to with some reluctance, and the pain immediately abated. . . .

"But I hasten to inform you how we proceeded on our voyage. I believe the wisdom of God intended that this should be a good schooling to our patience; for in addition to the usual trials of our faith, such as a leaky vessel, foul winds, heavy gales, dull lazy weather, and dark nights, we were chased by a French Corvette Privateer, which bore down upon us in a daring and warlike style. Although fighting and true religion are two things so widely different that it would be as difficult to reconcile them as to prove that they do not exist, yet on this emergency even the ministers of peace buckled upon themselves the harness of war, and our pious and truly esteemed Mr. Black, with his missionary marines, seemed disposed to give them as warm a reception as David gave to Goliath. Even good men, sir, may be converts to the doctrine of the Bible and sword. The Lord, however, spared us this trial, for when we lay to to receive our antagonist with our matches lighted, and every man at his post and gun, the myrmidon did not like our appearance, we being two in company, and our companion a fine large ship; so after hovering about us for some time like a snake upon the water, she thought fit to sheer off; and, giving loose to her canvas, left us only to admire the swiftness of her sailing and our own dulness; for we must needs go in chase, and by so doing (as the sea was tremendously high) we ran the risk of upsetting our ship."

Thomas Johnston lived through a somewhat similar experience in July, 1814, during a voyage from Greenock to Quebec in the brig *Emily*:

"On the 30th, when at supper below, we were alarmed by a loud cry of 'All hands on deck.' Terror struck, we hastened up the hatchway, but our panic still increased on beholding our captain and whole crew in a state of agitation, and a large ship less than a league to the leeward, which they supposed to be a French privateer. She fired twice, but our captain showed no inclination to strike. Having passed us, she fired a third time, but, finding us unwilling to lie to, she began to tack about. Expecting to be made prisoners, the passengers put themselves in their best apparel that they might appear more respectable before the enemy. Amongst our number we had an old Highlandman and his wife, who seemed most alarmed. They had a bag of money consisting of some gold, silver, and a considerable quantity of counterfeit halfpence, which probably was their all. After they had spent some time in hiding it amongst the lumber in the hold, they came upon deck. . . . The enemy's vessel, in endeavouring to tack, had missed her stays, fortunate for us. We immediately set every sail, and being favoured with a good breeze and approaching night, escaped."

More enjoyable than a race for life with an enemy ship was the

THE TANG OF THE SEA

friendly rivalry of chance companions. The *John Dennison* engaged in such a competition for the better part of a day, greatly to the amusement of passengers and crew. There was, on the other hand, a leisureliness about some vessels' progress that must have been irritating. Captain Cunningham of the *Mary Ann Bell* had all of Samuel Pepys' curiosity, and eagerly seized every opportunity to get to the bottom of possible mysteries. The diary of a passenger records that on May 17, 1817, "a small cask or barrel floating on the waves" was sighted, so the captain "took boat in pursuit of it, and on examining found a human body contained therein." On June 16th another discovery is described:

"This day a slender pine tree, about 18 feet long, was seen floating on the waves; the captain took a boat and brought it aboard; I never saw such a curiosity before. On this tree grew small shells, so thick as to cover every part of it, their form not unlike the head of a young bird, with a yellow edge; in these shells the bird called the Barnacle commences its existence; it is nourished from a long tube connected with the shell, and very like a large worm; I was quite astonished at its singular appearance. I suppose it had been driven to and fro these several years."

The opportunities for the study of nature were extensive. "Mother Carey's chickens" hovered about the ship in search of garbage, and strange birds lighted in the rigging, which one observed, caught, or shot, according to inclination. One passenger participated in a shooting excursion in the jolly-boat, practising for the "excellent sport in America shooting wild turkies." Whales, sharks, dolphins, porpoises, and flying fish provided no end of interest. Richard Weston passed the time shooting porpoises and baiting sharks with beef. Sharks, he was told, "smell disease in a ship, and follow it to prey on the dead." One was caught and hauled on deck, and after "frightful convulsions" it died and was minutely examined by the passengers. Dolphins in pursuit of flying fish, and the nautilus, or "Portuguese Man-of-war," provided interesting spectacles.

"The Argonauta or nautilus," one traveller relates, "was often seen by us in fine weather. It is a sea-snail which possesses the faculty of swimming or diving. Its appearance in sunshine, being of a light violet colour, is very beautiful. As soon as a storm commences, it draws into its shell, taking in as much water as will carry it to the bottom; and on the approach of fine weather reascends to the surface, putting up a small sail and guiding its movements by its tail as a rudder."

Richard Weston captured one, and it badly blistered a boy who touched it, ignorant of its power to raise a painful blister by exuding a fluid. A fellow-traveller thereupon picked it up and threw it into the sea—receiving the same treatment for his impetuosity!

Many a traveller was intrigued by natural phenomena which varied from snowstorms to "St. Elmo's Fire." One man wrote home: "On the 25th of May we had snow four inches thick on the deck, and we snow-balled one another till we got wet through." Such an event was unusual enough in May in the Gulf of St. Lawrence, but it was quite remarkable to experience a snowstorm on May 2nd, when the New York packet *Hannibal* was off the coast of Devonshire.

The Aurora borealis or Northern Lights were frequently particularly beautiful on the ocean. A traveller on a plague-ridden ship in 1847 records that he was suddenly awakened from a deep sleep by the captain, who shouted to him to come on deck quickly. Somewhat alarmed, he hastened from his berth and was well recompensed

"by the magnificence of the glorious scene I beheld. The northern portion of the firmament was vividly illuminated with a clear though subdued light, while across it shot fiery meteors from different directions; now rushing against each other as if engaged in deadly warfare; again gliding about in wanton playfulness. Disappearing for a while, and leaving behind a faintly luminous trail, they would again burst forth upon their stage, lighted up by a sudden flash for the igneous performers. I watched with delight until the lustrous picture was finally enshrouded in darkness."

Storms at sea were sometimes accompanied by beautiful electrical discharges: "So vivid was the lightning that from pitch darkness the sea as far as the eye could reach was suddenly lit up so as to appear like an ocean of flame." Captain R. G. A. Levinge describes similar effects during a stormy passage in the winter of 1837-1838. Jack o' Lanterns—halos of light like balls of fire—illuminated the ship's course; and a violent hail storm suddenly coming on, the combination of lightning, meteors, and hail was "awfully sublime." During a heavy midnight thunderstorm in August, 1835, a very vivid stroke of lightning lit up the whole sky so completely that every sail and spar of the ship *Tennessee* could be plainly seen. Immediately afterwards occured a phenomenon—St. Elmo's Fire—which the captain said was so rare that to see it once in fifty Atlantic crossings would be a fair average. James Hopkirk considered it was "one of the most splendid sights I ever saw in my life," and wrote a vivid description of it in his diary:

"Was awoke this morning about 2 o'clock—tremendous noise from thunder and lightning squall—dressed hurriedly and went on deck. Found captain and all hands reefing and hauling down the sails—the heavens as black as it is possible to conceive—suddenly the most vivid flash of forked lightning illumined the whole heavens, we could see the smallest rope for a second—the rain pouring down in torrents, all as dark as pitch. Suddenly one of those extraordinary phenomenons called by the philosophers St. Elmo's fire fixed itself at the very top of the foremast, where it remained, I suppose, 30 to 40 minutes. I went out, at the price of a complete drenching, to the foot of the mast and saw it, like a luminous ball of lambent fire—it was steady, not flickering, and very bright—not dazzling—more like a lump of phosphorus than anything else. . . . I was very fortunate in witnessing it."

James Taylor's *Narrative of a Voyage* smacks more of the sea than most accounts, for he had an intimate knowledge of sailing. His passage illustrates the uncertainty of travel by sail. He left Hull on April 11, 1843, in the ship *Queen Victoria*, expecting to go *via* the north of Scotland; but a sudden change in the wind made it necessary to go about and enter the English Channel. When crossing the Boston Deeps the vessel lost her main and fore yards during a severe hail storm. The crew made everything secure, and a distress signal brought repairs from shore. Another shift in the wind brought about a renewed attempt to sail around Scotland; but after several hours in that direction the breeze veered once again "chuck in our teeth," and the *Queen Victoria* steered westward. Heavy squalls in the vicinity of the Isle of Wight, fine weather near the Eddystone Lighthouse, and a fresh contrary wind at Land's End, provided variety along the south coast; but after proceeding some distance out to sea, the ship was driven back during the night by a hurricane.

On the morning of April 24th the *Queen Victoria* once more passed the Lizard Lights and "the Land's End of old England" and entered the Atlantic. Continued heavy winds forced her to sail closely reefed. At midnight of the 26th she lost a jib sail, and a few hours later shipped a heavy sea, "which found its way into the galley, smashing our crockery and upsetting every moveable, and, making its escape at the opposite side of the vessel, merged into its own element." A second jib sail was lost during a sudden midnight storm which called all hands from their berths; but more agreeable weather set in the following day, and the unfurling of the top-gallant sails enabled good headway until a heavy thunderstorm deluged the vessel with water. The vicissitudes of a seaman's life, and the exemplary manner in which he performed his duty at all hours of the day and night, evoked in James Taylor a feeling of admiration, and "a hearty desire for a revival in the marine trade, in order that the merits of those brave fellows might be better rewarded."

A new moon on April 30th brought a change of wind, and

during the same day a sail was sighted, a welcome occurrence when it was not unusual to travel ten or twelve days without seeing a vessel. Another storm that night forced all hands aloft to take in the sails, and Taylor observes that they were then "in total darkness, except when the broad sheets of lurid flame revealed the awful scene around us. The vessel at the time lay top-rail of the leeward bulwark forward under water, and deluges of rain poured down upon her prostrate form." A lull was followed by a tempest which "threatened us every moment with instant destruction"; but the sun rose on a clear sky and a quiet sea, and for two weeks the voyage was without incident. A dense fog, cold weather, and high seas greeted the *Queen Victoria* at the middle of May, when she was in sight of Newfoundland; but the sail through the Gulf of St. Lawrence was uneventful, and on May 24th, "after a stormy passage of six weeks," she cast anchor off Quebec.

CHAPTER XII

THE CABIN PASSAGE

"The chief cabin, or saloon, is lined with satin wood, in panels, banded with rose and zebra woods and American bird's eye maple, and the ceiling is in white and gold."
"The New American Line Ship *Victoria*," *Illustrated London News*,
August 12, 1843

We enter a new world when we leave the steerage and approach the cabin section, for many sailing-vessels provided excellent accommodation for those who wished to live almost as well as they could on land, and who were willing to pay handsomely for the privilege. It is probable that many emigrants who travelled steerage would never have left home at all, or at least would have spent extra money upon a cabin passage, if they had had any idea of the misery and suffering that was to be their lot in the ship's hold; but so great was the variation in ships, accommodations, and weather that no one could tell in advance just what the fates held in store.

Of some 11,000,000 people who emigrated from the British Isles to North America between 1770 and 1890, comparatively few travelled cabin class. Exact figures can not be compiled, but from available information it would appear that about 98 per cent were in steerage quarters. Between January 1st and October 12th, 1844, a total of 20,023 people landed at Quebec, and of these 19,460 were steerage passengers; in 1847, 90,410 persons left the United Kingdom for British North America, of whom only 684 were in the cabin; and in 1849, of 153,902 who left the port of Liverpool, 4,639 travelled cabin class.

There was at the time a pronounced distinction between "emigrants" and "colonists," the latter being, of course, those of higher class and, frequently, of independent means, some of whom undoubtedly considered that they were conferring a distinct favor upon the new land by removing to it. In most parts of America divisions arising from birth or rank are largely ignored; while in the British Isles class distinctions were (and still are) a matter of inheritance, and are in general taken for granted. The attitude in the days of the great emigrations is well shown by the activities at Blackwall, England, before the departure of the *Randolph* to establish a settlement at Canterbury, New Zealand. An elaborate fête brought together the local gentry and nobility in honor of the "colonist" cabin passengers, while the "labouring emigrants" in the steerage were given a humble dinner on another occasion.[1] On some vessels the implied inferiority of steerage passengers was at times an excuse for visits of inspection by those in the cabin, "as though they were passing through a menagerie"; and many a poor man of inherent worth was humiliated by the "swaying elegant superiority" of those who, in the words of Shakespeare, were "low peasantry . . . without the stamp of merit."

"Colonists" of means were advised that it would be preferable to take servants to the new land, rather than expect to obtain good ones there; for democratic feeling often made them too independent, or otherwise objectionable. A gentleman settler wrote from Portland, Maine, that he would "particularly recommend" the bringing of "a servant on whose attachment to your family you could depend; perhaps there is nothing in this country so unpleasant to an English family as the Servants which they must put up with here. Their wages are very high, and in general they have such an idea of the equality of mankind that their service is trifling." Those, however, who had no servants could usually obtain help during the voyage from among the steerage passengers. Mary Jane Watson received four dollars for waiting on ladies in the cabin while her parents travelled steerage; and Francis Thomas mentions in his diary that the hardships of his family were greatly lessened because he had procured an Irish girl as a servant.

In spite of the apparent superiority of cabin accommodations, they varied almost as much as steerage conditions, for there were many types of vessels; and a good steerage passage on one ship might be at least equal to the cabin accommodation on another. In general three main types of vessels provided cabin quarters: (1) merchant ships carrying passengers as a means of extra revenue; (2) vessels primarily engaged in the emigrant trade, or,—like many ships trading in square timber—depending upon emigrants for a return cargo; and (3) regular packets, which gave less of the feeling of privacy which was the best recommendation of the merchant vessel.

The cabin in an Irish emigrant ship of 1847 was merely the captain's quarters. About ten feet square and so low that only

[1] *Illustrated London News*, August 3, 1850, p. 108. As Robert Louis Stevenson found by experience, "In the steerage there are males and females; in the cabin ladies and gentlemen." (*The Amateur Emigrant*, 14 *et seq*).

under the skylight could one stand upright, it had a berth on either side,

"both of which were filled with the mistress' boxes, the captain's old clothes, old sails, and sundry other articles which were there stowed away and concealed from view by chintz curtains trimmed with white cotton fringe. The ceiling was garnished with numerous charts rolled up, and confined by tapes running from beam to beam; from one of which,—carefully covered by a cotton handkerchief,—was suspended the captain's new hat. A small recess above the table contained a couple of wine glasses, one of them minus the shank; also an antique decanter, resting upon an old quarto prayer-book, and guarded by a dangerous looking blunderbuss, which was supported by two brass hooks, from one of which hung a small bag containing the captain's spectacles, rule, pencil, and compass. At each side of this recess was a locker: one of them containing a crock of butter and another of eggs, besides tobacco and soap; the other held a fine Cheshire cheese, a little keg of sprats, and other articles too numerous to mention. An unhappy canary, perched within a rusty cage, formed a pendant from the centre of the skylight, but a much more pleasing picture decorated one of the panels,—a still-life, admirably delineating an enormous flitch of bacon, which daily grew—less. A small door led into the captain's stateroom; the ceiling of which was tastefully ornamented by several bunches of dipt candles; while the narrow shelves groaned under the weight of jars of sugar, preserves, bottled porter, spices, and the other usual necessaries for a long voyage."

Among the most successful and public-spirited immigrant settlers in the 1820's and 1830's were half-pay military or naval officers, who were probably in A. J. Christie's mind when he suggested that "many of those who were, from various reasons, compelled to hold a certain rank in society, and from their limited means unable to do so, have been obliged, (though with reluctance), to collect the shattered remains of their fortunes, and seek an asylum in Canada." These reserve officers, their incomes greatly reduced, were much impressed by the possibilities of the new land where, they were informed, the establishment of an "estate" on a scale impossible in Britain was a matter of no difficulty. A few of them, ambitious to imitate the nobility of the Old Land, settled in some remote and unpromising district the only advantage of which was its scenic beauty and the facilities for hunting, hawking, and fishing. In their voyage to America these and other fairly well-to-do passengers frequently travelled in the cabin, sometimes with servants, and their hardships were comparatively few.

Faced with the alternative of crossing the Atlantic in an emigrant ship "literally swarming with passengers, chiefly of the lower class of Highlanders," the Traills chose a fast-sailing brig, the *Laurel*, which was not in the regular service, and paid £15 each for the passage to Montreal. This they considered a high rate, but it included all expenses, and for it they received a cabin "neatly fitted up," as well as "the luxury of a handsome sofa, with crimson draperies, in the great cabin." They had also the use of the "state cabin," which contained narrow berths on either side. Somewhat similar was the cabin accommodation which the Stewarts and Reids, "their servants, and all imaginable requisities in the way of tools and implements, household furniture, etc., etc.," obtained on the *St. George* in 1822. Mrs. Stewart wrote:

"We have one very large cabin, in which all the Reids sleep. Mr. Reid and Thomas swing in the middle in cots. In this cabin we eat, and in bad weather we sit there. I have the little state cabin for my party; there are two good and very wide berths in it, in one of which I sleep with my nurseling. My maid, Anna Maria, and Ellen have the other. I am very comfortable here and quite independent; and though I have only just room to stand up and dress myself, I am much happier than if we were all together."

James Hopkirk of Glasgow left Scotland in 1835 because of reverses suffered by his family when the slaves were freed in Jamaican plantations. He arranged at a cost of £50 a cabin passage from Liverpool to New York for himself, his wife, two children, and a servant, on the *Tennessee*, an American vessel of 415 tons under Capt. G. W. Robinson. Originally constructed for the passenger service, the *Tennessee* had been altered to carry largely freight, but there was a crew of nineteen, seven cabin passengers, and eighty-three in the steerage. The cabin accommodation consisted of "the lady's cabin in the stern," and two small staterooms off it; and there was also "an open, airy house on deck," possibly because the vessel had formerly traded into the Gulf of Mexico. Hopkirk records in his diary that "the stores and provisions of every kind are most excellent," and that "nothing can be better than the fare we have always got—breakfast with tea, chocolate, delicious butter—finest fresh eggs"; for dinner "roastmeat or corn beef boiled, fowls, ducks, cabbage, potatoes—dumpling or pudding," and for tea "cold meat, ham, herrings, etc."

The mate of the *Tennessee* harpooned a large porpoise and distributed a good deal of it among the steerage passengers, who were short of food. A portion was kept for the cabin, and the steward consequently prepared for breakfast "a sort of stew made of potatoes and the porpoise sweetbreads which was exceedingly good." He was apparently well versed in the art of cookery, for he also made

"cakes of the brains which also tasted well. One would never have discovered they were fish, of which they had no taste. The sweetbread was something like kidneys, but a great deal more delicate, the brains tasted like those of lambs. We had to dinner today steaks made of the flesh of the porpoise. In appearance it was exactly the colour and look of beef steaks, in taste it more nearly resembled wild duck than anything else; had my eyes been blindfolded I should have taken it for this."

The porpoise steak was possibly "a little tough and dry," but had a pasty been made of it and eaten with red currant jelly, it was James Hopkirk's opinion that it "could be scarcely distinguished from a venison pasty." Typically, the last we hear of the porpoise was at the next dinner, when was served "a sort of stew or hash made of pieces of porpoise and potatoes, which with red currant jelly was most excellent. I should scarcely have known it from hare."

Quite elaborate was the provision made by the Rev. James Magrath, who, in May, 1827, accompanied by his wife, five children, a cousin, and a female servant, sailed in the brig *Donegal* of Whitehaven. The party engaged for £50 "the accommodation of the entire state cabin, containing six berths and two state rooms, with the service of a steward." In this instance, as not infrequently in vessels on the Quebec route, food was not supplied by the ship, and the additional cost of provisions for the voyage from Liverpool to Quebec was calculated on the basis of 80 days and amounted to £20.

The chief cabin on the *Duncan Gibb* having already been engaged, Mrs. William Radcliff and her party had to submit to miserable accommodation,—a cabin, "if it can be so called," housing 31 persons, who endured "the crowd and heat and various difficulties with tolerable patience and good humour." Fortunately some of the passengers proved to be "respectable and well informed," but even this advantage was of little value when everyone was sick and miserable during most of the voyage. Mrs. Radcliff was soon convinced that they had made a mistake in taking their own provisions: "By so doing you are excluded from the attention of the Captain or his steward, . . . your stores are useless while you are sick; and, before you are well, either spoiled or *stolen*—we have been nearly a month at sea, and during that time have been able to enjoy but one comfortable dinner, which was on the first day of our embarkation. This is to be remedied by a little sacrifice of economy to comfort, in paying to the Captain a bulk sum for accommodations, attendance and provisions." Storms, fog, cold weather, and bad water, with occasional diversions, rounded out the voyage; and while Mrs. Radcliff considered she had suffered severely, yet upon the whole her experience must be taken as much less arduous than that endured by the most fortunate of steerage passengers.

Cabin meals on such vessels were by no means as luxurious as on the regular New York packets, but were in general quite good. Salt pork was one of the staples, and biscuit the only type of bread. Apparently tea and coffee were seldom enjoyed, for a guide-book observed that the tea was "often boiled instead of being infused—and boiled as black as can be. . . . It is scarcely suited for the stomach of a rhinocerous." While the coffee, being generally roasted on board ship, was "often too much and often too little roasted; and when ground, although fresh enough, the aroma of that favourite beverage is no more like the fragrance of pure, properly roasted mocha than it is of a piece of boiled gutta percha. . . . It is a standing disgrace to ship-owners that such shamefully-cooked rubbish should be offered to passengers." On that account "pure cold water, or water and milk mixed, are the only liquids used by many throughout the voyage."[2]

The poor quality of the water supply aboard the *Duncan Gibb* forced Mrs. Radcliff to try various expedients. At first its taste could be improved by the addition of wine, spirits, raspberry, vinegar, tea, or coffee; but all of these together could not smother or disguise what had soon become "abominable" and "disgusting." She advised those who could afford it to bring a profuse store of bottled ale and porter as the only wholesome beverage on shipboard —"temperate advice, you will say, from a delicate lady!!—but the more delicate the ladies the more applicable the recommendation." She also advised the inclusion of a "filtering machine" among one's cooking utensils. Among other suggestions was that "almond milk" proved the best substitute for cream in tea, even though it had a peculiar flavor. Bottles of prepared milk were found satisfactory at first, but useless later in the voyage.

Life in the cabin of these vessels varied, as in the steerage, with the weather encountered and the efforts of the captain and crew to make the passage more agreeable; but in any event improved accommodations and more congenial fellow-passengers tempered the inconvenience and softened the hardship of conditions which in the steerage were often almost unbearable. Mrs. Traill's account of her voyage emphasizes the seasickness and monotony which followed the first feeling of exhilaration:

[2] *Canada and the Western States,* part II 18-19. Robert Louis Stevenson observed in 1879 that tea and coffee were "surprisingly alike. . . . I could distinguish a smack of snuff in the former and dishcloths in the second. As a matter of fact I have seen passengers, after many sips, still doubting which had been supplied them." (*The Amateur Emigrant,* 5.)

THE CABIN PASSAGE

"I was much pleased with the scenery of the Clyde; the day we set sail was a lovely one, and I remained on deck till nightfall. The morning light found our vessel dashing gallantly along, with a favourable breeze, through the North Channel; that day we saw the last of the Hebrides, and before night lost sight of the north coast of Ireland. A wide expanse of water and sky is now our only prospect. . . .

"Though we have been little more than a week on board, I am getting weary of the voyage. I can only compare the monotony of it to being weather-bound in some country inn. I have endured the horrors of *mal de mer* and except when the weather is fine I sit on a bench on the deck, wrapped in my cloak, and sew, or pace the deck with my husband and talk over plans for the future. . . . Every space is utilised in a ship. The bench on which the bed of cloaks is spread for me covers the hen coop. Poor prisoners to be killed and cooked as needed!"

The *Laurel* had a small library, but Mrs. Traill found that it was composed chiefly of "old novels and musty romances." No bad storms were encountered, and a month after leaving port the ship came in sight of Newfoundland.

Mrs. Traill's brother, Samuel Strickland, sailed from London on March 28, 1825, in the brig *William M'Gilevray*, and on several occasions the weather was so stormy that he was drenched with water while in his cabin. Once a sudden hurricane caused a rude awakening of this kind, and the pumps had to be used; while on another occasion during a heavy sea there was "a foot of water in the cabin, and all hands were at the pumps to lessen the growing evil." At other times Strickland enjoyed himself catching beautiful birds in the rigging, cleaning the captain's guns, and playing draughts with the mate. Once he took a shot at a whale, which "made the water fly in all directions"; but it was too rough to catch cod-fish off the Banks of Newfoundland, and the latter part of the journey was spent largely in admiring the icebergs and the scenery of the Gulf of St. Lawrence. A pilot was taken on near the Island of Bic, and the *William M'Gilevray* reached Quebec in due course.

An excellent account of a cabin passage from Bristol to New York is to be found in the unpublished letters of Mary Gapper, later the wife of Colonel E. G. O'Brien. She was 24 years old when she sailed for America in the Bristol trader *Warrior* in 1828. Cultured and highly educated, the daughter of a rector and squire of Somersetshire, she wrote vividly, and her journal contains a detailed description of her experiences over many years. The voyage, which was comparatively uneventful, commenced on August 31st, and for some days the weather was faultless. "The gentle heaving of the vessel," she wrote, "is like the breathing of some large animal on which we seem to be resting." The appearance of the sea by starlight and twilight, and phosphorescent phenomena fascinated the diarist. She passed much of the time in her "mighty cosy" cabin, reading or singing in German (she could read Spanish, Italian, and Greek as well); but her "highest enjoyment" was "that of writing my journal; . . . all manner of gossip, which I fancy will give you something of the same pleasure."

"A glorious saffron sunset" drew forth a description on one occasion, and again she notes that she is "making great friends with the Capt., who is so fond of his wife that he excites one's sympathy"; and the members of the crew and their varied activities even during calm weather are fully recorded. On September 4th she awoke to find

"an almost breathless heaven and waveless ocean which became thro' the morning more and more tranquil, till it seemed impossible in gazing on it to imagine that this scene of perfect beauty might in a few moments become one of indescribable horror. . . . To-day one half of the sea reflected the blue of the heavens whilst the sunbeams rested on the other with a uniform splendour gradually increasing till it was blended with the glowing mist of the horizon."

But although there were no great storms, the wind increased and the passengers experienced "various bodily discomforts, of which sickness was the least." Once the sea burst through one of the stern windows, frightening the ladies; and we are told that "Grandmama has discovered that sailing is nearly as much exercise as riding on horseback." Tables, chairs, and chests moved about from time to time, but it was all so mild and good-mannered that one could hardly compare it with the miserable experiences which most emigrants suffered. On Sunday, September 14th, the passengers "had service on deck under the magnificent temple of the sky—the Capt. & 2nd mate officiating—as the wind was steady we had an unbroken sabbath." On the 30th they could "smell the land," and were soon off the New Jersey coast. When the *Warrior* reached New York on October 4th Miss Gapper was sorry to leave the ship: "Ocean is to me the region of rest and peace."

Millicent and Ellen Steele recorded in their letters a voyage in which music and dancing provided plenty of diversion for those who were not too seasick. Their vessel, the *Thames*, "served in the most liberal manner—we have claret, Sherry, Port, every day, with the addition of Champagne on Sundays and Thursdays, and those that are ill may have sago, gruel, arrowroot, lemonade, as often in the day as they like to order them." Another writer, recalling the period of his own seasickness, advised those about to

Illustrated London News

ON DECK AT SEA

On the better vessels steerage passengers were permitted to use the deck at specified times.

Illustrated London News

FAMILY SALOON CABIN ON THE "GREAT EASTERN"

Similar luxurious accommodations were available on the best sailing packets.

Illustrated London News   *Morel Fatio, After a Sketch by the Prince de Joinville*
THE BURNING OF THE "OCEAN MONARCH," 1848
Most of the 440 on board lost their lives when a raging fire destroyed the *Ocean Monarch* shortly after she left Liverpool.

THE CABIN PASSAGE

make the Atlantic crossing that they would find "a stock of good thick cake ginger bread, gingerbread nuts, and oranges and apples a very good thing at sea. You can sometimes swallow a nut, or suck an orange when you would turn in disgust from anything else. Ginger tea, too, acts very kindly on a distressed stomach." Some cabin passengers, no doubt, made some such provision, but in general they relied entirely upon the ship's service, which was usually good.

The passage to Quebec was frequently from ten to twenty days longer than that to New York, and the latter route was consequently patronized by many who could afford to travel in the cabin, whether their ultimate destination was in the United States or in the British Provinces; for there was a distinct advantage also in the much quicker journey into the interior. Mrs. William Radcliff learned of the excellent service on the New York route after taking nearly three weeks longer to reach Quebec, so she wrote her father-in-law in Ireland to "warn any friends that mean to follow us to come by New York. It may appear more expensive; but I believe in the end, when the cost and great waste of private provisions is taken into consideration, the difference of expenditure will be but trifling, that of comfort and health excessive."

The cabin-class packets between Liverpool and New York usually carried but few passengers, but they were especially built for that purpose, and had more able, though brutal, commanders, and competent, but tough, crews. The Black Ball Line, instituted in 1815, was the first, and her four 500-ton ships offered a scheduled service, sailing irrespective of weather on the first day of each month—and the chanty *Blow the Man Down* was the happy result of such disrespect for the elements. The vessels, however, were comparatively small and the accommodations cramped. Numerous other lines followed the lead of the "Black Ballers," among them the Dramatic Line—consisting of the *Sheridan, Garrick, Boscius,* and *Siddons*. Several considerations gradually resulted in the construction of vessels of greatly improved type. The use of steam tugs made it easier for sailing-ships to approach the docks of the great ports; while the race for Chinese tea and Australian and Californian gold was an incentive to the development of fast clippers. There was, too, an increasing demand for a speedy service between British ports and New York.

In 1832 regular packets left Liverpool on the 1st, 8th, 16th, and 24th of each month, weather permitting. The average passage westward was 38 days, while that eastward was only 25 days; and activities during the voyage were highly developed for the times. James Stuart crossed to New York on the *William Thomson* in July-August, 1832, along with 14 cabin and 2 steerage passengers, and a crew of 31. The cabin fare was 35 guineas, inclusive of wines and liquors. Upon remarking that the staterooms and beds were very narrow he was informed that they were "purposely contracted to prevent accidents happening, by the inmates falling out of bed in a rolling sea." The cabin passengers were allowed to arrange the hours of their meals, so they decided upon 8.30 for breakfast, 12 for luncheon, 4 for dinner, and 7 for tea. There was a cow on board, "which supplied us with many luxuries." In the forenoon the passengers read or walked on the deck; they spent about two hours at dinner and whiled away the rest of the day in rubbers of whist or "the daily stock exchange." The captain sailed north of Ireland because of a southerly wind, and upon reaching New York 38 days later he learned that other packets which had taken the southern route had not yet arrived, even though they had left Liverpool from ten to fifteen days earlier.

One of the most consistent performers among the Liverpool-New York packets was the *Ontario*, which over a period of ten years averaged only 24 days for the passage. A gentleman who crossed on a similar liner wrote that everything was "admirable": "Eatables (what a sensualist is man!) of the most excellent description—fowls of all kinds—prime beef and mutton—capital hams, and puddings of all sorts and sizes. Dried fruits, etc., etc., —port and sherry every day *ad libitum*, and on Sundays and Thursdays claret and champagne." It is from William Lyon Mackenzie, however, that we obtain a full description of the meals on the *Ontario*:

> "We have breakfast at nine, consisting of black tea, green tea, coffee, biscuit, bread, hot rolls, fish, fowl, ham, cold mutton, eggs; sometimes we have chocolate, etc. A lunch follows, at noon, consisting of bread, cheese, cold meat, tongue, wine, porter, liquors, etc. Dinner comes on at four in the afternoon,—soups, fresh mutton, beef, pork, and sometimes veal, barn-door fowls, bacon, plum-pudding, preserves, pastry, etc. The dessert—oranges, raisins, almonds, Spanish nuts, figs, prunes; wines, *viz.*, excellent madeira and port, and also claret, are always on the table; and occasionally (say, every other day,) champagne, a very fair and genuine sample is served round after the cloth is removed."

A dinner menu of the first cabin of the ship *Lightning* when it was a week out from Liverpool shows that the fare on such vessels was very similar to the service in the best hotels of the day:

THE CABIN PASSAGE

Soups—Vermicelli and macaroni.
Fish—Cod and Oyster sauce.
Meats—Roast beef, *boeuf à la mode*, boiled mutton, roast veal, boiled turkey and oyster sauce, roast goose, roast fowl, boiled fowl, minced escallops, veal and ham pie, haricot mutton, ham.
Sweets—Plum pudding, rice pudding, roll pudding, tarts, orange fritters, small pastry.
Dessert—Oranges, almonds, Barcelona raisins, figs, etc.
Wines—Champagne, sparkling hock.

Life on board these fast packets approached in many respects that on the modern liner. Mackenzie found a library of several hundred volumes. He also notes that the tipping system was well organized, a sovereign each being raised among both men and women as a gratuity for the steward and female attendant. Charles Daubeny outlines some of the amusements on board the *Mediator* in 1837. Some played chess, others gambled, and to others shuffleboard was the chief diversion. Mr. Daubeny was more interested in conducting all sorts of scientific tests of the air and water; and a Mr. Horncastle wrote a song, *On Board the Mediator*, for the enjoyment of the passengers, among whom were Solicitor-General Draper of Upper Canada, and Major (later Sir Richard) Bonnycastle.[3]

In many first-class packets a band provided music for dancing, as well as concerts. Each evening the polka and quadrille were in full swing. The *Lightning* carried a six-piece "German band." Negro melodies (usually called "coon songs") such as *Old Black Joe, Carry Me Back to Old Virginie,* and *Stop Dat Knockin'* were popular, as well as Scottish and Irish folksongs, English choruses, and sailors' ditties—*A Life on the Ocean Wave, The Death of Nelson, I'm Afloat,* and *Cheer, Boys, Cheer.* Towards the close of a voyage there was usually a concert combining all talent from the first cabin down to the steerage. Among the entertainments organized were plays, mock trials, and debating and choral societies; while quoits and deck billiards provided sport for some, and cards, dominoes, draughts, and backgammon amused others who preferred to pass the time in the cabin.

But the packet passage at its best had numerous crudities in comparison with a modern liner. The long-boat was usually a pen for geese, sheep, and pigs, while on deck near by was a stable for the cows,[4] which were very important passengers. The water supply,

[3] Daubeny, *Journal of a Tour*, 3-7. Many a modern cabin passenger has cursed the tyranny of organized amusements arranged under the high pressure of social hostesses. For purposes of comparison see J. E. Middleton's essay, *The Well-known North Atlantic.*
[4] "Hoisting the cow aboard" was an interesting and characteristic spectacle at the port of embarkation in sailing-ship days. A lively description of the process is given by William Hancock in *An Emigrant's Five Years in the Free States of America*, 5-6.

kept in an iron tank, had to be carefully conserved; no freshwater baths were available even to the cabin passengers. Often, as on American river steamers, those in the steerage were in reality "deck" passengers, for in fine weather they were allowed to live and eat their meals in the open air. One stewardess was usually carried to wait upon cabin passengers. In cold weather the passengers crowded around one or two open grate-fires—if the captain thought it necessary to light them. The Rev. Isaac Fidler observed in 1831 that during all his voyage, "till three days before our arrival, there had been no fire in the cabin, but the intensity of cold was at last so great that fire could be no longer dispensed with."

Patrick Shirreff, an insular and somewhat puritanical agriculturalist who was seasick most of the voyage, saw but little to praise on the *Napoleon* except its American commander, Captain Smith. He was disgusted at the immoderate smoking of "segars" (one man used 150 in 14 days, he states), by the copious amounts of saliva to be found in many parts of the vessel, and at the amount of time most of the cabin passengers spent in "sensual gratification," by which he meant eating and drinking. The day was filled by "the noise of calling the steward and drawing of corks," and he wondered at the excessive amount of food and liquor which "some individuals stowed under their belts."

A Toronto commercial traveller, C. C. Taylor, who crossed in 1847, chose a sailing-ship, hoping that such a voyage might be more attractive than one by steamer. The idea was soon dispelled, for the business man in him greatly objected to the inertia of a dead calm. He notes that Captain Cornish of the *Sheridan* was a harsh man, and "those of the steerage had a hard time." They were fortunate that the passage lasted but 26 days.

Robert Playfair crossed from Le Havre to New York in the *New York*, one of a line of "splendid packets, . . . show-ships elegantly fitted up." The boat was "a truly elegant vessel" of 1400 tons with a cabin fare of £26. The staterooms were "commodious little apartments, entering from the eating saloon, each containing a sofa and two beds, one above the other, with a bull's-eye window towards the sea, which could be opened and shut at pleasure." There were 250 steerage passengers aboard, largely German, and an infectious disease among their children necessitated eight burials at sea—a disaster which might have been avoided had there been a surgeon on board. When the ship reached the Grand Banks, Captain Lines boarded a fishing smack, "and procured for us a

THE CABIN PASSAGE

supply of fresh fish, which proved very acceptable, as well as two newspapers."

A winter passage was usually an arduous undertaking. Captain R. G. A. Levinge experienced a remarkably stormy voyage during the winter of 1837. When four or five days on her way the *St. Andrew* encountered "an uninterrupted hurricane for thirty-three days"; during this period the ship lay to, "without a stitch of canvass set," a small piece of tarpaulin threaded through the mizzen-rigging being sufficient to steer her. She drifted several hundred miles out of her course, and "passed a Frenchman in great distress. . . . A sea had carried away the whole of her stern, over the wreck of which they were nailing canvass; but the sea ran so high that we dared not go near her. What made it more distressing was to learn from the signals she made that the whole of one watch had been washed overboard." Partial lulls were succeeded by "the most tremendous hail-squalls"; and at night Jack o' Lanterns illuminated the ship's course. Levinge observed that "the effect of the angry monsters of waves, beat down for a time by the violence of the hail to a comparative smoothness, lighted up by these meteors, and by vivid flashes of lightning, was awfully sublime. On one occasion a sea struck the vessel a little abaft the bows, clearing away the boats, bulwarks, hurricane-house and all, flush with the decks, and knocking over the men at the wheel." After sixty-five days the *St. Andrew* reached New York, having made the second best time among sixteen liners which had left Europe at the same time. Captain Levinge described the ship as "magnificent," and the life on board "perfect"; and, though there were more passengers than had been anticipated, "still we had everything equally good to the end of the voyage. Champagne, burgundy, porter, soda, selzer-water, sardines in oil; and what is the greatest luxury of all at sea, the old cow did her duty to the end of the journey." But during a large part of the voyage,

"so much was the old vessel out of the perpendicular that many of the passengers were afraid to leave their berths for days, taking what rest they could get by placing their feet in a *slantingdicular* position against the top of their berths, to steady themselves during the time they contrived to stow away a certain quantity of nautical food called *lobscouse*, an excellent conglomeration of the fag-ends of ham and smashed potatoes, capable of being conveniently conveyed to the mouth with a spoon."

Some long winter passages were rendered miserable not only by the elements but also because of a shortage of food—even in the cabin. T. R. Preston's ship from Portsmouth in late November,

1836, was hardly out of the Channel before she was struck by a terrific storm which very nearly put a sudden and disastrous end to the voyage. In the midst of it the captain was thrown violently to the deck by the wind, and was in bed for several days. When the storm finally subsided, gales drove the vessel hither and thither, and no appreciable progress westward was made. The captain, hoping to find the southern route less stormy, veered off the regular course and approached the Azores. There were about 100 passengers aboard, some twenty of whom, including Preston, were in the cabin. Neither the ship itself nor its steerage passengers were provisioned for a longer voyage than 30 days, and after the first month at sea there was an acute shortage. At first those in the cabin took up a subscription to relieve the hunger in the steerage by purchasing some corn from the captain; but it was only a few days before the cabin service was reduced by one meal per day, and then to a subsistence upon various dishes of cornmeal. Preston, having paid a fare of 35 guineas, objected to such a menu; but complaints were useless, and there was soon a very real danger of "dying of starvation on board a New York packet." Finally the ship approached the coast of America, but she was well to the south, off Virginia. A coastal vessel supplied some provisions, but soon after the liner ran on a shoal off Norfolk. After much difficulty a passing boat got her off, and she proceeded northward. The crew had meanwhile been mutinous because of harsh treatment and short rations; and to cap the climax the vessel, in the absence of a pilot, overshot Sandy Hook and narrowly escaped shipwreck. She eventually reached New York after 63 days[5] at sea, and Mr. Preston observed that while everyone on board was miserable enough, the steerage passengers were terribly emaciated and "but shadows of their former selves."

Almost as tempestuous, though with some pleasant compensations, was the voyage of John Duncan, who set sail from Greenock on February 2, 1818, and "after six weeks' tossing upon the boisterous ocean" found himself "amidst the orange groves of Fayal," one of the Azores Islands. An unfavorable wind at the start, and a succession of heavy gales and storms of sleet and rain, stove in the greater part of the bulwarks and carried away parts of the rigging, and the *Fanny* had covered twenty degrees of latitude before she made any headway westward. Consequently the captain thought it best to take refuge in the Azores and refit and re-

[5] In contrast it is of interest to note that the British liner *Queen Mary*, after fighting "a typical North Atlantic gale all the way," reached port on December 22, 1936, only 13 hours behind schedule.

THE CABIN PASSAGE

provision the ship. Seventeen days out from Fayal she reached Sandy Hook, and Mr. Duncan congratulated himself upon having seen a part of the world he had never expected to visit.

An American packet, the *Victoria*, which entered the service in 1843, was noted for its luxuriousness. Upon her arrival at St. Katharine Docks, London, after her maiden voyage, a distinguished group of personages accepted the invitation of the captain, and after a tour of inspection sat down to a *dejeuner* in the best of style, regaled with toasts, speeches, "the delicacies of the season," and the music of Prince Albert's Band. The vessel, which was described by an English publication as "a superb work of structure and design," was 170 feet long, 36 feet in breadth and 22 feet in depth, and of about 1,000 tons. A writer fond of statistics stated that she weighed 2,000,000 pounds, required 34 tons of iron and 6 tons of copper, "besides a great number of treenails"; and that the mainmast was 155 feet in height, and supported "over an acre of canvas" made from 24 tons of hemp. It contained in the forecastle a good library for the crew, and sailed "on temperance principles entirely." A generous sprinkling of French was considered essential by a contemporary newspaper in describing her outstanding features:

"The ladies' cabin is distinguished by the extreme elegance of the fittings; indeed, no drawing-room or boudoir on terra firma presents a nicer specimen of decorative art or appropriate upholstery than does this *bijou* of ship-joinery. The style of the apartment is that of Louis Quatorze or Quinze, in the most delicate white and gold, the carved framework of the panels being well executed. The *meubles* are in correspondent taste; the couches, *fauteuils*, etc., being stuffed in silk damask of exquisite pattern and colour—light blue and white, with carpet to match. There is a centre table of choice white marble. The apartment is lit through ground glass; and one of the large panes bears a picturesque view of Windsor Castle, and at the opposite end is Buckingham Palace, surrounded by the rose, shamrock and thistle. The decorator has not, however, lavished all his taste upon this apartment, for the berths are fitted *en suite*: the ceiling is in white and gold, and the handles of the doors are of glass."

CHAPTER XIII

Shipwreck and Disaster

"Now would I give a thousand furlongs of sea for an acre of barren ground—long heath, brown furze, any thing. The wills above be done! but I would fain die a dry death."

William Shakespeare: *The Tempest*

The hazards of ocean travel in the days of the sailing-ship were, of course, very great. The danger of collision with other vessels or with icebergs is, because of increased speed, present in a greater degree today than it was a century ago, though it has always been dangerous sailing amid the fog and ice of the Banks of Newfoundland and the Gulf. On the other hand the fire hazard and the danger of shipwreck have decreased with the construction of large steel vessels, and the danger of death through epidemics or starvation no longer exists. There are well-authenticated instances of small sailing-vessels being capsized and even wrecked by whales.[1] In 1840 shipwreck and disease made the normal death rate of passengers crossing the Atlantic to British America 1.005 per cent, but the rate on Irish ships was usually much greater than this. In the late 'forties, when half a million people died in Ireland of famine or pestilence, the death rate on the crowded ships bound for America was nearly 17 out of every 100, inclusive of those who died almost immediately after arrival. Conditions gradually improved and a less destitute type of emigrant entered upon the great adventure; while with the easing up in numbers a more thorough inspection was enforced, and the death rate fell still lower as the traffic passed to the steamship. By 1863, when over half of the trade was in steam vessels, it was only .19 per cent—no higher than if the passenger had remained on land.

There were many cases of extreme misfortune in the sailing-ship period. In 1819 a vessel *en route* to Quebec spent 15 weeks on the Atlantic before she reached Richibucto, New Brunswick. There a family short of provisions and ill with fever was forced ashore. After walking a long distance to another port they took passage in a boat heavily laden with plaster of paris, but the ship

---

[1] See, for example, the account of the wreck of the *Waterloo*, in the *Illustrated London News*, April 7, 1855, p. 316.

SHIPWRECK AND DISASTER 125

grounded a few days later and all perished. An early settler in Upper Canada related a remarkable series of unfortunate events connected with his ocean travel. After some unsuccessful years in the new land he determined to return to Ireland with his family on a timber ship sailing from Quebec to Liverpool. It was late in the autumn, and snow and sleet made the early part of the passage disagreeable. A very heavy storm was encountered in mid-ocean, and the vessel was so badly damaged that it became a mere derelict; and as it sprang a leak and began to fill, those on board saved only two eight-pound pieces of salt pork, a few biscuits, a little cream of tartar, and a cask of water which had been lashed on deck. Their experiences in the days that followed are described in the narrative of "Mr. G.," as related to Samuel Strickland:

"Our ship's company consisted of the captain, mate, and six seamen, besides a medical man, myself, and my poor wife and two children, who were cabin passengers. We made several unsuccessful attempts to procure a supply of provisions; consequently it became absolutely necessary to give out what we had on the smallest possible rations. The fourth night was ushered in by another storm, more terrific even than the last. A heavy sea struck the vessel, sweeping overboard the captain and three seamen; and the poor doctor's leg was broken at the same time by a loose spar. We passed a fearful night; nor did the morning add to our comfort, for my daughter died from exposure and want just as the day dawned. On the seventh morning the doctor, who had suffered the greatest agony from his swollen leg, sank at last, the paper of cream of tartar I had in my pocket being the only relief for his dreadful fever during his misery. My poor wife and remaining child soon followed. We now had fine weather, which was some relief to our intolerable misery.

"On the twentieth day the last of our provisions was consumed. I had an old pair of deer-skin moccasins on my feet: these were carefully divided amongst us. We had now serious thoughts of drawing lots to see which of us should die for the preservation of the rest. I, however, begged they would defer such a dreadful alternative to the last minute. On the twenty-first night of our disaster I had a most remarkable dream: I thought I saw a fine ship bearing down to our assistance, and that she was called the *London of London*. I related my dream to my companions, in hopes it might raise their spirits, which, however, it failed to do; for nothing was to be seen on that dreary waste of water, though we scanned the horizon in every direction. For upwards of two hours after we scarcely spoke a word, when suddenly the sun, which had been obscured all the morning, shone out brightly and warm for the season of the year. I mechanically raised myself and looked over the bulwarks, when to my astonishment and delight, I beheld a ship, the very counterpart of the one I had seen in my dream, bearing down directly for the wreck.

"It is not easy to describe our various feelings on this occasion: we could scarcely believe our senses when the boat came along side. We were so reduced by famine and exposure that we had to be lifted into her. In this state of exhaustion every attention was paid us by the humane captain and crew. As soon as I was on board I asked the name of the vessel, when I was surprised to find she was called the *Portaferry of Portaferry*. Although the name was not that borne by the vessel of which I had dreamed, it must be considered at least a remarkable coincidence. Great care was taken to prevent us eating too ravenously at first: we received every kindness our weak condition required; but, notwithstanding these precautions, two of my companions in misery died before we reached Ireland. When we arrived at Strangford, in the north of Ireland, I was entirely destitute—I had lost everything I possessed. Fortunately for me I belonged to the honourable fraternity of Free and Accepted Masons, who kindly furnished me with clothing and money sufficient to take me home, which I reached in safety."

A comparison of conditions in Ireland with those he had left in Upper Canada suggested that Mr. G. return again to America, and he

"accordingly embarked with the young wife I had lately married, and the three children I had formerly left in Ireland with my parents. We sailed early in the spring of 1825. My ill luck still attended me; for owing to the dense fogs we experienced on the Banks of Newfoundland we got out of our course and our ship struck the shore near Cape Ray: fortunately the sea was smooth and the weather fine: so that when daylight broke we were able, without much difficulty, to be landed on that most inhospitable shore,
'Where the bones of many a tall ship lie buried.'
"We saved little or nothing from the wreck; for as the day advanced the wind freshened into a gale which, blowing on shore, soon settled the fate of our gallant bark. The shore was soon strewn with casks, bales, and packages, some of which we were able to secure. Our captain chartered a small fishing-vessel, which landed us at last safely at Quebec."

A detailed narrative of the hardships of shipwreck is given by Francis Thomas in his unpublished "Journal of a Voyage from London to Quebec, with an Account of the Shipwreck near Cape Ray on the Coast of Newfoundland." On the morning of July 11, 1833, the ship *Hebe* ran upon a ledge of rock, and the passengers were terrified to see "breakers close to us, and the waves dashing over them in a most tremendous manner and not more than 20 or 30 yards distant. . . . We were in imminent danger—the bustle and confusion which now took place was beyond description." Like the others, Thomas rushed below to warn his family and secure his most prized possessions. With a sudden shock "like that of an earthquake," the *Hebe* was driven further in upon the rocks, and the screaming of women and children rose above the general din as the vessel shook and rolled "in a dreadful manner." Although many were injured as they were hurled from their feet, the condition of the ship was not as bad as it appeared, and in a short time a rope was thrown ashore, enabling the transfer of passengers and crew to a place of safety.

The *Hebe* did not immediately break up, and Thomas, among others, returned to secure as much as possible of his baggage, but the greater part of it was lost. It was a desolate shore, and such crude shelter as could be provided proved but a poor protection

SHIPWRECK AND DISASTER 127

from the elements. Next day the captain ordered a march towards Poyle Bay. "A more rugged path," says Thomas, "I think impossible." Only the women and children were conveyed thither, the men remaining encamped on the rocks. Another trip was made to the wreck, but it was the last, for the wind arose and the *Hebe* broke up, all remaining articles salvaged being claimed by whoever found them. The 96 men remained six days on the rocky shore, their supplies becoming depleted to an alarming extent. But finally the captain engaged the 120-ton sloop *Nimrod* to pick up the women and children at Poyle Bay and proceed to Rose Branch harbor, where the men would join their families aboard. Two days later, after an unpleasant trip, the passengers were landed at Sydney, Cape Breton, "dirty in our persons, and nearly worn out with sufferings and fatigue of various kinds." Lodging at a small tavern for ten days, Thomas finally engaged passage to Quebec on the *Mercury*, providing himself with two weeks' supplies for the voyage, which, again, was anything but pleasant, for the ship's officers proved to be "harsh, uncivil, unfeeling men, who treated us more like convicts transported for their crimes than as unfortunate distressed immigrants."

The brig *James* appears to have been fated to suffer disaster. In 1827 she set sail from Ireland with 160 emigrants, all of whom suffered from typhus fever during the passage. In 1834 she was wrecked off the Banks of Newfoundland, only eleven escaping death out of 267. She had sailed from Limerick on the 8th of April, and experienced nothing but a series of mishaps. Storms carried away the topmast, studding-sail boom, jib-boom, main-sail, fore-sail, and yard, and the *James* began to ship water. The narrative of the surgeon, Henry Downes, describes the events of the last hours on the sinking ship:

"On Sunday, the 25th, at six a.m., they set about pumping the ship out, but were not long thus engaged before the pumps were found to be choked with the passengers' potatoes, which, from the rotten description of the bags in which they were kept, went adrift about the hold, filling the pump wells and preventing the possibility of working the pumps, which were hoisted on deck and a great quantity of potatoes brought away from them; and to prevent a recurrence of this, tin kettles, with holes made in them, were laid on the heels, which proved ineffectual; after which baskets were substituted, with as little success.

"Finding the water to increase to an alarming extent, and a gale from the N. W. springing up, with a heavy sea, the ship straining very much, we had recourse to the expedient of baling her out from the fore hatch with buckets and a provision made fast to a tackle; but the water casks, which were floating about there, excited the apprehensions of the people, and one passenger, Henry Morgan, getting three of his fingers broken between two of them, the attempt was abandoned.

"About four o'clock p.m. she shipped a sea which carried away the lee bulwarks, and was soon after struck by a second still heavier, with the force of which she listed, canting her ballast, and never returned to an erect position. The water having reached the between-decks, and no chance of saving her presenting itself, the Captain, at five o'clock, ordered the longboat and skiff to be lowered, as a sail tacking to the southward made its appearance. The passengers crowded into the skiff while she was in the long-boat, and by this means made it difficult to lower the latter, which when drawn from the after-chock, came against the stancheons; after which they did not seem inclined to take further trouble with her. At half past six we lowered the jolly-boat, in which eleven of us were picked up by the *Margaret*, of Newcastle, Capt. Wake, to whose kindness and humanity since we are indebted for our preservation."

A similar statement was made by Captain Laidler, who also was among the rescued. He stated that when the ship became so full that she would not answer her helm he considered it useless to remain on board, and "exhorted the passengers to assist the crew in getting the long-boat and skiff out; but their answer was, the sea is so rough we are sure to be drowned, and may as well die on board as in the boats." The *Margaret* was only two or three miles away at the time, and after learning of the disaster from the ten men and one woman who saved themselves in the jolly-boat, she cruised up and down all night in the vicinity, but nothing was afterwards seen of either the *James* or her boats.

The same year seventeen vessels on the Quebec route were wrecked, and many hundreds of lives lost. In announcing three disasters—the *Fidelity*, the brig *Edward*, which sank after striking an iceberg, and the barque *Astrea*, wrecked on the rocks off Louisbourg with a loss of 208 out of 211 on board—the *Quebec Gazette* commented that the recent shipwreck of half a dozen vessels, with a death list of some 700 for the three worst disasters, suggested that there should be rigid regulations insuring the seaworthiness of emigrant ships, which, in general, were quite the worst in the Atlantic service. Those sailing from Ireland were commonly the most defective of all, and had frequently to put back to port when only a few days out, having sprung a leak, lost a mast, or been otherwise crippled; while hardly a season passed in which several vessels were not wrecked.

Lifeboat accommodation was commonly provided only tor cabin passengers. During the years 1847-1851, forty-four passenger vessels, out of 7,129 from the British Isles, suffered shipwreck, and 1,043 lives were lost, with the result that legislation was adopted to give assistance to those rendered destitute. One of the worst disasters was the wreck of the 320-ton *Exmouth*, sailing from Londonderry for Quebec with a crew of eleven and 240 emigrants, mostly women and children who were hoping to join relatives in Canada. According to the law this vessel was limited to 65½ passengers, but the numbers were swelled by the provision which allowed children to count as half an adult, or less. A terrific storm of several days' duration carried away the long-boat and parts of the rigging, and the captain had no alternative but to seek some haven on the Scottish coast. He lost his bearings and was driven upon one of the rockiest shores of the Isle of Islay. As the vessel crashed against the cliffs three men who were on the mainmast were hurled upon a rock by the force of the waves, but the ship was quickly dashed to pieces, and there were no other survivors. A contemporary account offers the following comment upon the disaster:

"Had the wreck remained in the chasm where it was originally thrown, and from which the three survivors escaped, the mainmast might have been used as a bridge by the others; but, unhappily, this last possibility of relief was taken away. . . . There was no cry from the multitude cooped up within the hull of the ill-fated brig; or at least it was unheard, for the commotion of the elements was so furious that the men on the top could scarcely hear each other at the top of their voices. The emigrants, therefore, must have perished in their berths as the rocks rapidly thumped the bottom out of the vessel. . . . At the latest date of our advices from Islay about 20 of the bodies had come ashore. They were principally females, with one little boy amongst them; and as many of them were in their night clothes, the probability is that they were those who rushed upon deck at the first alarm caused by the striking of the ship."

Three weeks later the *News* gave an account of the recovery of the bodies. By the exertions of five inhabitants of the island,

"no fewer than 108 bodies have been recovered and interred. These persons, slung over the rock by turns, succeeded in hooking the bodies in the surf, wrapped the women, all of whom were naked, in sheets, and had them thus hoisted up to the summit of the cliff. The bodies were dreadfully mutilated; some without faces, others without heads or limbs, and all in a far advanced state of putrefaction. . . . They are all buried in a beautiful spot— soft green turf, surrounded by wild rocks."

Some ships, however, appear to have had lifeboats enough for their passenger list. In 1841 the 296-ton brig *Minstrel* was wrecked between Limerick and Quebec, only 4 out of 141 emigrants being saved. The *Cobourg Star* of June 9th states that when the vessel struck Red Island Reef about 100 of the passengers embarked in her small boats, but before the painters could be cast off, the ship suddenly sank by the stern, carrying them all to their deaths. Eight, however, were at the time towing astern in the gig, and these escaped when their rope fortunately broke. It was possible to publish a list of the passengers, for in compliance with "a late regulation" it had been sent to the Emigration Agent at Quebec. Over a third of the passengers were children.

Another notable Irish shipwreck occurred in the late fall of 1850. In spite of the season, the *Edmund* set sail from Carrigaholt, on the Shannon, with 207 emigrants. Hardly had she commenced her voyage when "the wind tossed her wildly, until every thread of canvass was rent to atoms, and two of her masts carried away; she became perfectly unmanageable, and drifted along at the mercy of the waves." Striking Duggerna Rocks, she was held there for some time; but was soon washed off by a furious sea, and the captain tried to cast anchor at the entrance of the bay. An eyewitness wrote a vivid description of the last terrific crash: "Holding to for some time, the waves rolling over her hull and spars, she dashed in a perfect broadside against the rock, breaking her back right through the centre, and plunging her only remaining mast clear on the shore." By the aid of the mast and some of the inhabitants of the rocky region, the crew and a few passengers were able to crawl ashore; but the stern, half torn from the prow, bounded off to sea, carrying with it pieces of spars, cords, and sheathing, together with several of the passengers, whose piercing shrieks could be heard above the roar of the storm; while the prow, holding to the anchor, was crushed to pieces against the sharp rocks "until it was ground to fragments, which the waves and the storm hurled into the air."

Captain Wilson heroically "clung to the wreck while there was a stave to stand upon or a life to be saved; and when the last plank was shivered from his feet, he took an aged woman, who still clung to the plank, and, flinging her on his back, plunged into the sea and succeeded in reaching shore." On shore was another hero, Richard Russell, who "stood upon the rock throughout that terrible night, drenched by the sea, and almost exhausted by his superhuman labors, bearing in his arms the half-dead creatures who had crawled to the rocks, and rescuing many of them from certain death." Ninety-six lost their lives in this disaster, which left an appalling sight on the coast: heaps of scattered fragments of planks, staves, canvas, trunks, scraps of clothes, all literally ground to pieces. Of the vessel nothing was left but a torn, mangled, mass —"the completest wreck that writer ever described, or eye ever witnessed—not a plank together to tell her name or destiny."

But on some occasions officers and seamen showed extreme

SHIPWRECK AND DISASTER

cowardice and a lamentable disregard for all the rules of the sea. The *John*, bound for Quebec with 149 adult passengers and 114 children, was wrecked off the south coast of England on the very day she left Plymouth Sound, May 3, 1855. The greater part of the emigrants were natives of northern Devonshire, from which large numbers were at the time leaving for America. The captain sailed too close to shore between the Falmouth and Lizard Lights, and the *John* struck the rocks with such force that she ran right over one reef and crashed upon others farther in. The captain then ordered her to be run aground still further, but the sea washed her down the coast. Her anchor was then dropped, and an attempt made to launch some of the four boats, into one of which the master, one passenger, and four seamen immediately jumped. But finding her deficient in rigging, the captain climbed on deck again, and the boat made for shore without him. After some difficulty it landed, and contact was established with the coastguard through the efforts of the one passenger. It was too rough to launch any lifeboats at the time, but the life-savers were more successful the following morning. Meanwhile a disgraceful scene was in progress on the ship. Most of the crew were drunk, and the captain urged the emigrants to remain aboard while they might have escaped during low tide, the shore being only a few hundred feet distant.

"Before two the sea broke heavily over the vessel, dashing the boats to pieces, each wave carrying its victims into eternity amidst the most terrific shrieks of the rest, expecting every moment to meet the same doom. One hundred and ninety-six men, women and children were swallowed up, and about eighty saved. The crew, with the exception of the steward, evinced the greatest apathy throughout this dreadful scene, and did not render the slightest assistance to the passengers. When the shore boats arrived, about half-past three or four o'clock, they were the first to try to get into them, with their bags, showing a greater anxiety to secure these than to save the lives of the emigrants. Not a seaman perished."

A jury considered the conduct of the crew inexcusable, and returned a verdict of manslaughter against Captain Rawle, who was subsequently arrested. That the hazards of sailing in this locality were great enough at any time—without the addition of negligence—is apparent from a reference in the *Illustrated London News* in 1846. In one month of that year no less than 28 merchant and fishing vessels were wrecked between Plymouth Sound and Land's End, and altogether only two men and a boy were saved.

The east coast was not free from disasters. In the early spring of 1849 the American vessel *Floridian*, from Antwerp with about

200 German mechanics and farm laborers aboard, was wrecked on the Long Sands, near Harwich. The event is described as "one of the most frightful catastrophes that ever occurred on the English coast." The vessel struck

"with such terrific force that her planks and false keel immediately rushed up alongside. The emigrants hastened on deck in frantic dismay. Within a few minutes of the vessel's striking, the sea broke into her hull, blowing up the hatchways, and sweeping many of the poor creatures overboard, while others were drowned in their berths, being unable to rise from the effects of sea-sickness."

A desperate rush towards the ship's two boats capsized both of them. The crew took to the rigging, to which they lashed themselves; while the emigrants crowded the quarter-deck. In an hour's time the ship broke in two, the mainmast fell with a tremendous crash, and, as a frightful shriek arose, the heavy sea carried away the whole of the quarter-deck, the emigrants being precipitated into the sea. Some contrived to hold on to packages and staves for a while, but all had disappeared before night set in. Twelve survivors clung to the rigging of the foremast, which still remained upright. They endured great suffering all night, the cold sea breaking over them continually. By morning six were frozen to death, and their bodies were dangling in the rigging. Three sailors and one passenger retained their hold on life all that day and most of the next, when, almost frozen and deranged in mind, they were rescued by her Majesty's revenue cutter *Petrel* at great peril to herself; for another vessel had earlier lost five hands in an attempt to save the perishing emigrants. Some 200 ships set out from neighboring ports for the scene, in the hope—not of rescuing passengers—but of picking up some of the cargo.

Collisions with other vessels were not usual in sailing-ship days, though the fogs off Newfoundland and in the Gulf of St. Lawrence frequently made sailing very tedious and, where there were icebergs or islands, extremely dangerous. Francis Thomas states that his ship missed another by a margin of "only about 8 or 10 feet." The danger became more prominent after the introduction of steamships. In 1849, the mail steamship *Europa* ran down during a heavy fog the brig *Charles Bartlett*, carrying 162 steerage passengers from London to New York. The sailing-ship quickly sank, drowning 136 persons. The report of her captain stated that a dense fog set in during the afternoon of June 27th, and that consequently he

"ordered a good look-out from the top-gallant forecastle; also directed the

WRECK OF THE BARQUE "EDMUND," 1850

Ninety-six Irish emigrants were drowned when the *Edmund* crashed on the Duggerna Rocks, County Clare.

Illustrated London News

THE DISABLED "MARTIN LUTHER" SAVED BY THE "TAGUS"

The *Martin Luther*, carrying 498 passengers, narrowly escaped shipwreck on the French coast in 1857.

SHIPWRECK AND DISASTER 133

man at the wheel to look sharp to windward. At 3.30 p.m., being on the weather side of the poop deck, heard a rumbling to windward like distant thunder; turned my ear to the windward and my eye to the horizon; the man at the wheel, noticing that I was listening, looked to windward and cried 'Sail, ho!' I at once saw what I supposed was a ship about one point forward of our beam, about four hundred yards distant; I ordered the helm up, thinking if she did not discover us, that we should have time to clear her before she came into contact. All hands shouted at the same time to alarm the ship, and I ordered the bell to be rung, and called to the ship to port her helm, as I saw that that was the only chance of escape. There were nearly one hundred passengers on deck at the time. All was of no avail, for in one minute from the time that we saw the ship she was upon us, going at the rate of twelve knots, striking us abreast of the after main shrouds.

"The crash and the terrible scene which ensued I am not adequate to describe. I was knocked to leeward with the man at the wheel. I recovered myself in a moment, shouting for every person to cling to the steamer as their only hope. I caught hold of a broken chain on the bow and hauled myself up, shouting at the same time to the crew and passengers to follow. I had barely time to get on the steamer's bow; and while getting up, I noticed that her bow was into the ship within a foot of the after hatch, and that she was stove clear to the lee side, and that full twenty feet of her side was stove in. There must have been nearly 50 persons killed by the collision; and every exertion was made by Captain Lott, his officers and crew, and the passengers on board the steamer. The boats were lowered as soon as possible; unfortunately only about ten were saved by the boats; the balance, making thirty-three more or less, saved themselves by hanging to the bow. The steamer lay by the scene as long as there was any hope of saving any."

About £350 was collected on the *Europa* for the survivors, who were taken back to England; and the steamship company volunteered to send them to America free of charge by steamer.

Hundreds of passengers of sailing-vessels facing certain destruction were saved by the providential arrival of steamships. In 1857 the large 1240-ton ship *Martin Luther* narrowly escaped disaster. She sailed from Liverpool for Quebec on April 9th with 498 passengers; three days later a great storm carried away two masts, necessitating, as conditions became worse, the cutting away of all that was left of the rigging, except the foremast. It was impossible to steer the ship, and she was blown, entirely out of control, towards the French coast. The only hope of avoiding shipwreck was that some vessel would pass close enough to see her signals of distress; otherwise she must soon be dashed to pieces on the rocky shore. Fortunately the Peninsular mail steamer *Tagus*, bound for Southampton, sighted the wreck and, coming close, lowered her lifeboats. The wind was very heavy, however, and rescue work was attended with great danger. Lieut. Cartwright, R. N., volunteered to lead the efforts to save the ship, and after surmounting great difficulties the men under his direction succeeded in getting lines to the crippled vessel. The *Tagus* then took her in tow, and reached Plymouth in safety. The emigrants were naturally overjoyed at their preservation from what appeared to be certain death, and presented a silver cup to their captain, Thomas J. Gordon, "for his energetic and humane conduct." Lieut. Cartwright, too, who at the risk of his life led in the rescue of over 500 souls, received the thanks of the Admiralty and the blessings of the passengers and crew of the *Martin Luther*.[2]

In the days when the commerce and, to a considerable extent, the industries of the world were based upon wood, fires at sea were by no means uncommon, in spite of regulations and precautions. In November, 1849, the American emigrant packet *Caleb Grimshaw*, 1,166 tons, with 427 passengers and a crew of 30, took fire when some 300 miles north-west of the island of Flores, in the Azores group. An effort was immediately made to extinguish the fire by pouring water down the fore-hatch, but the chief result was that clouds of smoke pervaded the steerage and threw the passengers into a panic. While some helped the crew fight the fire, others swung out a boat, and in their hurry to get into it twelve men were drowned. Soon afterwards a group of the crew provisioned another boat and left the ship, though they kept close to the stern for several days. As the fight against the fire began to appear hopeless, the remaining four boats were launched, accommodating some 50 or 60 people, including a number of women cabin passengers. Observing that there was no likelihood of their being taken off in the few boats, some of the steerage passengers and crew commenced the construction of rafts. During the next few days conditions became worse and worse, the frantic passengers screaming and wailing, emptying water casks and creating a scarcity of that invaluable commodity, and in general acting like madmen. Thirty of them sailed away to their death on a raft, and the rest began to suffer from hunger and thirst. After five days, during which the Azores might have been reached had the captain known his business, a sail was sighted and contact established with the 537-ton Nova Scotian barque *Sarah*, whose captain, David Cook, immediately approached the *Grimshaw*. Those in the boats were taken aboard, but the saving of lives came temporarily to an end when night and a heavy wind intervened.

Many feared that the burning ship would founder during the night, but the *Sarah* kept as close as possible in a rough sea, and in the morning, when the wind died down, the rescue work recom-

---

[2] *Plymouth and Devonport Weekly Journal*, quoted in the *Illustrated London News*, May 2, 1857. Lieut. Cartwright was a grandson of Dr. Edmund Cartwright, noted inventor of the power loom.

SHIPWRECK AND DISASTER

menced. During that day 163 passengers, mainly women and children, were removed from the burning vessel. Nothing could be done at night, however, and during the next three days stormy weather prevented any further rescue of passengers, who were now suffering severely from a shortage of water. On the ninth day after the fire, Captain Cook of the *Sarah* decided that an effort must be made to get more sail on the *Grimshaw* in the hope that Flores, only fifty miles away, might be reached before the ship sank. Volunteers from the *Sarah* succeeded in effecting this, and learned that forty persons had died from thirst during the previous three days. Relieving five exhausted men, a fresh crew of half a dozen sailed the *Grimshaw* to the lee of the island, and there the rescue work was completed during the night. The enfeebled women and children had to be transferred to the *Sarah* in slings and bags. The abandoned vessel was soon afire both fore and aft, and the crowded rescue ship proceeded to Fayal, 120 miles distant, the approach to Flores being deemed impossible since that island was dead to windward.

When the *Sarah* reached Fayal with the 356 survivors, she was held several days by quarantine regulations, the passengers, meanwhile, being in a very weak and miserable condition on board the small ship. Finally, through the good offices of the British and American consuls, supplies were sent out, and some of the cabin passengers were allowed to proceed to New York in another vessel. The following day one hundred of the sick were conveyed ashore, greatly relieving the overcrowding and distress. Great anxiety was then caused by a sudden storm, but finally, just as it appeared that ship must be wrecked on a rocky shoal, the wind veered and she escaped.

After two weeks in Fayal harbor the *Sarah* sailed for New York with 343 passengers, arriving there 36 days later, on January 15, 1850. The fame of her rescue had already reached port, and captain and crew were accorded a notable reception. The leading merchants raised a large sum of money and each member of the crew received a gift of $100, the officers larger amounts, and Captain Cook $5,000, "for his humanity and noble exertions in saving so many lives at the peril of his own." An account of his reception at the Wall Street Exchange notes that "the cheering was most rapturous and protracted, and a scene of enthusiasm followed which was rare indeed in a meeting of New York merchants"; and Captain Cook, "greatly affected, was hardly able to reply through emotion, but made the usual sailor's rejoinder that he had merely done what he considered was his duty." Upon his next visit to his home town, Yarmouth, Nova Scotia, David Cook was similarly honored by a public reception and the presentation of an address of appreciation, and the marine sensation of the day passed into the pages of history as one of the great epics of the sea.

One of the most terrible disasters by fire was the burning of the *Ocean Monarch* in 1848. The vessel had left Liverpool with 91 first- and second-cabin passengers, a crew of 42, and 307 steerage emigrants, and was hardly out of the Mersey when fire was discovered. The captain was immediately informed by a seaman, who stated that a passenger had lit a fire in one of the ventilators in the after part of the ship. But there were several theories, the Captain himself believing that steerage passengers were smoking; while one of the sailors said the fire resulted from the carrying of an unprotected candle by a fellow-seaman. In any event the conflagration was soon beyond control:

"A brief unavailing endeavour was made to save the ship, but the flames were unconquerable, and the vast multitude on board surrendered themselves to despair. The burning element progressed from stern to stem; spars and masts, wrapt one by one in the living flame, fell, crushing in their descent the shrieking masses on the deck, and numbers in desperate frenzy sought safety but to find death in the waves around. The yacht *Queen of the Ocean* and the Brazilian steam frigate *Affonso*, which were in the vicinity, hastened to render assistance, and by their boats rescued numbers; but yet the lamentable fact must be recorded that of the vast multitude on board a large proportion perished."

An eye-witness, Thomas Littledale of the yacht *Queen of the Ocean*, described the scene as "most appalling and harrowing," and such as he hoped never to witness again:

"The flames were bursting with immense fury from the stern and centre of the vessel. So great was the heat in these parts that the passengers, men, women and children, crowded to the fore part of the vessel. In their maddened despair women jumped overboard; a few minutes more and the mainmast shared the same fate. There yet remained the foremast. As the fire was making its way to the fore part of the vessel, the passengers and crew, of course, crowded still further forward. To the jib-boom they clung in clusters as thick as they could pack—even one lying over another. At length the foremast went overboard, snapping the fastenings of the jib-boom, which, with its load of human beings, dropped into the water amidst the most heart-rending screams both of those on board and those who were falling into the water. Some of the poor creatures were enabled again to reach the vessel, others floated away on spars, but many met with a watery grave. . . .

"We must not omit to mention an act of heroism exhibited towards the close of this melancholy scene. When only a dozen helpless women and children remained on the burning wreck, paralysed with fear and totally incapable of helping themselves by descending from the tottering bowsprit to the boats which in the midst of the heavy sea and wreck in vain offered their assistance below, an Englishman, Frederick Jerome, a native of Portsmouth, a seaman of the American ship *New World*, stripping himself naked, made his way through the sea and wreck, and with a line in his hand succeeded in lowering the last helpless victims safely into the boats, being the last man to leave the wreck."

CHAPTER XIV

NEWFOUNDLAND AND THE GULF

"I was called on deck to *smell the land*—and truly the change was very sensible. . . . It was the breath of youth and hope and love."
Diary of Mary Gapper

The last days of the emigrant's voyage to America form a period apart. As the first evidences of land become apparent, there is an immediate change in attitude, and hope succeeds despair in the hearts of all but the most miserable. To Mrs. Catherine Traill, never had anything seemed "so refreshing and delicious as the land breeze that came to us, bearing health and gladness on its wings. I had become very weak, but soon revived as I felt the air from the land reaching us, and some winged insects came to us— a welcome sight." Even the captain's gold-finch was delighted: "He sang continually, and his note was longer, clearer, and more thrilling than heretofore; the little creature, the captain assured me, was conscious of the difference in the air as we approached the land. 'I trust almost as much to my bird as to my glass,' he said."

On most vessels the first land sighted was Newfoundland, and, as one man observed in commenting on his fellow-passengers' "great delight," "They were under the impression that they were near their destination, little knowing the extent of the Gulf they had to pass, and the great river to ascend." When the cry of "Land!" was heard on another ship, all the passengers put on their "most elegant" clothes, so that many of them could not be recognized. "The people," wrote the Rev. James Wilson, "now seem to forget all the misery, sickness, and sensible trials they have passed through, as all enjoy health and are looking forward with eager desire to a speedy deliverance, and are thereby comforted, expecting to reap the benefit of an exertion truly great and awful—in leaving one kingdom for another." The approach to Newfoundland was not, however, pleasurable from the point of view of navigation. Many a vessel was wrecked off the rocky coast, and it was a time for cautious sailing, foghorns, and sounding lines:

NEWFOUNDLAND AND THE GULF 139

"The gloom spread around by the impenetrable fog was heightened by the dismal tone of the fog-horn, warning us of the vicinity of some fishing-boat, numbers of which were scattered over the banks. The mate being unable to make an observation, we were obliged to depend upon his 'dead reckoning.' . . . The captain having given orders for sounding, Jack was sent to find the reel and line. . . . The sails having been put aback, so that the brig stood motionless upon the bosom of the water, the reel was held by a man at the stern, and the line being uncoiled was drawn outside the ropes of the rigging until it reached the bow. The lead was then attached and carried by a seaman to the point of the bowsprit, where the sailor sat swinging the weight, like a pendulum, until, upon the order to heave, he cast it forth upon its mission. Bottom having been found at thirty-four fathoms, the line was placed upon a pulley and drawn up; when there was found imbedded in the grease with which the lead was filled, fine white sand, as laid down in the chart. . . . The captain had a great dread of the coast of Newfoundland, which being broken into deep bays divided from each other by rocky capes, is rendered exceedingly perilous; more especially as the powerful currents set towards this inhospitable shore."

On another ship "heaving the lead" was accomplished only by sending out a small boat:

"The fog was so penetrating as to soak with moisture the blankets in our state-cabins: and yet no one caught cold; and so dense was it that sometimes we could not see the length of our small vessel. Not being certain of our position, a boat, into which I jumped, was sent out to sound. The sailors soon learnt where they were from the nature of the bottom. During our absence kettles, bells and bugles were kept sounding terrifically on board the good ship, or we never should have found it again, for at twenty yards' distance we lost sight of her. I shall never forget the vast magnifying effect of the mist on the ship, her spread sails, shrouds and cordage. She loomed into sight an immense white mass, filling half the heavens."

Various passengers wrote about fishing off the Grand Banks. A. D. Ferrier recalled the good cod-fishing which the passengers of the *Rebecca* enjoyed in May, 1830: "Altogether, what with the log line, the deep sea line, and the various substitutes, we caught 118 fish." The Rev. William Bell similarly refers to the "seasonable refreshment" derived from the cod-fishing off the Banks; and Francis Thomas, whose voyage in 1833 was in most respects a miserable experience, notes that eight or ten fish were caught, of which his family enjoyed part of one. Thomas Johnston describes how his vessel was becalmed off the Banks, and the passengers amused themselves at the sport, catching

"a few cod and a great number of dog fish; the skin of which is used to polish wood, and answers some other useful purposes; they were in general about two feet in length, and might weigh from six to nine pounds. As we had eaten nothing but salt beef and biscuit in the passage, and of course were in need of fresh provision, we boiled some of these dog fish, which are not used but in cases of necessity, and to us, in our present circumstances, they were delicious enough."

The emigrants on the *John Dennison* in 1833 were more fortunate than most, for there was a pronounced community spirit in evidence among passengers and crew. At times the rum-drinking and dancing extended far into the night, to the annoyance of the more sober, but the fishing off the Banks resulted in a great dinner for all on deck. Even on a fever-infested vessel in 1847 the fishing provided a pleasant break in an otherwise most miserable passage, though the steerage passengers had no proper equipment for the sport:

> "The captain having provided himself and me with lines, we spent that afternoon fishing for mackerel, which were so plenty that I caught seventy in about two hours, when I had to give over, my hands being cut by the line. The captain continued, and had a barrel full by evening. They were the finest mackerel I ever saw, and we had some at tea, which we all enjoyed as a delicious treat after six weeks of salt beef and biscuit diet. Many of the passengers having noticed our success followed our example, and lines were out from every quarter; all the twine, thread, etc., that could be made out being put into requisition, with padlocks and bolts for weights, and wire hooks. Even with such rude gear they caught a great number; but their recreation was suddenly terminated, a young man who was drawing in a fish having dropped upon the deck quite senseless, and apparently dead. He was carried below and put into his berth, there to pass through the successive stages of the fever."

The Radcliffs on the *Duncan Gibb* in 1832 had log-lines and hooks "of a strength that was laughed at, leaving home." Their success in fishing is recorded by Mrs. Radcliff:

> "The Captain has just succeeded in catching an immense cod-fish—our people are putting out their lines. Two o'clock—we have had the amusement of seeing fish taken—four of them by your own sons and our servant, whose success was transcendant. The fish he hooked weighed 40 lbs. and measured in length four feet. The others were about 10 lbs. each. We dressed two of them, which gave 18 people, great and small, a plentiful dinner. . . . I never tasted any thing so delicious. . . . Our fishing goes on with great success; amongst the captures of this day is an immense Hollybut, 70 lbs. weight; we are to have it for dinner. . . . Nine more cod-fish taken by our party! We fished (observe how I identify myself with the sport) in fifty-fathom water, which is considered the best."

On many ships, of course, there was no fishing. Samuel Strickland states that the weather was too rough and the fish wouldn't bite; while on another vessel the captain purchased some instead. When the *Tennessee* reached the Banks in 1835 it was very foggy and cold, but one morning "there were 150 sail of fishing craft in sight. The decks of those we passed near enough to see were loaded with splendid cod. We spoke to two Spaniards and a Frenchman—they had had a splendid take of fish. We should have liked much to have some, but we were getting on too well to stop to buy even fresh fish for dinner."

NEWFOUNDLAND AND THE GULF

The last week or two of the voyage was—in spite of hopeful expectations and the fishing interlude—usually an unpleasant and dangerous experience. Fog, storms, and cold weather[1] made it monotonous and tedious, and everyone was impatient. One traveller records that although his vessel reached Cape Breton on the 28th day out from Dumfries, they had to spend eight days more beating up and down the Gulf in bad weather before it was possible to land at Prince Edward Island. The cold in the vicinity of Newfoundland is largely due to the Labrador Current and accompanying masses of ice. Captain Cunningham of the *Mary Ann Bell* ascended to the topmast to obtain a good view of "a large mountain of ice," but he came down in a hurry to avoid a collision with it.[2] Samuel Strickland was greatly impressed by the grandeur of icebergs encountered off the Banks:

"A more magnificent and imposing spectacle cannot be conceived; but it is very fearful and sufficiently appalling. Suddenly we found ourselves close to an immense body of ice, whose vicinity had been concealed from us by the density of the fog. Our dangerous neighbour towered in majestic grandeur in the form of a triple cone rising from a square base, and surpassed the tallest cathedral in altitude. The centre cone, being cleft in the middle by the force of the waves, displayed the phenomenon of a waterfall, the water rushing into the sea from the height of thirty feet."

The dangers of the Gulf passage commenced at the very entrance. Isle St. Paul, some ten miles beyond Cape North, between which and Cape Ray lay the passage into the Gulf, was described in 1847 as

"a huge rock, dividing at top into three conical peaks. Rising boldly from the sea, there is a great depth of water all round it, and vessels may pass at either side of it. It has been the site of numerous shipwrecks; many vessels, carried out of their reckoning by the currents, having been dashed against it when concealed by fog, and instantly shattered to atoms. Human bones and other memorials of these disasters are strewed around its base."

Upon passing this dangerous island a ship entered, in the words of Jacques Cartier, "a goodly great Gulf, full of islands, passages and entrances, towards what wind soever you please to bend."

The next points of interest in the Gulf were the Bird Rocks, three in number, "so called from the immense number of geese and aquatic birds which resort thither to rear their broods. These rocks rise to the height of 400 feet perpendicularly from the sea. The fishermen, nevertheless, continue to climb them for the sake of the eggs." Another traveller who observed the rocks wrote that

---
[1] This disagreeable atmospheric condition off Newfoundland went by the name of "bank weather," according to [Beaufoy], *Travels through the United States*, 5.
[2] Wilson, *Narrative of a Voyage*, 11. The vessel is called the *Mary and Bell*, which is presumably a printer's error.

they appeared at a distance "to be clothed in white, on account of the prodigious quantity of ordure and feathers with which they are covered; and the birds, when compelled to take wing, completely obscure the water, over which they fly, with the shadow of their numbers."[3]

Even more dangerous than St. Paul's Isle was Anticosti, a large island without bay or harbor, "the grave of many a tall ship." Like St. Paul's it had a lighthouse in the 1840's, but earlier there was merely a house at either end, equipped and provisioned to shelter the shipwrecked. Approaching it in a fog and drifting with the tide without the aid of a pilot, the *Brunswick* was in great danger of grounding upon it. Every captain, in fact, who found himself within ten miles of the island immediately sheered off on another tack, for it is surrounded by sunken reefs. A writer at the middle of the century found its surface "low and level, and covered with a pristine forest through which prowls the bear, undisturbed except when hunted by Indians, who periodically resort hither for that purpose."

During the sail through the Gulf many steerage passengers were too ill and miserable to enjoy the scenery, or were busy preparing the scanty remnant of their food supply in order to be in readiness for the bateau trip up the St. Lawrence. If the weather was fine, however, the time could be spent pleasantly enough in ascertaining the names of islands and scanning the shore line:

"I am now able," wrote Mrs. Traill, "to trace distinctly the outline of the coast on the southern side of the river. Sometimes the high lands are suddenly enveloped in dense clouds of mist, which are in constant motion, rolling along in shadowy billows, now tinted with rosy light, now white and fleecy, or bright as silver as they catch the sunbeams. So rapid are the changes that take place on this fog-bank that perhaps the next time I raise my eyes I behold the scene changed as if by magic. The misty curtain is slowly drawn up, as if by invisible hands, and the wild, wooded mountains partially revealed, with their bold rocky shores and sweeping bays. At other times the vapoury volume, dividing, moves along the valleys and deep ravines like lofty pillars of smoke, or hangs in snowy draperies among the dark forest pines."

Edward Talbot, in common with a few others who were not used to rugged scenery, did not find the shores of America attractive. He wrote that

"perhaps no country on earth exhibits a more wild and repulsive aspect, or affords greater sources of enjoyment to the lovers of terrific scenery.... Its appearance is most uninviting, and awakens in the mind few feelings except such as are the most unpleasurable and repugnant. Unfruitful soil, frowning

[3] Talbot, *Five Years' Residence in the Canadas*, I 31-2. See also *The Ocean Plague*, 53. Jacques Cartier saw the Bird Islands in 1534, observing that they were "as full of Birds as any field or meadow is of grass."

rocks, stunted trees and roaring cataracts are the most prominent and *engaging* features which it offers for attraction."

From another point of view, however,—as a place for the unfortunate of the Old Land to start life anew—he found the prospect pleasant enough:

"This far-famed land,—the asylum alike of friendless poverty and enterprising wealth—the reputed nurse of liberty—the patron of arts, science and literature—the genial soil of piety, philosophy and peace—the enemy of oppression—the mother of equality—and the seat of independence—was then the object of my immediate contemplation; and never did any man of whom it might be said
  'Fair Science smiled not on his humble birth,'
derive more real delight than I did from the indulgence of such a train of ideas as were presented to my mind on this occasion."

Before reaching Anticosti the captain signalled for a pilot by firing off a gun; but one did not always come, and the delays and perils of the last stages of the voyage were thereby increased. The pilot, who usually approached in a small schooner, brought with him the quarantine regulations. Most pilots were French; one is described as "a heavy, stupid fellow—a Canadian speaking a horrible *patois* and broken English." Although 200 miles of the voyage still remained, the scenery gradually became more intimate as the river narrowed. "Many charming tributary streams," wrote one traveller, "rolled along sweet valleys, enfolded in the swelling hills whose sides were clothed with verdure. I would fain explore each of these enchanting vales, but too soon we passed them, and some jutting cape would hide from view the little settlements at each embouchure." As the *British Tar* sailed onward during the night "a succession of fires arising from the burning of trees in clearing, on each bank of the river, lighted and cheered us on our way." Dr. John Bigsby's vessel anchored off Apple Island, some 65 miles below Quebec, and while she awaited a favourable tide a boat put out for shore

"and found the island loaded with ripe bilberries, and in its centre a spring of pure fresh water, bubbling up from beneath a smooth brown rock. The sugar-loaf mountains of New Brunswick were on the south-east in the remote distance, and a low rugged wilderness on our north, with a few fishermen's huts on the margin of the water. Only those who have been pent up among the evil scents and dissonant noises of a ship can estimate the pleasure of a wash, a fragrant stroll, and a banquet upon the juicy fruit of America for the first time."

The following day, however, a "first-rate river-hurricane" struck the vessel as she continued up the St. Lawrence. Two sails were "blown to rags," but the ship made 18 miles per hour under bare poles. Several whales could be seen thashing about, and altogether it was "a most animating scene."

Very different from Dr. Bigsby's excursion to Apple Island was the visit of Edward Talbot to the Isle d'Orleans in 1818:

> "Immediately after landing on the shore we proceeded to the house of a Canadian pilot for the purpose of soliciting permission to inter another one of those little ones in whose burial we were then daily employed. . . . After apologising for our intrusion we acquainted her in English with the mournful object of our mission. She replied, with a smile, *'Je ne puis pas parler Anglois.'* One of the company then addressed her in French. She very politely acceded to our request, sent a man to point out a spot in which we might deposit the body, and afterwards kindly invited us to return and partake of some refreshment. . . . Of this rare and unexpected treat we partook with delight."[4]

The closer one approached Quebec the more company was in evidence. "It was a pleasing sight," wrote a cabin passenger, "to see such a number of vessels, continually passing each other, and each evidently endeavouring to gain upon the rest every tack. We had a large fleet of ships, barques and brigs, two of which were transports with troops." But it was a time of varied emotions:

> "I have seen many a beautiful sunset, but all fade before the exquisite beauty of that which I witnessed this evening. . . . We weighed anchor at noon, and gently glided through a scene of indescribable loveliness. . . . I remained on deck long after all had retired to rest, and watched the gray twilight creeping over day, until it was illumined by the pale moon, which soon smiled upon one of earth's most beauteous pictures. . . . A few miles further sail brought us among a number of beautiful islets—so beautiful that they seemed like a fairy scene. . . . A vast fleet of vessels lying at anchor told that we had arrived at Grosse Isle; and after wending our way amongst isles and ships we dropped in the ground allotted for vessels upon arrival, and hoisted our ensign at the peak as a signal for the inspecting physician to board us."

[4] Talbot, *op. cit.*, I 34-5 and 27. During a voyage of six weeks twenty-four children who had previously been "cheerful and healthy, the hope and delight of their parents," were buried from the *Brunswick*.

CHAPTER XV

"Purification" at Grosse Isle

"You may imagine yourself looking on a fair or crowded market: clothes waving in the wind or spread out on the earth; chests, bundles, baskets; men, women and children asleep or basking in the sun, some in motion busied with their goods, the women employed in washing or cooking in the open air beside the wood fires on the beach."
Catherine Parr Traill

During the early period of more leisurely emigration there were no restrictions upon immigrants entering either the United States or the British Provinces. For the first twenty years of the nineteenth century work was available for all who came, and many who had long been destitute in the Old Land were surprised to find employers competing for their labor in the new. Before the establishment in 1831 of the quarantine station at Grosse Isle vessels usually proceeded direct to Quebec, where they were visited by a surgeon to see that there was no fever on board. Having been properly entered at the custom-house, a ship was at liberty to discharge her cargo and passengers or to proceed to Montreal. The health inspection was less rigid than that of later years, one narrative stating that some passengers were allowed to land before the examination, and were merely told by the captain to return to the ship a few hours later. Fever patients were either detained on board until they recovered, or were removed to a hospital.

The means taken to avoid difficulties with the customs were sometimes shrewd, though exceedingly heartless. In his *Report* Lord Durham records that a shipmaster informed him that he had come up the St. Lawrence with some thirty cases of fever among the passengers, many of whom were in a state of delirium:

"Fearing that on his arrival in port he should get into trouble, he quietly landed fourteen of the most violent of his poor wretches on the Island of Orleans to shift for themselves. The harbour-master boarded him on his arrival, but he persuaded the other passengers who were not ill to come on deck and get up a fight, in the noise and hubbub of which the screams and cries of the sick never reached the ears of the officer, who was glad to escape from the scene of uproar. When night came on he landed the remainder with their luggage in the usual way."

Until 1823 Roman Catholic organizations took care of most immigrants arriving at Quebec in distress, but in that year, and subsequently, the great increase of the sick and destitute necessitated government provision for special hospital accommodation and more adequate care of the needy. In 1830 a fever hospital was opened at Point Levi, and in 1831, when an outbreak of Asiatic cholera devastated the north of England, a second quarantine hospital was established at Grosse Isle, by which it was hoped, in the words of Lord Durham, to prevent "the accumulation of wretched paupers at Quebec, and the spread of contagious disease." Grosse Isle was an unoccupied island 33 miles below Quebec, and the structures first erected upon it were of a temporary nature, well described by their usual appellation—"the sheds."

In ordinary times "purification" at Grosse Isle was not very arduous. "We performed Quarantine only 2 hours, as we were all healthy," wrote Francis Thomas in his diary. As at embarkation, cabin passengers were not required to appear for examination, the assumption being that even if they were among "the halt, the lame and the blind," they would have friends to look after them. Usually they were requested to send their bedding to be cleaned. Mrs. Traill states that a servant washed hers to the satisfaction of the inspectors. Among crowds of people scrubbing themselves and their clothes she observed children "pursuing each other in wanton glee, rejoicing in their newly-acquired liberty"; while here and there appeared "the stately form and gay trappings of the sentinels," the whole picture being heightened by the thin blue smoke of wood fires rising above the trees.

Everything was not as pleasant as a distant view might suggest, however. One of the officers from the fort thus commented upon the illusory picturesqueness of the scene:

> "Believe me, in this instance as in many others, 'tis distance lends enchantment to the view. Could you take a nearer survey, . . . you would there behold every variety of disease, vice, poverty, filth and famine—human misery in the most disgusting and saddening forms; such pictures as Hogarth's pencil only could have portrayed, or Crabbe's pen described."

Mrs. Traill Sister, Susanna Moodie, surveyed the scene at closer range. Several hundred immigrants had been landed a few hours before. Those who were sick had been confined in sheds resembling cattle-pens. Some of the well were tramping upon their bedding in tubs or in holes left by the receding tide; while others were variously occupied in the water or on the rocks, at one stage or another of clothes-washing:

"PURIFICATION" AT GROSSE ISLE

"The confusion of Babel was among them. All talkers and no hearers—each shouting and talking in his or her uncouth dialect, and all accompanying their vociferations with violent and extraordinary gestures. . . . The Indian is one of Nature's gentlemen—he never says or does a rude or vulgar thing. The vicious, uneducated barbarians who form the surplus of overpopulous European countries are far behind the wild man in delicacy of feeling or natural courtesy. The people who covered the island appeared perfectly destitute of shame, or even a sense of common decency. Many were almost naked, still more but partially clothed. We turned in disgust from the revolting scene."

A soldier informed the Moodies that the night scenes "far exceed those of the day. You would think they were incarnate devils, singing, drinking, dancing, shouting, and cutting antics that would surprise the leader of a circus." But perhaps one may take the charitable view that a very considerable amount of "letting off steam" might be excused after the terrifying experience of a voyage in the steerage of an emigrant ship.

In the plague years the congestion and suffering at Grosse Isle made the performance of quarantine an ordeal of great severity. Except upon vessels where the passengers were demoralized, an effort was usually made to clean up the ship in preparation for its inspection. During the year 1834 there was in addition to a large number of shipwrecks, a recurrence of typhus fever, measles, and cholera, which had created so much misery in 1832. In the late spring the inhabitants of Quebec were becoming alarmed over the situation, and the following statement was consequently issued "by good authority" in an effort to dispel the anxiety:

"The undermentioned vessels at present lying at Grosse Isle are detained under strict quarantine in consequence of their having had sickness or death on board during the voyage, or upon their arrival; and no vessel arriving at the Quarantine Station under similar circumstances will be permitted to proceed on her voyage to Quebec until it can be done with the most perfect safety to the Public Health:—*Mary* and *Brutus*, from Cork; *Thetis* and *Priscilla*, from Limerick; *William Fell*, from Newry; *Recovery* and *Penelope*, from Youghall; *Hercules*, from Annan; *British Tar*, from Portsmouth; *Friends*, from Dublin. The number of deaths which have taken place at Grosse Isle since the opening of the navigation amount to ten; five of which were children, the eldest six years old, and some of them in a dying state when landed. No case of Cholera has occurred either on shore or afloat at the Station this season."

Some conception of the defective system under which these vessels performed quarantine may be gained from contemporary descriptions. A short announcement was made a week earlier concerning the *Mary*:

"The barque *Mary*, from Cork 12th April with 300 emigrants, is detained to perform quarantine at Grosse Isle in consequence of having several cases of fever on board, who have landed, and the usual precautions adopted with regard to cleansing and purifying the vessel."

There was, however, much more suffering behind the statement than this apparently innocent announcement would indicate. In pressing for the provision of a hospital "for the reception of the dying sick," a correspondent of the *Quebec Gazette* mentions the case of the *Mary*: "On landing the passengers there (Grosse Isle) the captain had to throw the bedding of straw overboard, but unfortunately no fresh supply was sent from the Island; and those who returned convalescent, having no beds to lay on, became again invalids." The Master of the *Mary*, Henry Deaves, gives a detailed account of the circumstances in the next issue of the *Gazette*. The vessel arrived on May 18th, with 40 cases of measles and typhus fever. One man and six children had died during the voyage, the Captain stating that the children died from lack of proper care while their parents were seasick. The rest were detained a few days at Grosse Isle and sent back to the vessel, which, after cleaning and fumigation, had only eleven beds for the 250 passengers,

"and they are now obliged to lie on the boards, without a covering, the greater part having nothing on the passage but their wearing apparel, which they are obliged to keep on to prevent the boards from cutting their hips. There are mothers and children in this state. It is inconsistent with reason to expect them to remain healthy while they are in this state. There is no constitution able to bear such treatment in these piercing nights. There are fifty of my passengers in hospital at present, and the remainder must be soon there if something is not done for them. The people ought to be kept on shore till the vessel is liberated. . . . It is a sad thing to detain the vessel here such a length of time."

And the Captain was also most unfairly treated by being required to victual the passengers all this time, particularly since he had received only 30 shillings per passenger for the voyage.

As a consequence of the disease, dirt, poverty, and misery which attended the influx at its height, British immigrants were soon in great disfavor in America. A head tax was for several years enforced to provide funds to take care of those who arrived destitute, for the expense had become an intolerable burden upon the benevolence of individuals and municipalities. In 1832 the tax at Quebec amounted to 5s. for adults, half that amount for children from seven to fourteen, and 1s. 8d. for those under seven. A contemporary writer notes that one-fourth of this money was

"placed at the disposal of the Emigrant Society, and is applied by it for the relief of Emigrants possessing large families, and who have not the means of providing for themselves on landing. The remainder of the tax is supplied to the support of the Marine and Emigrant Hospital, where all

Public Archives of Canada   *Captain Ralph C. Alderson*
GROSSE ISLE CHOLERA HOSPITAL AND TELEGRAPH, 1832
A monument commemorates the burial there of 3,424 victims of typhus who, "flying from pestilence and famine in Ireland in 1847, found in America but a grave."

Illustrated London News
ICEBERGS OFF THE GRAND BANKS
"Bank weather" and the fishing diversion were other prominent features off the coast of Newfoundland.

From Christian Schultz's Travels on an Inland Voyage, 1810
POLING BOATS UPSTREAM
Various types of bateaux and Durham boats were indispensable in the ascent of the St. Lawrence and many other North American rivers.

John Ross Robertson Collection *Captain B. Beaufoy*
QUEBEC IN 1830
The great mass of Canadian immigrants debarked at Quebec, but the wise engaged a passage to Montreal.

"PURIFICATION" AT GROSSE ISLE

emigrants are admitted free of expense and receive every medical advice and assistance they may require."

In the early plague years—1832 and 1834—all steerage passengers, whether healthy or ill, were forced to land at Grosse Isle, and the sick frequently infected the well. By 1847, however, it was usual to send ashore only those who suffered from disease, the others being transferred to steamships, or proceeding in their own vessel to Quebec or Montreal. Hugh Johnson experienced quarantine on Grosse Isle in 1847, after a voyage from Glasgow in the *Euclid*, which was infested with smallpox:

> "Bad as it was on board, it became infinitely worse when we reached quarantine. On our arrival at the dock, ropes were stretched across the dock so as to leave a passage in the middle. A doctor was stationed on each side of this passage and only one person was allowed through at a time. All those who showed any symptoms of the disease were forced to go into quarantine, while others were sent ashore. The only exceptions made were in the cases of well mothers, who were permitted to accompany sick babies. I am an old man now, but not for a moment have I forgotten the scene as parents left children, brothers were parted from sisters, or wives and husbands were separated, not knowing whether they should ever meet again."[1]

Conditions on the island itself were very bad. An eye-witness called it the Isle of Death, and found a strange contrast of beauty and suffering, of levity and sorrow:

> "There were 2,500 at that time upon the island, and hundreds lying in the various vessels before it. . . . After a long pull through a heavy swell, we landed upon the Isle of Pestilence; and climbing over the rocks passed through the little town and by the hospitals behind which were piles upon piles of unsightly coffins. A little further on, at the edge of a beautiful sandy beach, were several tents, into one of which I looked, but had no desire to see the interior of any others. We pursued our way, by a road cut through a romantic grove of firs, birch, beech and ash, beneath the shade of which blossomed charming wild flowers, while the most curious fungi vegetated upon odd, decayed stumps. . . . We arrived in front of the superintendent physician's cottage, placed upon a sloping bank at the river's side, on which were mounted two pieces of ordnance guarded by a sentinel. The view from this spot was exquisitely beautiful—upon the distant bank of the broad river were the smiling, happy-looking Canadian villages, backed by deep, blue hills, while the agitated water in front tossed the noble vessels that lay at anchor. . . .
>
> "Upon our return we called at the store licensed to sell provisions upon the island. It was well stocked with various commodities, among which were

[1] Reminiscences quoted in Smith, *Pioneers of Old Ontario*, 208-9. Similar impressions of the enforced division of families are recorded in *The Ocean Plague*, 83 and 88-90. Typical of numerous advertisements to be found in the press of the day is the following from the *Montreal Transcript* of September 11, 1847:
"Information wanted of Abraham Taylor, aged 12 years, Samuel Taylor, 10 years, and George Taylor, 8 years old, from County Leitrim, Ireland, who landed in Quebec about five weeks ago—their mother having been detained at Grosse Isle. Any information respecting them will be thankfully received by their brother, William Taylor, at this office."

carrion beef, and cattish mutton, bread, flour, cheese, etc. . . . There was a vast concourse of mates, stewards, seamen and boys, buying his different articles and stowing them away in their boats. The demand for bread was very great; and several batches were yielded from a large oven while we remained. Hearing the music of a fiddle accompanied by the stamping of feet in time, I walked up to the shed from which it issued. . . . There were two men dancing a jig in a trial of skill, . . . and around the dancers was a circle of 'habitans' and sailors, who encouraged them by repeated 'bravos.' I did not remain long, nor could I enjoy the amusement in such a place. . . .

"Vessels were arriving with every tide. . . . Two ships from Bremen came in the morning and were discharged at once, having no sickness. . . . More than thirty in quarantine. . . . Boats were plying all day long between the several vessels and the island; and the sea being high the miserable patients were drenched by the spray; after which they had to clamber over the slimy rocks, or were carried by sailors. There was also an almost unbroken line of boats carrying the dead for interment; then there was the doctor's boat unceasingly shooting about; besides several others containing captains of ships, many of whom had handsome gigs with six oars and uniformly-dressed rowers. . . . To complete the picture the rigging of the vessels was covered over with the passengers' linen, hanging out to dry; by the character of which as they fluttered in the breeze I could tell with accuracy from what country they came; alas! the wretched rags of the majority told but too plainly that they were Irish. . . . It was indeed a busy scene of life and death."

Many of those who left the British Isles, a citizen of Montreal believed, were "half dead before they embark; and the surrounding influences when on board the vessel . . . bring rapidly about what, to these poor, lost, dejected and forlorn creatures, must be a happy consummation." But death, he found, came to many only after weeks of intense suffering on the voyage over, and a miserable reception at Grosse Isle:

"I have frequently visited the sheds, impelled by strong feelings of sympathy for my keenly suffering fellow mortals, and done my best to cheer up their drooping spirits with the hope of prosperity in this life, and of eternal happiness in the next, and in some instances have seen beams of gratitude in the eye when the tongue had ceased to speak; and never in my life, in this country or the old, have I witnessed such a melancholy mass of suffering humanity. After passing through nearly two thousand adults in the different stages of disease, you come to two or three hundred infant orphans, some only fifteen or twenty days old, and many of them taken from the side, and some from the breast, of a dead mother, and I envy not the feelings of the man whose stony composition can move through such a heart-rending scene of human woe without being touched with the deepest feelings of sympathetic love."

A typical report of a day's news from Grosse Isle at the height of the plague is most illuminating:

"We are in possession of the latest news from Grosse Isle. The hospital statement yesterday, the 9th, was 2,240. There is a large fleet of vessels at the station, and amongst them some very sickly, as it may be seen from the following statement:

"PURIFICATION" AT GROSSE ISLE

Vessel	Port of Sail	Passengers	Deaths	Sick
Bark *Ellen Simpson*,	Limerick,	184	4	—
Brig *Anna Maria*,	Limerick,	119	1	1
Bark *Amy*,	Bremen,	289	—	—
Brig *Watchful*,	Hamburg,	145	—	—
Ship *Ganges*,	Liverpool,	393	45	80
Bark *Corea*,	Liverpool,	501	18	7
Bark *Larch*,	Sligo,	440	108	150
Bark *Naparima*,	Dublin,	226	7	17
Bark *Britannia*,	Greenock,	386	4	25
Brig *Trinity*,	Limerick,	86	—	—
Bark *Lilias*,	Dublin,	219	5	6
Bark *Brothers*,	Dublin,	318	6	—

"A full-rigged ship just coming in—not yet boarded. The hospitals have never been so crowded, and the poor creatures in the tents (where the healthy are) are dying by dozens! Eleven died on the night of the 8th, and one on the road to the hospital yesterday morning. Captain Read of the *Marchioness of Breadalbane* died in hospital on the 7th. The captain of the *Virginius* died the day after his arrival at Grosse Isle. We regret to learn that the Rev. Mr. Paisley is in a critical state. He was dangerously ill this morning.[2]

"Since writing the above we learn that 60 new cases were admitted into hospital, and 300 more, arrived on the 8th and 9th, remain to be admitted."

The Irish were by far the greatest sufferers, while German immigrants were not affected by the plague. While at Grosse Isle "A Cabin Passenger" observed the inspection of a German vessel containing 500 passengers,

"all of them, without a single exception, comfortably and neatly clad, clean and happy. There was no sickness amongst them, and each comely fair-haired girl laughed as she passed the doctor, to join the group of robust young men who had undergone the ordeal. . . .

"As we repassed the German ship, the deck was covered with emigrants, who were singing a charming hymn, in whose beautiful harmony all took part; spreading the music of their five hundred voices upon the calm, still air that wafted it around. . . . As the distance between us increased, the anthem died away until it became inaudible. It was the finest chorus I ever heard,—performed in a theatre of unrivalled magnificence. . . . Although it was pleasing to see so many joyous beings, it made me sad when I thought of the very, very different state of my unfortunate compatriots; and I had become so habituated to misery, disease and death that the happiness that now surrounded me was quite discordant with my feelings."

It is greatly to the credit of the *Quebec Chronicle* that it carried the names and ages of all those who died at Grosse Isle, permission to do so having been obtained from the authorities when it appeared that no official list was being published. There seems, in fact, to have been more effort to hide the facts than to make them known. In the spring of 1848, when a revival of the fever plague threatened, all publication of reports from Grosse Isle was for-

---

[2] The Rev. Richard Anderson and the Rev. Charles Morris were among the clergy who died as a result of their ministrations at Grosse Isle. Doctors and captains were also victims.

bidden, as was also the issuance of any official reports by the Quarantine Station—a policy which the press described as "as arrogant as it is absurd and mischievous," and making it possible, in the absence of authentic information, for "wild and exaggerated rumours" to gain credence.

While the congestion at Halifax, St. John, and minor ports was not usually so great, conditions in the plague years differed only in degree. When the epidemic of 1847 was at its height the Quarantine Station on Partridge Island, near the entrance to the harbor of St. John, contributed more than its share to the misery of long-suffering humanity. Investigators found, in addition to a deplorable lack of food, water, beds, and hospitals supplies, that

"many of the emigrants have slept all night in the open air upon the damp ground, with no other covering except their wearing apparel. We found patients suffering from fever and dysentery in this destitute and neglected condition. . . . In reference to impurities upon the island we may state in the first place atmospheric impurity arising from the filthy condition of the tents, the filthy habits of the people, and the exhalations from the burying-ground, where upwards of forty bodies are deposited in one hole, without a sufficient covering of earth, and many others are buried with only a few inches of earth over the bodies, which are not protected by a coffin."[3]

The breakdown in the facilities for the reception and inspection of emigrants to the British Provinces was in no respect the fault of officials in charge of the quarantine stations, but must be laid upon those who permitted a relaxation in the enforcement of the regulations under which they left the Old Land. The station doctors exercised the greatest humanity in administering their disagreeable duties, though it must be admitted that they consisted more in attempting to protect their country from contamination than in relieving the distress of those who sought admittance. The quarantine system, never particularly effective even in ordinary times, could not withstand the strain of an invasion of vast hordes who were famished when they left Ireland, exposed to every species of misery on the Atlantic, and in the last stage of wretchedness when they reached America.

From time to time minor changes were made in the levy collected from immigrants at the port of debarkation. As a result of the great exodus from Ireland a graded tax varying with the season was enforced in Lower Canada in 1848, in the hope that the greater number would arrive when outdoor employment was plenti-

[3] *Papers Relative to Emigration*, printed December 20, 1847, pp. 122-3. The Commissioners of Immigration of New Brunswick reported that 94 vessels landed 15,269 passengers during the season, and the deaths at sea on these vessels numbered 662.

"PURIFICATION" AT GROSSE ISLE 153

ful. The inducement was provided by a tax of only 10s. from March to August, while that for September was 20s., and for the rest of the year 30s. This ingenious experiment was apparently not successful, for it was not repeated, the tax being reduced to a uniform amount of 7s. 6d. in 1849. The same purposes were served by the proceeds from this taxation as in earlier years, and there were no further changes of importance in the sailing-ship period. The quarantine station at Grosse Isle was, however, greatly improved and made permanent in 1850, and the whole island, instead of a part, was used for immigration purposes thereafter.

When quarantine had been performed by the passengers, and the ship given a clean bill of health, it was legally possible for it to proceed. Immigrants had still a sail of a day or two before they reached Quebec, but if they were healthy and happy enough to enjoy beautiful scenery they found no lack of it:

"A more beautiful panorama I never beheld than the country through which we passed,—the churches of St. Thomas' and St. Pierre's, surrounded by handsome cottages and beautiful fields. . . . At sunset we had reached the eastern extremity of the Isle of Orleans; and an hour after dropped anchor before St. François, a sweet village composed of quaint-looking cottages whose walls were as white as snow, with red roofs, bright yellow doors, and green venetian window blinds. . . . We again set sail soon after daybreak this morning with a breeze against us, which compelled us to take about. I did not regret this, as I had many near views of the southern bank of the river, and of the beautiful shore of Orleans Island, with its luxuriant orchards and well cultivated farms sloping down to the water's edge, and dark forest upon the crest of its elevated interior. . . . At 8 a.m. we passed St. Vallier and St. John's; the latter upon the island, consisting of entirely white cottages, which are chiefly inhabited by the branch pilots. . . . At noon we dropped anchor again, before St. Michel's, where we lay until 6 p.m., when we once more renewed our tacks, passing the sheltered cove called Patrick's Hole, in which a fine ship rode previous to leaving port for sea. . . . We passed next Beaumont, where the south bank becomes elevated, increasing in height to Point Levi. . . . The magnificent Fall of Montmorenci then was revealed to view, in a sheet of tumbling snow-white foam set between the dark green banks, covered with fir and other trees. . . Night spread its curtain over the splendid picture when we reached the mouth of the River St. Charles, where we dropped anchor."

After passing through the narrow channel between Isle d'Orleans and the south shore the vessel neared Quebec, and "a most splendid panorama" burst into view:

"To the left we had the pine-clad rocks, scattered white houses and trim churches of Point Levi; to the right the lengthy village of Beauport, and the graceful cascade of Montmorenci, screened by purple mountains. Before us, in front, was the fine city of Quebec, crowning a lofty promontory, and alternately in gloom and gleam with the scud of the tempest; while the battlements of Cape Diamond, overlooking the city, were seen to extend out of sight up the now contracted river. Some vessels of war, with crowds of merchant-ships and steamers, fringed the shore."[4]

One more inspection was essential before anyone dare land at Quebec—the Harbour Master and the Medical Inspector must first discharge the ship from quarantine. They approached one vessel "in a long six-oared boat, with the Union Jack flying in her stern," and demanded the ship's papers and clean bills of health. Upon an inspection of these the vessel was released, and merchants from shore might approach or the passengers leave at will. How would the immigrants be received at Quebec? Not that many gave much thought to the matter, though there was the important consideration, in one writer's opinion, that "Canadians are a shrewd, selfish people: even juveniles are in general too old for one-half of the newly-arrived adults."

[4] Bigsby, *The Shoe and Canoe*, I 8. Dr. Bigsby notes the interesting coincidence that another vessel left Portsmouth the same day and reached Quebec within three hours of his ship, neither having seen the other during the voyage.

CHAPTER XVI

QUEBEC AND MONTREAL

"They commonly established themselves along the wharfs and at the different landing-places, crowding into any place of shelter they could obtain, where they subsisted principally upon the charity of the inhabitants. . . . Daily drafts of from 10 to 30 were taken to the hospital with infectious disease."

Evidence of Dr. Morrin, Inspecting Physician at Quebec

"It is a curious and rather painful sight," wrote an eye-witness, "to watch the emptying of a newly-arrived cargo of emigrants on the unknown shore. Squalid, thinly clad, and far from clean, you instantly distinguish the bony Irishman with his wife and all the children, dragging an ill-packed bundle tied with a bit of rope, which is made long enough by the help of a strip of ticking or a list border. They slide their bundle—their all of worldly wealth —down a plank, and having drawn it aside on the dock, they hang helplessly around it, the children tumbling on it, till the ship has disgorged her motley company, and all are ready to appear at the Emigrant Office. Next you will see a pair of stout, thickly-clothed Germans, letting down their heavy chest, well nailed and corded, with a parcel of bedding on the top. And again a rosy, round-cheeked Englishman, with his deal box, painted red. Each pours forth with a load to carry or care for, like the busy population on an ant-hill, and group after group sit or watch by their slender store. What will become of them all?"

When the emigrant disembarked his journey was not at an end; and it was the sad experience of thousands that the trip inland to their chosen place of settlement cost as much—both in money and suffering—as the Atlantic passage. There was, of course, a great variation in their condition upon arrival. Some were well able to take care of themselves; while others were without the means of moving away from the wharves. The Immigration Agent estimated in 1827 that, of some 75,000 settlers in Upper Canada who had arrived at Quebec during the previous fifteen years, on the average they did not possess half a dollar a head on landing. While passengers entering at colonial ports were permitted by law to remain 48 hours on the ship after arrival, it was another matter to enforce the observance of the statute, and those who did not take the first opportunity to debark were usually assisted by the crew in no uncertain manner. Immigrants who were without means would in any case be but little better off by delay in landing; and in addition to the suffering which large numbers of "pauper" emigrants experienced on the Atlantic, disillusionment and disappointment was frequently their lot on being dumped ashore at Quebec.[1] The evidence of Dr. Morrin, Inspecting Physician, outlines the miserable existence of these deluded people and many other destitute immigrants. Scattering themselves along the waterfront, they were dependent upon charity for subsistence, and subject to every disease:

> "The mortality was considerable among the emigrants at that time, and was attended with most disastrous consequences; children being left without protection, and wholly dependent on the casual charity of the inhabitants of the city. As to those who were not sick on arriving, I have to say that they were generally forcibly landed by the masters of vessels, without a shilling in their pockets to procure them a night's lodging, and very few of them with the means of subsistence for more than a very short period. . . . For six weeks at a time from the commencement of the emigrant-ship season I have known the shores of the river along Quebec, for about a mile and a half, crowded with these unfortunate people, the places of those who might have moved off being constantly supplied by fresh arrivals, and there being daily drafts of from 10 to 30 taken to the hospital with infectious disease. The consequence was it spread among the inhabitants of the city, especially in the districts in which these unfortunate creatures had established themselves. Those who were not absolutely without money got into low taverns and boarding-houses and cellars, where they congregated in immense numbers and where their state was not any better than it had been on board ship. This state of things existed within my knowledge from 1826 to 1832, and probably for some years previously."[2]

A guidebook, in warning prospective emigrants that they would still have to look after themselves upon arrival at Quebec, yet gave the experience of several hundred Scotch weavers as an example of the philanthropy of Canadian compatriots and the aid of the government. Observing that many in previous years had been under the erroneous impression that they would be supported and forwarded at the public expense to any quarter in which they wished to settle, this authority stated that 663 people from Glasgow and Paisley, chiefly weavers and mechanics and their families, were enabled to emigrate in 1840 largely through the efforts of societies,

---
[1] See in this connection *The Ocean Plague*, 106; "A Citizen," *Thoughts on Emigration*, 15; and letter of Adam Ferrie in *Papers Relative to Emigration to the British Provinces in North America* (1848), 36-7. Among others accused of misrepresentation were the agents of Lord Darnley and Lord Palmerston. A denial by J. Kincaid, agent of Lord Palmerston, follows Adam Ferrie's letter. In a letter in the *Cobourg Star* of June 27, 1849, the Hon. Adam Ferrie says that for "nineteen years I gratuitously visited the Emigrant Sheds, administering to the comfort of the sick." He states that he rendered himself immune from cholera by "having impregnated my body with sulphur." It would appear probable from its similarity to his letters that he was the author of the above-mentioned pamphlet published anonymously by "A Citizen," and "Addressed to the Right Honourable Lord John Russell, Prime Minister of England."

[2] Evidence quoted in Lucas edition of Lord Durham's *Report*, II 244. Other instances of destitution, as well as efforts on the part of citizens to relieve it, are described in the *Quebec Gazette* of June 2, 1834. "An Old Countryman," apparently believing that religious consolation rather than material advice was the need of the unfortunate immigrants, accordingly printed his *Friendly Advice to Emigrants from Europe, on their Arrival in Canada*.

QUEBEC AND MONTREAL 157

and were "very poor and destitute" on reaching Quebec. About sixty of them took up land in the townships of Leeds and Ireland, some fifty miles from Quebec, aided by the Immigration Agent, Mr. Buchanan, and by "some influential Scotch gentlemen in this city," who assisted them through the first winter. The rest of this emigration were not nearly so successful, having great difficulty reaching the interior, and in finding employment when they finally arrived in Upper Canada through state aid.

Perhaps William Lyon Mackenzie's impressions of the steerage of the *Airthy Castle* when she docked in April, 1831, may be considered a fair example of conditions on an emigrant ship of a somewhat better class:

"One forenoon I went on board the ship *Airthy Castle*, from Bristol, immediately after her arrival. The passengers were in number 254, all in the hold or steerage; all English, from about Bristol, Bath, Frome, Warminster, Maiden Bradley, etc. I went below, and truly it was a curious sight. About 200 human beings, male and female; young, old and middle-aged; talking, singing, laughing, crying, eating, drinking, shaving, washing; some naked in bed, and others dressing to go on shore; handsome young women (perhaps some), and ugly old men, married and single; religious and irreligious. Here a grave matron chanting selections from the last edition of the last new hymn book; there a brawny ploughboy 'pouring forth the sweet melody of Robin Adair.' These settlers were poor, but in general they were fine-looking people, and such as I was glad to see come to America. . . . It is my opinion that few among them will forget being cooped up below deck for four weeks in a moveable bed-room, with 250 such fellow-lodgers as I have endeavoured to describe."

Those who had any choice in the matter were warned against undue haste in disembarking:

"Take it patiently; let the ship come quietly to anchor; and be in no hurry to get upon the shore. Give no money for it: the ship will bring you to the edge of the wharf at the next tide, or the next tide but one, and then take your family and things on shore without any expense worth speaking of, and save yourself the expense of boats, from which I verily believe more accidents arise, on an average, than from the ships themselves."

Boats were frequently swamped when their occupants insisted on going to shore in a strong wind. The captain of Mrs. Moodie's vessel refused under such circumstances to land passengers at the order of an immigration official, but during the same evening she saw eleven persons drowned while attempting to reach land from a neighboring vessel. Some left their ship before they had even taken proper care of their baggage or sought information as to their best course of action, and as a result their possessions were scattered or the vessel gone when they returned, and they had to spend their remaining cash on lodgings.

The bringing of liquor aboard the *David* caused considerable trouble shortly after she reached Quebec. John M'Donald states that the captain ordered the mate to see that nothing of the kind occurred, but

"some of the passengers who had gone ashore returned with some rum, which was taken from them and thrown overboard. This circumstance caused no small disturbance, and produced blows between the sailors and the passengers, and even amongst the sailors themselves; and till the scuffle terminated, it was indeed a very disorderly night."

The passengers, however, were allowed to sleep on board, and in the morning transferred themselves and their effects to a steamship bound for Montreal. It was not until 1835 that the newcomer was given official advice and aid in the matter of baggage transference, and protection from the clutches of the unprincipled "runners" who infested the wharves; for as one man observed, Quebec abounded with "the lowest of the low, who are aptly, although not elegantly, designated 'land-sharks,' and to such demons in human form the loitering stranger is almost certain of becoming a prey."[3]

To avoid all such crimps and to retain one's self-control in a land where one might literally drown himself in whisky and rum were the chief items of advice in guidebooks, some of which contained lengthy exhortations on the many evils attendant upon intemperance:

"Many upon landing feel elated at having once more fixed their feet on firm land, and all sorts of spirituous liquors being cheap, when their prices are compared with those for which they are purchased at home, they are often led to indulge too freely in the use of them; not always with the intent of pursuing such a course of intoxication, but to gratify the desire of the moment; when, alas! a vicious inclination gratified, even for a short time, more generally leads to a confirmed habit, and this brings on, as its necessary consequence, poverty, disease, and all sorts of misery, which by a very natural combination must eventually secure the death of their unhappy victim! Hundreds, yea thousands, have in these provinces been hurried to an untimely grave by this habit."

A contemporary newspaper announces the sailing from London in 1832 of the *Caroline*, which included among its passengers some fifty or sixty "who will bring out from £15,000 to £20,000," as well as "a choice selection of all kinds of breeding stock, agricultural implements, grass seeds, etc." For such fortunate persons the transition to the new land might, with good luck, resemble a triumphant march, although disillusionment amid the hardships of

---

[3] Warr, *Canada as It Is*, 25. Even captains robbed their passengers by illegally collecting the Capitation Tax after the expiration of the Act on May 1, 1834. A. C. Buchanan forced a number of them to disgorge their money. See *Quebec Gazette*, May 12 and June 2, 1834.

QUEBEC AND MONTREAL 159

"bush" life could be avoided only by settlement on cleared land, the price of which placed it far beyond the reach of the average immigrant. Perhaps the comment in an issue of the *Quebec Gazette* in 1834 may be taken as representative of the general attitude towards immigration, and at the same time as descriptive of the stirring scene of activity presented by the Quebec wharves in spring and summer, and of typical groups of newcomers as they passed through the city *en route* to Upper Canada:

"The bustle of business, usual on the arrival of our spring vessels, has now fairly commenced. Emigrants for embarkation for Upper Canada covered the steamboat wharves the whole of the past week. The *John Bull* took up more than six hundred on her last trip; the *Voyageur* upwards of four hundred, and the *Canadian Patriot* about two hundred, on Saturday evening. The number already arrived in port exceeds 4,000, and little less than 1,000 are known to be at Grosse Isle.

"Generally speaking they are a respectable class, and those who have thus landed within a few days have conducted themselves in a peaceable and orderly manner. What may be the general character of those yet to come, the total of which seems now likely to exceed that of last year, we can only gather from the masters of vessels vith whom we have conversed on the subject. These are unanimous in the opinion that most of the emigrants from Great Britain will be well able to provide for themselves; some are in affluent circumstances. On board the *Westmoreland*, Capt. Knill, arrived Saturday, four families have from 700 to 1000 sovereigns each; others 200, and there is scarcely one family that had not 100. They have brought with them great quantities of implements of husbandry, seeds, etc., for their own use. All of them intend residing in Upper Canada, where they will be joined shortly by upwards of six hundred others from Yorkshire, most of them practical farmers with sufficient capital to purchase cleared lands or stocked farms. The latter were to sail from Hull between the 10th and 25th of April in the following large vessels for Quebec: *Aurora, Triton, Harmony, Victory, St. Mary,* and *Forrester.*"

These immigrants would be most likely to call at the agent's office or that of the Canada Company, in order to avoid the pitfalls which entrapped so many; and to such people of means the Exchange Coffee House or the Neptune Inn would afford "very respectable" accommodation while they remained in Quebec.

The next stage of the immigrant's pilgrimage took him to Montreal, and as it was invariably made by river boat it sometimes differed from the ocean passage in little but length. Some were far-sighted enough to engage a passage to Montreal direct, and so avoided the expense and trouble of transferring to another vessel at Quebec; but the majority took no such precaution. In the very early period of emigration, prior to the close of the War of 1812, bateaux of large size, barges, or small schooners provided transportation to Montreal, and this method of ascending the lower St.

Lawrence was employed by some of the poorer immigrants in later times, when most travellers used river steamers.

In normal times immigrants made the Quebec-Montreal lap of their journey in from one to two days. When first introduced the steamships were very slow,[4] and might take three or four days against the current. Two or three steamers a week comprised the Quebec-Montreal service in the early 'twenties, and the 180-mile trip took from 36 to 44 hours; but in later years several vessels a day made the journey in faster time, frequently over night. Sometimes the river steamer came alongside the sailing-vessel, but more frequently the immigrants were landed at the wharves, where they made arrangements for their journey westward. Baggage could be carried by barges if the steamship was too crowded. It was advisable to throw away all boxes and barrels in which the provisions had been carried, for their transport further would be costly. A little boiled beef or pork and some fresh bread were provided before embarking by those who were able, and hot water to make tea could generally be obtained on the steamer.

The cost of the Quebec-Montreal passage varied greatly at different periods. In 1819, when steam travel was still something of a novelty on the St. Lawrence and the passage took nearly two days, steerage or deck passengers paid 15s. and supplied their own provisions and beds; while those who travelled cabin class were charged £2 10s., for which they received meals and berths, though paying in addition for whatever "porter, liquor, or lemonade" they wanted. This, however, was the period of leisurely emigration, and the rates were subsequently reduced by competition for an ever-increasing trade. In 1834 the steerage rate was only 5s., and even this was occasionally lowered by cut-throat competition. The *Quebec Gazette* notes in May of that year that the *Voyageur* was getting too much of the business to suit the *Patriote*, which thereupon reduced her rates to 2s. 6d. The *Voyageur* lowered to 2s., and soon left with 400 aboard. The *Patriote* then loaded up, but charged everyone 5s., in spite of the promise to accept half-price.[5]

In general the short voyage was comparatively pleasant; while for the cabin passenger it was a sight-seeing excursion:

"The accommodations are of the very best order, the rate of travelling

---

[4] John Molson's *Accommodation*, 1809, the first steamship in Canadian waters, required more than a week to negotiate the passage from Quebec to Montreal, and it was necessary for ox-teams to aid her through St. Mary's Current, below Montreal.

[5] *Quebec Gazette*, May 23, 1834. Ten years later the *Charlevoix* carried deck passengers for 2s., while a cabin passage was 10s., meals included.

expeditious, the viands extremely good, and the company generally respectable. . . . The country now wears a more pleasing aspect—neat villages and some very good farms appear, and the lands are generally in a tolerable state of cultivation. The scenery of the St. Lawrence is agreeably diversified by the appearance of the steamboats and other vessels passing to and fro. Occasionally an immense raft of timber comes from the upland country, covering at least an acre; and then the light canoe, gliding gaily over the surface."

The cabin passage in the 'thirties was usually 26s. sterling (six dollars), and is described as "well found, and with excellent accommodations." The best of wine and porter might be obtained at 3s. a pint and 1s. 3d. a quart, respectively. One guidebook emphasises that the passenger should remain on board at stops or he may suddenly find himself left behind:

"After leaving Quebec, the first place the boat stops at is a small town called Three Rivers, containing about fifteen hundred inhabitants, ninety miles distant, or halfway between Quebec and Montreal. The boat merely stops here to land and receive passengers, and to take a fresh supply of fuel; so you had better not go ashore, as they start at a moment's notice, and will not wait for anyone. There is nothing to engage your attention here, but I have heard of many persons being separated from their friends and their baggage by gaping about, and suddenly finding the boat gone without them. Proceeding on, you go through what is called Lake St. Peter, and shortly after reach the small town of Sorel, or William Henry, where the boat also stops to land and receive passengers and take more fuel; the same observations may apply here as at Three Rivers. You are now only forty-five miles from Montreal, which you accomplish in about six hours; making the whole passage from Quebec to Montreal in from twenty to twenty-four hours.

"The steam-boat landing at Montreal is both convenient and roomy; but do not be in too great a hurry to land: a little patience here may save you both trouble and imposition from carters, porters and landlords. There is sometimes a little delay in getting the boat into her berth at the wharf, but it will not be long before everything will be conveniently arranged for landing both yourself and luggage."

In bad weather, however, and particularly among the crowds of deck passengers, the lack of sleeping accommodation made the voyage a miserable experience. William Peacock spent two nights on board a steamship packed with 800 passengers. Francis Thomas "passed one night on board the steamer in our voyage to Montreal, when we encountered a most dreadful thunder storm. I certainly did at one time feel very considerable alarm for our safety, as it was so very violent, and the river was both very broad and deep; but providentially no accident happened, except that a poor man fell overboard and was drowned." Thomas was pleased to find

"a most wide difference in the behaviour of the Captain and men of the steamer to what we had for a long time been used to at sea. Here we were met with civility, attention and even politeness, which, ever since we left London, we had been strangers to. . . . Early the following morning we arrived at Montreal, and landed in health and safety after having suffered numberless trials and hardships, just 12 weeks from our leaving the London docks."

In the early period immigrants at Montreal were not beset with as many difficulties as later, although there were always crimps about the waterfront to mislead and defraud the unwary. As crowded emigrant ships began to pour out their ever-increasing quota upon the docks of Quebec and Montreal the dangers increased. Many of the most destitute found shelter at "the sheds," near the entrance to the Lachine Canal. For others who could afford to pay, lodgings might be obtained from 4d. to 6d. per night, and meals at from 10d. to 1s. each; though William Peacock paid 4s. 6d. a night to an unscrupulous Montreal tavern-keeper for the privilege of "laying on our own beds" on the floor.

In the plague years Montreal presented a strange appearance. Mrs. Susanna Moodie reached the city in 1832, when the cholera epidemic was at its height, and she observed that the streets, in addition to being dirty and ill-paved, had all the sewers opened up "in order to purify the place and stop the ravages of the pestilence." In her opinion, however, this scheme resulted chiefly in "rendering the public thoroughfares almost impassable, and loaded the air with intolerable effluvia, more likely to produce than stay the course of the plague, the violence of which had, in all probability, been increased by these long-neglected receptacles of uncleanliness." Her other impressions of Montreal center around the all-pervading fear of death:

> "The sullen toll of the death-bell, the exposure of ready-made coffins in the undertakers' windows, and the oft-recurring notice placarded on the walls, of funerals furnished at such and such a place at cheapest rate and shortest notice, painfully reminded us at every turning of the street, that death was everywhere—perhaps lurking in our very path; we felt no desire to examine the beauties of the place. With this ominous feeling pervading our minds, public buildings possessed few attractions, and we determined to make our stay as short as possible."

Just as her sister, Mrs. Catherine Traill, was about to leave the city she was stricken with the disease and forced to remain in her hotel for several days. Becoming hourly worse, she suffered "extreme torture" and "mortal agony," but the various remedies applied—bleeding, opium, blue pill, and salts—eventually proved effectual and she recovered sufficiently to proceed westward. During her illness she had plenty of attention from servants, hotel attendants, and her husband,—as well as a physician,—so that her sufferings were small in comparison with those of poorer immigrants whose very poverty, coupled with the suspicion natural to the times,

QUEBEC AND MONTREAL 163

led to their being shunned by everyone. Some were fortunate enough to be taken to a hospital; others died in the streets or on the wharves and were buried in a nameless grave. That many, even in ordinary times, disappeared without any knowledge of their fate ever reaching their friends is apparent from the experience of members of the McKee family. In 1840 Martha McKee contracted fever *en route* from Ireland to Quebec, and was detained for eight weeks in a hospital. Her brother, who had settled a few years earlier in Hastings County, Upper Canada, proceeded to Quebec to meet her, and, we are told by her son,

"He interviewed the doctor in charge, but was informed there was no such person there. However, the doctor took him through the hospital and as they walked by my brother's cot she thought she recognized her brother, but was too weak to get their attention. On their way back she made a desperate effort and succeeded, to the untold satisfaction and happiness of both."

In the great ship fever year, 1847, many thousands of the most destitute were crowded into steamships as if they had been so many cattle, and forwarded at government expense into the interior, where they arrived more dead than alive. Citizens at lake ports recalled with horror the sight of the sick, lying in groups on the open wharves, and actually overrun with the rats which until modern times infested the decaying wooden piers of Canadian harbors. But even if he was ill and dispirited, penniless and exhausted, the immigrant must contrive in some manner to push forward.

"And as he progresses up the country," says a guidebook, "he will find himself gradually gathering strength; and change of air, of scenery, of diet, and of the mode of travelling, will relieve him from the lassitude with which he was at first oppressed. Although on his first landing among us, the Emigrant may regard the scene with a languid eye, and move forward with a faltering step, yet he should never suffer his resolution to be shaken, or his purposes abandoned from momentary doubt or suffering. Let him continually keep in vivid remembrance that state of dependence and hopelessness, it may be poverty and want, from which he has escaped, and never for once lose sight of the tranquillity and competence which he may yet secure by reasonable perseverance and industry."

CHAPTER XVII

Ascending the St. Lawrence

"During this short period each of us encountered greater difficulties, endured more privations, and submitted to stronger proofs of our fortitude than had been our lot in all the preceding years of our lives. We were obliged by day, in consequence of the great weight of our luggage, to assist the sailors in towing the boat up the rapids, often up to our armpits in water; and by night to rest our enervated and shivering limbs on the inhospitable shores of this river of cataracts."

Edward Talbot

To an exceptional degree the ascent of the St. Lawrence was an epic of navigation. Avoided by the Indians on account of its rapids, the river long defied the mastery of the white man. By using specially-constructed boats, various ingenious expedients, and frequent portages, a slow and hazardous journey might be effected. First used was the bateau[1]—an open flat-bottomed craft about 40 feet long and 6 to 8 feet wide, usually constructed of pine boards. It was propelled by French-Canadians using oars, setting poles, grappling-irons, and a lug sail or two, as conditions necessitated. Where the current was too strong for navigation it was hauled by men or horses; while the passengers tramped across the portages, over which the boats were dragged, carried, or floated through primitive locks. Shortly after 1800 the bateau was joined by the Durham boat, a larger sloop-like craft introduced on the Delaware River about the middle of the eighteenth century.[2] Slowly propelled against the current by setting poles and square sails, these clumsy-looking undecked boats, sometimes 90 to 100 feet long, had a capacity of 350 barrels of merchandise.[3] In such crude vessels thousands of immigrants laboriously worked their way up the St. Lawrence to Prescott in from six to twelve days.

While their baggage was being carted for five or six shillings from Montreal to Lachine, nine miles away, the passengers tramped alongside or travelled by stage or wagon. At Lachine the immigrant

---

[1] The word, spelled by most early writers *batteau*, had no exact meaning as to the type of craft, but merely signified all boats smaller than barques or schooners, exclusive of canoes.

[2] Named for its inventor, Robert Durham of Pennsylvania, a celebrated builder of river boats.

[3] A detailed account of Canadian transportation and travel—from Indian trail to air mail—may be found in the author's *Early Life in Upper Canada*, 373-613.

Public Archives of Canada
WINTER STAGE-COACH ON THE ST. LAWRENCE
Many Canadian settlements were accessible only in winter.

From De Roos' Personal Narrative of Travels, 1827   *Lieutenant J. F. F. De Roos*
WATERLOO INN, BETWEEN BALTIMORE AND WASHINGTON, 1826
The stage-coach provided the speediest means of land travel until the coming of the Iron Horse.

From Bigsby's The Shoe and Canoe, 1850   *John Bigsby*
ANDREW'S TAVERN, ABOVE BROCKVILLE
Those who could not afford to patronize wayside inns slept in barns or under the stars.

From Willis' Canadian Scenery, 1842   *W. H. Bartlett*
BATEAUX UNLOADING AT COBOURG, UPPER CANADA, IN 1840
Cobourg, on Lake Ontario, was early prominent as a port of entry for immigrants proceeding to the interior.

was advised by a guidebook to go to Messrs. Grant and Duff's, merchants,

"who will forward his baggage to Kingston, consigned to Mr. H. C. Thomson, in whose store it will be perfectly safe until his arrival. . . . An inventory should be kept of the contents of every package. The emigrant will have leisure to make this out during the passage from England to Quebec. At La Chine he can go to Mrs. Campbell's Inn."

At the head of the Lachine Rapids they took to the boats, which were aided by sails through Lake St. Louis. There was a small lock at the Cascades, but if traffic was congested the boats would be dragged through the rapids or along the shore, while the immigrants aided in the towing. The Split Rock and Cedars Rapids were next surmounted, and at the head of the Cedars the boats were reloaded, most of the goods having been carted thither from the Cascades. The Coteau du Lac might be avoided by the first lock constructed on the river—one cut through limestone in 1780-81. Lake St. Francis was navigated by sails, supplemented by oars and poles. Above Cornwall was the turbulent Long Sault, surmounted by means of locks or the portage road, particularly between Mille Roches and the head of the rapids. There were no difficulties above Prescott, and bateaux might be sailed, rowed, and poled into Lake Ontario; but there were several points below where "tracking" the boats was impossible owing to steep banks, and the expedient of a skidway of small rolling logs was necessary; while windlasses, horses, and oxen supplemented man-power at Pine Tree Point and Point Iroquois.

The French-Canadian crews were no gentle characters, and added to the disagreeable nature of the trip. Sir Richard Bonnycastle mentions their pilfering: "Still they are above stealing—they only tap the rum cask or the whisky barrel, and appropriate any cordage wherewith you bound your chests and packages." John Howison observed the crews as they reclined around the camp-fire at the close of the day's work, "talking barbarous French and uttering the most horrid oaths"; or, as another put it, "such repeated blasphemy and most horrible new-invented oaths that Lucifer and all his train perhaps could not exceed." Altogether, as they sat around the encampment singing troubadour songs,

"They resembled a band of freebooters. Most of them were very athletic, and had the sharp physiognomy and sparkling eyes of a Canadian. The red glare of the fire communicated additional animation to their rude features; and their bushy black beards and discordant voices rendered them a rather formidable-looking set of people."

As the brigades of bateaux and Durham boats commenced their ascent of the St. Lawrence at Lachine, there was sometimes a delay while the traveller made his arrangements. In 1821 a Scottish emigration waited four days while fifteen bateaux were obtained to accommodate 366 persons; two horses towed each boat where the current was strongest. A Durham boat was even slower than a bateau. Samuel Strickland in 1825 found the crew such "a rough set of customers" that he left his boat at the Cedars Rapids, walking along the shore as far as Prescott and waiting there two or three days until his baggage caught up with him! In 1818 Edward Talbot found that the accommodations of his Durham boat "were so poor that our situation during the thirteen days of our voyage from Lachine to Prescott was in reality 'below the reach of envy.' To make room for my mother and the children in the wretched little hole of a cabin, my brother and I were frequently obliged to sleep on the shore in the open air." Between the 18th of August and the 1st of September the journey of 120 miles was completed, but not without hardships which he considered greater "than had been our lot in all the preceding years of our lives." When for variety Talbot and some others struck into the woods to tramp for a mile or two, they wandered into an impassable swamp, and did not catch up with the boat again until the following day. They fortunately chanced late at night upon a log house, and had been allowed to sleep on the kitchen floor; but the boat continued on its journey without the slightest interest in their whereabouts.

The intense suffering endured by many thousands is apparent from the description given by one poor immigrant:

"Our travelling this way is very tiresome and took us eight days to get to Prescot: the first night we reached a village, and after begging hard we prevailed with them to let us lay on their floor: we carried our beds and slept there, at the charge of 6d. each: at break of day we went on board, and stopped at night where there was no house: we borrowed the sail, and as many as could get under it did; the others made a large fire, and sat or slept by it: the next day it rained all day, and at night we stopped at a village and prevailed with some poor people to lodge us, a house full, on their floor: they let us make tea, and dryed our clothes: in the night I was taken ill with spasms, and a fever followed; I did not eat one mouthful of food for eight days; only drank a little port wine often. I could not hardly get in or out of the boat, nor did I think I should ever see Adelaide. We at last came to Prescot, *sleeping on the ground every night but two:* the boatmen were all Frenchmen, and no way obliging; we could not make the kettle boil by the fire. When we came to Prescot we were all very wet with rain, and went to a tavern, hoping to dry ourselves; but we were so many, standing in their way, they did not want us there, so we was forced to remain as we was."

ASCENDING THE ST. LAWRENCE 167

Those who could pay for accommodations were sometimes able to obtain them, though they had their drawbacks. One woman describes in her letters that in 1822 she and her husband spent one night at a tavern, "but between the heat and the visitations of troublesome insects we could not sleep." In spite of such experiences, however, she bravely wrote that they "met with no hardships and but few difficulties." Many, unaccustomed to fresh water during much of the ocean voyage, died from "the bloody flux," a disease resulting from drinking too much river water. John M'Donald refers to several deaths among the members of his party, and states that sleeping in the open air was the cause of much sickness: "I have found in the morning my night-cap, blankets and mat so soaked with dew that they might have been wrung."

Even state-conducted emigrations were not free from delays. Many of the Scots who had given up their homes in April, 1815, were still far from their locations a year later. They were finally settled in the spring and summer of 1816, but their disposition along the St. Lawrence during the previous winter is outlined in a despatch of Sir Sidney Beckwith to Sir Gordon Drummond:

"I have the honor to report to Your Excellency that of the settlers recently arrived from Scotland in the transports *Dorothy, Atlas* and *Baltic Merchant*, and since forwarded to the Upper Province, eight or nine hundred unmarried men have proceeded to Kingston and are there employed by the Engineer's Department on the King's works. At Brockville, thirty large families are accommodated in the barracks, in some adjoining huts hired by themselves, and in the neighbouring farm houses, where most of them have procured employment. . . . At Fort Wellington there are a few families, whom it is contemplated also to settle on the Rideau. . . . At Cornwall I found about three hundred of the settlers and their families. For these there was no adequate accommodation. The Barracks and hired buildings had been given up and were in bad condition, but as cover was indispensably necessary before winter, I was obliged to direct three of the buildings being re-engaged, a few stoves to be placed in them, the windows to be repaired, and some of the berths to be replaced. . . . In the small barrack at the River Raisin are about fifty settlers, including their families, who are comfortably lodged for the winter. At Coteau de Lac are three families, who are artificers and employed with Your Excellency's permission to repairing the locks under the Engineer's Department. At Montreal are a few families whom the confinement of their wives or the sickness of their children rendered unable to proceed."

Before the introduction of steam navigation on Lake Ontario in 1817, immigrants usually continued by bateau or Durham boat through the upper St. Lawrence and lower lakes, the total cost of transporting a family direct from Montreal to York being about £3 15s. Until the early years of the century travellers bound for Niagara or Detroit often made the long trip from Quebec entirely by bateau. Although tedious, the voyage was not without interest if one enjoyed a wild carefree life. Dr. William ("Tiger") Dunlop found the mode of travel "far from unpleasant, for there is something of romance and adventure in it." All supplies were carried, and camp was pitched at night in the mouths of creeks or at other sheltered spots. The crew was made up of "seven stout, light-hearted, jolly, lively Canadians, who sang their songs all the time they could spare from smoking their pipes. Often they sang and danced all night, for if the Frenchman has a fiddle, sleep ceases to be a necessity of life for him." It was possible, however, except in the very early period, to transfer at Prescott or Kingston to a sailing-vessel, which would reach the lake ports more quickly under favorable weather conditions.[4]

Prescott, above which there were no rapids, was consequently a great stopping-place for immigrants bound westward or northward. In January, 1832, the sum of £270 was voted by the Upper Canadian Legislature for the relief of immigrants there. Most of them encamped in open fields near the town, where the more destitute frequently remained for weeks—sometimes even into the winter months. In July, 1821, this encampment included over 1,000 people, largely Scottish, who were destined for the vicinity of New Lanark, 62 miles inland from Brockville by a bush road. M'Donald, a member of the emigration, observed that "an episcopal chapel and a Presbyterian meeting-house" were then in course of erection in the town, but that

"the only place of worship, as far as I could learn, which previously existed, was a school-house, the master of which gave a discourse in the forenoon to the few who attended. It is, however, seriously to be lamented that the Sabbath, the holy and honourable of the Lord, is so little respected there. Many were employed in singing, in playing on flutes, and drinking. A few of us asked the school-house for the purpose of religious worship, which was readily granted, and each took his turn. We met here three Sabbath days and sung the Lord's song, read his word, and approached his throne of grace, pleading the fulfilment of his gracious promise that where two or three are met together in his name, he will be in the midst of them to bless them and do them good. We found those days to be the most pleasant of all the days we spent in a foreign land."

Among the saddest episodes in the history of Kingston are those relating to the suffering and death of immigrants on their way westward. When Peter Robinson's Irish emigration was delayed there for several weeks in 1825, over 300 cases of fever broke out and there were thirty-three deaths. Still worse were

[4] William Dummer Powell and his family, for example, travelled by schooner between Kingston and Niagara and from Fort Erie to Detroit, the ascent of the St. Lawrence, as well as the Niagara portage, being accomplished by bateau, "calash" (*calèche*), on horseback or on foot. (See Riddell, *Old Province Tales, Upper Canada*, 64-92.)

the plague years of 1832 and 1847, when many hundreds died. A monument was erected in 1894 to the memory of some 400 Irish immigrants who were buried there during the latter year. Although Kingston had sheds for the shelter of destitute immigrants, it was not usual for them to remain long, for there were numerous vessels sailing to Cobourg, York, and other ports up the lake.

After the introduction of steamships on the more open portions of the St. Lawrence and Ottawa rivers it was quite usual for bateaux and Durham boats to be towed part of the way. The resulting advantage in speed was offset by the discomfort of the night travel which it enabled, as is apparent from the following:

"At Coteau-du-Lac our steamer took seven bateaux in tow, in one of which I counted 110 immigrants of all ages, who were doomed to pass the night on board. Men, women and children were huddled together as close as captives in a slave-trader, exposed to the sun's rays by day, and river-damp by night, without protection. It was impossible to look upon such a group of human beings without emotion. The day had been so intensely hot that the stoutest amongst them looked fatigued, while the females seemed ready to expire with exhaustion. Conversation was carried on in whispers, and a heaviness of heart seemed to pervade the whole assemblage. Never shall I forget the countenance of a young mother, ever anxiously looking at twin infants slumbering on her knee, and covering them from the vapour rising from the river, and which strongly depicted the feelings of maternal affection and pious resignation. Night soon veiled the picture, and, I fear, brought no relief to the anxious mother."

Large numbers of immigrants who could not afford transportation trudged wearily along the roads, subsisting upon charity. After outlining the difficulties and expenses of travel by wagon and bateau, the author of a guidebook recommends with considerable enthusiasm the "easy and cheap" method of tramping thirty miles a day:

"The third way of travelling from La Chine to Prescott and Kingston during the summer months is on foot. For single men it is eligible, easy and cheap. There are farm-houses and inns on the great west road for the whole distance. By subsisting principally on bread and cheese and milk, or Sepaune and milk, the expense of each person will not be more than three shillings sterling a day, having sent his baggage forward from La Chine to Kingston by a bateau from Messrs. Grant and Duff's. If travellers call at farm-houses they will not be charged as much for provisions and beds as at the inns. Even women and children might travel in the same manner by easy stages, and by sometimes hiring a waggon for a few miles, which can always be procured of a farmer on the road."

But travel by wagon or stage was too expensive for the average immigrant, though those bound for the Eastern Townships might find it to their advantage "to buy a horse and cart to carry the family and baggage from the city to those parts." The cost of hiring a wagon with a team of horses was usually $3 per day in the 1840's, while travel by stage was from 2½ to 3d. per mile; but in earlier times it was much more expensive. There was an irregular service over the portages as early as 1808, and during the winter of 1816-1817 Barnabas Dickinson and Samuel Purdy co-operated in providing through stages from Montreal to Kingston and York. Six days was the scheduled time, and the fare totalled about $35 for the two parts of the trip. It was usual at first to discontinue service during the season of navigation.

In the 1830's the improvement of steamship engines enabled their use on the less turbulent sections of the lower St. Lawrence, and these, supplemented by stages, composed the "steam-and-stage" line for travellers who could afford to pay 31s. 6d. to reduce the time of the Montreal-Prescott lap to one strenuous day's travel. Mrs. Susanna Moodie was one of nine passengers crowded so closely in the stage that the journey was most unpleasant. Mrs. Traill was similarly "dreadfully fatigued" and "literally bruised black and blue," but she considered, nevertheless, that the steam-and-stage line was operated "with as little trouble to the passengers as possible." Mrs. William Radcliff, who used the steam-and-stage route in 1832, found that "the new coaches (drawn by six horses) are very showy, and by no means ugly in their appearance." There were three rows of seats, each of which would accommodate "four *moderate* persons, but *three* Radcliffs." Mrs. Radcliff found sitting in the rear seat to be "dreadfully" fatiguing, while front-seat travel was "remarkably easy with an agreeable swinging motion."

Some travellers preferred the less tedious "American line of conveyances." In 1833 Patrick Shirreff proceeded

"by stage to Lachine, from thence to Cascades by steam, from Cascades to Coteau du Lac by stage, and again by steam to Cornwall. On reaching Cornwall I immediately proceeded on board the American steamboat *Dalhousie*, which conveyed us across the Hoogdensburgh. From thence we were conveyed to Ogdensburgh by land. At five in the morning the *United States* steamboat left Ogdensburgh for Brockville and Kingston."

Upper Canada was somewhat more easily reached when the Rideau Canal from Bytown (Ottawa) to Kingston was completed in 1832. Immigrants took a wagon or steamer at Lachine, where bateaux had to be towed about 40 miles to Carillon, continuing up the Ottawa by steamship or Durham boat, and thence southward to Kingston *via* the Rideau. In 1834 the *Quebec Gazette* described the advantages of this route, stating that four days was sufficient instead of the six or more by the St. Lawrence. The

ASCENDING THE ST. LAWRENCE 171

Rideau route was both cheaper and safer, and since it was unnecessary to unload and reship goods, damage was less likely and there was less need of insurance. This roundabout, triangular method of reaching Kingston was, however, exceedingly tiresome. Most immigrants relied largely for their provisions upon farmers and merchants along the route; but others, unable to finance such a journey all at once, hired out from time to time as farm laborers. Soon after the opening of the Rideau Canal, John Treffry and his family, who settled in Oxford County, Upper Canada, had an uncommonly eventful voyage on it:

"The first adventure occurred when the steamer sprang a leak and it became necessary to borrow a pump from a barge in tow to keep the water under control. Two days later the engine broke down and the captain took two of the Durham boats, which the steamer was also towing, and started for Kingston to secure assistance. Meanwhile those on board ran short of provisions and had to make good the deficiency by fishing. They even tried to capture a deer which appeared on the bank, but failed in the attempt. The situation was not made brighter when the cook mutinied. Finally the captain returned with help and provisions, and the *Enterprise* was able to reach Kingston by the thirteenth of May, seven days after leaving Bytown."[6]

Early travel by sailing-ship on the upper St. Lawrence and Lake Ontario was by "the King's Ships"—the British armed vessels. They first carried passengers in 1791, charging two guineas, wines included,—a moderate fare for a voyage from Kingston to Niagara which might last from 22 hours to a week. A steerage passage cost one guinea. In 1796 Isaac Weld found the accommodations quite pleasant, and "the cabin table well-served, including port and sherry wine." Lieutenant-Governor Simcoe and his wife travelled from Kingston to Niagara in three days on the *Onondaga* in July, 1792. The Duc de la Rochefoucauld-Liancourt observed that the King's Ships were "built of timber fresh cut down, and not seasoned," and that consequently they never remained in use more than six or eight years. First-class passengers and officers were accommodated aft in small two- and three-berth cabins, badly lighted and ill-ventilated. Steerage passengers managed without berths.

After the War of 1812 the King's Ships gradually passed out of use. Numerous merchant craft were available to passengers, though seldom subject to schedule. Edward Talbot took passage on the small schooner *Caledonia* at Prescott in 1819 and was six days

[6] John Treffry's diary quoted in Smith, *Pioneers of Old Ontario*, 195-6. Francis Thomas went over the Rideau route in 1834, proceeding in a tedious manner from Montreal by barge, the steamer *Ottawa*, another barge, the steamship *Shannon*, and finally on the *Enterprise* to Kingston. He found it "a dismal course, nothing for miles together but wood and water," and he counted 48 locks along the canal. (Diary of Francis Thomas, supplementary note.)

reaching York. With favorable weather sailing-ships provided satisfactory service, but the Rev. Isaac Fidler's experiences in sailing from Oswego to York in 1831 were not unusual:

> "I agreed with the captain for $9 for myself, family and baggage, and he on his part assured me that he would land me safe in 24 hours. Our provision was included in the fare. Instead of reaching York in one day we were five days on the lake. . . . The cabin of the vessel served for the sitting, eating and sleeping room of passengers, captain and crew. . . . The food generally placed before us for dinner was salt pork, potatoes, bread, water and salt; tea, bread and butter, and sometimes salt pork for breakfast and tea; no supper."

The *Frontenac*, the first steam vessel on the upper St. Lawrence and Lake Ontario, was considered a floating palace. In 1819 John Howison travelled to York on her and thoroughly enjoyed the trip, especially after the hardships of the bateau trip up the St. Lawrence:

> "I could not but invoke a thousand blessings on the inventors and improvers of the steamboat for the delightful mode of conveyance with which their labours have been the means of furnishing mankind. It required some recollections to perceive that I was not in the Kingston Hotel."

Mrs. Susanna Moodie embarked at Prescott upon the *William IV*, "a fine new steamer, crowded with Irish emigrants proceeding to Cobourg and York." She travelled cabin class, anticipating an enjoyable trip, but it was

> "too stormy to go upon deck—thunder and lightning, accompanied with torrents of rain. Amid the confusion of the elements I tried to get a peep at the Lake of the Thousand Isles; but the driving storm blended all objects into one, and I returned wet and disappointed to my berth. . . . The gale continued until daybreak, and noise and confusion prevailed all night, which was greatly increased by the uproarious conduct of a wild Irish emigrant who thought fit to make his bed on the mat before the cabin door. . . . The following day was wet and gloomy. The storm had protracted the length of our voyage several hours, and it was midnight when we landed at Cobourg."

When Patrick Shirreff was a passenger on the popular *Great Britain* in 1833 the "night-scene on board formed a counterpart to that of the bateau on the St. Lawrence, almost every inch of surface being crowded with reposing individuals. . . . The aged and infirm sought shelter down below; the boys clustered round the chimney-stalks for heat, while the more hardy stretched themselves on the upper deck with almost no covering." The fare was sometimes $5 cabin and $3 deck from Kingston to Toronto, but competition occasionally cut it down; for a short time in 1843 cabin passage could be secured for 1s., and a deck trip (or steerage) for

ASCENDING THE ST. LAWRENCE 173

6d. Many of the poorest could not pay even this small fare, so they were forced to pawn some of their goods; and quite often considerate friends redeemed them at the end of the journey. When immigrants landed in small numbers it was sometimes possible to get accommodation at an inn; but in Captain Hale's *Instructions to Emigrants* we find that "when a large party are together they commonly get housed in a barn, which is seldom charged for and may have offers of employment."

As the stranger approached the interior, he was still liable to imposition and fraud. The *Upper Canada Herald* describes a despicable trick:

"We have seldom found a more flagrant instance of dishonourable cupidity than has been brought under our notice in the following facts. Last Sunday fortnight the American steamboat *William Avery* took on board a number of English Emigrants at Kingston, and the Captain engaged to take them to Toronto. Instead of doing this he took and landed them at Rochester, and after staying there two or three days they had to take a boat and come to Port Hope. But this circuitous route and consequent delays and expence were not all the evil. By being landed at Rochester the Emigrants had to pay the States heavy duties on all their goods, paying on a gun more than it cost in England." The *Herald* expressed the hope that "some of our townsmen will attend the *William Avery* when she comes, and prevent her captain from entrapping our countrymen in his toils."[6]

In almost all centers of population in the British provinces—and in many cities of the United States—were to be found the National Societies of St. George, St. Patrick, and St. Andrew, which served the double purpose of keeping green the memory of the Old Land and of assisting their compatriots. Many a family owed their start in the New World to these societies, or other kindhearted individuals. Citizens of Cobourg living within recent years recalled that their parents used to go to the harbor with baskets of provisions for the sick and weary travellers, for whose accommodation some buildings in the vicinity were also provided. At York these philanthropic activities were carefully organized.

In 1822 the Stranger's Friend Society spent £110 in the relief of sick and destitute immigrants. It was recognized that "the great expense attending the passage of emigrants and their families up the St. Lawrence frequently exhausts their means, depresses their spirits, and, added to the great fatigue of the journey and the exposure of the weather, produces sickness among them ere they reach York." James Fitzgibbon, the secretary, reported that 7,898 rations had been distributed and 215 families relieved during the

[6] Toronto *Upper Canada Herald*, June 11, 1834. (The town of York became the city of Toronto in March, 1834.) The account was reprinted in the *Quebec Gazette* of June 17th as a warning to immigrants.

year. In 1829 the same organization was known as the Society for the Relief of the Sick and Destitute; while in the autumn of 1830 an "Emigrants' Asylum" was erected. Two years later the York Emigrant Committee, appointed by the Lieutenant-Governor, assisted in facilitating settlement and employment.

The Rev. Anson Green who was in Cobourg in October, 1825, when one section of the Peter Robinson emigration reached the village, observed that the beach west of Division Street was

"covered with small white tents, filled with Irish immigrants. . . . There was no wharf in Cobourg then, and the landing was somewhat difficult. . . . These white tents presented a beautiful and attractive appearance. They stretched along on the sand beach lying between the lake and a forest of small cedars which covered the worst part of the swampy ground east of Ham's Mills."

The greater part of these immigrants were Roman Catholics, but the zealous Methodists discovered that fourteen families were Protestants, and though the priest in charge of the majority objected, the Irish did not lack evangelical gospel.

A few years later thousands of immigrants entered lake ports every week, and many citizens did a thriving business. David Wilkie, who visited Toronto shortly after it had assumed that name and city status, observed that although there were "many extensive establishments and dozens of minor houses of entertainment, all are generally fully occupied." We see groups of weary travellers on the beach just after the arrival of a steamship:

"It is a scene of no common interest, and exhibits a very singular taste in the ideas of economy. You will see, probably, a few old chairs not worth half a dollar each, which have been brought nearly or quite five thousand miles; with old bedsteads and other pieces of common furniture that could have been disposed of at home for nearly as much as the new would cost here, for wood being so very abundant in Canada these common articles of furniture are very cheap in most parts of the Province."

Many died on the very threshold of the Promised Land. In 1821 the father of a family was drowned while bathing in the St. Lawrence. At Fort Wellington the widow and her eleven children were delayed while wagons were being obtained to carry them to the interior, but the mother, "overcome with grief and fatigue," was taken ill and died, leaving the children without any guardian. "But in this country," observed Mr. Bell, "orphans need never be destitute of a home. Farmers who have few or no children of their own, readily take them and bring them up for the benefit they receive from their labour."

In the plague years the immigrant's progress into the interior

ASCENDING THE ST. LAWRENCE

was made still more arduous by the fear and suspicion with which every stranger was regarded. Patrick Shirreff describes the experiences of one woman and her family:

"Arriving at Montreal when cholera was raging in a dreadful manner, and her husband being in a delicate state of health, no time was lost in pursuing their route. In passing up the St. Lawrence with her family and luggage, the boat admitted water so freely that she was forced to walk by the river side with an infant on her back. The population being panic-stricken at the havoc cholera was making, shut their doors on emigrants, who, they imagined, had introduced the disease into the country; and she was under the necessity of making bread for her family with her own hands and firing it under a tree."

How death stalked these poor people—and those whom they infected as they proceeded—is well shown by a statement of cases and deaths in various settlements along the St. Lawrence and Lake Ontario, as reported in the *Cobourg Star* of July 4, 1832:

STATE OF CHOLERA UP TO THE PRESENT DATES

Settlement	Date	Cases	Deaths
Quebec	June 25	694	429
Montreal	" 26	3,411	970
Cornwall	" 28	—	15
St. Regis	" 28	34	5
Prescott	" 26	46	16
Brockville	" 28	4	3
Kingston	" 23	121	39
Cobourg	July 4	6	2
Port Hope	July 4	2	1
York	June 30	48	23
Hallowell	July 1	6	3

The human tragedy behind such a list of casualties is brought to mind by experiences like that of Henry Smart, whose family came from Sussex in one of the emigrations financed by the Earl of Egremont. After describing how his son was stricken with fever on the Atlantic, while his wife, approaching her confinement, gave him great cause for anxiety due to continued illness, he relates that a daughter was born to them, and buried where she was born—in the harbor of Quebec:

"Then we started up the river in a Durham boat. . . . We were in the boat 7 days, when we landed at Prescot. We stopped at Prescot three days, . . . but the third I was very sick. . . . About four o'clock she was taken very ill, and said if there was not an alteration soon she would soon be gone. . . . The doctors told me it was no use: she had the cholera and could not live but a few hours. . . . She told me all she wanted of me was to promise to take as good care of her child as I had done of her. So she died that day. . . .

"About an hour before she died Frederick was taken very ill with the bowel complaint, and died 8 days after. I was obliged to go on to Hamilton on account of the cholera, and I was still very ill then; but still I kept about. I buried my wife at Prescot; and my child at Hamilton. I am as much as two hundred miles from where I buried my wife but my child I can look upon every week."

John Capelin's letter to his brother in England in 1832 gives details in elaboration of his sad statement, "There was 32 of us that came up into the woods together, and there is 12 of the 32 dead":

"I take the opportunity of writing these few lines to you to inform you of our distress and trouble. After a very rough passage of twelve weeks, by the help of the Almighty God we arrived safe to land; except the loss of two babes, Ned Luff's youngest, and ˉVm. Tickner's youngest child; but we then thought ourselves safe, but the Almighty was pleased to send a very great affliction upon us. In a few days after we arrived at our intended place of settlement I lost my poor little Mary for the first; then my dearest wife; then my two youngest and little Edmund; all in the space of eight days: but, dear brother, I am not the only one the Almighty was pleased to send the affliction on: poor Joseph Kinshott was the first; and his sister, Nathan Morley's wife was next; and I am very sorry to inform you that my poor brother-in-law, poor Bob is gone: likewise the two young Lander's. The complaint was cholera morbus; they all died in the space of a fortnight: there [was] none laid ill but a few days."

A man who accompanied emigrants to America in 1847 in order to observe their condition at first hand, wrote as follows concerning their journey towards Toronto:

"I have seen small, incommodious and ill-ventilated steamers arriving at the quay in Toronto after a 48-hours' passage from Montreal, freighted with fetid cargoes of 1,100 or 1,200 'Government emigrants' of all ages and sexes, the healthy who had just arrived from Europe mixed with the half-recovered convalescents of the hospital, unable during that time to lie down, almost to sit. In almost every boat were clearly marked cases of actual fever, in some were deaths, the dead and the living huddled together. Sometimes the crowds were stowed in open barges, and towed after the steamer, standing like pigs upon the deck of a Cork or Bristol packet. A poor woman died in a hospital here in consequence of having been trodden down, when weak and fainting in one of those barges. I have, myself, when accompanying the emigration agent on his visit of duty to inspect the steamer on her arrival, seen him stagger back like one struck, when first meeting the current of fetid infection exhaled from between her decks. It is the unhesitating opinion of very many I have spoken to, including Government officials and medical men, that a large proportion of the fever throughout the country has been actually generated in the river steamers."[7]

The inhabitants of Toronto—like those of Kingston, Bytown, and other interior towns—could not escape the disease under such conditions. The Toronto *Standard*, in announcing that the City Council had decided to spend £5,000 to erect a House of Refuge

---

[7] Stephen E. De Vere to T. F. Elliot, in *Evidence before the Select Committee of the House of Lords on Colonisation from Ireland*, 1847, pp. 45-8. The Inspector-General of Canada reported that £35,450 was expended upon the transport of immigrants to the interior in 1847. In later years free transit by railway was sometimes available in Canada to the most destitute immigrants, but cheap fares were substituted when it was found that many posed as penniless in order to qualify.

ASCENDING THE ST. LAWRENCE 177

for immigrants and other destitute persons who were then crowding into the city, describes the spread of the fever:

"The health of the city remains in much the same state as it did several weeks ago. The individual cases of fever have abated nothing of their violence, and several families have caught the infection from having admitted emigrants into their houses. The greatest caution should be observed in this respect, as it does not require contact alone to infect a healthy person. Breathing the same atmosphere with the infected, or coming under the influence of the effluvia rising from their clothes, is, in some states of the healthy, perfectly sufficient for effecting a lodgment of the disease in the human frame."[8]

As the St. Lawrence Canals were gradually completed in the 1840's, the hardships of the ascent of the river became less and less. In 1843 those who could afford $12 for first-class accommodations could proceed from Lachine to Kingston by steamship in 26 hours. The average immigrant, however, did not patronize this service. "The ordinary conveyances up the country," wrote James B. Brown,

"are the small steamboats and barges departing from the Lachine Canal, which commences at Montreal Harbour; and proceeding up the St. Lawrence and Ottawa Rivers, and through the Rideau Canal, reach Kingston, a distance by this route of about 250 miles, and which is usually accomplished in three days by the steamboats when they take no barges in tow. The barges, and those steamers towing them, take about six days. The fare by steamboat is usually three dollars steerage; and eight dollars cabin, including meals. The fare of the barges is from one to two dollars."

In the second edition of his guidebook, 1851, James B. Brown omitted almost all reference to the old types of transport, stating that

"on arriving at Quebec emigrants may go direct from the ship's side on board of commodious steam vessels, without its being necessary for them to go on shore, or to spend a shilling for transporting their luggage, or for any other purpose: and in those steam vessels they can be conveyed to their destination, to any of the main ports on the St. Lawrence or the Great Lakes without trans-shipment, and with great rapidity."

In from seven to ten days the traveller might now proceed in one vessel direct from Quebec to Chicago at a cost of 35s., exclusive of meals, while a few years earlier he might have been as long reaching Kingston, or even Prescott. Smaller steamers and barges charged from one to two dollars steerage and eight dollars cabin class for the trip from Montreal to Kingston. The passage to Chicago without trans-shipment made the St. Lawrence route for the

---

[8] Quoted in "A Cabin Passenger," *The Ocean Plague*, 104. In Toronto alone 863 Irish died during the summer and autumn of 1847. It is estimated that 7000 were buried in Montreal, Prescott, Kingston, and other settlements as they made their way inland.

first time more advantageous than that by the Hudson River and Erie Canal—more satisfactory in many respects than the long railroad journey by way of Philadelphia or New York; and large numbers of German immigrants bound for Illinois, Wisconsin, or Minnesota patronized it. But every type of transport has its day, and no sooner was the St. Lawrence system open for through service than the railway era began. The nine-mile Lachine portage railroad was soon merely a small link in the Grand Trunk Line, which reached Brockville in 1855, Toronto in 1856, and Sarnia by 1859. Stage lines gave way before the "Iron Horse"; while the steamship felt the competition of the railway with ever-increasing severity. The sailing-ship as an emigrant carrier was disappearing just as the "emigrant train" was becoming the usual means of travel to the interior of America.

CHAPTER XVIII

ENTERING AT NEW YORK

"The entrance to the bay of New York is one of the most beautiful sights in the world."
[Beaufoy]: *Travels through the United States and Canada*

"The truth is, Sir, I am ashamed to say that some of these citizens ain't over and above good characters; they'd cheat a fellow out of his eye-teeth while he was opening his mouth to take a chaw."
"A Young Adventurer": *Voyage in an Emigrant Ship*

Vessels which entered at New York were near their destination at the first sight of land. In some instances "the hills of Neversink, on the Jersey coast, which rise 300 or 400 feet above the sea," were first observed. When the *John Dennison* approached Long Island, the first to see it won the prize of a bottle of rum amid "three hearty cheers given at the sight of the land of liberty and equality." In general, Fire Island, upon which was a lighthouse, was the first land seen. One man, who anticipated debarkation as welcome relief from a floating prison, considered his first sight of Sandy Hook and Staten Island "one of the happiest moments of my life," and he observed that

"even the brute animals that formed part of our stock seemed to partake in the joy of their more rational companions. The hogs frisked about, the cow lowed, and all appeared sensible (the sailors said by smelling) that we were now approaching land."

The *John Dennison* was in most respects a well-regulated vessel, and while she was still some distance from shore her crew were busily engaged in holystoning the deck, scraping and painting the masts, blackening the yards and tarring the rigging. The passengers, too, were advised to get their possessions in order for inspection, and were mustered on deck so that the captain might collect from each 5s. "hospital-money." This aroused strong protests, for their tickets stated that they were to be landed without further expense, but the captain swore vociferously and threatened that he would put the ship about and give them all another month's sailing. One woman resisted to the last, but the rest met the demand, learning later that the legal amount to be assessed was $1 for steerage passengers and $1.50 for those in the cabin, so that the captain received some £6 extra for his assiduity in collecting the tax.

The arrival of a pilot was an important event as a vessel approached land. When a short way off from the *John Dennison*, the foresail of the pilot's small, decked vessel was backed for a moment, and a small two-oared yawl was lowered over the side, which brought him to the ship. A few hours later "emissaries of two morning newspapers" came aboard to get the news of the voyage and the names of the cabin passengers.

Richard Weston describes the pilot as "a dandyfied personage," but he soon showed he was no mean seaman; nor did his clothes and appearance prevent him from swearing with the best in the trade, as was quite apparent when he tested the crew on their ability to manage the ship. The next arrival was the inspecting officer from the quarantine station. One girl was seriously ill, so "her mother had put on two gowns that she might pass muster on her own account, and then, throwing off one, might personate her daughter, which was accordingly done, and, the daughter having been removed to a concealed situation, the deception was not discovered." The inspector then ordered the passengers to wash all clothes, "pronounced an eulogium on our respectable appearance," and expressed the hope that all would become useful citizens of the United States. Upon his departure, old clothes were thrown overboard and clothes-washing continued throughout the night. Lines were set up between the masts, but the breeze carried away some of the wash and it became advisable to hire the sailors to fasten clothing securely in the rigging, the usual payment for such services being rum. The nearer the vessel approached the Quarantine Station the more ships were in evidence, and "the spectacle of clothes fluttering in the breeze was to be seen on all sides."[1]

New York shared with Quebec the rather doubtful honor of being the great dumping ground for European emigrations.[2] As in Lower Canada, the care of the needy was left entirely to charitable persons during the first quarter of the nineteenth century; but in 1824 New York led the way in protecting itself from the influx of the destitute by bonding shipmasters and subtracting from the

---

[1] Weston, *A Visit to the United States and Canada*, 45 et seq. A traveller of some twenty years later gives an almost identical description of the pilot. Dressed in "white coat and spotless linen, the close-fitting unmentionables, the silk hat and patent boots," he gave no promise of ability; but soon proved to everybody's satisfaction that he was "fearless, reliable and effective." (Hancock, *An Emigrant's Five Years in the Free States of America*, 18-19.)

[2] The chief other American ports of entry were New Orleans, Boston, Philadelphia, and Baltimore in the order named.

From painting by Samuel B. Waugh, Courtesy Museum of the City of New York

The Bay and Harbor of New York in 1847. At the right is a ship discharging immigrants. Castle Garden is the round building on the left. Anchored off it is a Chinese junk.

Illustrated London News
THE "SOVEREIGN OF THE SEAS," 1853

A Currier and Ives print *Daniel McFarlane*
THE "DREADNOUGHT" OFF TUSKAR LIGHT, 1856
Two of the finest clipper-ships of the Golden Age of Sail.

bond the cost of the care of poverty-stricken passengers. The most prominent result of this legislation, however, was the development of what would now be termed a "racket"—the disreputable trade of insuring captains against the forfeit of any part of their bond. This was achieved by lodging the destitute in the worst of boarding-houses, where they experienced the harshest treatment amid degrading conditions; but as their care did not fall upon the city, ship captains saved a great deal of money that would otherwise have been forfeited, although at the same time the intent of the law was almost entirely evaded. In 1832 a tax of one dollar per immigrant was made optional, and was collected from shipmasters who preferred the direct levy to the former method. A few years later $2.00, and then $2.50, was the amount of the tax, which was either included in the passage money or charged directly to the immigrant; while the trade of providing disreputable accommodations and insuring the captain against loss went on, over three-fourths of the money collected finding its way, apparently, into the pockets of captains or brokers. At the middle of the century, when emigration from the British Isles reached its peak, the tax was $1.50 per passenger.

The Quarantine Station on Staten Island, nine miles from the city, was better organized and less congested than those in the British Provinces, as would be expected in a country so much further advanced economically; and the immigrants were consequently not subject to the same inconveniences and delays. "You will be pleased," states a guidebook, "with the exceeding beauty of the scenery all around, and the magnificent bay before you, where as many as 100 sails are to be seen lying at anchor." Though he had no opportunity to make a close personal inspection, James Hopkirk bore out the truth of this statement, finding that "nothing can be more beautiful than the appearance of the Hospitals—the buildings are handsome and are surrounded by very beautiful weeping willows." Richard Weston was similarly impressed, but found that "on a nearer view the charm was lost," though everything was "remarkably clean." The sick were kept in quarantine until they had fully recovered, while on Ward's Island was the clearing-house where "healthy emigrants are sent to wait until they can be disposed of at work in the interior of the country. Here they rest, with light employment and under good regulations till they recover from the effects of voyages made in crowded ships." The delay on Ward's Island, however, was not as lengthy as here intimated, but in a day or two the well steerage passengers usually proceeded to New York.[3] In 1855 Castle Garden became the great immigrant depot, and Ward's was the site of the hospital where those were sent whose illness or destitute circumstances might result in their becoming a public charge. In September, 1858, "a disgraceful riot" occurred on Staten Island. The report having been spread that there were a number of yellow fever patients at the Quarantine Station, a group of the inhabitants of the island, "anxious to get rid of the whole establishment, used sword, pistol and fire to accomplish their vicious purpose." The buildings were destroyed, but the State Government decided to rebuild them on the same site, "although to the annoyance of a few individuals." It was not until 1891 that Ellis Island became the Quarantine Station.

There was also the Customs examination at Staten Island, but it was to a large extent a good-natured formality; and while their less fortunate fellow-travellers of the steerage were suffering detention, the cabin passengers, as at Quebec, were being accorded preferential treatment and proceeding into the country with but slight interruption. Thomas Need refers to the courtesy and speed of the inspection, and James Hopkirk considered that "nothing could be more gentlemanlike" than the cursory examination which his luggage received; while Charles Dickens, who landed at Boston, and who certainly could not be said to have gone out of his way to compliment the people of the United States, was high in his praise of the conduct of officials at the ports of entry:

"In all the public establishments of America the utmost courtesy prevails. Most of our Departments are susceptible of considerable improvement in this respect, but the Custom-house above all others would do well to take example from the United States and render itself somewhat less odious and offensive to foreigners. The servile rapacity of the French officials is sufficiently contemptible; but there is a surly, boorish incivility about our men, alike disgusting to all persons who fall into their hands and discreditable to the nation that keeps such ill-conditioned curs snarling about its gates. When I landed in America, I could not help being strongly impressed with the contrast their Custom-house presented, and the attention, politeness and good humour with which its officers discharged their duty."[4]

In common with other ports, New York suffered severely during the epidemics of cholera and fever. Immigrants who arrived in the late summer of 1822 found that an epidemic of yellow fever had

[3] The *Tennessee* was held in quarantine three days, and the cabin passengers, who had gone on by steamer, had to wait in New York until their luggage came up with them. (Diary of James Hopkirk, September 2-5, 1835, in Calvin, *Atlantic Crossing, 1835*.)
[4] Among the few who were not in agreement with these sentiments was Thomas Ashe, an early traveller who says he experienced "search, extortion and pillage." (*Travels in America Performed in 1806*, I 60.)

frightened the inhabitants so greatly that "out of a population of 120,000, not more than 7 or 8000 remained in the city." The streets were "nothing endued with life" except "here and there a cat, . . . the only inhabitants of a great part of the city."[5]

The course of events in the ship-fever year, 1847, indicates careful management on the part of the Commissioners of Emigration which contrasts very favorably with the congestion at Grosse Isle. In the first place stringent sanitary regulations and other restrictions were enforced at American ports, so that when the plague broke out, many overcrowded vessels bound for New York altered their destination to the St. Lawrence, where two or three times as many might be landed as in the United States. Such protective measures saved American ports from the calamity which descended upon Montreal, though the disease was widespread enough to require extensive hospital accommodation. In New York all the quarantine hospitals were first filled with the ill and destitute; then all spare rooms connected with the City Almshouse were rented at $1 per week for those who were destitute and $1.50 per week for the sick. But the risk attendant upon placing fever patients in the Almshouse led to the construction of special buildings on Staten Island. As these were still inadequate, the buildings on the Long Island Farms were leased, but the fear of contagion so alarmed the neighborhood that they were burned by incendiaries. The United States Government then permitted the use of warehouses at the Quarantine Station; and when they were almost immediately filled, all the chief hospitals, public and private, were called into requisition. Finally, at the height of the plague, a large stone building on Ward's Island was leased, which, with structures subsequently added to it, afforded ample accommodation for all.

The Commissioners did not, however, stop at the provision of shelter. Between May and the middle of September, 10,308 pieces of clothing were made under their direction on Ward's Island and furnished to destitute immigrants; while hundreds of men were given employment in the interior of the state, or were forwarded to the West free of charge. Over 100,000 immigrants entered at New York between May 5th and September 30th, 1847, of whom 43,208 were German and 40,820 Irish. A total of 6,761 were sent to hospital or otherwise relieved, and of these nearly 60 per cent were Irish. The deaths in the same period were 703, and almost

[5] [Beaufoy], *Travels through the United States and Canada*, 9-10. John Duncan refers to the same epidemic, and states that the village of Greenwich, "about a mile above the city," was established as a retreat from yellow fever. (*Travels through Part of the United States*, 311.)

the only oversight in the work of the Commissioners appears to have been the failure to publish the names and other particulars relative to the dead, and to make any provision for the erection of memorials over their graves.[6]

The approach to the city of New York has always been very impressive. "The sail up the Hudson," wrote James Hopkirk, "is truly beautiful—fine hills—magnificent trees—it resembled most the Largs side of the Clyde at that place. In short, one might fancy the Hudson and its Banks like a man in the prime of manhood, and the Clyde an infant—bearing such resemblance as an infant bears to a man." A few years later a more famous visitor, Mrs. Frances Trollope, whose seven weeks' voyage from London to New Orleans in 1827 was "favourable, though somewhat tedious," wrote that her imagination was "incapable of conceiving anything of the kind more beautiful than the harbour of New York. Various and lovely are the objects which meet the eye on every side. . . . I doubt if even the pencil of Turner could do it justice, bright and glorious as it rose upon us." Perhaps this impression was the more remarkable since it came from one who saw little to praise, and whose estimate of most things American was, like that of Charles Dickens and a few lesser writers, rather insultingly critical.

As the *John Dennison* sailed up the harbor after passing the medical inspection, a lighter approached and transferred the steerage passengers and their baggage to Staten Island for Customs examination. This proved to be the usual cursory inspection, and baggage and immigrants were once more stowed aboard the lighter. Richard Weston describes subsequent events:

"At sun-down we made sail for New York. The wind chopt round right a-head of us; we had to beat, but the tide was with us; the spray broke incessantly over us, and the rain began to descend. It was half-past ten before we arrived at the quay. Here we were landed in the dark, the rain pouring upon us, and our luggage strewed all around. The shops, if there were any at hand, were all shut, and we had no one to direct us where to proceed. We had therefore no alternative than to pass the night where we were in the open air. As the spray was occasionally dashing over the wharf, I constructed a barricade of the trunks belonging to myself and two fellow-passengers, . . . over which I put some deals which were lying on the wharf. Under the lee of this shed we placed the female passenger who was ill of a fever; and having procured a pitcher I proceeded into the town in search of water, and some wine for the woman. This I procured from a shop which I found still open, together with a bottle of brandy and some bread and cheese. Myriads of rats kept squeaking and frisking about and

[6] *Report of the Commissioners of Emigration at New York, October 1st, 1847.* The number of fever patients admitted to the Deer Island Hospital, Boston, up to January 26, 1848, was 2,230, of whom 347 died and were buried on the island. (Report of the Deer Island Hospital, Boston, for the week ending January 26th, 1848.)

over us all night; one of them captured a piece of cheese from my knee while I was at supper.

"Here then were we, one hundred and sixteen souls, landed with our luggage in a wet, cold, and stormy night on a wooden quay in New York, where we had to bivouack under the canopy of heaven. . . . Indeed we got a cold reception—yet we had each paid five shillings as hospital money, and God knows such a night as this was sufficient to have fitted one and all of us for the benefits of that institution. In fact two of our party only survived a few days. Our Captain had taken a dexterous method to get quit of us. . . . Having recruited ourselves by eating bread and cheese and drinking some spirits and water, . . . we creeped under the lee of our barricade of chests and trunks and endeavoured to compose ourselves to rest, for to sleep was out of the question. . . .

"About 3 a.m. the rain ceased and the wind lulled considerably. At length day broke, and objects soon became visible. We found that we had been put ashore at the south end of Washington Street, near the Battery. . . . I went into the town and inquired for a furnished room. On going along the quay, I passed two other encampments of emigrants in Washington Street; some of them were lying huddled together under carts, some within the recesses of doors, and some on the bare pavement. I enquired at a good-looking elderly woman who was lying on the pavement—her head bare, and her long grey hair fluttering in the breeze—how long it was since she landed; and she answered in German that it was six nights, and that her party had lain all that time in the streets."

Upon his return Weston found that two scoundrels were making off with his baggage, which he secured only by threatening to run them through with his umbrella. He was, in fact, in no pleasant mood: for an innkeeper had just attempted to cheat him out of his change for a three-penny glass of rum; and that night, in a room with three others, "bugs and fleas were creeping over me in every direction." Twenty hours after he and his companions had been dumped ashore in this miserable fashion, the ship which should have brought them to the docks appeared at the quay, but nothing could then be done about the matter.

William Brown describes a debarkation of a more usual nature. As the vessel approached the wharves a rope was thrown and tied, whereupon "a gang of 300 or 400 ruffians, calling themselves runners," jumped on board and, "in the style of plunderers or pirates," seized all baggage and endeavored to persuade the passengers to go to such-and-such a lodging-house. There followed swearing, fighting and general confusion "as great as ever was heard at Babel." The appearance of the men was "as disgusting as their horrid oaths." They were "without coats, without cravats, with shirt necks flying open, a large roll of tobacco in each cheek, the juice from which, exuding down the corners of their mouths, adds to the unsightliness of their cadaverous aspect. They principally seem of a mongrel breed, half Indian and half Irish." They received a York shilling (6½d.) per head for alluring travellers to the various inns and grog-shops; and made the remainder of their living "by stealing trunks from passengers, which they call *playing at Trunk loo*. . . . The steerage passengers of our vessel lost about twenty-seven trunks by these gentry, and some contained all the money they had in the world."

"It would," wrote a commentator, "literally require volumes to recount the nefarious doings of these prowling harpies. . . . A runner is a man who is desirous of assisting you with your baggage, who professes to know a great deal, and who advises you to go to a particular hotel, eating-place or boarding-house with which he is connected. In reality he belongs to a class of tormentors, cheats and money-suckers—as annoying and far more dangerous than if you were threatened with an attack by a wolf, offered up to the stings of a hive of wasps, or seduced into the folds of a rattlesnake."

Stories of misadventure at the hands of such people soon exaggerated the danger. "Hundreds of pickpockets were on the lookout," wrote George Moore in his diary in describing his arrival at New York; while thirty-five years later, in 1879, Robert Louis Stevenson was "at first amused, and then somewhat staggered, by the cautious and grisly tales that went the round" as the iron sail-and-steam ship upon which he was travelling approached New York. An apprehensive attitude had become traditional, the natural result of the villainous activities of several generations of sharpers, and many considered it best to regard all but officials as potential swindlers; though since 1855 the Castle Garden immigrant clearing-house had greatly improved conditions of entry.

Earlier used as a fort, as a circus, a theater, and as a place of public meeting, this depot was financed largely by the head tax levied on immigrants, together with a commission of 20 per cent paid by transport companies on the sale of tickets. As a guidebook says, "No one can properly appreciate the interest it takes in the emigrant and the assistance it renders him, . . . unless he had been witness to the truly fearful scenes which occurred on the landing of a shipload of emigrants, with their baggage, previous to its establishment." Here the stranger was given information to guide him to his destination, and sold the proper ticket to enable him to reach it in the most expeditious manner; if he was sick he was transported to Ward's Island, where he was maintained at the public charge until his recovery; while if he wished to obtain advice as to suitable boarding-house or hotel accommodation it was available without the very questionable help of "runners." The authorities approved "3 boarding-houses where British emigrants, and 3 others where German emigrants can be recommended to go."

Loss of baggage was a common disaster before the opening of

Castle Garden. Upon a vessel's arrival she was boarded by an official who issued checks for all baggage, which was then claimed by the owner at his convenience. Many remained a few days at Castle Garden rather than spending their remaining cash for accommodations, and at times 2,000 people slept on bench or floor, and availed themselves of washing-rooms, free hot water, and supplies of milk, bread, cheese, sausages, tea, and coffee at lowest possible prices. The institution was in charge of a superintendent appointed by the Emigration Commissioners, and was carefully organized in the matter of registering the immigrants. The penniless were loaned sums varying from $2 to $50 on the security of their baggage, for terms of from a few weeks to two years, without interest. Small children, sent to join relatives, were taken under the charge of officials, and, "with a label fastened round their bodies showing their destination, forwarded like express parcels." There were, of course, plenty of cases of misfortune and disappointment, but the American was quite justified who, thinking of conditions at British ports of debarkation, observed that "Great Britain has something yet to do in affording some such protection and assistance, . . . and out of the books of Castle Garden, in republican New York, we think she may take a lesson or two with some advantage."

Various private agencies also worked to alleviate distress among immigrants. The Ohio Philanthropic Association, with headquarters in Cleveland, had a branch in New York, and others in various important centers—even in Liverpool. In the early 1840's an association composed of "respectable English residents of New York" made an effort to protect immigrants from waterfront crimps. One lady wrote home that although her family had but 4s. 6d. when they reached America in 1816, yet they were well dressed and "several genteel persons stopped us to kiss the children and bid us welcome"; while her husband obtained immediate work as a stone-cutter.

New York, the great melting-pot of the nation, presented many contrasts which seemed peculiar even to those who had seen something of the world; though others were characteristic of North American cities and surprised only such visitors as were entirely unfamiliar with the customs of the new land. Richard Weston emphasizes the distinctions of the latter class:

"The pavement was composed partly of brick and partly of flag-stones, but in considerable disrepair. . . . At half-past 4 a.m. the people began to stir. . . . The newsmen were running about with newspapers. . . . Numbers of pigs were strolling about in every direction.⁷ . . . I counted sixty-seven lottery offices in Broadway. . . . Several cows were going about picking their food from the refuse on the streets; indeed they and their swinish brethren seemed to enjoy the liberty of the country, and were often to be seen lounging about in the most fashionable places. . . . A fire-engine passed me drawn by a number of men, some of whom carried speaking-trumpets and roared through them most hideously. . . . After church on Sundays the aristocracy of New York have an opportunity of attending either of two concerts held in the gardens, one in the Bowery, called Vauxhall Gardens, and the other in Broadway, a little beyond Broome Street, on the same side with the Park. The music is very melodious; and between the interludes the bar-rooms are crowded. You are charged one shilling for refreshments, but nothing for the singers—the bar-keeper pays them. Smoking and spitting are carried on to a great extent. . . . During the forenoon I went to a church on Broadway. Few were yet present; and I went to an empty seat. Shortly thereafter several females came to the same seat and stared at me, but went into one either before or behind me. . . . I thought, surely the American women must be chaste when they will not sit and worship God beside a man."⁸

But while Richard Weston was in no mood to see the best side of things, many others were more favorably impressed. James Hopkirk, while depreciating the lighting and paving, admired the City Hall and Broadway, which a century ago bore considerable resemblance to the Boulevards of Paris. When Mary Gapper approached the harbor in 1828, most of the city was concealed by trees, and upon landing, it appeared to her "very like the children's plaything city." She was surprised to find "everything and everybody so perfectly English." The Earl of Carlisle considered New York "a very brilliant city. To give the best idea of it I should describe it as something of a fusion between Liverpool and Paris— crowded quays, long perspectives of vessels and masts, bustling streets, gay shops, tall white houses, and a clear brilliant sky overhead."

William Brown accepted the recommendation of a friend as to a lodging-house on South Street with "good accommodation" for immigrants. "But next morning," he wrote, "we were in a most woful state; the beds were full of bugs, which bit some of us severely. We had also a legacy of great grey lice; and worse than all, the mosquitoes sung all the night, and bit every one of us upon every part which was exposed. That night was indeed a torment." Mary Gapper, on the other hand, was fortunate in being conducted by the captain to a boarding-house "at one end of the famous

---

⁷ W. N. Blane also emphasizes the hogs, referring to the lower part of the town as "notoriously filthy." (*An Excursion through the United States*, 12.) William Brown observed that the odor in the streets was "so insupportable that almost every merchant of condition lives out of town." (*America: a Four Years' Residence*, 5.)

⁸ In a similar vein Sir Richard Bonnycastle states that "an especial Act of Congress" forbade American ladies to admit "such words as *naked* or *legs* into their vocabulary." (*Canada and the Canadians*, II 149.)

ENTERING AT NEW YORK

Broadway," where she greatly enjoyed the meals and service, criticising only the "lack of implements" to eat with.

The hotels supplied more luxurious accommodation for those who could afford it. In 1820, and for some years afterwards, the City Hotel was "the best and most fashionable place of resort for travellers." John Howison described it as

"a large brick building, four stories high, containing a splendid dining saloon and a magnificent drawing-room, each 85 feet in length, a billiard room, several suites of apartments for private families, and more than 100 bed-chambers. Upwards of 80 people breakfast and dine there every day at the public table during the summer months; and the charge for board and lodging is ten dollars a week, for which four meals a day are furnished in the best possible style."

But Howison strenuously objected to *table d'hôtes*, where everyone ate the same food at the same time and in a public place. It was possible, however, if you chose to pay more than double the rate, to have food served to you at other than meal times. Lieutenant De Roos stopped at the City Hotel, "the principal inn," in 1826, and found much to condemn:

"The house is immense and was full of company; but what a wretched place! The floors were without carpets, the beds without curtains; there was neither glass, mug, nor cup, and a miserable little rag was dignified with the name of towel. The entrance to the house is constantly obstructed by crowds of people passing to and from the bar-room."

As the years passed, more and more hostelries competed for the trade. James Hopkirk stayed at Holt's Hotel in 1835 and, like many another Britisher, he disliked American cooking and the speed with which meals were eaten. By 1847 there was the Astor House, "unrivalled as to extent and splendour," while the Howard Hotel was one of those "quite as comfortable" but "more circumscribed in its dimensions and moderate in its charges." In the late 1850's the Brevoort House, at Fifth Avenue and 8th Street, was recommended as "very comfortable and quiet, . . . fitted up for 100 guests. . . . Largely patronized by English families, . . . who prefer the European plan. . . . Has a magnificent 'coffee-room' where all meals are served." The Clarendon Hotel, Union Square, had "no less than 80 bath rooms," and "parties can be accommodated comfortably in elegant apartments." Lefarge House, Broadway opposite Bond Street, was "one of the most magnificent white marble-fronted hotels in New York, elegantly furnished and fitted up."

Thousands of immigrants did not know where to turn for work.

An Address to the People of Ireland[9] warned against those by whom many a person had been "plundered of his money or induced to invest it in some unsafe and tottering business; or enticed away, if a labourer, to some unwholesome spot, where, after a brief career of toil and vain regrets and unavailing complaint, he falls a victim to the malaria. . . . We need not add that for all persons—in all occupations—temperance, integrity, and the love of peace are indispensable, and that Father Matthew's pledge is as good as the best letter of recommendation."

The inordinate use of liquor was considered the grave of thousands of immigrants. One writer, in stating that it had been "ascertained as a fact" that over one-third of all newcomers died within three years of taking up residence in the United States, waxed eloquent over the evils of intemperance—usually the first step to the poorhouse or the prison:

> "At present, as soon as they land in the seaport town, they are beset with as many harpies as surround the unhappy sailor when he first touches the shore, especially by the keepers of low taverns and dram-shops. By them they are decoyed to their houses, made drunk under the pretext of a welcome and hospitality, their money taken from them if they have any, and, if they have not, a debt for board and drink contracted against them. They then roam about the city in search of employment, where little or none is to be had; they become inspired with a distaste for the country, where alone a sure and certain harvest awaits them; and like the moth which lingers around the flame until consumed by what dazzles it, they hang about the skirts of the cities and the grog shops till their poverty tempts them to crime, when they become the inmates of the poorhouse or the prison, and there end their days in neglect and misery."

The advice to all immigrants was "Go West," for prices were frequently four times as high along the Atlantic seaboard; and while there were comparatively few chances of employment, there were many opportunities to contract vicious habits. But those who sought to get out of New York without delay were not always able to escape misfortune, even if they had ready money; for there were "agents" who sold illusory tickets to imaginary places, or who collected steamboat fares to Albany—but the captain charged you over again, and had a pleasant way of holding your baggage until you paid. There was nothing these people could not offer the immigrant: "One of them could let him have a house and store, if he turned his thoughts to merchandise; another could supply him at a low price with the workshop of a mechanic, a methodist-meeting, or a butcher's shop, if either of these articles would suit him." Then there were the "land-sharks," who recommended that

---
[9] Between 1820 and 1850 two-fifths of all immigrants into the United States were Irish; and during the eighteen-fifties one-third.

you "become a *land-jobber*; and to buy of them a hundred thousand acres on the borders of the Genessee country, and on the banks of *extensive* rivers and *sumptuous* lakes," . . . "which they will describe as the most desirable spots on the continent of America; . . . but lend you a deaf ear to them, or you are sure to be a sufferer." You would shortly find yourself, in the words of another, "located in some rocky, mountainous district, or made fast in a swamp. . . . In Ohio there are farms called *fast* properties—some fair to look at, but which, once paid for, cannot be resold." In short the immigrant had to contend with "a shrewd, knavish people. . . . I am sorry to suggest a relaxation of morality, but you that go had better leave the greater part of that article at home in England."

CHAPTER XIX

THE HUDSON ROUTE

"The whole course of the river is singularly beautiful."
Earl of Carlisle: *Travels in America*
"Equal to any of our European waters—the Rhine not excepted."
G. W. Warr: *Canada As It Is*
"By taking walks along the banks at certain times, travel by Erie Canal tow-boat is altogether as pleasant as any person not in a hurry could wish."
William Brown: *America: A Four Years' Residence*

The "lordly Hudson" long provided the easiest as well as the most beautiful approach to the interior of America. It allowed 150 miles of clear sailing, unobstructed by rapids necessitating portages. John Duncan made the voyage in 1818 in the finest steamship of the day—the 496-ton *Chancellor Livingston*. She was 165 feet long, and with a favourable wind and tide her Fulton engine of "75 horses" drove her along at 12 knots an hour. Built when materials and workmanship were very high, she cost $25,200. The accommodation for passengers is described as follows:

"The principal cabin is 54 feet long and 7 feet from the floor. It accommodates with ease two parallel ranges of dining tables of the full length of the apartment. The Ladies' cabin is upon deck, immediately over the other, and is 36 feet long. The forward cabin is entirely a sleeping apartment, 40 feet long with a longitudinal partition in the centre. The sleeping berths are along the sides of the vessel, in two tiers, ... in all 118, but these are often inadequate to the accommodation of the passengers, and mattresses are laid out upon settees on the floor."

Shortly after leaving the New York wharf the ship passed Hoboken, then Weehawken, a noted duelling-ground where "men of honour, by eluding the laws of men and defying those of God, unanswerably demonstrate the extremity of their courage." In 1818 there was a small white obelisk marking the spot where General Hamilton fell by the hand of Colonel Burr, but it was "going rapidly to decay." Weehawken was described as "a romantic spot about 200 feet above the level of the river, from which a most commanding prospect is enjoyed of the bay and surrounding scenery." About a mile above New York was Greenwich Village, in which were "many neat buildings, the greater part of which, as well as the village itself, were erected in former times as a retreat from the yellow fever." The banks on the right were thickly wooded, while on the left broken and precipitous cliffs soon gave way to "an abrupt wall of granite"—the Palisades—"while here and there a solitary pine tree, 'moor'd on the rifted rock,' seems, like the banner of a citadel, to wave a proud defiance from the edge of the cliff." Tappan Bay—the Tappaan Zee of Dutch times—with woodland banks of rich luxuriance, provided scenery of another kind, and "country seats and snug farm houses, flanked by capacious barns," as well as Sing Sing prison, were to be seen on its shores. Along the banks were a multitude of "thriving little towns" with wharfs projecting into the water, at which sloops and barges were forever loading or discharging. Rounding Verplank's Point, the steamship was soon surrounded by the Highlands of the Hudson, and Fort Putnam, prominent in the Revolutionary War, was passed on the left, to be closely followed by West Point Military Academy. Sugar Loaf Mountain, Crow's Nest, Butter Hill, and Anthony's Nose were soon in the rear as the *Chancellor Livingston* paddle-wheeled along; and during a moonlit night the Kaatskills, together with a number of little towns, were passed. Albany was reached at 9 a.m., just 24 hours from New York.

Most early immigrants did not go by steamship, however, for the fare was high. John Duncan paid $7, plus a state tax of $1 to aid in cutting the Erie Canal. His cabin passage included a berth and three meals, but there was no second cabin or steerage; poorer travellers went by barge or sloop. Hudson River sloops were described as

"proverbial for their neatness. They are not deep in the water, but very broad in the beam and sharp in the bows; carrying a large cargo and giving space for a comfortable cabin, but drawing little water and sailing fast. The rigging is abundant and in excellent order, the vessel clean, showily painted, and occasionally decorated with a handsome figurehead; altogether very superior in appearance to any of our (Scottish) river craft. The number that are employed upon this river has been estimated at 2,000 of 40 tons and upward."

Before the introduction of steam, a sloop took from two to five days to reach Albany and usually charged from $6 to $10, including meals and berths but not baggage.

The open nature of the Hudson made towing easy, and one or more tugs frequently hauled a "floating town" of canal boats, hay barges, or ice boats, four or five abreast and perhaps stretching out nearly half a mile. In one case 108 vessels were towed in one group. Many immigrants travelled by barge. A settler in New York State wrote that he engaged passage in a tow-boat "and slept on board that night. As she did not start for several days, we saved the expense of hiring lodgings. I gave 1 dollar each, half-price for children, and 6d. per 100 lbs. of luggage to Albany, 160 miles." A typical "runner" fraud was the sale of railway or steamboat tickets which turned out to be for barge and canal boat. Many destitute immigrants worked their way up the Hudson by tow-boat, and in 1826 the *Albany Advertiser* protested against the presence of large numbers of them in the city:

> "The picture of distress which these immigrants present on their arrival here is almost indescribable; and by many of our citizens great blame is attached to the commanders of our river craft for bringing them from New York and landing them upon our wharfs, knowing them to be destitute of a single cent to secure themselves a mouthful to eat; the consequence of which is they are next seen begging through our streets in the most loathsome and abject state of filth and misery. It appears that they beg in the city of New York until they get a few shillings, or sufficient to induce a captain of a tow-boat or some other craft to bring them to Albany, where they are left to depend upon Providence, or their ingenuity in the art of begging, in which, by the way, most of them are adepts."

One early traveller, however, found the town itself almost as forlorn as the worst of immigrants. The Capitol was "an unfinished proof of poverty—broken windows, broken steps without railing, . . . a shade in summer and shed in winter to pigs, cows, marbles, tops and schoolboys." Originally considered attractive for passengers because of immunity from "bursting boilers," tow-boats shortly became almost as large and palatial as steamers. Attached to the stern of a steamship by two six-foot timbers bolted across her bow, the luxurious barge *Lady Clinton* carried Thomas L. McKenney up the Hudson in June, 1826:

> "I was struck with the admirable invention, and with the extent and variety and perfection of the accommodations. . . . The Cabin in which we dined is below, and 180 persons can sit down at once. . . . Towards the bow is a bar, most sumptuously supplied with all that can be desired by the most fastidious and thirsty. The berths occupy the entire sides of this vast room; they are curtained in such a way as to afford retirement in dressing and undressing. . . . Next above these are the ladies' cabin and apartments—staterooms rather—furnished in the most splendid style, and in which a lady has all the retirement and comfort which the delicacy and tenderness of her sex requires. . . . It is not possible for New York to furnish in her best hotels a better dinner than we sat down to yesterday, nor in a better style of preparation. . . . Taken altogether I question whether the world ever witnessed anything so perfect in all that relates to the accommodation and comfort and pleasure of passengers."

Possibly Mr. McKenney travelled on a pass, to account for his enthusiasm! Otherwise he was fortunate, for travel by barge

> "was not always the height of enjoyment. Progress was slow, and the boats

THE HUDSON ROUTE

latterly carried a varied cargo of farm products, baled hay and livestock. Calves and lambs bound for the city slaughter houses, and horses for the New York street car lines—the Third Avenue line had three thousand horses in its stables alone—frequently made such a chorus of 'bahing,' bleating and neighing that rendered futile any attempt to sleep in the 'stateroom' in the 'grand saloon' on the upper deck."

The world's earliest successful steam packet was Robert Fulton's *Clermont*, which ran on the Hudson in 1807. Sloop and stage-coach travel suffered considerably, and the sloops took revenge by obstructing the *Clermont's* passage and fouling her. Progress could not be held back by such methods, however, and by 1826 there were sixteen steam vessels on the Hudson. With their development the activities of "runners" were intensified. Originally it cost as much as $10 for a passage to Albany, but the rivalry of competing ships sometimes forced the fare down to 10¢—or nothing at all, provided one spent a little for meals or accommodation. So intense was the competition that a man sometimes travelled by one line while his "carpet bag" went by another; and the inducements offered varied from the promise of a steamboat journey all the way to Buffalo to the assurance of nervous old ladies that the steamships had no boilers to burst! The departure of a steamer from New York provided an amazing scene for the British traveller:

"Fifteen minutes before the starting of the boat there is not a passenger on board. . . . The American arrives on the narrow pier at the same instant with seven hundred men, ladies and children, besides lapdogs, crammed baskets, uncut novels, and baggage for the whole. No commissioner in the world would guarantee to get all this freight on board in the given time, and yet it is done, to the daily astonishment of newspaper hawkers, orange-women, and penny-a-liners watching for dreadful accidents. The plank is drawn in, the wheels begin to paw like foaming steeds impatient to be off, the bell rings as if it was letting down the steps of the last hackney-coach, and away darts the boat, like half a town suddenly slipping off and taking a walk in the water. The 'hands' trip up all the little children and astonished maids in coiling up the hawser; and the black head-waiter rings a hand-bell as if he were crazy, exhorting 'them passengers as hasn't settled, to step to the Cap'n's office and settle.' "

In 1840 there were about 100 steamships on the Hudson, varying from the "magnificent floating palace" downwards. For about twenty years they were at the height of their glory, making the trip to Albany in from 9 to 12 hours, carrying as many as 1,000 passengers. Many boats offered popular music by steam calliope—an expensive nuisance that exhausted the steam essential for the paddle-wheels. The average Britisher was rather shocked at the speed with which meals were eaten. William Brown, who travelled on the *Empire*, "largest in the world," describes meal-time as follows:

"The meals are spread in an immense saloon, and partaken of by all who chose to pay. The sight of a meal as set out upon one of these boats is worth seeing. I had never beheld so large a company, nor a table set out in so superb a style. . . . But this entertainment was very transient. I should think that after the supper had commenced not five minutes had elapsed before one-half of the guests had 'got fed' and were leaving their seats. . . . When you sit down to a meal in America at a public table you must proceed to business instanter; . . . scarce a word is spoken, and everybody falls to upon what is before or near him, . . . and minds nobody's business but his own. All sorts of meat, beef, pork, pickles, apple sauce, butter, cheese, potatoes, tomatoes and pudding are all on their plates at once; and when they arise from the table there is perhaps twice as much on each plate as each guest has eaten. . . . No quarter is given or asked."

Another contrast was apparent in the American's chivalry towards women. An Englishman noted that while in English steamboats "the ladies are generally worse accommodated than the stronger sex," it was quite the reverse in America:

"No man is admitted into the dining saloon until all the ladies are seated at the table, when they rush in pellmell. After that, should a lady require either, the chair is without ceremony taken from you and the plate from before you. . . . The Americans pride themselves on their courtesy to women and consider it a sign of high civilization; and they are no doubt right, but it seemed to me to be carried to an extreme; that women are treated like petted children, and that they must often feel rather annoyed than pleased by the excessive politeness and consideration shown them."

In spite of the cheapness of the fare, there were ways of cheating the passenger, particularly the unsuspecting immigrant. "On the American lakes and rivers," wrote Sidney Smith, "the steamers and canal boats swarm with miscreants who lie in wait either to steal the emigrant's money or to cheat him out of it." Although William Brown was told that the 25-cent fare included his baggage, on approaching Albany he was charged $7 for extra weight, and his goods were held until he paid it, a procedure which he considered "direct robbery."

The approach to Albany provided an imposing scene. One traveller wrote that

"a distant view of this city from any quarter is rich, but particularly from the river side, from which the noble gilt and tinned domes of two of the public buildings appear splendid in the extreme. The effect is much heightened by the rich gold colour of the one being contrasted with the silver white of the other. The City Hall is a fine white marble structure which adds greatly to the ornamental part of the city."

The immigrant's impression of Albany was possibly colored by less attractive features than the scenery, however. The association

From Willis' American Scenery, 1840   *W. H. Bartlett*
THE PALISADES, HUDSON RIVER

Navigation by sloop, barge, and steamship was highly developed.

From Willis' American Scenery, 1840   *W. H. Bartlett*
ALBANY IN 1837

The spires and domes of the New York State capital were among the many attractive landmarks.

"LOW BRIDGE!"
In spite of certain inconveniences, travel by canal packet was "altogether as pleasant as any person not in a hurry could wish."

From Willis American Scenery, 1840   W. H. Bartlett
THE ERIE CANAL NEAR LITTLE FALLS

On a moonlit evening in this romantic region, travel by tow-boat to the musical accompaniment of the captain's organ was indeed the poetry of motion.

THE HUDSON ROUTE

that many of them vividly recalled was "that of having lost a portmanteau there." We have a lively description of the landing:

"The north-river steamboats land you with from three to seven hundred passengers upon a narrow pier in the dusk of the evening, where you find from three to seven hundred individuals (more or less), each of whom seems to have no other object in life than to persuade you, at that particular instant, to go to a certain conveyance, or to stop at a certain hotel. . . . One of the most amusing scenes in the world, if it were not so distressing, is to see a large family of rather respectable emigrants landed by the steamer in Albany. They yield their children and baggage to the persuasive gentleman who assures them that all is right. . . . At the end of five minutes the crowd thins a little, and he looks about for his family and effects. A stagecoach is dashing off in one direction, with his eldest daughter stretching out of the window and crying in vain that there is some mistake; his two youngest are on board a steamboat just off from the pier, and bound eight miles further up the river; the respectable part of his baggage has entirely disappeared; and nothing but his decrepit grandmother and the paternal bedstead (both indebted for their escape to being deaf and not portable), remain of his family and chattels. For his comfort the gentry around him inform him that his children may be got back in a day or two, and he may find his baggage somewhere on his route to the West!"

Before the construction of the Erie Canal the modes of travel on the lakes and rivers northward and westward from Albany were as various and primitive as on all other North American waterways. In fur-trading days the Hudson, Mohawk, and tributary rivers formed the canoe route from New York and Fort Orange (Albany) to Chouéguen (Oswego),—the name Canada Creek implies the trail to Canada. By this route hundreds of United Empire Loyalists escaped northward, and other early emigrants to Upper Canada followed. Thomas Horner, who settled in Oxford County in 1796,

"packed his goods in two small roughly-made boats which he launched on the River Hudson near Albany, proceeded up the Hudson to the River Mohawk, and up said river about 100 miles; then carried goods and boats across the Norval Creek, thence down the Norval Creek to Lake Oneida, across the lake to the Oswego River, thence into Lake Ontario."

Flat-bottomed vessels of various sizes were used on the Mohawk system. The "dorms" were similar to Durham boats; while Schenectady boats and flatboats were much the same as those employed on the Susquehanna, and like the Canadian bateaux. Laboriously rowed, poled, and sailed along, they provided a slow but fairly satisfactory means of transit for heavy freight. To reach Schenectady, however, it was necessary to travel from Albany over a "very good turnpike road." On this fifteen-mile stretch large numbers of wagoners, who had the reputation of being "great rogues," hauled freight. Those who could afford it would continue north-westward by wagon in preference to the more tedious flatboats. In October, 1818, John Duncan went to Buffalo by stage in six days "with great ease and comfort," and again in May, 1819, in ten days "with great difficulty and distress."

After many years of construction the Erie Canal system was opened in 1825. The inauguration of the 362-mile waterway connecting the Hudson River and Lake Erie occurred on October 26th, when a gay flotilla of canal boats set out from Buffalo for New York. The marriage of fresh-water Lake Erie and the salt-water Atlantic was solemnized by the pouring of a barrelful into the ocean. New York City and other centers celebrated with grand illuminations and fireworks. No public improvement had so captured the public imagination for many a year. Wallpaper illustrated scenes along the completed canal, and bandboxes of similar design commemorated the opening of the waterway.

The route of the canal and the points of interest are well described by John Duncumb, who made the trip when canals were at the height of their usefulness. After leaving Albany there was some delay while the boat weighed in at the dock; whereupon the horses towed the boats along with but little interruption. The next point of interest was the United States Arsenal, near "the large and flourishing town of Troy." Rocky and precipitous banks attracted the attention. At the junction with the Champlain Canal there were double locks, and the "hurry and bustle" of the canal men as they locked boats through was of great interest to the average immigrant.

The canal now changed its direction westward, and the scenery became "more delightful as the splendid cataract of the Mohawk River gives animation to the scene." An aqueduct over 1,000 feet long carried the waterway over the Mohawk, which was recrossed on another shortly after. As Schenectady was approached the scenery became "romantic in the extreme" and "truly terrific," "highly imposing" and "almost indescribable." The 27-mile trip took 11 hours and there were some twenty locks, but Mr. Duncumb considered that the beautiful scenery more than compensated for the delays of canal travel.

The first point of interest beyond Schenectady was Schoharie Creek, "wild and inhospitable." Owing to a very rapid current a "singular rope ferry" was necessary to cross the Mohawk: "A wheel turned by a horse moves a rope which is stretched double across the river and is carried round a wheel on the opposite side; a line attached to this draws the boats, and another rope keeps them in their course." Soon after, the tow-boat passed St. Anthony's Nose, "a name apparently particularly pleasing to the Americans, for it is the third mountain from hence to New York which bears that name." Fort Plain, once a stronghold of the Oneidas, recalled Butler's Rangers and the atrocities of Cherry Valley; and there followed Little Falls, "a great treat to the admirer of wild scenery." After passing through the "improving town of Utica," the canal ran 70 miles without a lock. The Mohawk was crossed once more, and "innumerable log-built villages" caught the eye at frequent intervals; and for some sixty miles "rapid but recent acts of industry" showed that much of the country was in process of settlement.

At Syracuse many bound for Upper Canada took the Oswego Canal northward. Because of its extensive salt works the town was "destined to be an important place." Between Syracuse and Rochester was "a long tract of wild country, low, swampy and unhealthy." Stagnant water held back by the canal embankment had killed the trees for many miles along the route, and they presented "a world of naked masts, . . . a most melancholy and dreary appearance." Rochester, dating from 1812, had had an "astonishingly sudden growth." An aqueduct described as " a grand work of immense magnitude" carried the canal over the Genesee River. Sixty-three miles beyond was Lockport, where there was a rise of 62 feet by double locks, the canal being blasted through solid rock which rose from five to forty feet high on either side for several miles. The next important town was Black Rock, where travellers for Niagara Falls and Canada crossed the river by steam packet to Chippewa, while the Erie Canal continued three miles farther to Buffalo, terminating on the shores of Lake Erie.

Tow-boat transport differed from bateau travel largely in being more civilized: for while the crews might at times merit the description, "the greatest blackguards in language and manners of any in the world," they were an improvement over the undisciplined bateaumen; and the accommodations and the absence of exceptional difficulties made the Erie Canal journey in many respects a pleasure trip. One traveller was impressed by the absence of "perceptible motion, jar, or smell of steam"; and he considered this type of transport, although "the least popular," "the most delightful of all modes of travelling in America." In the heyday of the canal some 35,000 people were employed during the navigation season, spending the other five months chopping wood, threshing grain, or loafing in boarding-houses, where they lived upon the summer's wages or "the proceeds of sundry trunks which travellers occasionally lose sight of," and then finished the vacation "on the credit system." Some 10,000 horses towed the boats, which numbered at least 5,000. There were four main types of tow-boat, with a speed corresponding to their size and use. Flat-bottomed scows, each with a stable and three or four horses aboard, provided a regular freight service. Large privately-owned barges were operated by individual companies, and averaged about forty miles per day if they did not have to make an undue number of stops. Passenger vessels, which usually carried freight as well, were known as line boats and fly boats. Relays of two horses every eight or nine miles enabled the line boats to travel sixty miles a day; while the packets or fly boats might make eighty miles a day by the use of three horses.[1] It was usual to travel throughout the night.

The typical passenger tow-boat was 60 feet long and 11 feet wide. In the bow was the men's cabin, 12 feet by 10, which contained four double and eight single berths. The ladies' cabin, also in the bow, was 6 feet by 10 and had ten berths. A traveller refers to them as "like shelves in a library," and he found the cabins "beautifully fitted up" and "as convenient as is possible in such small vessels."[2] The center of the boat was usually filled with freight, while the stern was "at once the dining room and serves also for a sleeping room for the captain and men, occasionally for passengers also." "On the best line of passenger tow-boats," observes the same writer, "provisions may be had on board at about 18 cents per meal, but the cheapest plan will be to purchase your own provisions, which you may do at any of the towns as you pass along."[3] Passengers who drank "not infrequently fell into the canal or otherwise forfeited their lives."

The rates on the canal varied from 1 or 1½¢ per mile for an ordinary passage to from 2 to 3 cents for a cabin trip, including meals. Railway competition sometimes forced the fare as low as 1 cent a mile, including "three good meals." Baggage to the amount of 40 pounds was carried free, and children under twelve paid half fare. Immediately after leaving port the passenger was required to

---

[1] John Duncumb states that they travelled 6 miles per hour, which was no doubt correct over a short distance and without any allowance for stops or lockage. In any case the trip of 362 miles to Buffalo usually took 7 or 8 days.
[2] Brown, *America: a Four Years' Residence*, 7-13. Charles Dickens gives an intimate and entertaining account of the accommodations, meals, etc., with which he was supplied on a tow-boat trip in the Susquehanna region. (*American Notes*, Chapters 9 and 10.)
[3] John Duncumb observed that the stores were about four miles apart. His excellent account of the Erie Canal trip may be found in his *The British Emigrant's Advocate*, 327-43.

pay his fare; and it was prohibited to place baggage on the bedding, or to lie down on berths, lockers, or settees with boots on. No smoking was allowed in the cabin, nor any loitering in the stern during cooking hours. Those wishing to board "by the single meal" were requested "to bespeak them in due season." Passengers carrying their own food could not eat it in the fore cabin, but were allowed the use of the table and the kitchen furniture. "Indecorous behaviour or language" was prohibited, especially on the Sabbath; and there was to be no blowing of horns, shouting, nor "anything to offend or disturb the respectable or graver part of the community."

Tow-boat progress, though leisurely, was not without danger. "No passenger is allowed to walk the decks after dark," stated the regulations, "under the penalty of being knocked off by the bridges." William Brown, in the 1840's, quickly discovered that "one great annoyance on this canal is the number of very low bridges you have to go under, when, if you are on deck, you are obliged to lay yourself flat down while you pass through; and many accidents happen to strangers before they understand the shout of the steersman, 'LOW BRIDGE!'" Many bridges were so low "that the smallest trunk can hardly remain safe on the top of the boat"; and so callous was the crew that the knocking off of a passenger was an accident "of daily occurrence, and thought a trifle." Boats were carelessly handled at the locks, where the water was allowed to pour in "in a frightful current." As a consequence, observed John Duncumb, "the cabin was flooded with water" at Fort Plain Locks, and there resulted "great damage to several of the passengers' packages," while the water "had nearly sunk the boat." One captain, although warned by passengers that there was smoke issuing from the cabin, laughed at the suggestion until it was too late to save the boat, which quickly burned to the water's edge, destroying all the possessions of the passengers and leaving them destitute. But accidents were quite exceptional, and there are poetic accounts of the packets' progress through romantic regions like Little Falls in the moonlight—to the accompaniment of music from the captain's organ.

Many travellers on the Canal were bound for Upper Canada, for the route was long preferable to the ascent of the St. Lawrence. There were a number of points where immigrants might leave the main route. At Albany they were advised to obtain a porter or hotel footman to direct the way to canal boats, stage-coach line, or railway station; for even in the early 1830's "Steam Coaches" were available to Schenectady, covering the 16 miles in 1¼ hours —ten less than the 30-mile tow-boat trip. If they had but little baggage it might be preferable to take the railway, but otherwise the best plan was to go direct to the Erie Canal Station, and join other families bound for the same destination. The usual fare from Albany to Oswego was from $2 to $3. From Oswego schooners and steamships sailed to Canadian lake ports, a cabin passage to York being about $6, including meals, and the steerage fare $2. Some immigrants bound for the Eastern Townships of Lower Canada proceeded northward by the Champlain Canal from Troy, continuing by steamer through Lake Champlain and the Richelieu River to St. John's, from which the Champlain and St. Lawrence Railway carried them to La Prairie, and a steam ferry across the river to Montreal. In an earlier day travel over this route was chiefly by large, tulip-wood canoes propelled by poles. Another route to Canada was along the Erie Canal to Lockport, where for about $3 wagons could be hired to convey the women, children, and baggage 21 miles to Young's Town, while the men tramped alongside. At Young's Town the Niagara River could be crossed by ferry, and a steamship passage to York obtained for $1.

In his guidebook of 1844, James B. Brown outlines the railway service available from Albany to Utica, but as the train reached Utica at an inconvenient hour of the night, he advised immigrants "that comfort and economy perhaps may be both consulted by proceeding on the railway no further than Schenectady, about 17 miles from Albany, and here taking a canal packet-boat . . . on board of which the traveller may rest for the night."[4] It was possible, however, for those who could afford it to go by rail from Albany to Buffalo in 25 hours for $11 first class or $5.25 by "emigrant train."

By the middle of the century the whole complexion of interior transport had changed. Two railways were competing for Hudson River traffic, a railroad to Whitehall on Lake Champlain was taking most of the trade from the Champlain Canal, and the Western Railway to Buffalo was providing a faster and cheaper service than the Erie Canal tow-boat. "These boats," observed Mr. Brown in 1851, "are frequently very inconveniently crowded. This, together with their limited and uncomfortable accommodation and length of time on the way, make them anything but a satisfactory means of accommodation for families, or even single persons." The St.

---

[4] Brown, *Views of Canada and the Colonists*, 1844 edition, 265. John Duncumb states that the trip by rail to Schenectady cost only 63 cents.

Lawrence route to Chicago by steamship without trans-shipment was now more expeditious than the Hudson; though in about the same time a steamboat and rail trip from New York might be effected at a slightly higher cost, with the added inconvenience and risk of transferring baggage from Hudson River steamship to railway, and then at Buffalo to steamer again. A few years later, however, both routes had to give way to the comparatively speedy—if most unpleasant—"emigrant train" for the "Far West," a term applied to Chicago at the middle of the century, Omaha or even Salt Lake City ten years later, San Francisco in 1870, and the Canadian prairies in the 1880's.

CHAPTER XX

PROCEEDING TO THE SETTLEMENT

"Cheer up, brother, as we go
Over the Mountains, westward ho!
When we've wood and prairie land
Won by our toil,
We'll reign like Kings in fairyland,
Lords of the soil."
An immigrant chant

It is the merest accident that millions of inhabitants of North America are living in their particular locality, for the considerations that led their ancestors to Virginia, Upper Canada, or the shores of the Missouri were frequently unbelievably trivial. A ship sailing on the day they reached the seaport, the destination of a chance acquaintance, or the suggestion of a propagandist led thousands to embark for New York, Quebec, or New Orleans; while others after their arrival settled the matter of whether they were to be Americans or Canadians—canal laborers, Kansas squatters, prairie farmers, or lumbermen in the wilds of New Brunswick or Minnesota. One writer after investigating wrote that nine-tenths of the immigrants

"have scarce an idea of what they are going about. Of the whole of the emigrant passengers that sailed in the same ship with me, and all of whom were possessed of some means, from £200 to £1000, not one knew where he was like to settle, or anything respecting the country or its productions."

Before the days of steam, interior travel was exceedingly primitive. Many of the earliest to push westward—like the thousands who, following the lead of Daniel Boone, moved from Virginia into Kentucky during the last quarter of the eighteenth century—did not even choose the most expeditious route:

"They shunned the continued proximity of rivers, crossed a stream or valley instead of following it, climbed mountains, and went stubbornly onward. They moved like an army of ants, and, fixing their eyes towards a distant land, marched as directly as the country and their own powers would let them, surmounting each obstacle as it appeared until they reached their goal."

But in every region from Hudson Bay to the Gulf of Mexico the ingenuity of man gradually devised some means by which difficul-

PROCEEDING TO THE SETTLEMENT 205

ties were overcome and a sure if slow journey to the promised land effected.

Whenever possible water travel was chosen. Judged by modern standards, travel to the interior appears excessively slow; while the danger of death through climatic conditions or mere hardship was always present, and the possibility of attack by hostile natives or jealous squatters by no means imaginary in many regions. The river boats varied with the difficulties to be surmounted, but were in general an adaptation of raft or flatboat. On comparatively slow-moving waterways like the Delaware or Susquehanna it was not difficult to use pole-boats against the current; but upon others like the St. Lawrence and Mississippi the traffic upstream was possible only through the most laborious exertion.

The typical pole-boat was 20 to 30 feet long, 3 to 5 wide, and 2 or 3 deep, and was commonly constructed of pine. Since it was flat-bottomed it drew less than a foot of water even when heavily laden, while a pointed bow and stern lessened the resistance of the water. Originating on the Connecticut and Delaware rivers, these vessels were propelled by a crew of from four to eight men using ash or hickory poles shod with iron spikes. In the larger craft particularly, each crewman commenced at the bow, and, facing the stern, bent low as he placed the button to his shoulder and walked along the narrow gangway, shoving the boat its own length on each trip. The helmsman, as he worked a large sweep, corrected any zigzag course. The largest of such vessels was the Durham boat. Similar craft were often employed on the Susquehanna and Mohawk as arks, or under the name "dorm" or "dorem," and their use quickly extended to the St. Lawrence, where bateaux were the earliest boats apart from the birch canoe.

Of heavier construction were arks, scows, and barges for downstream transport only. These were usually built of large timbers, and were commonly broken up and sold as lumber at their destination. Keelboats, sometimes long and slender, were used on the Ohio, and, like the Schenectady boat on the Mohawk, and the Hudson's Bay Company York boat, were variations of the bateau or flatboat. There were also Ohio-boats, broadhorns, Kentucky-boats of from 50 to 60 feet in length called "fresh-water frigates," and the even larger New Orleans boats. On the Mississippi, Ohio, and their tributaries there were, besides, large log canoes called perrogues (or pirogues), skiffs, bateaux, and rafts.

In many instances the larger flatboats were floating houses. Almost all had some sort of shelter or cabin, particularly in southern waters. Even a voyage down the Mississippi with the strong current took four months by flatboat from St. Louis to New Orleans, while the ascent was often a journey of unparalleled hardship and suffering, as shown in the following account concerning a group of Connecticut farmers, the survivors of which eventually became successful planters in the vicinity of Natchez, Mississippi, having "handsome dwellings, large estates, and scores of slaves."

"Reaching New Orleans, August 1st, 1776, they begin to ascend the Mississippi in open boats. Day after day passes; and they are yet dragging their heavily-laden craft against the furious current, through sickly airs and under the exhausting southern sun. The malaria of the swamps begins its fearful work, and one and another of the hardy emigrants sicken and die; while the fated survivors, with diminished strength, more slowly drag the heavy boats upstream. Boat after boat is left—the crew too feeble to draw it—fastened to the willows or anchored in the current. . . . The remainder of the party at last reaches the site of the intended settlement, . . . having been almost a hundred days in making the trip from New Orleans."[1]

The descent of the Ohio or Mississippi was accomplished with comparative ease, if disease was avoided. A guidebook advises those who planned to settle on their shores to build "rafts of white pine boards, which, if properly constructed, are as safe and more convenient for a family than a common boat." But they were admonished that to start after the first of May would be "ruinous" owing to the prevalence of fever. Many immigrants, however, constructed flatboats, almost square and partly roofed over, which they guided by sweeps at the stern and sides. Whether they drifted along on raft or on flatboat the boards of their vessel finally served in building their first shanty.

A malaria region would hardly seem to attract settlers, but every district had its proponents. Samuel Brown suggested that "emigrants suffering from rheumatism or consumption" might find themselves much improved in Indiana. "There are now living in Vincennes," he wrote in 1817,

"four Frenchmen who were at the defeat of General Braddock, who have lived in that place between fifty and sixty years. There are also two French women between eighty or ninety years old, and one person of the name of Mills lately died aged 115 years. These instances may show that there is nothing peculiarly destructive to human life in that country."

And there was, besides, "the ease and safety with which families can descend the Ohio, . . . the great thoroughfare of emigration to the south-western states." Loss of health or life in reaching In-

[1] Milburn, *The Pioneers, Preachers and People of the Mississippi Valley*, 214-7. A traveller of a century ago observed that the sandy swamps of New Orleans "are so noxious that they may be likened to the gates of death"; but he stated that if the immigrant were not overtaken with "imbecility of mind" he might quickly "realize a fortune." (Weston, *A Visit to the United States and Canada in 1833*, 120.)

diana, he goes on to say, is due more to "the injudicious manner of performing that navigation, than to the unhealthiness of those countries." The river, Brown warned, should be descended in autumn after the frosts have commenced, "for by that time the offensive smell from the shores will have abated." River water must be filtered before use; and diluted with cider or strong beer to make it more palatable. He advised taking plenty of provisions, for a good diet will save a doctor's bill. "Go not in a vessel with a bad roof; . . . bending their boards over head is not sufficient." Take but little spirituous liquor, for "every excess debilitates the system." If the weather turns warm beware "the smell of bilge water." If you must go in the spring,

"Remember you are fleeing for your lives. . . . Nail boards over head to keep off the heat of the roof, for sometimes it will remind you of an oven. . . . The effluvia of the shores is poison. . . . To get wet and lie out all night is little short of madness."

Travel in the north also had its difficulties. Particularly arduous was the journey of some 200 Highland Scots to the Red River colony in 1811-1814. Lord Selkirk, hoping to alleviate distress and suffering among Scottish Highlanders, early in the nineteenth century secured from the Hudson's Bay Company 116,000 square miles in the valleys of the Red and Assiniboine rivers. The vanguard of the settlers made a 61-day Atlantic Passage in 1811, "the longest ever known, and the latest to Hudson's Bay." Arriving on September 24th, when it was too late to proceed inland, they built log winter quarters, for York Factory could not accommodate so many. The long winter was spent largely in cutting firewood and hunting game, but towards spring preparations were made to continue their pilgrimage to Assiniboia in bateaux and birch canoes built under the direction of Indians and traders. Laboriously tracking their boats up the swift-flowing Hayes River, they proceeded through the entire length of Lake Winnipeg and ascended the muddy Red River. Towing the boats up St. Andrew's Rapids, they reached Fort Douglas a month after leaving the Bay and were welcomed by traders and Indians, the latter expressing wonder that people would cross "the Great Waters" merely "to dig gardens and work lands." A later emigration suffered from an outbreak of typhoid fever which caused many deaths. The Red River settlers passed through many vicissitudes because of crop failure and the proximity of rival traders and jealous Indians, but this small body of hardy Scots not only laid the foundation of the great midwestern city of Winnipeg but also formed the nucleus of the first permanent settlement in the Canadian West.[2]

Whether on foot, horseback, ox-cart, wagon, or stage—as the routes of travel advanced from trail to road—the immigrant's progress to his place of settlement was never a pleasure trip.[3] Samuel Brown described bush roads in the western states as "good in winter, horrible in April, tolerable in summer." The difference, in fact, between an Indian trail and the average colonization road lay largely in the imagination. John M'Donald describes the experiences of those who came to Upper Canada with him in 1821, as they proceeded to the interior by wagon over a bush road from Brockville to "New Lanark and New Perth":

> "One boy was killed on the spot, several were very much hurt; one man got his arm broken, and our own wagoner, in spite of all his care and skill, was baffled, his horse having laired in a miry part of the road where he stuck fast; and even after he was loosed from the yoke the poor animal strove so much to no purpose that he fell down in a state of complete exhaustion three times in the mire. The mire was so tenacious, being a tough clay, that we were compelled to disengage his feet from the clay with handspikes before we got him freed. . . . Fortunately a team of oxen came forward, which the owner loosed from the yoke and fastened to our wagon. With these and the horse together the wagon was at length pulled out. . . .
>
> "Next morning, . . . when we came again to the road it appeared so very bad that it put us to a complete stand, seeing no way of getting through it. We at last concluded that the only alternative left us was to pull up the farmers' fences, which we did in two places, and thus got through and then closed them up again. This was a new mode of travelling to us, but the only one by which we could at all hope to get through. Every now and then we were compelled to cut down the fences, as it was wholly a region of woods through which we had to pass."

Wagon travel was most highly developed in cross-continent journeys by the "prairie schooner," or Conestoga wagon. First used in Pennsylvania about the middle of the eighteenth century, this covered wagon transported thousands of German-Dutch from that state to Upper Canada in the early years of the next century,[4] and, as an alternative to rounding Cape Horn in a sailing-vessel, was an important vehicle of travel at the time of the California gold rush of 1849. "Emigrant trains" were sometimes half a mile in length.

The Peter Robinson emigration of Irish to Peterborough County, Upper Canada, suffered many delays in pushing north-

[2] The most comprehensive work on the Selkirk settlements is Martin's *Lord Selkirk's Work in Canada*.
[3] Richard Weston describes travel in the United States by horseboat ferries, covered toll-bridges of corduroy, and cart and wagon of various types and in several localities, in his *Visit*, 101 *et seq.*, and 141 *et seq.*
[4] In the period 1800-4 Peter Reesor travelled from Pennsylvania to Markham Township, Upper Canada, on horseback, exchanged his horse for a piece of land, and walked back; shortly afterwards he conducted a group of settlers to the same locality by wagon. The settlement of Waterloo County by Pennsylvania Germans is the *motif* of Mabel Dunham's novel, *The Trail of the Conestoga*.

ward some thirty miles from Cobourg, on Lake Ontario. After they had been encamped for some time on the lake shore, the immigrants started inland thirteen miles to Sully, on Rice Lake, over an almost impassable trail. Only by repairing the roadway as they went was it possible to use ox-carts to carry the baggage, while the men and women tramped alongside. With great difficulty three large bateaux were portaged to Rice Lake, but the water of the Otonabee was too low to use them; consequently eight days was spent in building a large flat-bottomed scow, sixty feet long and eight feet wide, which drew only a few inches of water. Thirty of the healthiest immigrants accompanied twenty old settlers on the first trip to Scott's Mills (later named Peterborough), but all of these suffered severely from ague and fever, and two died. Another was drowned during the delay at Rice Lake, but after many journeys across the lake and up the river the 2,000 members finally reached the headquarters at Scott's Mills, where they were accommodated in rude wigwams of branches, sods, and slabs of wood of their own construction.[5] The water route was the only practicable means of access to the place of settlement during the summer, though in winter a bush road provided a much easier and speedier approach, even though it required two or three days to proceed 35 miles.[6]

John Watson reached New Brunswick on the *Wellington* in 1819 after a disagreeable voyage during which two men were killed by lightning. Watson found the winter too severe, and in the early spring of 1820 set out westward. He wrote to a friend:

"I therefore, with my wife, got a hand-sleigh, in which I placed the children, and drew them on the ice up the St. John's River, about 360 miles, Mary and myself walking, drawing the children after us. You must also recollect that 100 miles of this was not settled, being all wood. We arrived at the head of St. John's River. We travelled on in the same manner, across snow and ice, to the great River St. Lawrence, about 180 miles below Quebec; there we found the country, along the bank, thickly settled. I then built myself a light waggon, and had all our people provisioned during the time of making the waggon for 'I thank you,' the good people, who were French-Canadians, wishing us very much to stay with them. In this waggon our children were drawn by myself for upwards of 400 miles, to Kingston at the mouth of Lake Ontario. There (as every other place) we met with uncommon kindness: a gentleman, quite a stranger, not only sent us by the steamboat, free of all expense, to Fort George (Niagara), but put six or seven dollars in our pockets besides."

[5] See the Hon. Peter Robinson's evidence in *Report of the Select Committee on Emigration* (1827), 345-7. From the summer of 1825, when they left Ireland, to March, 1826, a total of 102 members of this emigration had died from attacks of seasickness, ague, dysentery, or fever.
[6] See the account of Mrs. Frances Stewart's journey in her *Our Forest Home*, 2nd edition, 25-9. Thomas Choate's trips on foot and by ox-sled from New Hampshire to Upper Canada are described in Guillet, *Early Life in Upper Canada*, 492-3.

Watson and his family decided to locate in the United States, a few months later proceeding (apparently on their nerve, as before,) to Aurora, Indiana, where they were soon satisfactorily established through the kindness of neighbors. They had travelled between 2,000 and 3,000 miles and were greatly elated at the abundance of food, the lowness of taxes, and the general improvement over their condition in England.[7]

As travel improved, there was a continual rolling back of the frontier, and enterprising immigrants pushed farther and farther into the West. To the stream which poured in from northern Europe were added large numbers from settled districts in the East, who gave up valuable holdings for what in many instances proved to be an illusory paradise in the wilds.[8] Prominent among propagandists of the early period of western settlement was Morris Birkbeck, who promoted the Illinois Territory. A contemporary observed that he had inveigled to the district "every devoted lunatic furnished with money, and possessing a head unfurnished with brains."[9] John Howe was enthusiastic about "the banks of the Red River, which empties itself into the Mississippi about 225 miles above New Orleans." The man of capital, he considered, could best amass wealth in the Southern States; but he advised poorer emigrants, "Do not go to any states south of Pensilvania."[10]

The introduction of steam on the Mississippi by the *New Orleans* in 1811-14 partially solved the problem of its ascent; but it was a difficult trip, and it was not until 1817 that the *Etna* reached Louisville and some years later before a boat steamed into St. Paul. For about thirty years steamship travel progressed slowly, the raft and the scow being much too convenient for downstream traffic to be displaced entirely. Birkbeck advised emigrants to Illinois to sail to New Orleans, from which it was a month's voyage to Shawnee Town by steamship, then 50 miles overland to English Prairie, after which the stranger had merely to "inquire the road" to his destination.

---

[7] A series of Watson's letters, 1819-1828, may be found in [Smith], *Twenty-four Letters from Labourers in America to their Friends in England*, 9 *et seq*. A few are also quoted in Cobbett, *The Emigrant's Guide*, 47 *et seq*.

[8] Richard Weston accompanied a group of "Mononites" (Mennonites) from Boston to Indiana in 1833. They were travelling in three two-steer wagons, with several cows following. (Weston, *op. cit.*, 117.)

[9] Wilson, *The Wanderer in America*, 2nd edition, 6. A similar comment is made by C. F. Grece in his *Facts and Observations Respecting Canada and the United States*, 2; while Richard Weston criticizes the territory severely in his *Visit*, 117 *et seq*.

[10] Howe, *The Emigrant's New Guide*, 14 *et seq*. James Stuart's *Three Years in America* was another work that was considered much too exaggerated in its praise of the new land. "He has flattered hundreds to their ruin," said a settler to Richard Weston, "and many are the murmurs already breathed out against him." (Weston, *op. cit.*, 49 and 123.)

PROCEEDING TO THE SETTLEMENT

Steamship travel on the Mississippi and other southwestern waters had but little in common with that on the Hudson. The boats were frequently constructed of green wood and fitted with poorly-made boilers, which were carelessly repaired when they developed holes; but a goodly outside of gilded panels covered interior deficiencies, and the ships, although usually negligently operated, were loaded on every passage. On the down trip they kept to the center to obtain the advantage of the current, while upstream they followed a course closer to shore, the wheels lashing the river as the steam hissed high in the air, and clouds of cinders and black smoke trailed in the rear. In the 1830's a cabin passage from New Orleans to Pittsburgh was $50, while the *hoi polloi* on deck travelled much more cheaply, and those who were not above lending a hand to load on wood at the stops were carried for still less. C. D. Arfwedson ascended the river in 1834 on the *Louisiana*, of the Mississippi and Ohio Mail Line, which he stated was the "only one in all the Western States in which it is possible to travel with any degree of safety." Of nine ships leaving New Orleans the same day, only three arrived at their destination without some kind of disaster. "It is almost a miracle to escape with life on these trips," observed Mr. Arfwedson. Fires and explosions, stumps and snags gave the Mississippi a reputation for danger unsurpassed by the Atlantic crossing by sailing-ship, or even a voyage to China; while the bar-rooms and the cabins were crowded with people of all classes—tourists, speculators, planters, and slave-dealers. In the more humble quarters were immigrants, peddlers, and other lesser folk, dancing, gambling, wrestling, singing, and reading the Bible far into the night.[11]

As early as the last years of the eighteenth century there were packet-boats on the Ohio River with separate cabins for women and men, making round trips from Cincinnati to Pittsburgh in four weeks. These vessels were well armed against the Indians. Later immigrants who reached Buffalo by Hudson River steamship and Erie Canal packet, were able (if they escaped alive from the "ball alleys" described by William Brown![12]) to

[11] See Chevalier, *Lettres sur l'Amérique du Nord*, II 1-28; and Arfwedson, *The United States and Canada in 1832, 1833, and 1834*, II 80-141. The latter traveller made a twelve-day passage from New Orleans to Louisville in the *Louisiana*, and then continued by lesser vessels to Wheeling on the Ohio. The events of the voyage are narrated in an interesting manner and in considerable detail. Similar descriptions are given by Charles Dickens in his *American Notes*, chapters 11 and 12.
[12] He found the town "abundantly supplied with 'ball alleys', where resort hundreds of blacklegs from noon to midnight, ready to pick the pocket of any unfortunate green-un who should ignorantly stray into one of these dens of infamy." The game was formerly Nine Pins; but an Act of the New York Legislature having forbidden it, another pin

continue to Cleveland by steamer, and thence by canal to the Ohio and Mississippi, on which they might reach New Orleans by steamship in about seven days. Transportation was not as highly developed in Upper Canada, but every advantage was taken of American routes where available. John Linton travelled from New York to Oswego by tow-boat in 1833, thence by schooner to Hamilton, Upper Canada, and finished his trip to the Canada Company's "Huron Tract" by wagon. The total cost of his journey from New York to Hamilton was £1 6s. 3d., with a slight additional charge for baggage. He paid $1 a hundredweight for his baggage by wagon, which was no doubt the most difficult part of his journey; but his total outlay was much less than that by the slow and laborious 700-mile St. Lawrence route.

Proceeding westward from Guelph, Upper Canada, in 1828 by ox-cart, Mrs. Samuel Strickland's party made fairly satisfactory progress the first two days; but when they entered a newly-blazed section of the roadway difficulties commenced, and in the next five miles the wagon was twice upset. There was still more than 60 miles to go, and they walked the entire distance, covering about 15 miles a day, Mrs. Strickland carrying her child. Two of the remaining four nights they camped out, and finally, after an exhausting trip, reached Goderich on the morning of the sixth day.

But even "backwoods" districts in process of settlement had sometimes a shelter for the long-suffering immigrant. To the north of the Huron Tract, in "the Queen's Bush," was the village of Sydenham in the 1840's, and among its primitive buildings stood "Government House"—not a vice-regal mansion, but merely an asylum for destitute strangers. Upon making application for accommodation a family was given a section of the building and could remain until they were able to provide for themselves. It was "fitted up with sleeping cribs, cooking stoves, etc., fuel being to be had for the chopping." If the supply of space was not equal to the demand, those who had been there longest had to vacate.

Throughout the entire period of emigration large numbers who entered the British Provinces were merely birds of passage to the United States,[18] though only before the opening of the Erie

---

was added and the game went on apace—an example of "Yankee ingenuity" which was "too much for the lawmakers." (Brown, *America: A Four Years' Residence,* 15.) Richard Weston made a similar comment sixteen years earlier. (*Op. cit.,* 173.)

[18] Statistics show that in some years only from one-fifth to one-sixth remained in the British Provinces.

From The Progress of the Republic   *N. Johnson*
THE PUBLIC LANDING AT LOUISVILLE
Two flatboats may be seen in the center foreground.

A Currier and Ives print   *Fanny Palmer*
MIDNIGHT ON THE MISSISSIPPI
The *Natchez* and *Eclipse* racing for port at 6 knots per hour!

BROADWAY, ST. LOUIS, DURING MIGRATION TO THE FAR WEST

In 1849 Stanislaus Lasselle was six and a half months travelling by "prairie schooner" over the Santa Fé trail from Logansport, Indiana, to California.

Reproduced by courtesy of the Union Pacific Railroad
THE RAILWAY-BUILDERS PUSH THROUGH NEBRASKA

On May 10, 1869, the Union Pacific and Central Pacific railroads met near Ogden, Utah, but the Canadian Pacific Railway was not completed until 1885.

PROCEEDING TO THE SETTLEMENT 213

Canal, and at the middle of the century when the St. Lawrence canals were first available, could there be any definite advantage, and then only to those bound for central or western states. At times large numbers found it cheaper to enter Canada at Montreal and proceed southward to the United States *via* St. John's, the Richelieu River, and Lake Champlain; thousands were reported by the Chief Agent of Emigration to have followed this route in 1846. Much later, immigrants bound for the Canadian West were forced to go by way of northwestern United States,[14] a route upon which railroads were available long before the Canadian Pacific Railway was completed across the continent in 1885.

The early railways achieved a speed of 15 to 20 miles per hour, which was exceedingly fast at a time when the average overland conveyance covered but little more ground in a day. William Hancock set out in 1853 from New York for Piermont by steamship, and continued to Dunkirk by train; here he took passage to Sandusky in a freight steamboat carrying half a dozen cabin passengers and the rest on deck; but they were unexpectedly put off at Cleveland and had to conclude the journey by train. Mr. Hancock found the eastern portion of his rail trip "a mode of travelling not to be recommended on the score either of comfort or dispatch" but the rate for immigrants was cheap—½d. per mile; and the delay and inconvenience was "scarcely felt by people who have already 'roughed it' for a month or six weeks at sea." Everyone got as close as possible to "a stove in the centre of the carriage," and put in the two nights smoking and in fitful attempts to sleep.

Western railways, observed Mr. Hancock, were of necessity cheaply constructed, and consequently afforded "not the most pleasant travelling." The line from Cleveland to Sandusky had frequent "deviations from the level," and—like a corduroy road —the effect on the passenger was similar to "being jolted over a ploughed field in a farm-cart innocent of springs." The speed of rail travel averaged from 7 to 8 miles per hour, progress being retarded by frequent stops, one of which was "midway between two of the stations, at a dilapidated shanty, to leave a demijohn of whiskey for its owner." As he worked farther into the West Mr. Hancock observed immigrants pressing into Minnesota, but

[14] The military expedition to the Red River in 1870 could not, of course, travel through the United States, and was forced to proceed by bateaux over the laborious route from Prince Arthur's Landing (Port Arthur), earlier famous as the Grand Portage of the fur-trader. An account of the difficulties surmounted by Colonel Wolseley's expeditionary force may be found in Guillet, *Early Life in Upper Canada*, 720-34.

he considered that "civilization has as yet scarcely extended beyond the banks of the Mississippi and its tributaries; half naked savages walk about the streets of St. Paul, and the settler not infrequently finds on his return from market his farm a smoking ruin, and a group of Sioux dancing round it."[15] But settlers were pushing into Nebraska and Kansas in large numbers, the Mississippi having been crossed by a railway bridge over a mile in length at Davenport, Iowa. From the railheads settlers pushed on by "prairie schooner" to Utah and California.[16] On January 1, 1859, there were 27,819 miles of railroad in the United States, and it was possible to travel from New York by rail to such diverse points as New Orleans (1,950 miles), Kansas City (1,480 miles), Vicksburg (1,559 miles), and to various points in Iowa, Wisconsin, and Minnesota upwards of 1,500 miles distant. When Robert Louis Stevenson passed westward to California in 1879 transcontinental railways were available, but he found travel by "emigrant train" a miserable experience—"far worse" than the Atlantic passage; though of course he crossed by steamship, not by the already antiquated sailing-vessel.

[15] Hancock, *An Emigrant's Five Years in the Free States of America*, 229 and 297. The quick growth of western settlements is exemplified by St. Paul. In 1842 it was the site of but one trading-post; in 1847 "the rude cabins of a few half-breeds marked the spot"; but ten years later it was an extensive city, though the fur trade still predominated. (*Canada and the Western States*, part I 134.)

[16] Among the Lasselle Papers in the Indiana State Library is the diary of Stanislaus Lasselle, describing an overland journey by wagon from Logansport, Indiana, to California. The trip took six months and two weeks. This narrative is printed in Dunbar, *History of Travel in America*, Appendix M, Volume IV, pp. 1427-1443.

CHAPTER XXI

The Promised Land

My Hame

I canna ca' this forest hame,
    It is nae hame to me;
Ilk tree is suthern to my heart,
    And unco to my e'e.
      .   .   .   .
If I cou'd see the primrose bloom,
    In Nora's hazel glen;
And hear the linties chirp and sing,
    Far frae the haunts o' men:
      .   .   .   .
If I cou'd see the lane' kirk yard,
    Whar' frien's lye side by side:
And think that I cou'd lay my banes
    Beside them when I died;

Then might I think this forest hame,
    And in it live and dee;
Nor feel regret at my heart's core,
    My native land, for thee.

By an anonymous resident of Otonabee Township, Upper Canada.
Cobourg Star, December 27, 1831

It is not easy to estimate the comparative advantages of midwestern American states and the British provinces in the "pioneer" period; but there is no doubt that economic conditions in the older portions of the United States were upon a different plane from those in the Canadas.[1] Lord Durham's *Report* may be taken as an unbiased document. Referring at first to Upper Canada, and then to all the British provinces, he wrote:

"A very considerable portion of the Province has neither roads, post-offices, mills, schools, nor churches. . . . Their means of communication with each other, or the chief towns of the Province, are limited and uncertain. With the exception of the labouring class, most of the emigrants who have arrived within the last ten years are poorer now than at the time of their arrival in the Province. . . . Even in the most thickly peopled districts there are but few schools, and those of a very inferior character; while the

---

[1] One of the most remarkable comments is that of C. H. Wilson. "I cannot but wonder," he says, "why England retains so unprofitable an appendage in her dominions. . . . One half is boundless snow, and the other half literally a wilderness." He did, however, see one ray of light, for he conceded that "the only answer that can be made is *Timber*." (Wilson, *The Wanderer in America, or Truth at Home*, 61-2.)

more remote settlements are almost entirely without any. Under such circumstances there is little stimulus to industry or enterprise, and their effort is aggravated by the striking contrast presented by such of the United States as border upon this Province, and where all is activity and progress. The forest has been widely cleared; every year numerous settlements are formed, and thousands of farms are created out of the waste; the country is intersected by common roads; canals and railroads are finished, or in the course of formation; the ways of communication and transport are crowded with people, and enlivened by numerous carriages and large steamboats. The observer is surprised at the number of harbours on the lakes and the number of vessels they contain, while bridges, artificial landing-places, and commodious wharves are formed in all directions as soon as required. Good houses, warehouses, mills, inns, villages, towns and even great cities, are almost seen to spring up out of the desert. . . . Their fine churches, their great hotels, their exchanges, courthouses and municipal halls, of stone or marble, would be admired in any part of the Old World. On the British side of the line, with the exception of a few favoured spots where some approach to American prosperity is apparent, all seems waste and desolate; a widely scattered population, poor and apparently unenterprising, though hardy and industrious; . . . living in mean houses, drawing little more than a rude subsistence from ill-cultivated land, and seemingly incapable of improving their condition, they present the most constructive contrast to their enterprising and thriving neighbours on the American side."[2]

Misrepresentation was one of the greatest evils of the American colonization period. Referring to Upper Canada the Rev. William Bell wrote that "some of the flattering accounts you have seen of the state of the country are more like descriptions of what it may be like fifty or a hundred years hence than of what it is at the present time." Many of the better class would never have removed to the British provinces had they known the true state of things. Upon reaching Fitzroy Harbour, Upper Canada, in 1835, one immigrant recorded her disappointment in her diary: "In vain we looked for the realization of the picture that had been painted in such glowing colours!" Like many another newcomer, however, she found that "the warm welcome of our friends reconciled us to our exile home." Some were so disappointed that they immediately returned to the United Kingdom. John Palmer met two men who had attempted farming in the "backwoods" of Upper Canada, but had become discouraged and were on the way back to England. "It is a damned wild country, full of yankies and agues," volunteered one of them; and both insisted that home was home, and there was no place like home![3]

[2] Lucas, *Report on the Affairs of British North America*, II 184-5 and 212-3. Lord Durham's comparison has been criticized as unfair to the British provinces, but there seems to be no doubt of its general truth. On the other hand, however, the depression incident to the Rebellion of 1837 rendered appearances considerably worse than they were either before or after. The conditions of settlement and the impressions of immigrants described in this chapter are not intended to apply beyond the eighteen-sixties, when the sailing-ship era was drawing to a close.
[3] Palmer, *Journal of Travels in the United States*, 231. "Please to tell Mr. and Mrs. F―― that I think they were foolish in going back again," wrote Sophia Hill; "but

THE PROMISED LAND

One traveller observed when he was returning to Scotland on the *Camillus* after a visit to the United States that there were several families aboard who had been unsuccessful in America. Occasionally immigrants who could not support their families were deported. But few found it practicable to return voluntarily, and most were forced to make the best of their circumstances. Some of those not entirely destitute, becoming restless at their lack of progress, crossed the international border to try their fortune in other surroundings. The greater number moved from the British provinces to the United States.

"We happened to meet," says one observer, "a Scotch family returning from Canada to Columbus, Ohio, who had been decoyed away in that manner, with the offer of a lot of *land* for nothing—but which they found to be a complete *swamp*. When they got there, the wife and children were nearly tormented to death with mosquitoes—no road to their shanty—no friends within a considerable distance—nothing to be bought, and many other miseries we have not repeated."

Sheer lack of ability was a common cause of failure. The very fact that thousands had been "shovelled out" because they were a drag upon their fellows is a sufficient reason to account for any lack of success in America, whatever cause may be advanced for their condition in the United Kingdom. Observing that many people disliked the new land for a time—"some being love or mamma sick," and others constitutionally lazy or weak-minded, —a settler found a number who objected to their new circumstances because there was no overseer to whom they could apply for poor-relief. To place such persons indiscriminately on wild land and expect them to make good was unreasonable. "Many remain mere labourers," wrote Charles Shirreff, "and are fit for nothing else: . . . and thousands, so far from being capable of managing a farm, will be unable to regulate their own conduct." The Irish and Germans, observed another, were the "hewers of wood and drawers of water" in the United States, and obtained work on canal and railway projects or in other manual occupations, where they "soon pick up the better habits of this country." A *good* Scotch workman, says the same not altogether unprejudiced observer, will get along "if he is sober." In fact he advocated temperance for all immigrants, admonishing them "to leave the habits connected with the pint or quart measure, the gill and the mutchkin, behind them, as nothing will sooner lead a man to

---

that is the way of some people, they just come and look round and run back again before they know anything about it, and give it a bad name." (Letter in the *Quarterly Review*, September, 1835, pp. 426-7.)

dishonour and disgrace than the use of them here."[4] In some villages, reported a clergyman, one-third of the buildings were taverns.[5]

Continual misfortune or fraud was the cause of some failures. "Americans are a shrewd, enterprizing, speculating race," wrote John Duncan; "and he would need to have both wit and industry who enters into rivalry with them. . . . Of those who emigrate, hundreds have found, to their dear-bought experience, that gold neither paves the streets nor grows upon the trees." James Taylor refers similarly to Canadians, whom he found both shrewd and selfish. Richard Weston describes the deplorable plight of a family by the name of Moon, who purchased land some 300 miles from New York "before seeing it":

> "I called at their residence, a miserable log-house. . . . I observed many a chink between the stones of which the chimney was built, and also between the logs. . . . The furniture of the house was most wretched, and Mrs. Moon was dressed in coarse worsted stuff. She seemed completely broken down in her spirits. A daughter who had never recovered from sea sickness was dead; and the rest of the family had all taken the fever of the place and were now dispersed in various directions. Her husband had purchased land before seeing it, at the rate of three dollars per acre, but the soil proved to be completely useless. . . . They were now completely ruined. . . . Our flowery travellers never drew a picture like this; but such a sight became familiar to me in the course of my travels, and so it must have been to them. They, however, were filling their pockets by gulling the people at home, and therefore had not the honesty to take any notice of such scenes."[6]

Besides disappointment and delay in the securing of land grants, the performance of settlement duties, and the final obtaining of title deeds, there was an almost entire lack of communication and of decent living conditions, especially in the early period. Life was inevitably primitive for many years after settlement. Lord Selkirk's 800 hardy Scots at Prince Edward Island in 1803

> "lodged themselves in temporary wigwams, constructed after the fashion of the Indians, by setting up a number of poles in a conical form, tied together at top, and covered with boughs of trees. Those of the spruce fir were preferred, and, when disposed in regular layers of sufficient thickness, formed a

---

[4] *Canada and the Western States*, part II 44. "I think I shall be a teetotaler," wrote C. Jones from Buffalo in 1848, "for teetotalers are looked on well." (Quoted in Smith, *The Settler's New Home, or the Emigrant's Location*, 104.)

[5] Abbott, *Philip Musgrave, or the Memoirs of a Church of England Missionary in the American Colonies*, 1850 edition, 103 and 135. Mrs. Anna Jameson called drunkenness "the vice and curse of the country" (*Winter Studies and Summer Rambles in Canada*, I 76); while another writer found "every inn, tavern and beer shop filled at all hours with drunken brawling fellows; and the quantity of ardent spirits consumed by them will truly astonish you." ("An Ex-Settler," *Canada in the Years 1832, 1833, and 1834*, 25.)

[6] Weston, *A Visit to the United States and Canada in 1833*, 19 fn. On page 49 he refers to the similar circumstances of another woman, whose misfortunes are blamed upon a propagandist. The "flowery travellers" alluded to by Weston were men like Stuart, Howison, and Birkbeck. The last named, however, is said to have lost £15,000 through his investments in the Illinois Territory.

THE PROMISED LAND

very substantial thatch, giving a shelter not inferior to that of a tent. The settlers had spread themselves along the shore for the distance of about half a mile, upon the site of an old French village, which had been destroyed and abandoned after the capture of the island by the British forces in 1758. . . . I arrived at the place late in the evening, and it had then a very striking appearance. Each family had kindled a large fire near the wigwam, and round these were assembled groupes of figures, whose peculiar national dress added to the singularity of the surrounding scene. Confused heaps of baggage were every where piled together beside their wild habitations; and by the number of fires the whole woods were illuminated."

Many, particularly those who had been accustomed to better things, sank under the weight of their hardships and died years before the fruit of their toil was reaped by their children. He who had loved the rugged scenery of his native Scotland, or the quiet lanes and green meadows of the English countryside now found himself

"in a foreign land, far distant from his relations and friends, fixed in a desolate wilderness, shut up in a miserable hut called a shanty, the cold winter winds penetrating through its crevices and piercing his benumbed limbs with their chilly blasts; he will wildly look around the place he has chosen for a habitation for his beloved wife and family, whom he has, perhaps, dragged from home almost against their will; he views them with cheerless glances, and their returning looks of despair must wound his very soul,—all this he will have to endure with the prospect of spinning out a miserable existence."[7]

On the other hand there were those who, having never experienced its hardships, could wax most enthusiastic over the idyllic life in a log hut in the wilderness. How simple it all was, in theory, to burn up acres of timber and sow crops among the stumps! How easy, on paper, to raise a herd of cattle from one cow! The Attorney-General of Nova Scotia optimistically pointed out that a settler could not fail to be "in comfortable circumstances" in a few months, and reach "a tolerable degree of affluence" shortly afterwards. Some writers reached the heights of eloquence in describing the romantic attractions of "a country untouched by the hand of man":

"The individual who seeks the Canadas for a home has much to learn. . . . An emigrant blessed with strength and hardihood, and being, moreover, in the prime of life, will not consult his permanent interest by embarking his fortunes in an old settlement; a country untouched by the hand of man is before him, clothed in native verdure, and portioned with a native fertility—let him strip the forest of her gigantic mantle, convert the wilderness into the fruitful plain, and force the treasures from the bosom of nature. The virgin soil will repay the exertions of man by an abundant increase,

[7] Taylor, *Narrative of a Voyage to, and Travels in Upper Canada*, 80. Mrs. Susanna Moodie referred to log huts as "dens of dirt and misery which would be shamed by an English pig-sty." (*Roughing It in the Bush*, introduction to the third edition, 1854.)

and the proud reflection will be enjoyed of having carved out from a mass of incongruous materials the means of future support and comfort."

Among the many who were confused and disappointed amid "backwoods" conditions were commuted pensioners—old soldiers and sailors, personal servants, and the like. Aided to a limited extent in emigrating, they were provided with a log hut in the wilderness, but many of them had none of their pension left when they reached their land. One of them told a traveller in Upper Canada how his family had commenced life anew in America. They crossed in the great cholera year, 1832, and fifty-three passengers died before the ship docked at Quebec. Using the rest of his pension and selling his watch, the father arranged to transport the survivors of his family (the mother and one daughter had died at sea) to York. Here a schooner was supplied by the government to carry them farther westward:

"We had rations provided, and that brought us on to Port Stanley, far below Port Talbot; then they put us ashore, and we had to find our way and pay our way to Delaware, where our lot of land was; that cost eight dollars; and then we had nothing left—nothing at all. There were nine hundred emigrants encamped about Delaware, no better off than ourselves."

The general experience of such pensioners in attempting to adapt themselves to the strange new life is described by the same man:

"The government built each family a house, that is to say, a log-hut, eighteen feet long, with a hole for the chimney; no glass in the windows, and empty of course; not a bit of furniture—not even a table or a chair. . . . The first year we cleared a couple of acres and sowed wheat enough for next year. . . . We worked meantime on the roads, and got a half a dollar a day and rations. . . . Many of them couldn't stand it no ways. Some died; and then there were the poor children and the women—it was very bad for them. Some wouldn't sit down on their land at all; they lost all heart to see everywhere trees and trees, and nothing beside. And then they didn't know nothing of farming—how should they, being soldiers by trade?"

Some of these people were reduced to very straitened circumstances in later years. "A poor old pensioner," 68 years of age, who had fought through the Peninsular War and "lost the use of nearly every limb," stated that he was induced to commute his pension "in the hope of gaining in Canada a better livelihood for myself and wife—everyone knows what a misfortune that commutation has been to us old soldiers. Many of us have been reduced to starvation, and so great has been my distress that I have often wished for death. . . . Forced by want, we are driven to beggary." Finally, he says, their "deplorable condition" was made known to the Queen, and a "pittance of *fourpence halfpenny a*

THE PROMISED LAND

day" was allowed them; "and this is all I have to provide support for myself and aged wife, worn down with fatigue and hardships; and to find shelter from the piercing cold of winter, for these old limbs are now almost useless to me."

There were, of course, many minor, if not trivial, considerations which one person or another found objectionable in the United States or Canada. C. H. Wilson was of the opinion that the females of America, while "often very pretty," were "void of animation, and in complexion fading lilies — no tint of the opening rose, or crimson blush of the red cabbage." He also found it hard to get used to calling a cock a *rooster*, and "a female of the *dog* species a *slut* — and other ridiculous Republican innovations." Many of the well-to-do considered that the levelling process made servants much too independent; while the same "gentlemen colonists" found it no small matter to be forced by democratic feeling to mix with those of "inferior" social status.[8]

Of more importance was the unhealthful climate of many regions from the mouth of the Mississippi to Hudson Bay, particularly before the swamp lands had been improved by clearing and draining. One writer calmly observed that the winters of Upper Canada were "perhaps a little colder" than those of England! Among the diseases caused or aggravated by climatic conditions, tuberculosis and various types of ague ("the chills") and fever took the heaviest toll.[9] "A man out west was took so bad with 'the shakers' that every tooth rattled so in his head that you could hear the noise at the far end of a 50 acre farm"! Newly-arrived immigrants were particularly susceptible. "Unfortunately his very first season proved wet and unhealthy," runs the obituary notice of an early settler; "and the necessary exposure and fatigue operating upon a totally unprepared constitution soon brought him to a bed of

[8] In the unpublished diary of John Thomson, for example, it is recorded that certain men present at a bee, "being gentlemen, messed in the dining room, while the others, landed proprietors but no gentlemen, lived in the kitchen"; but as "envious feeling" arose among "certain Yankiefied personages," the gentlemen were constrained to mix with the rest of the party, "and did all we could to do away with any bad impression." This diary is in the Archives of Ontario, but the entries from April 19th to 24th, 1834, describing a three-day "raising bee" in which one man was killed in a fight, are quoted in Guillet, *Early Life in Upper Canada*, 286-7. One writer considered the difficulty of getting satisfactory servants, and the general "incivility and rudeness of the lower classes," as the two most serious drawbacks of the new land. With particular reference to the latter, "of which," he says, "we have all heard," he adds the following comment: "Believe me, this has not been exaggerated; their assumption not of equality only but even of superiority is very galling, and I consider it by far the most trying and disagreeable thing, as gentlemen, you have to encounter in America." ("An Ex-Settler," *op. cit.*, 24-5.)

[9] Observing that York, the capital of Upper Canada, was "better calculated for frog-pond or beaver-meadow than for the residence of human beings," Edward Talbot stated that "probably five-sevenths of the people are annually afflicted with agues and intermittent fevers." (*Five Years' Residence in the Canadas*, I 100-2.) Talbot, among others, stated that women lost their good looks and most of their teeth early in life, a condition probably due to a combination of lack of care, the climate, and the hardships of the life.

sickness, which his constant anxiety for a beloved wife and child, solely dependent upon his exertions, rendered ultimately fatal."[10]

The lack of religious observance in new settlements, and often for many years afterwards, was painful to many. John M'Donald found that his neighbors

"want one great cordial,—one of inestimable value in the time of distress,—and that is the gospel. But I am sorry to say that this is a gospel which few seem to relish or desire. To them it is an unknown sound. There are, however, many who have come here who know both its power and consolation. I hope their Christian brethren will feel it to be their duty to send them ministers. . . . It is certainly desirable to have a pious neighbour, to remind one of the weekly return of the Christian Sabbath, for some here forget its recurrence. . . . They come in with their waggons full and transact all their business on the Lord's Day."

An immigrant from Somerset observed almost the same lack in Yarmouth Township, Upper Canada, which had been much longer settled. He wrote home that "we should be extremely happy if there were a meeting near us. I want to be at Frome on Sundays and here other days. Now I hope you will make up your minds to come, and bring with you a number of religious people, and among them an humble preacher. I have no doubt that much good in a spiritual way might be done, for those who are not Quakers say they wish there was preaching here, as they do not like to go to the Quaker's meeting."[11] But as religious life developed it was noticeable, as John Watson pointed out in connection with Indiana, that while they had church services, yet there was "no parson to tythe us."

Women, particularly, suffered from loneliness and isolation and from the crudeness of wilderness life. Some died from no other cause. A careful observer, Mrs. Anna Jameson, was impressed by the lack of social intercourse in many sections. Referring to the London district she noted that "here, as everywhere else, I find the women of the better class lamenting over the want of all society, except that of the lowest grade in manners and morals. For those who have recently emigrated and are settled in the interior there is absolutely no social intercourse whatever."[12] Similarly, William Watson advised prospective emigrants that "society in the Wilderness is by no means good, as very few polite

[10] Obituary notice of Thomas Fenton, Otonabee Township, Upper Canada, in the *Cobourg Star*, July 11, 1832.
[11] Letter quoted in "Doyle" (William Hickey), *Hints on Emigration*, 76-7. Frome, in Somersetshire, had been a centre of the weaving industry for three centuries. During the Napoleonic Wars the inhabitants were busily engaged in the manufacture of cloth for the navy, but after Waterloo, their occupation gone, all weavers were on relief, and many consequently emigrated to America.
[12] Jameson, *op. cit.*, II 146-8. The life of the pioneer woman is well described in Isabel Skelton's *The Backwoodswoman*.

people are there to be found. Those who enjoyed the politeness and advantages of Irish hospitality, its intercourse and conviviality, must feel very solitary; no matter what merits or good conduct distinguished them heretofore, they are little valued or respected, but are obliged to associate with the most illiterate, unpolished and worthless sort."

Such a life, aggravated by poverty and a complete inability to adapt themselves to a "backwoods" existence, made the plight of "gentlemen" settlers particularly unfortunate. An observer went to some trouble to delineate the gradual deterioration of Captain L—— and his family, an aspect of pioneering which may still be traced among the descendants of highly cultured settlers in various parts of North America.

"The house stood on rising ground which was perfectly bare, all the trees having been cut down for many acres around. There was not even the pretence of garden before the doors, nor any enclosure, but the great shapeless old log house stood, in all its naked roughness, alone. Mrs. L——, I found, was an elderly lady of elegant manners. . . . Her dress struck me on entering. It had once been a superb satin, but that was very many years before. There was hardly anything to be called furniture in the house, a few old wooden chairs, supplemented by some blocks of wood, mere cuts of trees, serving for seats, a great deal table, and a 'grand piano'! (which, Mrs. L—— told me, they bought at Vienna), forming all that could be seen. The very dog-irons on which their fire rested were broken. Overhead I heard feet pattering on the loose open boards which formed the floor of some apartments, and was presently informed that the 'dressing-room' of the Misses L—— was above, and that they would soon be down. Not an inch of carpet, nor any ornament on the walls, nor anything, in fact, to take off the forlorn look of emptiness, was in the place; but the stateliness of language and manner on the part of the hostess was the same as if it had been a palace. . . . From one step to another the family sank into the deepest want, until Mrs. L—— was at last forced to try to get food by making up the wreck of her former finery into caps and such like for the wives of the boors around, and hawking them about till she could sell them for flour or potatoes."

Among other dangers were those arising from the almost entire lack of organized government. Such a condition prevailed in Tennessee and Alabama in the early years of the nineteenth century. Fresh water being scarce in some localities, immigrants encamped in large numbers around springs, or "squatted" there and cultivated small patches of corn. Under such circumstances there was soon fighting over the right of occupancy. Conditions almost identical were found later in most other central and western states as the frontier was gradually rolled westward towards the Pacific.

In spite of the many difficulties of pioneering in "the bush," the greater number of immigrants were far better off in the new land than they could ever have hoped to be in the old. Particularly was this true of the more destitute and the so-called "working-classes" —factory "hands," unskilled tradesmen, and agricultural laborers. Some of these gradually built up a trade or commercial enterprise which developed into one of the great corporations of today; while others, having heard of the great demand for labor in America, took the disastrous course of placing too high a value upon themselves. The Emigration Agent at Quebec observed that

"instances occur almost daily of persons who in their own country (Ireland) were glad to work for 10d. to 1s. per day, refusing employment here at 3s.; and they do not consider that, for the first season, until they become acquainted with the labour of the country, their services are worth little more than one-half to the farmer. Many, to my certain knowledge, have been offered several advantageous engagements in this neighborhood, but refused permanent employment, preferring to proceed, in hopes of better wages, but in which very many are disappointed."

"Emigrant" societies often acted as employment agencies, and in York, Upper Canada, there was an Emigrants' Asylum where shelter might be obtained, as well as information; and immigrants were advised in addition that "if they have children they wish to provide with situations the editor of the *Courier* paper will always put in an advertisement gratis and, I believe, the columns of the *Advocate and Canadian Freeman* are also open to them."[13]

Typical of the self-sufficient immigrant was a thrifty Scotchman who, arriving at Montreal with £300 in his pocket, immediately banked his savings at 5 per cent interest, and proceeded to the Eastern Townships of Lower Canada. He described his experiences as follows:

"After travelling about forty miles through the intricate mazes of Canadian roads I reached the settlement I was in search of. As it was too late in the season to commence upon land of my own, . . . after making some inquiries into the character of the inhabitants among whom my lot had thus accidently been cast, I attached myself to the family of one of them, a substantial farmer, a native of the country. I did not actually hire myself as a labourer, but by making myself as useful as I could, was to pay nothing for my board; this was certainly a foolish bargain, but, as I happened to fall into good hands, suffered no loss for my imprudence, for he gave me in stock and seed-grain as much as I could have expected had I stipulated for regular wages."

It was often advisable for the settler without capital to continue for a lengthy period to work a part of each year at lumbering, or for some well-to-do neighbor. In 1817 a considerable num-

[13] Cattermole, *Emigration*, 190. The *Cobourg Star* of July 9, 1840, announces to "Farmers and Others wanting Labourers, female servants, etc.," that "several Families of healthy Emigrants, arrived in Cobourg, are in search of employment. Apply at *The Star* Office, if by letter Post-paid."

THE PROMISED LAND 225

ber were enabled through the aid of the British Consul at New York to emigrate from the north of Ireland to Cavan Township, Upper Canada, and before they became well established they engaged in various types of work. Some were in the brickyards of York; others found employment each summer on American canals, and returned in the autumn with their wages; but in a few years, as their financial condition and the production of their land improved, it became more profitable for them to remain at home.[14]

The eventual success of individuals sometimes came only after years of difficulty and toil. John Brown, who became Surveyor-General of New Brunswick, recalled that he was 19 years of age on arrival in America, was without friends, but had a fair education, seven dollars, and two suits of clothes. He first worked with a farmer for his board and lodging; then at cellar- and well-digging; next as a member of a threshing outfit; and then hired out with a lumberer as a swamper. Finally after another season excavating cellars and wells, he bought a wilderness lot on shares with another young man; from which, with intervals of various types of labor, camping out "thirteen winters or parts of winters," and working "twelve springs at river driving," he gradually rose in the scale of human activity.

A small group of Irish emigrants from Cork and Waterford came to Nova Scotia in the 1820's. The Attorney-General of the province stated that the first five families who settled in "Irish Town" —in the wilderness between Subinacade Lake and the Windsor Road—had not five shillings among them when they entered "the bush." "They subsisted," he observed, "upon potatoes and herrings and other things which I gave them. About forty or fifty bushels of potatoes and half a barrel of herrings will be a sufficient provision for one of these families for a year; and next year they are able to provide for themselves." So much better was this meager diet than the food upon which many thousands subsisted in Ireland that "they move heaven and earth" to obtain a chance to emigrate to America, where they may rise (in the words of Archdeacon Strachan) from "an extreme degree of poverty" to "a tolerable degree of affluence."

[14] See Strachan, *Remarks on Emigration from the United Kingdom*, 51 *et seq.* These immigrants were aided to the extent of $10 each, and received a free grant of land in Upper Canada. The agent also secured a flat rate of $5 for their conveyance from New York. In 1823 a conducted emigration of 568 Irish settled along the shores of the Mississippi River, Upper Canada. Log houses "far superior to Irish cabins" were erected on their lots, and they were also provided with supplies until their crops were sufficient to support them. By February, 1826, Dr. Strachan observed, many of them were to be seen selling surplus produce in Brockville.

A group of Paisley weavers in Sullivan County, New York, avoided hardships by settling near a center of population. In 1844 they left Scotland, but on reaching New York purchased at 5s. an acre some uncleared government land about 100 miles from the city, instead of pushing westward a thousand miles or more, as was considered the thing to do when "the fever" (as Americans called emigration) was at its height. Though not by training adapted to chopping and logging, they set to work; and as they were within four or five miles of one of the trunk roads leading to New York, there was a ready market for their excess produce. A traveller found that fifteen years later they had about two-thirds of their land cleared, were producing fine crops of grain, vegetables, peaches, grapes and watermelons, lived on rolling land free from fever and ague, and had spring water and fuel in abundance at their door. But, best of all, the district had about it an air of the Highlands; and its inhabitants were "as independent as the wealthiest man in Christendom, with few anxieties about the future, and, as one of them declared to us, they never work more than 4 out of the 12 months." Even with eight months in which to enjoy life, one of the women (who still remained a "Paisley body") observed that she "had mair folk to gang and see" than she had time for.

The assimilation of millions of immigrants was not accomplished without difficulty, though the fact that so much of the continent was in process of settlement made it easier. Work was plentiful and land readily available, and in many localities the newcomer was more easily reconciled to his new life because of neighbors from the same part of the Old Land. Some difficulties were peculiar to certain districts. Settlers in states where slavery was a recognized institution had to be careful not to be too outspoken in criticism of it, particularly while they still ranked as strangers. It was always best to avoid the appearance of excessive self-conceit, "bounce," or "John-Bullism," no matter what the subject under discussion; for in "backwoods" regions particularly, there were rough-and-ready methods of mob persecution which might easily be aroused against the opinionated.

But upon the whole there was more to like than dislike about the new land. "Emigrants of a lower order," observed the Rev. Isaac Fidler, "are not tantalized by the presence of luxury from which they are excluded"; and they soon found that their labor was a type of capital which might yield them "numerous and daily-increasing comforts" that had been entirely beyond their

THE PROMISED LAND

grasp in the United Kingdom. Many of the downtrodden were pleased with the effect of the levelling process in democratic America. One woman wrote home that "they dont put up dinners in this Country, but they dine along with the masters and mistresses as you call them in England, but they will not be called so here, they are equals-like and if hired to anybody they call them their employers." William Baker wrote to his parents, with similar exultation, that they might "tell the farmers at Kirdford that if it please God I have my health, in three years time I shall be as well off as John Downer, at Marshall's, though he used to cut such a swell over us at the meetings." Others, however, disliked the new land for the same reason. "Democracy will never go down an old countryman's stomach," wrote one man to the folks at home; and he was still more emphatic when he found his young sons telling him "they guess they will do as they have a mind to."

Many of those who had never had much opportunity to enjoy nature—much less to hunt and fish—were greatly impressed with the wild life of America. After noting that while there were numerous birds of lovely plumage, yet he had never heard a bird sing, John Inglis observed that "our frogs are very merry, they mount the trees and croak; you can hear them half a mile; they are twice as large as Scotch frogs but they stay only in the marshes: I am glad we have none near our dwellings." As for game, he informs his friends in Auld Scotia that flocks of wood-pigeons almost "darken the air," while deer "come to the very door." In a similar strain, though with more enthusiasm than orthography, a farm-hand wrote to his father that he liked "the Contry very Much—I am at librty to shout terky, Quill, Pigons, Phesents, Dear, and all kind of Geam wch I have on My Back Wood."[15]

In most parts of America during the great period of immigration the distinctions of wealth and poverty were not apparent. While some were well-to-do, there were none living either on parish relief or in ostentatious wealth. Bitterness was frequently present in the minds of those who believed that the distress which led to their enforced emigration had been due to the class system. "This is the land of plenty, where industry is rewarded," wrote Jem and Jane Powell, formerly Chartists; "and not as in England, where some roll in luxury while others starve. . . . No hereditary titles and distinctions,

[15] Letter quoted in Cattermole, *Emigration*, 209-11. Recalling "insolent" gamekeepers, more insolent and tyrannical lords of the manor, and "country parson magistrates," uniting to transport men to Australian penal colonies, John Howe observed with some feeling, "Merciful God! that men, that Englishmen should witness such things and endure them!" (*The Emigrant's New Guide*, 39.)

such as lords, dukes and other nick-names; no fat bishops and state church to supply the rich gentry and fag-end of nobility with large salaries and nothing to do for it."[16]

It was the same with rent and taxes. Robert Slade was particularly pleased that he was in this respect independent: "We have no landlord to come at Michaelmas to say 'I want my rent'; no poor-rates to pay; we are in a free country. It is a pretty thing to stand at one's own door and see a hundred acres of land of his own." John Watson, in Indiana, had also a vivid memory of other times: "Those animals called in your country Excisemen are not known in this country, so that we boil soap, make candles, gather hops, and many other things, without fear, which you *must not do*."

The more equitable distribution of worldly goods appealed particularly to the women. "You can't tell which are lady's here, the women dress so fine," observes Jane Powell of Pittsburgh; and she adds in a burst of enthusiasm, "They literally hoop their fingers with rings and signets." John Down wrote from New York that even the poorest women had their veils and parasols; while Mary Jane Watson, who hired out as a "help" (not a servant!) and who very shortly married "a man in good circumstances," bragged that she had "good clothes, and I can dress as well as any lady in Sedlescomb. I can enjoy a silk and white frock, and crape frock and veil and Morocco shoes, without a parish grumbling about it. . . . The girls here that go out to do house-work dress as well as any lady in Sedlescomb."[17] The greater opportunities of the new land made for a more pronounced attitude of sociability and good feeling. A settler in Venango County, Pennsylvania, wrote that his neighbors were "constantly walking in and out of one another's houses. If you should stay to supper you are invariably pressed to stay all night. I like the people very much. An Englishman was taken suddenly ill; the neighbours all collected together, nearly thirty of them, and in two days got all his corn into the barn for him."[18]

[16] Letter from Pittsburgh, Penn., quoted in S. Smith, *The Settler's New Home, or the Emigrant's Location*, 104. That there was some justification for bitter statements is apparent from the fact that, prior to 1832, holders of sinecures and pensions who contributed nothing to the public service were drawing about £1,100,000 annually from the Treasury.
[17] [B. Smith], *Twenty-four Letters from Labourers in America*, 21 et seq. "I have bought a very handsome leghorn bonnet for 19s., a new hat for John, a pair of shoes each, two new gowns and aprons, a very handsome black silk shawl, and a pair of new trousers for John, and I have a pound to spare; and this is more than I should have had in Frome in a year." (Letter of Sophia Hill from Little York, Upper Canada, in the *Quarterly Review*, September, 1835, pp. 426-7.)
[18] Quoted in S. Smith, *op. cit.*, 103. It is said that only one Roman Catholic was settled among the Protestant Irish of Cavan Township, Upper Canada, but when he took sick at harvest-time the "Cavan Blazers" came secretly and prevented loss by

A Currier and Ives print THE ROCKY MOUNTAINS—EMIGRANTS ON THE PLAINS *Fanny Palmer*

When there was danger of Indian raids travellers proceeded cautiously in long wagon-trains.

Eighty Years' Progress in British North America

BEGINNING A HOME

The crude log shanty provided shelter until a log house could be built.

From Gelkie's Life in the Woods, 1864

OUR HOME IN THE WOODS

The log house was supplanted by an improved home of frame, brick, or stone construction as the settler became more prosperous.

The proverbial hospitality of Canada and the United States was due partly to well-stocked larders and to the co-operative feeling of pioneer life. John Howison advised the intending emigrant that he "must not expect to live very comfortably at first. Pork, bread, and what vegetables he may raise will form the chief part of his diet for perhaps two years"; but while travelling through Upper Canada he noticed that most settlers were soon able to vary their diet with venison, poultry, vegetables, milk, and various types of bread and cakes. Howison concluded that "the people live much better than persons of a similar class in Great Britain; and to have proof of this it is only necessary to visit almost any hut in the backwoods. The interior of it seldom fails to display many substantial comforts, such as immense loaves of beautiful bread, entire pigs hanging around the chimney, dried venison, trenchers of milk, and bags of Indian corn." E. A. Talbot, who spent five years in America, came to the same conclusion, but he expressed it in his own peculiarly snobbish style. He cordially disliked everything and everybody in the new land, and considered it humorous that

"Irish mountaineers or Scotch Highlanders,—who in their native country had seldom, except 'on some high festival of once a year,' sat down to a more luxurious meal than 'murphies' and buttermilk, or to an oaten cake and porridge,—surrounded a table in Canada which groaned beneath the weight of a profusion of sweetmeats and fine fruits, and 'did the honours' with all the politeness of newly-elected Aldermen."

Those settlers who had been accustomed to very little were astonished at the change in their condition. "We love this country well," wrote Thomas Thorley from Cirkland, Ohio; "I have lost the fear of ever wanting! or my children! We have been here at this house seven weeks, during that time one quarter of veal, three quarters of a sheep, two pigs, the one weighing 18 score 9 lbs., the other small, about 40 lbs.; so much for starvation! And then there is liberty. I can take my rifle down and fetch in a brace of large squirrels to make a first-rate pie, or a wild duck; these I fetched in ten minutes." . . . "I have a Good Sugger Bush that will inable Me to Make as much as a Tun of Sugger yearly if I like," wrote a laborer from Upper Canada; while John Watson of Aurora, Indiana, was pleased to note that while he was writing home his wife was "eating preserved peaches and

---

harvesting his crop. As for the practice of walking uninvited into one another's homes, it was frequently most objectionable, and especially when it was coupled with "the borrowing system." Mrs. Susanna Moodie devotes Chapter V of her *Roughing It in the Bush* to this aspect of pioneer sociability.

bread and washing them down with good whiskey and water." Meat, particularly, was more readily available in America. "You know that we could hardly get a taste of meat in England," wrote Charlotte Willard to her sister, "but now we can roast a *quarter* of meat." Patrick Shirreff was told by a Scotchman that "the beef of Canada was so tough that teeth could not chew it"; but however tough it may have been, there was the all-important consideration that while "in the Old Country he got beef only once a week, on Sunday, here he had it three times a day."

The abundance of food and drink aided in the development of a free and easy attitude in many regions. John Down wrote in 1830 that "they do not think of locking the doors in the country, and you can gather peaches, apples, and all kinds of fruit by the side of the roads. And I can have a barrel of cider holding 32 gallons for 4s., and they will lend me the barrel till I have emptied it.... I would rather cross the Atlantic ten times than hear my children cry for victuals once." Conditions in England had not been pleasant for James and Harriot Parks, but they wrote from Greenbush, New York, that "there's no sending children to bed without a supper, or husbands to work without dinners in their bags." Some found the cheapness of alcoholic beverages a great attraction. "You have a good many cold bellies to go to bed with," observed William Snelgrove somewhat crudely; "but if you were with us, for three half-pence your belly would be so warm that you would not know the way to bed." ... "A pint of gin for threepence, and no complaining in our streets," wrote Thomas Lister from Philadelphia in 1830; while Joseph Silcox had no hesitation in stating that "if Lord Bath was to give us Corsley farm rent free" it would not be an inducement sufficient to coax his family back to England. D. Jones of Southampton, Pennsylvania, made the same point, "I would not give my situation and liberties for any Lord's estate in England."

But the greatest recommendation which any land can have is suitable employment for all its inhabitants—a chance to get along in the world. Matthew Houston, a former Paisley weaver, wrote home from Carleton Place, Canada West, in 1841:

"I am very sorry to hear of your distress at home—so many going idle and have no work to do. We may be thankful that we have left the place and come here. We all have plenty of work to do here.... You know the state we were in when we left you—we had neither meat nor money,—but we have plenty of everything that we need at present."

"Urge my brothers to come out if ever they wish to free themselves from bondage," writes another; "this is the land of independence to the industrious—the soil that will repay the labourer for the sweat of his brow." George Hill was particularly pleased that his work as a farm laborer did not entail as much "driving" on the part of his employers as he had found usual in the Old Land:

"Dear father and mother, we left you almost broken-hearted, but you may be satisfied that we have bettered our condition by coming here. . . . We work here from sunrise to sunset, but we don't work so hard as we do at home: we rest through the day very often; they are not so particular here about losing a little time as they are at home."

C. Jones noticed a more fraternal attitude in Buffalo than he had been accustomed to: "Men are not kept under here as they are in England. The masters talk to them like talking to one another." Another immigrant, who was *en route* to Ohio from Queensbury, New Brunswick, in search of cheap land, observed that "an honest, industrious man can maintain his family better by 3 days work here than he can in England by 6." Travellers noticed the greater respectability of appearance and conduct among the "working classes":

"In workshops, generally, the men wear a sort of light overalls over their clothing, so that when work is over they throw these off and appear on the streets more 'respectable' in appearance than the mechanics of Great Britain do after work. . . . In every workshop here there are opportunities for washing after work is over, and in large establishments it is no uncommon thing to find a placard stuck up, with 'Men's Wash Room' upon it. . . . In the evenings and on Sundays the working classes walk about a great deal with their wives and children. . . . Instead of either husband or wife carrying a child in arms they have a light carriage or perambulator which the husband wheels along. . . . The well-dressed appearance of the working class is apparent at once to a stranger from Great Britain, and in most of the cities one fails to see that crowd of ragged unwashed men and women which are to be found about the lazy corners of London, Manchester, Liverpool, Glasgow and such cities."

The improvement in economic and social status soon became proverbial, and was the basis of no end of novels and romances. But it was founded on fact. "By adopting this country as the future home of myself and family," stated George Wood, "I am now a *master*, where I could never well expect otherwise than to see myself and my family as *servants*." A large family of children, which in the British Isles was often "a burthen to their parents and a nuisance to their neighbours, . . . first pilferers, then poachers, and eventually thieves upon a large scale," became instead "really a treasure to a man," . . . "a source of profit and wealth to him, as well as of domestic happiness." A settler located in Lower Canada among "a happy people, enjoying the fruits of their own industry and blessed with all the conveniences of life," wrote that he was "as comfortable as it is possible to be." Though the French Canadians were not "that pushing, enterprizing people, who by dint of strong exertions seek to amass wealth," yet he was pleased to assure his friends in the Old Land that he had seen no poverty among them.

The satisfaction of service was to many settlers a sufficient justification. The Rev. William Bell, the first Presbyterian minister at Perth, Upper Canada, did not regret the hardships of his life. After years of arduous toil as an itinerant preacher in "the bush," he wrote that

"in fulfilling my office, which, in this extensive settlement I can assure you is no sinecure, the heat in summer and the cold in winter have consumed me, till like Jacob of old, sleep has departed from my eyes; . . . though I have had many labours to undergo and difficulties to encounter, I have never once repented coming to this country."

Perhaps the spirit of the pioneer is best expressed by the remarks of the indomitable William Singer, formerly a bricklayer, but in America an agricultural laborer and lumberman:

"I have been very unfortunate, I've cut myself four or five times: I cut my hand in the summer whilst mowing with Meredith Orman on Mr. Silcog's field; I cut my foot very bad four weeks ago, it's not well yet. I cut two of my toes off: Mr. Silcog sewed them on again: they seem to be getting on very well considering the time. You must not think I dislike the country on account of my misfortunes, for if I was to cut my right leg off I should not think of returning to Corsley again, for I could do much better here with one leg than in Corsley with two."[19]

[19] See his letter, from Southwold Township, Upper Canada, quoted in "Doyle," *op. cit.*, 84. While most newcomers undoubtedly laboured under great disadvantages in "backwoods" life, yet there were some who were, by reason of their former occupation, quite handy in the use of new implements. Handloom weavers, for example, made excellent choppers, as they had become somewhat ambidextrous by throwing the shuttle and could cut either right- or left-handed. In the same way tailors became very satisfactory sheep-shearers.

CHAPTER XXII

THE PASSING OF THE SAILING-SHIP

"Sir, a ship is worse than a jail. There is, in a jail, better air, better company, better conveniency of every kind; and a ship has the additional disadvantage of being in danger. When men come to like a sea-life they are not fit to live on land."

Dr. Samuel Johnson

Sailing-vessels reached the peak in development at the very time they were being replaced in the passenger trade by steamships. But for many decades their architecture had been based largely upon tradition or storage capacity. Ships of war had long been built upon the lines of the Elizabethan galleon; while timber ships and other merchant craft were constructed more with a view to the cargo than for speed, good design, or the convenience of passengers. Many early emigrant-carriers were, in the words of a contemporary newspaper, "the worst of all the merchant ships of Great Britain and Ireland; with a few exceptions they are very old, very ill manned, very ill found; and considering the dangers of an early spring voyage to this port, from ice and tempestuous weather, it is perhaps astonishing that more serious accidents have not occurred."

A number of considerations brought about the improvement of vessels. The development of steam tugs, which provided an easy means of towing sailing-vessels out to sea, indirectly aided the development; while the ending of the East India Company's monopoly of trade in 1833, the opening of Chinese ports to foreign commerce in 1842, the repeal of the Navigation Laws in 1849, and the Californian and Australian gold rushes of 1848-51, were all conducive to the construction of better and faster vessels. In the race for tea and gold the American clipper-ship of the 1840's and '50's led the way in design and speed. This period is known as "the Golden Age of Sail." The *Lightning* made 436 miles in a day in 1854, an achievement which steamships could not equal for some thirty years. One of the fastest Canadian-built packets was the *John Bannerman,* which once sailed from St. John to Liverpool in 17 days. Several American ships, among them the *Red*

Jacket of 2,460 tons, made the Atlantic crossing in 13 or 14 days, but not with passengers, and usually only on the eastward voyage; while as early as 1815 the ship *Galatea* is reported to have sailed from Newfoundland to Portsmouth in 11 days without having made a single tack.[1] Probably the best performance of a sailing-ship on this route was that of the American clipper *Sovereign of the Seas*, which sailed the 1,668 miles from the Grand Banks to Cape Clear, Ireland, in 135 hours. This vessel made several other records. Although her greatest day's sailing was 430 miles—six less than the *Lightning's* record day—yet she was in a class by herself for sustained speed. In ten consecutive days she once sailed 3,144 miles, and completed a voyage of 6,245 miles in twenty-two days—a most remarkable achievement. The first iron sailing-ship was the *Ironsides*, 1838, but it was not until the 1850's that iron was replacing wood on a large scale.

One of the finest and most carefully constructed of sailing-vessels was the American line-ship *Cornelius Grinnell*, which was fitted out in Boston in 1850. In August of that year this ship arrived at London, where she excited much curiosity. A detailed technical description of the vessel appeared in the *Illustrated London News,* and indicates the great strength of heavy timbers and beams and the general excellence of structure which characterized the best in shipbuilding.

The *Cornelius Grinnell* was not a large ship, however. In 1855 the title "the largest in the world" was held by the American four-masted clipper-ship *Great Republic*. This magnificent specimen was 305 feet long, 53 feet beam, and her tonnage was 3,400. She drew 25 feet of water, and this, added to her huge size, made it impossible for her to enter the London docks. The management of the sails and other heavy work was facilitated by a steam engine of 8 horse-power. At the other extreme were the small craft in which the adventurous occasionally crossed the Atlantic. In 1857 the cutter yacht *Charter Oak* made the passage, and in the following year Charles R. Webb built the *Christopher Columbus*, of 45 tons, and with two boys reached New York from Southampton in 45 days. A newspaper commented that "a more frail-looking bark in which to cross the Atlantic it is scarcely possible to conceive."[2] Suggesting that the passenger vessels of the 18th

---

[1] All sorts of records and other curious information relative to Atlantic shipping, and particularly to early steamers, may be found in Maginnis, *The Atlantic Ferry: its Ships, Men and Working*.

[2] *Illustrated London News,* November 13, 1858, pp. 445-6. Some of the most noteworthy voyages of exploration were made in very small vessels. In 1610 Henry Hudson

THE PASSING OF THE SAILING-SHIP 235

century were dungeons, with the added disadvantage that you could not possibly get out, a newspaper of 1852 observed in an account of the 1,420-ton *Ben Nevis* that

"the wonderful developments of science, in their application to the purposes of social life, are nowhere more visible than in the progress of marine architecture, and in the accommodation now afforded to those whose business or pleasure leads them 'to go down to the sea in ships.' There is as much difference between a packet ship of the present time and its counterpart of twenty years ago as between an elegant modern villa and the rude hut of a peasant. The object seems to have been, by added accommodation and the perfecting of every arrangement, almost to make passengers forget that they are on shipboard, for it is certain that they may now sail to the Antipodes without missing one of the essential comforts of home."

The development of steamships was, of course, a great incentive to the best in sailing-vessels. In 1860 another notable clipper-ship, the *Great Australia,* entered the passenger trade. She was a three-masted three-decker of 1,660 tons, and was 204 feet long. On this vessel the third-class accommodation in "the spacious, well-ventilated and well-lighted 'tween decks" is described as "superior to anything that has ever been seen before. The berths are judiciously arranged, and everything about the apartment wears an aspect of comfort and cheerfulness. . . . Altogether this may be said to be a model passenger ship." A few years earlier, on January 17, 1856, the *Royal Charter* had provided the first important trial of the principle of a combination of clipper-ship and auxiliary steam power. She was also the first large English vessel to adopt the American plan of double topsails on each mast. Her accommodations for passengers were greatly improved, particularly in the third class or steerage. Instead of long tables midway between the rows of berths the *Royal Charter* had special mess-rooms, and the same arrangement applied, with more luxurious quarters, in the first and second cabins. As this ship was launched during the Crimean War she carried eight guns.

Auxiliary steam power had been applied to sailing-vessels many years before its use on the Atlantic. The first steamship of practical utility, the *Charlotte Dundas,* was in successful operation on the Forth and Clyde Canal in 1803, and by 1818 there were steamers on all the chief rivers of England and Scotland, as well as two which crossed the Irish Sea with mail. The coastal service was the next to introduce steam vessels, and, as construction and power improved, steamships travelled to neighboring countries,

reached Hudson Bay in the *Discovery,* of only 55 tons, and the same ship carried several subsequent expeditions to Arctic waters.

even as far as Scandinavia in the north and Madeira in the south. Scientists were, however, almost unanimous in the opinion that the ocean passage was not practicable by steam power, the greatest drawback being the apparent impossibility of carrying enough fuel to supply the engines.

Fortunately the opinions of experts did not prevent the attempts of enthusiasts. In 1819 the American Ship *Savannah*, fitted with steam and sails, crossed the Atlantic in 27 days; but sails alone were employed during 568 of the 648 hours, for after the engines had been used a few days there was sufficient fuel left only to enable her to steam impressively into Liverpool. During the voyage the British revenue cruiser *Kite*, observing the smoke, thought the *Savannah* was on fire and pursued her for an entire day in an attempt to rescue the passengers, but the *Savannah* steamed proudly on. A Canadian vessel, the *Royal William*, was probably the first to cross the ocean with steam as the main motive power. Built at Quebec in 1830-31, she traded on the Atlantic coast for some time, and then left Quebec for London in 1833. Stopping at Pictou for a short time, she then proceeded across the Atlantic, reaching London twenty-five days later. The voyage is referred to in some quarters as "the first complete passage wholly under steam"; but the *Royal William* was schooner-rigged, with three masts, and presumably used sails whenever advantageous. That she was the first to cross the Atlantic under steam has often been disputed, but Sir Sandford Fleming considered that "to my mind it is incontestably established that the memorable voyage of the *Royal William* in 1833 must be held to be the first passage across the Atlantic under steam"; and a later authority states that this conclusion "has now (1898) been generally accepted."[8] The *Royal William*, which had accommodation for only 60 passengers, was sold in 1834 to the Spanish Government and was converted into a warship.

Among other early voyages with steam as the main motive power may be mentioned those of the *Sirius* and *Great Western* in 1838. The *Sirius* left Cork on April 4th, arriving at New York on the 23rd; while the *Great Western* sailed from Bristol several days after the *Sirius*, but reached port only a few hours behind her. Both vessels were accorded a typical New York reception. The *Great Britain*, 1843-44, was the first large screw steamship,

[8] Hopkins (Ed.), *Canada, an Encyclopaedia of the Country*, III 340-1. On June 28, 1894, during a meeting of the Colonial Conference at Ottawa, a brass tablet was placed at the entrance to the Library of Parliament in commemoration of the event.

THE PASSING OF THE SAILING-SHIP 237

and had also the distinction of being the earliest transatlantic liner of iron construction.

The first Cunard liner, the *Britannia*, created quite a flurry of excitement when she arrived at Boston in 1840, and inspired at least one sermon, which also appeared in print. The approach of this vessel to the shores of America is represented by the clergyman, Ezra S. Gannett, as "fraught with issues of spiritual moment to the whole world," and the notable event is contrasted with the approach of the *Mayflower* 220 years earlier:

> "In 1620 the *Mayflower* entered Massachusetts Bay, after a tedious and perilous passage of more than two months' duration, across the then almost untravelled ocean, and cast anchor in sight of a sterile coast, amidst the bleakness of winter. In 1840 the *Britannia*, after crossing the same waters in little more than two weeks, approaches, amidst the splendours of summer, a city crowning the curve of that same bay, around whose whole extent may be seen flourishing towns and the promise of an ample harvest.... The hopes that were cherished in the little cabin of the *Mayflower* have been more than realized. God grant that the hopes which now swell the bosoms of a vast community be not disappointed!"[4]

The four earliest Cunard liners were of great importance in providing well-to-do emigrants to New York with passages by steam, though it was the late 'forties before the movement towards travel in steam vessels had gained impetus. The screw-propelled *Globe*, which started her maiden voyage on December 11, 1850, was another vessel which was influential in diverting passenger traffic from sailing-ships. Writing in that year, Dr. John Bigsby observed that "steamboats have now converted Atlantic passages into mere courses of good eating in good company for prescribed periods, except for ambassadors, governors of colonies, and such-like, who must still submit to the honours and headwinds of the Queen's frigates";[5] while some years later Sir William Butler found the "steam-and-sail" crossing "no longer a voyage" but merely "a run" of definite duration—though on her previous passage the *Samaria* broke her shaft and was missing

[4] Gannett, *The Arrival of the Britannia. A Sermon Delivered in the Federal Street Meeting-House, in Boston, July 19, 1840*. The pamphlet has been reprinted in facsimile by the Cunard Steamship Company, Ltd. In 1844 the *Britannia* was frozen in Boston harbour, and was released only when the inhabitants of the city cut a seven-mile canal to open water.
[5] Bigsby, *The Shoe and Canoe*, I 1. Of some interest in this connection is Lady Aylmer's account of her experiences on the frigate *Pique*. The vessel grounded on the Labrador coast, finally got off and proceeded towards England, but lost her rudder and had to steer by trimming the sails, the passengers being transferred to a passing vessel. The whole story, with the addition of many a pious hope and fear, is told in a rambling and incoherent manner by one who terms herself "a weak, helpless woman." (See her *Narrative of the Passage of the Pique across the Atlantic*.) The British Navy lagged behind both in the change from sail to steam, and from wood to iron, being eventually forced to follow the trend of the times because of the proximity of the more advanced French fleet.

for nearly a month. Robert Gourlay was perhaps unduly optimistic when he observed in 1849 that by steamship "any one may leave the County of Fife, be in Boston the eleventh day from departure, and within a fortnight bathe in the Ohio, the Mississippi, or Missouri." He recognized the increased cost of the faster passage, however, and suggested that by dispensing with superfluities and "crowding in" the emigrants it would be possible to reduce the fare from $125 to $30.

As an example of the gradual change from sailing packet to steam-and-sail the *Helena Sloman* may be taken. Prior to the construction of this screw steamship in Hull, England, in 1850, German emigrants to America usually travelled from Hamburg to Hull, thence across England to Liverpool, and by British or American ships to Quebec or New York. The *Helena Sloman*, the first of a line designed to carry passengers from Hamburg to New York, was of a model and rig "calculated equally for steaming and sailing," and her two 80 h.p. engines supplied steam "by tubular boilers on a new construction," which enabled a great saving in fuel, only 12 cwt. per hour being necessary to drive the ship at a rate of 9 knots against a head wind. She carried 600 tons of coal and a cargo, and had accommodations for 50 first-class passengers, 50 second-class, and 300 third-class. The hold was divided into six water-tight compartments, and the between-decks was six feet high, well ventilated, and fitted with iron bedsteads for the third-class passengers. For the accommodation of first-class and second-class there were not only "cheerful and convenient staterooms and berths," but also

"a spacious and handsome saloon, lighted from the sides and top, and entered from both the main decks and the poop, the latter entrance leading into a smoking-room apart from the principal saloon. . . . The panelling is of bird's-eye maple, highly polished, with gilt mouldings and spiral columns of the same beautiful wood, between which are placed several mirrors. The seats and sofas are also of maple, and covered with green velvet."

The transfer of passenger traffic from sail to steam (or, more accurately, to "steam-and-sail") was very rapid in the 1850's. Of 7,836 emigrants who entered the St. Lawrence in 1860, no less than 6,932 were on steamships and only 904 on sailing-vessels, though on the more open American route sails persisted a little longer, and a traveller might do much worse than book on "the Travelling Scotchman" or "one of Messrs. Hall's unrivalled Aberdeen clippers." The best of such ships—like the *Great Australia*—continued as emigrant-carriers in the Australian trade until the close of the century, but the traffic passed to the steamship much earlier on the Atlantic. It is an indication of the improved general condition of British emigrants that, although the cost of a steam passage was about one-third more than by sail, many were able to afford the faster service. In 1863 forty-five per cent of British emigrants to America travelled in steamships; while three years later the number had increased to eighty-one per cent. Sailing-ships continued to be patronized by small groups of the poorest emigrants in later years, particularly from the Irish ports at a distance from steamship service, but their numbers gradually decreased until they were a negligible quantity; for even a very low fare, unless inclusive of decent rations, could hardly compete with the much faster passage offered by the steamship.

Steamship service had been in operation for nearly twenty years on the New York route before it was inaugurated to Quebec and Montreal. Sir Hugh Allan led the way, but his first ships—the *Canadian* and the *Indian*—were immediately employed to transport troops to the seat of the Crimean War. In 1856 the Allan Line fortnightly Atlantic mail service commenced, and two years later four new vessels were added and the mails carried weekly. Intense competition, though it ruined many companies, was not the most serious problem with which they had to deal. As an example of the losses which most early steamship companies suffered the record of the Allan Line may be taken. The *Canadian* was wrecked in 1857 through the stupidity of a pilot; the *Indian* was lost in 1859 near Halifax; the *Hungarian* ran ashore near Cape Sable in 1860, and everyone on board perished; in 1861 a second *Canadian* was crushed in an ice-field in the Strait of Belle Isle, and the *North Briton* was wrecked in a snow storm; in 1863 both the *Anglo-Saxon* and the *Norwegian* were lost; and in the following year the *Bohemian* struck a rock off the state of Maine. Such a list of disasters[6] would ruin any company, and the Allan Line was kept solvent only by greater subsidies from the Canadian Government. In the meantime methods of navigation were gradually being improved. The introduction of the floating compass made the art of sailing a more exact science, and the hazards were further decreased by the employment of better pilots, the construction of more powerful engines, the extension of telegraphs, and the lighting of the River and Gulf of St. Lawrence,

[6] Between 1840 and 1890 about 120 steamships disappeared during the Atlantic crossing, and no trace of 24 of them was ever found.

with the result that the Allan Line lost only one vessel during the last thirty years of the century.

On the New York service, meanwhile, had come some notable ships. The true forerunner of the huge modern liner was the 22,500-ton *Great Eastern*, with paddle-wheels as well as screw, and six masts (five of them of iron) carrying some six or seven thousand square feet of canvas. Very much larger than any other vessel afloat, she was 705 feet long, nearly 90 feet wide, and had for a long-boat a steamship 100 feet in length. The periodicals of the day delighted in giving minute descriptions of the giant vessel, and the *Illustrated London News*[7] produced hundreds of engravings over the period which elapsed between her commencement in 1857 and her first voyage in 1860. Five funnels carried off the smoke produced by the fires essential to operate her engines. She had accommodation for 4,000 passengers—or 10,000 soldiers might be crowded in if necessary. Enthusiastically described as a "floating palace, . . . a series of first-class hotels," she had a protected promenade on the upper deck where the ladies of the saloon "may display the newest Parisian and London fashions with as much effect and to almost as many admirers as on a fine afternoon in Regent-street or the Esplanade at Brighton." The captain, we are informed, "will telegraph his orders," and even from a central position he "will have to use a telescope to see what is going on at the bow and stern." Lighted at night by gas manufactured on board, the ship also provided both warm and cold baths, and every other known luxury which cabin passengers might hope to enjoy. In fact a contemporary publication stated that it was estimated that

"her vast weight will effectually resist the attacks of storm and wind, and that seasickness will be a thing unknown in her experience. . . . This stupendous experiment will cost, ere the first trial is completed, nearly a million sterling. . . . Her success, if she does succeed, will inaugurate a new epoch in the history of steam navigation."

After all the publicity the ship was not the success confidently anticipated. Even the first attempts to launch her almost ended in disaster. She commenced her maiden voyage on June 17, 1860, and reached New York in eleven days, having on board only 36 passengers; and so much coal was consumed that it was impossible to show a profit from her operation. Her most notable achievement

---

[7] Over a period of several years the *Illustrated London News* covered in great detail the construction, launching, and operation of the *Great Eastern*. See May 30, 1857; June 13, 1857; November 7, 1857; and, among many others, the issues of December, 1858, January, February, August, September and October, 1859, and June 23, 1860.

THE PASSING OF THE SAILING-SHIP 241

was the laying of the Atlantic cable, and after a life of some 25 years she was broken up in 1886. The *Great Eastern* was a noble experiment, but too great an advance was attempted at one jump, and the vessel was consequently half a century ahead of her time. Her importance was greatest during the three years when she was under construction, when at times she almost monopolized the public interest to the exclusion of such world events as the War of Italian Liberation and the Sicilian Revolution.

The general characteristics of the Atlantic passage during the transition stage between sail and steam will be best shown by reference to voyages on a few of the more notable "steam-and-sail" vessels. Captain Barclay-Allardice crossed on the *Britannia* in April, 1841, and although the passage was stormy he considered that the vessel was well adapted for Atlantic navigation. He observed, however, that the absence of cargo, apart from the passengers, their baggage, and the mailbags, made her roll excessively, and there resulted a "constant crashing of plates, glasses, and other moveable articles." The ship was considered to be in "a crowded state," although there were only ninety passengers aboard; and the fare of forty-one pounds combined with the exclusion of steerage passengers to make the company not only "select" but "agreeable"—"There was, in fact, not a single *black sheep* on board." Fourteen days after leaving Liverpool the *Britannia* reached Halifax[8]—"a miserable dirty place; the houses all of wood and straggling in every direction; the streets narrow and a foot deep in mud." Eight hours later the ship left for Boston, which, in contrast with Halifax, Captain Barclay found "much to be admired."

Charles Dickens sailed for Boston on the *Britannia* in the winter of 1842, and wrote a lengthy account of his experiences. When he and his wife set out from Liverpool on their memorable discovery of America, a small steam tender carried them to the ship, which stood at anchor some distance off. A scene of great activity was presented in and around the *Britannia* as supplies, baggage, and passengers were conveyed on board and assigned by bustling stewards and lesser personages to their respective places. The main saloon was decribed by Dickens as "a gigantic hearse," heated by "a melancholy stove,"[9] and surrounded by long

[8] Halifax and St. John are the chief Canadian winter ports on the Atlantic, and Halifax was the port of entry for overseas mail.
[9] The development of heating in Atlantic passenger vessels was from open fireplace to stove, and thence to gas on the *Great Eastern*, and in later years to hot-water or steam radiators.

tables on which glasses and decanters were carefully fastened in place. Altogether it was so different from advertisements and expectations that the passengers "actually reeled beneath the blow." Similarly astonished at the cramped quarters of their stateroom, Mr. and Mrs. Dickens were soon resigned to the inevitable, and busily occupied themselves in examining (with some misgivings) its internal arrangements and conveniences. There was, in fact, no appreciable difference between the *Britannia* and the best sailing packets—with the exception of the speedier passage; and from Dickens' vivid description of a storm at sea it is apparent that the elements made no concessions to the more advanced method of navigation: "Words cannot express it. Thoughts cannot convey it. Only a dream can call it up again in all its fury, rage and passion." Better weather was always promised for the morrow, the fire in the saloon stove would frequently not burn, the lights were sometimes too poor for reading, the meals were not all appreciated, the fruit was sometimes a little mouldy, the paddle-boxes were smashed and the rigging knotted, tangled and drooping; but brandy-and-water, great-coats and rubbers of whist enabled the passengers to survive the voyage—which, it must be remembered, was in mid-winter.[10] Perhaps a more typical reaction was that of George Moore after his passage on the *Great Western* in 1844. Fourteen days after leaving Liverpool the ship was in New York harbor; and the detailed bill of fare of a "grand state-dinner" left little to be desired, and lost nothing in comparison to the extensive menu he sampled at the Astor, "the world's largest hotel."

With the change from sail to steam, emigration lost many of its old terrors, though the Atlantic crossing could not be pleasant and at the same time cheap. Disease and suffering now became unusual, and complaints and lawsuits infrequent. Rapacious and dishonest captains and agents, so general in sailing-ship days, were squeezed out of the trade when the expensive steamship, operated by large companies, replaced the sailing-vessels which were largely owned by individuals. It would be easy, however, to exaggerate the improvement in the accommodations supplied by early steamships, particularly insofar as the steerage passenger was concerned. Robert Louis Stevenson travelled to America in

---

[10] See the first two chapters of Dickens' *American Notes for General Circulation*. As eminent a contemporary reviewer as Lord Macaulay considered the *American Notes* "at once frivolous and dull, . . . vulgar and flippant," and that Buckingham's and Mrs. Trollope's descriptions of the United States, defective as they were, were much preferable. (Trevelyan, *The Life and Letters of Lord Macaulay*, II 109.)

1879 in the second cabin of an iron "steam-and-sail" ship, and found that his accommodation, as in the average sailing-ship, was little more than a separate section of the steerage. As he closely observed steerage conditions, as well as describing his own privileges and conveniences, his account makes an excellent companion-picture to Charles Dickens' narrative of a first-cabin passage in the *Britannia* thirty-seven years before, and enables comparison with the conditions under which millions made the voyage in earlier years.

The second cabin was "a modified oasis" in the heart of a group of five steerage compartments, and through the thin partition came the sounds of various activities, pleasant and otherwise. There were, however, advantages in the second cabin: complete, if somewhat crude furnishings were provided, and the diet was superior in theory if not always in practice. Porridge was a standard food; but soup, roast beef, Irish stew, potatoes, bread and pudding—some of them quite evidently rehashed from the remains of the cabin feasts—were dealt out in varying quality in second cabin and steerage. But how much better the meals were than in sailing-ship days! The steerage passage cost six guineas, however, and the second-cabin eight; but the extra two guineas provided not only better berths and meals but better air—in fact, second-cabin passengers were "ladies and gentlemen," those in the steerage merely "males and females."

Stevenson's account of his experiences indicates in what respects, besides the shortness of the passage, the life of the emigrant was on a higher plane than was possible in the sailing-ship. The majority of the steerage passengers were "hugely discontented" with the food offered, condemning it as "only fit for pigs" and "a disgrace," though it is suggested that they were unreasonable in this respect. But there is no doubt of the vileness of their quarters:

"A single night had filled them with horror. . . . The engine pounded, the screw tossed out of water with a roar and shook the ship from end to end. . . . Steerage No. 1 is lined with eight pens of sixteen bunks apiece. . . . At night the place is lit with two lanterns. . . . The yellow flicker of the lantern spun round and round and tossed the shadows in masses. The air was hot, but it struck a chill from its foetor. From all round in the dark bunks the scarcely human noises of the sick joined into a kind of farmyard chorus, . . . the hateful coughing and retching, and the sobs of children."

But in the daytime the hours were passed in chess, cards, dominoes, puzzles of various types, guesses as to the ship's progress (but never a bet), and games which on land would be considered childish; while spirits rose as the weather improved, a fiddler encouraged reels, jigs and ballads, and it was soon time for "grisly tales" of the predominance of sharpers at New York, whereby an immigrant might well "instantly and mysteriously disappear from the ranks of mankind."[11]

But little remains to be said of the passing of the wind-ship. While their use as passenger-carriers became unusual, they continued in the merchant traffic, visiting Montreal in greater number than steamships as late as 1880. In subsequent years, however, the replacement of the old type of navigation was very rapid. At the outbreak of the World War in 1914 there were forty-three clipper-ships surviving in the merchant trade, and only three of these were British. The oldest of them had been built in 1864 and the most recent dated from 1891, and it is perhaps unnecessary to add that they bore but little relationship to the great sailing-ships of the eighteen-fifties.[12] A few old schooners still ply the Atlantic—even engage in passenger traffic of a kind. Three of them sailed from American ports in the winter of 1935, bound for the Cape Verde Islands off the African coast and carrying passengers of Portuguese and African descent. An Associated Press despatch from New Bedford, Massachusetts, gives details of the trade, and expresses fears that two of the packets, fourteen or fifteen weeks out, had been lost:

"As two Cape Verde Island packets, the *John R. Manta* and the *Winnipesaukee*, with 45 men, women and children aboard, remained unreported to-night, demands were voiced here for some form of supervision and regulation of old windjammers engaged in the trade. While old salts muttered the reputed malign influence of the number '13,' others less influenced by superstitions felt the condition of the two old schooners might have had more to do with it, if they had foundered, than the fact they carried crews of 13.

"Both schooners are long overdue at the islands off the African coast. The *Manta* is 108 days out of Providence, R. I., and the *Winnipesaukee* 98 days out of New Bedford. Another packet, the former pilot boat *Trenton*, which sailed after the other two cleared, arrived at her destination a week or so ago. The *Manta* and the *Winnipesaukee* are two of a group of ill-assorted old sailing craft that serve many southern New England residents of Portuguese and African blood as a medium of travel to their native islands."

As for the steam liners which have supplanted the sailing-ship, they have continued to become larger, more powerful, more

---

[11] Stevenson, *The Amateur Emigrant*, Biographical Edition, 14 *et seq.* How interesting a steam-and-sail voyage might be, especially on paper, may be seen from an account in *Canada and the Western States*, part II 18-26.
[12] A list of these survivals of another age may be found in Lubbock, *The Colonial Clippers*, appendix, 416.

Illustrated London News
THE "GREAT BRITAIN," 1844
Notable as the first large screw steamship and the earliest transatlantic vessel of iron construction.

Illustrated London News
THE SALOON OF THE "GREAT EASTERN" IN A STORM, 1861
It was confidently expected that the 22,500-ton "steam-and-sail" *Great Eastern* would be entirely immune from the effects of storms!

Reproduced by courtesy of the Cunard-White Star Line
THE "BRITANNIA," 1840, AND THE "QUEEN MARY," 1936, IN NEW YORK HARBOR

THE PASSING OF THE SAILING-SHIP 245

magnificent. After 1870 the invention of the compound engine and improvements in condensers not only reduced the cost but enabled speedier transportation; and the development of cheap steel by Bessemer soon rendered out-of-date the use of iron in the construction of ships. All sorts of improvements and innovations in accommodation were gradually introduced, among which perhaps the least important was that (credited to the White Star Line) of providing special bridal chambers, "as in this age of rapid transit a trip across the Atlantic is not too extensive for a honeymoon."[13] In 1874 two large Cunard liners accommodated a greatly increased number of steerage passengers, but at the sacrifice of speed. Other vessels continued to reduce the time necessary for the crossing. In 1881 the *Servia* reached New York from Queenstown in 6 days, 23 hours, and 50 minutes, and three years later nearly a day was cut from this record; while we approach modern times and modern speeds with a 5½-day average in 1898.

The employment of sails to supplement the power generated by steam continued, however, long after their use was essential to maintain good speed, and almost all Atlantic steamships of the 1880's were rigged as barques or schooners. It is thought that the first vessel to cross the Atlantic under steam alone was the Cunard Royal Mail steel screw liner *Umbria*, which, although fully equipped with sails, made no use of such supplementary aid during a voyage in 1884. In 1888-1889 the Inman and International Line produced two twin-screw steel steamers, the *City of New York* and the *City of Paris*; the former was the first twin-screw ship to cross the Atlantic. The type of construction was almost completely transformed by these vessels, three polemasts with but little sail-power all but ending any dependence upon the wind. The twin screws, as an authority relates with some feeling, had "sounded the death-knell of all the timehonoured and romantic associations of the glistening sail and flowing sheet"; for the reason for the retention of sailing equipment had been the possibility of the crippling of the ship in midocean by the failure of a single power plant. This partial abandonment of sail power was carried still further by the White Star liners *Teutonic* (1889) and *Majestic* (1890), which have a very modern appearance, though even the latter was rigged as a three-

[13] Maginnis, *op. cit.*, 76. An account of a passage to New York on the White Star liner *Germanic* in 1878 is of considerable interest in this connection. See "Incidents of a Journey Round the World," in *The Sunday at Home*, 1880, pp. 22-6.

masted schooner; and it was only a matter of a short time before sailing equipment was entirely omitted, the masts being replaced by flagpoles or derricks.

As has already been described, the period 1850-1870 saw the gradual transference of the emigrant trade from sailing-ships to "steam-and-sail"; while the use of sails as auxiliary power may be assumed to have passed by 1890. Sailing-vessels predominated until the end of the 1863 season, during which 55 per cent patronized them; but in subsequent years the steamship quickly assumed the lead, and by 1870 the number of sailing-ship passengers was negligible. Allowing for the overlapping of the two types of transport, the total of some eleven millions who crossed the Atlantic between 1770 and 1890 is fairly evenly divided between sail and "steam-and-sail." The following table is as accurate as it is possible to compile from available data:[14]

Period	British Provinces	United States	Total
1770-1814 (estimated)	500,000	400,000	900,000
1815-1863	1,243,040	3,301,489	4,544,529
1864-1890	606,311	5,247,052	5,853,363
1770-1890	2,349,351	8,948,541	11,297,892

A reference to the largest liners in the world today will enable comparison with early sailing-vessels and steamships. The French liner *Normandie* established new records for both westward and eastward crossings. Her maiden voyage to New York, completed on June 3, 1935, was made in four days, 11 hours, 42 minutes for the passage of 3,192 miles from Southampton to Ambrose Light. She averaged 29.64 knots or almost 35 miles per hour throughout the passage, and made another record of 754 miles within 24 hours. The eastward voyage, which from sailing-ship days has always been made in faster time, was completed at the record average speed of 30.31 knots per hour, or 4 days, 3 hours, 28 minutes for the passage from Ambrose Lightship to Bishop's Rock. The gross tonnage of the *Normandie* is 82,000, and her

[14] Fragmentary figures only are available for the period prior to 1815, when official returns were first made, and the totals given are consequently merely estimates. There was a considerable movement westward in the early seventeen-seventies, but it was slowed up by the Revolutionary War; while after the seventeen-nineties the wars with Napoleon resulted in the official prohibition of emigration, though small groups are known to have left from time to time without permission. It is, perhaps, unnecessary to state that a large proportion of those who entered colonial ports proceeded immediately to the United States; in some years only from one-fifth to one-sixth remained in the British provinces. There were, on the other hand, comparatively few who entered at New York and proceeded across the international border. Detailed annual returns since 1815 may be found in Carrothers, *Emigration from the British Isles*, Appendix I, 305-6.

THE PASSING OF THE SAILING-SHIP

length almost one-fifth of a mile. It took 4,000 men four years to build her, and the cost was about $53,000,000. Although 2,170 passengers paid handsomely for the privilege of crossing to New York on the maiden voyage, it is anticipated that a large deficit in her operation will be met by a subsidy from the French Government, for the cost of fuel oil and motor oil is $167,000 for each round trip, and the wages of the crew of 1,400 amount to $76,000 monthly. A three-story pier was specially constructed for her at New York at a cost of $4,275,500.

The Cunard-White Star liner *Queen Mary*, with a length of 1,018 feet (11½ less than the *Normandie*) and a gross tonnage of 80,773, left Southampton on her maiden voyage on May 27, 1936. Her engines developed 200,000 horse-power as against 160,000 generated by her rival of the French Line. Almost every room on the *Queen Mary* has a private bath and telephone, and many of them have been individually designed by famous artists and finished in rare woods and fabrics. Two acres of open deck space and a magnificent dining-room which will seat 800 guests are among other notable features of this twelve-deck giant ship. Her 140-ton rudder alone exceeds the tonnage of many an early sailing-ship. Her westward record is 4 days, 7 hours, and 12 minutes, or 4½ hours better than the *Normandie's* record crossing; at the same time her average speed was 30.01 knots per hour as compared with the 29.64 knots of the *Normandie*. Similarly the record for the eastward passage to Bishop's Rock was lowered to 3 days, 23 hours, and 57 minutes, at the average rate of 30.65 knots per hour; and as her best day's travel stands at 766 miles her supremacy over the *Normandie* is unquestionable.

In the modern period it has been usual for the largest and fastest vessels to cater more or less exclusively to first- and second-cabin passengers, leaving the emigrant trade to the slower boats. Since the outbreak of the World War, moreover, immigration into America has been greatly restricted, both naturally and artificially. As for the ships themselves, oil-burning boilers are to a considerable extent replacing those using coal, and Diesel internal combustion engines are offering strong competition. The most notable development in accommodations has been the "tourist third-class" passage, used by thousands of voyagers who would· not wish to travel steerage, and who cannot afford, or for one reason or another dislike, the cabin passage. While the service still has its dangers and its disasters—like the loss of the great

Titanic in 1912—the passage, no matter how disagreeable, is speedily over; and it is apparent, in spite of all sentimental memories of the days of sail, that no one was the loser when the ancient mode of ocean travel disappeared, for upon close inspection the glamour of the sailor's life usually fades into misery.

SOURCE REFERENCES

This compilation of source material is arranged by chapter and page to facilitate reference. Items are given in the order of the appearance of quotations or citations to which they refer. The name of the author, or the pseudonym under which he wrote, indicates his work, which is given only where more than one title appears under his name in the Bibliography; while abbreviated titles are given for works published anonymously. In the few instances where other than the first edition is cited this is indicated, but the edition is not repeated at every subsequent citation. Sources given in the footnotes are not repeated here, but corroboratory and supplementary references are included where they are considered of special value. The *Illustrated London News* is referred to as the *News*, and the titles of official reports and other sources which admit of abbreviation are similarly shortened.

Chapter I

Page 1—MacLeod's Memoirs, 1785, appended to Boswell's *Journal*.
Page 2—Boswell, I 137; Johnson, XV 156 and 185; Bell, "A History" (MS.); Public Archives of Canada, Q 328, p. 143.
Page 3—Quoted *Edinburgh Review*, January, 1828, pp. 224-5; Evidence of Mr. Hulton, *ibid.*, 225.
Page 4—*Edinburgh Review*, December, 1826, p. 49, and *Quarterly Review*, September, 1835, pp. 413-17; "A Canadian Settler," 3-5.
Page 6—*News*, August 6, 1842, p. 193; J. Buchanan's *Project*; Bannister's *Sketches of Plans*.
Page 7—Alexander, *Sketches*, II 223; *News*, October 20, 1849, p. 257.
Page 8—London *Times*, August 26, 1847, p. 4, and September 17, 1847, p. 4.
Page 9—*Littell's Living Age*, September 7, 1850, p. 492; Mooney, quoted *ibid.*, p. 497.

Chapter II

Page 10—Report to a Parliamentary Committee, 1802-3.
Page 11—Henry, preface, V; Lamond, 47; Neilson, 32; 43 Geo. 3, c. 83.
Page 12—Public Archives of Canada, Q 135, p. 91; 56 Geo. 3, c. 83; Public Archives of Canada, Q 135, p. 106.
Page 13—Bell, 19-22; 4 Geo. 4, c. 83; *Edinburgh Review*, December, 1826, p. 62.
Page 14—*Report of the Select Committee on Emigration, May 26, 1826*, 172-3, 38, and 41; 7 and 8 Geo. 4, c. 116; 9 Geo. 4, c. 21.
Page 15—5 and 6 Will. 4, c. 56; Levinge, I 3 fn.
Page 16—Report of the Emigration Officer at St. Andrews, 1847; Letter of J. and E. Thorpe, quoted in Cobbett's *Guide*, 78-9; 10 and 11 Victoria, c. 103; *Chambers' Edinburgh Journal*, April 13, 1844, p. 229.
Page 17—Report of the Emigration Agent at London, 1838; *Chambers' Edinburgh Journal*, April 13, 1884, p. 229; 12 and 13 Victoria, c. 33; 5 and 6 Victoria, c. 107; 15 and 16 Victoria, c. 44; 16 and 17 Victoria, c. 84; 18 and 19 Victoria, c. 119.
Page 18—Lubbock, 2; Foster to Hobart, *Colonial Land and Emigration Commissioners' Annual Report*, 1851.
Page 19—Quoted in Durham's *Report*, Lucas, II 250-3.

Chapter III

Page 20—M'Donald, preface to 5th edition; Talbot, I 6 fn.
Page 21—*Sussex Emigrants for Canada*, VIII; Proclamation, February 22, 1815, Public Archives of Canada, Q 328, p. 143; Talbot, I 17 et seq.
Page 22—M'Donald, 3-5; Quebec *Mercury*, June 12, 1821; *Edinburgh Review*, December, 1826, p. 49.
Page 25—A. C. Buchanan, 19 et seq.
Page 28—B. Smith, preface, IV; Scrope, 9; "A Citizen," *Thoughts on Emigration*, 15.
Page 29—*News*, January 15, 1853, pp. 39-42; Gourlay, *Emigration*, 3-4.
Page 30—Gourlay, *Emigration*, 3-4.
Page 31—Cobbett, *Rural Rides*, II 81, and *Weekly Political Register*, March 12, 1831; "A Cabin Passenger," 25 and 29; Quoted in Durham's *Report*, II 250.
Page 32—Evidence of Mr. Jessop, Durham's *Report*, II 250.
Page 33—*News*, April 13, 1844, p. 230, and December 21, 1844, p. 398

Chapter IV

Page 34—*News*, July 6, 1850, pp. 16-21; *News*, April 25, 1857, p. 384.
Page 35—Howe, 27-8; A. C. Buchanan, 89; Watson, 20.
Page 36—Mudie, 199; S. Smith, 12 and preface; Hill, 285; Diary of F. Thomas, June 22, 1833; Letter of James Tewsley, quoted in Barclay, 33.
Page 37—Shipping records cited in S. C. Johnson, 70; *Quebec Gazette*, May 19, 1834, and May 23, 1834; McGregor, I 456.
Page 38—"Doyle," 47; Linton, *Backwoodsman*, 17-18; Quoted in "Doyle," 83; W. Singer, quoted ibid., 85; E. Prongley, quoted ibid., 81; *Letters from the South Side of the Hills*, 10; Rose, II 245-7.
Page 39—Lewellin, 32; Cattermole, 94; *Letters from Emigrants sent by the Petworth Committee*, 11; Quoted in Barclay, 43; ibid., 25; Rose, II 245-7; Mudie, 206; "Doyle," 46.
Page 40—A. C. Buchanan, 88; Rose, II 247; Evans, 118; Rose, II 244-9; *Letters from Canada*, 51-2.
Page 41—Duncumb, 26-7; Dunlop, 32-52; Inches, 161-5; Cobbett, 100; Evans, 119.
Page 42—*Sussex Emigrants for Canada*, VI.

Chapter V

Page 43—Letter of Robert Stevenson, quoted in Abbott, *The Emigrant*, 60; Boswell, II 39.
Page 44—*News*, December 21, 1844, p. 398.
Page 45—*News*, May 10, 1851, pp. 386-8, and "A Cabin.Passenger," 106.

Chapter VI

Page 47—Mrs. Turnbull, quoted in *The American Traveller*, 20; "An English Farmer," 10 and 12-13.
Page 48—*Chambers' Edinburgh Journal*, April 13, 1844, pp. 228-9; Buchanan, 86; Colonial Office circular, February 9, 1832; *News*, July 6, 1850, pp. 19-20.
Page 49—Colonial Office Records, quoted in Cowan, 211; *Emigrant's Informant*, 27; Weston, 9; Cobbett, 37 and 102-5.
Page 50—5 and 6 Will. 4, c. 56; Palmer, 1.
Page 51—"A Citizen of Edinburgh," 7-8; Rose, II 243; "A Citizen of Edinburgh," 3-4; Cobbett, 105.
Page 52—Neilson, 36-7; Cobbett, 112; Palmer, 5; C. H. Wilson, 7.
Page 53—Cattermole, 85; C. C. Taylor, 40; *Chambers' Edinburgh Journal*,

SOURCE REFERENCES 251

April 13, 1844, pp. 228-9; S. Smith, 36; Buchanan, 86-7; S. Butler, 44; J. Wilson, 7-8.
Page 54—S. Butler, 44; Buchanan's Report to the Governor-General, 1841; Butler, 45; Abbott, *The Emigrant*, 107.
Page 55—J. Wilson, 6-7; Howe, 28; Picken, appendix, XLVII; Letter quoted in *Counsel for Emigrants* (Butler, 45-6).
Page 56—Letter of J. and H. Parks, quoted in Cobbett, 68; Buchanan's Report, quoted in Butler, 45; *Guide*, quoted in Butler, 47-8.
Page 57—J. Wilson, 7; *Guide*, quoted in Butler, 46-7; Cobbett, 106-7, and "An English Farmer," 14-15; Buchanan, 87; Bell, 165-6.

Chapter VII

Page 58—Stevenson, 14-16; Radcliff, 62; "A Citizen of Edinburgh," 7; Bell, 2.
Page 59—Diary of Mary Jane Tripp, quoted in *Arnprior Chronicle*, August 31, 1933; Johnston, *Pioneers of Blanshard*, 107, and Hancock, 2-4; "A Cabin Passenger," 19; Bigsby, I 1-2.
Page 60—"A Citizen of Edinburgh," 8-9, Duncumb, 18, and Hancock, 2; *News*, April 13, 1844, pp. 229-30.
Page 61—*News*, August 12, 1848, pp. 94-6.
Page 62—Weston, 1-7.
Page 65—*Littell's Living Age*, September 7, 1850, pp. 492-7, and *News*, July 6, 1850, pp. 16-21.

Chapter VIII

Page 66—Letter of Wright, in Barclay, 22; *Chambers' Edinburgh Journal*, April 13, 1844, p. 230; Cobbett, 109.
Page 67—Bell, 4-7; Lubbock, 3.
Page 68—*Montreal Advertiser*, quoted in Niles' *Weekly Register*, September 27, 1834; *News*, April 13, 1844, and December 21, 1844.
Page 69—J. Murray, 26; *Colonial Land and Emigration Commissioners' Annual Report*, 1848; Weston, 12.
Page 70—Brydone, 3 *et seq.*; *Colonial Land and Emigration Commissioners' Annual Report*, 1848; Hopkirk diary, July 26, 1835; Prout diary, in *News*, January 20, 1849, p. 41; Finan, 17-18; Bell, 4-5; "A Cabin Passenger," 41-2.
Page 71—"A Cabin Passenger," 31; "A Citizen of Edinburgh," 11-12; *Blackwood's Edinburgh Magazine*, November, 1821, p. 457; Hopkirk diary, August 3, 1835.
Page 72—Evidence before a Parliamentary Committee on Emigration, 1844; Thomas diary, June 16, 1833; Evidence before a Parliamentary Committee on Emigration, 1844.
Page 73—"A Cabin Passenger," 25, 28, 40; *Blackwood's Edinburgh Magazine*, November, 1821, p. 457; Bell, 12 *et seq.*; Letter quoted in B. Smith, 28; Lewellin, 29; Warr, 24.
Page 74—"A Cabin Passenger," 42; Weston, 12; *News*, April 13, 1844, pp. 229-30; Prout diary, *ibid.*, January 20, 1849, pp. 39-41.
Page 75—Bell, 26, and Thomas diary, June 16, 1833; J. Wilson, 9.
Page 76—"A Cabin Passenger," 62 and 88; Cobbett, 109-10; Johnstone, *A Series of Letters*, 5-7, Radcliff, 62, and Playfair, 7; Mudie, 215-6.
Page 77—*Emigration. Practical Advice*, 33; J. B. Brown, 2nd Ed., 421; *Quebec Gazette*, June 13, 1834, and A. Jameson, II 164; Hopkirk diary, August 16, 1835; "A Cabin Passenger," 32; Weston, 33.
Page 78—Mudie, 204-5; C. C. Taylor, 40; W. Brown, 1.
Page 79—Weston, 14; "A Cabin Passenger," 43; Prout diary, *News*, January 20, 1849, pp. 39-41.
Page 80—Thomas diary, June 25, 1833; "A Citizen of Edinburgh," 50-1;

252   APPENDIX

Weston, 32-3; *Canada and the Western States*, II 21; Weston, 21; C. H. Wilson, 10-11.

Chapter IX

Page 81—Letter of J. and H. Veness, in Cobbett, 73.
Page 82—Knight, II 358; *Blackwood's Edinburgh Magazine*, November, 1821, p. 457; J. Wilson, 5; "A Citizen of Edinburgh," 13 and 15; Weston, 289-306.
Page 83—"A Citizen of Edinburgh," 22-4; Bell, 7-8; Philips, 11; Bell, 8; Weston, 13-16; "A Cabin Passenger," 58; Letter quoted in *Sussex Emigrants for Canada*, 34; Letter of Charlotte Willard, quoted in Barclay, 20, also M'Donald, 4, and Lamond, 46.
Page 84—Bell, 7; Jameson, II 161-6, Weston, 277-8, and "A Cabin Passenger," 51 and 62; "A Citizen of Edinburgh," 38 and 41.
Page 85—Reuben Switzer, quoted in W. Johnston, *Pioneers of Blanshard*, 107; Thomas diary, June 16 and 27, 1833; Letter in Barclay, 18; Thomas diary, June 22, 1833; Quoted in Barclay, 21, and J. Wilson, 8 and 11.
Page 86—Weston, 25-6; Quoted in Cobbett, 72; Thomas diary, July 3, 1833; *Canada and the Western States*, II 20; Duncumb, 14-15; Weston, 27 and 30; Riddell *Diary*, May 16, 1833.
Page 88—"A Young Emigrant," 1-31.

Chapter X

Page 89—"A Cabin Passenger," 86 and 18; Hansard, 2nd Series, XVIII 962.
Page 90—*Evidence in Return to an Address . . . , 9 July, 1839*, pp. 34-9; London *Times*, June 15, 1832; A. Jameson, II 161-6.
Page 91—Weston, 277-8; *Colonial Land and Emigration Commissioners' Annual Report*, 1848.
Page 96—Shipping reports in Quebec *Mercury*, August 10, 1847, *et seq.*; Report of the Montreal Board of Health, August 12, 1847; London *Times*, September 17, 1847.
Page 97—De Vere to T. F. Elliot, *Evidence . . . on Colonisation from Ireland, 1847*, pp. 45-8; "A Cabin Passenger," 79; *Ibid.*, 12.
Page 98—London *Times*, September 17, 1847.

Chapter XI

Page 99—Cobbett, 116; *Emigration. Practical Advice*, 40; Johnstone, *A Series*, 5-7; Weston, 281 *et seq.*
Page 100—Shirreff, 5-7; Weston, 39, and J. Wilson, 16; Talbot, I 61-2, also "An English Farmer," 38, and Hopkirk diary, 56.
Page 101—Thomas diary, June 13, 1833; C. C. Taylor, 40; *Blackwood's Edinburgh Magazine*, November, 1821, p. 457, and Weston, 10; "A Cabin Passenger," 67; Hopkirk diary, August 16, 1835.
Page 102—Weston, 22-3 and 36; *Canada and the Western States*, II 21; J. Stuart, I 1-13, and *Canada and the Western States*, II 21; Thomas diary, June 25, 1833; Playfair, 12.
Page 103—"A Cabin Passenger," 64; C. C. Taylor, 40; Diary of Eliza Jane Tripp, quoted in *Arnprior Chronicle*, August 31, 1933.
Page 104—Marsden, 6-15; T. Johnston, 6-7.
Page 105—Weston, 34; J. Wilson, 3 and 10-11; Weston, 28, 23-4, 29, and 35; J. Stuart, I 7.
Page 106—Weston, 28-9; John Ayling, in *Letters from . . . the South Side of the Hills*, 8; Tudor, I 3; "A Cabin Passenger," 56, and J. Stuart, I 9-10; C. C. Taylor, 39-40; Levinge, II 88-100.
Page 107—Hopkirk diary, August 29, 1835.
Page 108—J. Taylor, 1-12.

SOURCE REFERENCES

Chapter XII
Page 109—Emigration Agent's Report, Quebec, October 12, 1844; Official Returns of Emigration, 1847; Official statistics, Port of Liverpool, 1849.
Page 110—*The American Traveller*, preface; Letter of Elizabeth Watson, quoted in Cobbett, 56; Thomas diary, June 2, 1833.
Page 111—"A Cabin Passenger," 36-7; Christie, 31-2.
Page 112—Traill, *The Backwoods of Canada*, 1929 Ed., 27 *et seq.*; F. Stewart, 2nd Ed., 1.
Page 113—Hopkirk diary, *passim.*
Page 114—Radcliff, 16-17 and 60 *et seq.*
Page 115—Traill, 27 *et seq.*; Strickland, I 1-4.
Page 116—Letters of Mary Gapper, August 31 to October 4, 1828; M. and E. Steele's *Diary of a Voyage.*
Page 117—Rose, II 240; Radcliff, 108.
Page 118—J. Stuart, I 1-13; Radcliff, 111; Mackenzie, 214-5.
Page 119—Lubbock, 101; Mackenzie, 111; Lubbock, 99 *et seq.*
Page 120—Rogers, Ch. VII; Fidler, 5; Shirreff, 5-7; C. C. Taylor, 39-40.
Page 121—Playfair, 5-12; Levinge, II 88-100.
Page 122—Preston, I 1-21.
Page 123—J. Duncan, I 3-22; *News*, August 12, 1843, p. 108.

Chapter XIII
Page 125—Quebec *Mercury*, July 9, 1819.
Page 126—Strickland, I 114-9.
Page 127—Thomas diary.
Page 128—*Quebec Gazette*, May 23, 1834; *Ibid.*, June 2, 1834.
Page 129—*News*, May 8, 1847, p. 295, and May 29, 1847, p. 348.
Page 130—*Cobourg Star*, June 9, 1841; *News*, December 7, 1850, p. 436.
Page 131—*News*, May 19, 1855, pp. 475-6; *Ibid.*, May 2, 1846, p. 295.
Page 132—*News*, March 10, 1849, pp. 151-2; Thomas diary, July 7, 1833.
Page 133—*News*, July 7, 1849, p. 2.
Page 136—Wallace, *In the Wake of the Wind-Ships*, 200-9.
Page 137—*News*, September 2, 1848, pp. 137-8.

Chapter XIV
Page 138—Gapper diary, September 30, 1828; Traill, 32; "A Cabin Passenger," 52; Arfwedson, I 11-12; Wilson, 15-16.
Page 139—"A Cabin Passenger," 47-50; Bigsby, I 5; Ferrier, 1923 Ed., 5; Bell, 29; Thomas diary, July 8, 1833; T. Johnston, 8.
Page 140—Weston, 31; "A Cabin Passenger," 54; Radcliff, 66-9; Strickland, I 4; Playfair, 12; Hopkirk diary, August 14-16, 1835.
Page 141—Johnstone, *A Series of Letters*, 7; J. Wilson, 11; Strickland, I 4; "A Cabin Passenger," 52-3; Strickland, I 5.
Page 142—Talbot, I 30; "A Cabin Passenger," 55; Traill, 33.
Page 143—Talbot, I 29-33; "A Cabin Passenger," 60 and 61; Brydone, 7.
Page 144—Bigsby, I 6-7; "A Cabin Passenger," 64-74.

Chapter XV
Page 145—Traill, 41; J. Wilson, 19; Durham's *Report*, appendix, 280.
Page 146—Durham's *Report*, Lucas Ed., II 247; Thomas diary, July 11, 1833; Traill, 41.
Page 147—Moodie, 1923 Ed., 29-31; *Quebec Gazette*, May 26, 1834.
Page 148—*Quebec Gazette*, May 19, 1834; *Ibid.*, June 11, 1834; *Ibid.*, June 13, 1834, also Brydone, 9.
Page 149—Neilson, 37-8.
Page 150—"A Cabin Passenger," 82 *et seq.*; "A Citizen," 6 *et seq.*

APPENDIX

Page 151—Quebec *Mercury*, August 10, 1847; "A Cabin Passenger," 91-2.
Page 152—*Kingston Chronicle,* June 17, 1848.
Page 153—"A Cabin Passenger," 93-7.
Page 154—"A Cabin Passenger," 97; J. Taylor, 79.

CHAPTER XVI

Page 155—Evidence quoted in Durham's *Report,* II 244; M. L. Duncan, 274-5; A. C. Buchanan, appendix, 117.
Page 157—Butler, 57-9; Mackenzie, 179-80; Cobbett, 117; Moodie, 23.
Page 158—M'Donald, 5; Evans, 32-3; *Cobourg Star,* February 8, 1832.
Page 159—*Quebec Gazette,* May 19, 1834.
Page 160—"An English Farmer," 42.
Page 161—Henry, 4-5; Murray, 17 and 23; *Letters from Settlers in Upper Canada,* 4.
Page 162—Thomas diary, July 11, 1833; *Letters from Settlers in Upper Canada,* 4; Moodie, 52 and 57; Traill, 56-64.
Page 163—Reminiscences of T. M. Henry, Toronto; Neilson, 38.

CHAPTER XVII

Page 164—Talbot, I 87-92.
Page 165—"An English Farmer," 46; Bonnycastle, *Canada and the Canadians,* I 93; Howison, 3rd Ed., 41-2.
Page 166—M'Donald, 6; Strickland, I 11-13; Talbot, I 87-92; Quoted in Brydone, 20.
Page 167—F. Stewart, 11-14; S. Butler, 234; M'Donald, 7-8; Public Archives of Canada, C 621, p. 103.
Page 168—Dunlop, 53-4, and Hadfield *Diary,* in D. S. Robertson, 49-107; M'Donald, 8-9.
Page 169—Shirreff, 143; "An English Farmer," 48-9; Grece, 73.
Page 170—Moodie, 60-1; Traill, 74; Radcliff, 94-110; Shirreff, 143; *Quebec Gazette,* May 23, 1834.
Page 171—Brydone, 14-20; Weld, 284-8; Simcoe *Diary,* July 23, 1792, *et seq.,* Ed. J. R. Robertson; Rochefoucauld-Liancourt, I 271-6 and 289-90.
Page 172—Talbot, I 95; Fidler, 253-6; Howison, 62; Moodie, 62-5; Shirreff, 146-7.
Page 173—Hale's *Instructions* quoted in *Sussex Emigrants for Canada,* 80; *Upper Canada Gazette,* December 12, 1822.
Page 174—Green, 58-9; Wilkie, 197; Henry, 108-9; Bell, 155.
Page 175—Shirreff, 165; *Cobourg Star,* July 4, 1832.
Page 176—Letter in *Sussex Emigrants for Canada,* 37-9; Letter *ibid.,* 16.
Page 177—J. B. Brown, 260; *Ibid.,* 2nd Ed., 431-5.
Page 178—Kohl, 321 *et seq.*

CHAPTER XVIII

Page 179—Beaufoy, 8; *Chambers' Edinburgh Journal,* April 13, 1844, pp. 228-9; J. Stuart, I 10; Weston, 39; Beaufoy, 7-8.
Page 180—Weston, 35 *et seq.*; J. Duncan, I 22-3.
Page 181—*Canada and the Western States,* II 26; Hopkirk diary, September 1, 1835; Weston, 44-8; M. L. Duncan, 276-7.
Page 182—*Canada and the Western States,* II 26; Need, 1-2; Hopkirk diary, September 1, 1835; Dickens, 37.
Page 184—Hopkirk diary, September 1, 1835; Trollope, 3rd Ed., I 1 and II 188.
Page 185—Weston, 51 *et seq.*
Page 186—W. Brown, 3-4; *Canada and the Western States,* II 42; Moore, 7; Stevenson, 104; *Canada and the Western States,* II 28.
Page 187—*Canada and the Western States,* II 30; Gourlay, *Emigration*

SOURCE REFERENCES

and Settlement, 19-20; J. B. Brown, 265; Letter of Mrs. Turnbull, quoted in *The American Traveller*, 20.
Page 188—Weston, 56 *et seq.*; Hopkirk diary, September 2-5, 1835; Gapper diary, October 4, 1828; Carlisle, 27; W. Brown, 4-5.
Page 189—Gapper diary, October 4, 1828; Howison, 329-30; De Roos, 5; Hopkirk diary, September 2-5, 1835; Warr, 28; *Canada and the Western States*, II 91.
Page 190—*Address*, quoted in S. Butler, 103 *et seq.*; James Buckingham, quoted *ibid.*, introduction, XI; W. Brown, 4; Ashe, I 60-1.
Page 191—Ashe, I 60-1; Howe, 13; Gourlay, *Emigration and Settlement*, 11; C. H. Wilson, 103 and 108.
Page 192—Carlisle, 27; Warr, 30; W. Brown, 7; J. Duncan, I 303-20, also B. Hall, *Travels*, I 46 *et seq.*, and Arfwedson, I 46 *et seq.*
Page 193—J. Duncan, I 314-15; Schultz, II 2 *et seq.*, and C. H. Wilson, 35.
Page 194—Letter of James Tewsley, in Barclay, 28; *Albany Advertiser*, quoted in Carrothers, 74; C. H. Wilson, 35; McKenney, quoted in Buckman, 94-7.
Page 195—Buckman, 98; Willis, *American Scenery*, I 14-15.
Page 196—W. Brown, 6-7; Reginald Fowler, quoted in Buckman, 25-6; S. Smith, 36; W. Brown, 6; Duncumb, 326.
Page 197—Willis, *American Scenery*, I 22-3; Guillet, *Early Life*, 373-94; Shenston, 30; Schultz, II 2.
Page 198—J. Duncan, II 3-27, also Abdy, I 328 *et seq.*; Duncumb, 327-43.
Page 199—Duncumb, 327-43, also *The Emigrant's Informant*, 55-66; Duncumb, 328; Willis, *American Scenery*, I 119.
Page 200—W. Brown, 9 and 7.
Page 201—Rules and Orders, in Duncumb, 331; W. Brown, 8-9; Duncumb, 327-43.
Page 202—Guillet, *Early Life*, 397-8; J. B. Brown, 2nd Ed., 446-7.

Chapter XX

Page 204—Buchan, 71 fn., Dunbar, I 161.
Page 205—Dunbar, *passim*, also Schultz, I 16 *et seq.*, 129 *et seq.*, and II 73 *et seq.*, also Guillet, 373-464.
Page 206—S. R. Brown, appendix, 352-5.
Page 207—Brown, *ibid.*
Page 208—Brown, 355; M'Donald, 10-11.
Page 210—Birkbeck, 79.
Page 212—Linton's journey cited in *Letters and Extracts of Letters*, 15-16; Strickland, I 266-70; Rose, I 222.
Page 213—*Papers Relative to Emigration* (1847), 11; Hancock, 219 *et seq.*
Page 214—Stevenson, preface, X.

Chapter XXI

Page 216—Bell, 153-4; Tripp Diary, in *Arnprior Chronicle*, August 31, 1933.
Page 217—Weston, 277 *et seq.*; *Canada and the Western States*, II 6; William Simpson quoted in *Letters from Settlers in Upper Canada*, 2; C. Shirreff, 15.
Page 218—J. Duncan, II 340-1; J. Taylor, 79.
Page 219—Selkirk, 190-2; R. J. Uniacke, *Report of the Select Committee on Emigration, 1826*, 38-40.
Page 220—Henry, preface, XV; Sholto quoted in A. Jameson, II 161-8, and III 347.
Page 221—Letter in *Cobourg Star*, July 9, 1840; Wilson 32 and 34;

APPENDIX

Scrope, *Extracts of Letters from Poor Persons*, 10-11; *Canada and the Western States*, II 67.
Page 222—M'Donald, 25; Letter of Watson, in Scrope, 15.
Page 223—Watson, 22; Geikie, 174-6; S. Brown, appendix, 357.
Page 224—Emigration Agent's Report, Quebec, July 31, 1841; Memoranda quoted in S. Butler, 76 *et seq.*
Page 225—J. Brown, *New Brunswick*, 9 *et seq.*; Quoted in John Strachan, 52-4.
Page 226—*Canada and the Western States*, II 63-4; *Ibid.*, 44; Fidler, 363.
Page 227—Charlotte Willard, in Barclay, 19; Letter in *Continuation of Letters*, 16; Quoted in Cattermole, 169; Quoted *ibid.*, 197-206.
Page 228—Letter of Slade, *Quarterly Review*, September, 1835, p. 428; Letter of Watson, in Scrope, 13-14; Letter of J. Powell, in S. Smith, 105; Letter of Down, in Scrope, 21.
Page 229—Howison, 270; Talbot, II 11; Letter of Thorley, in S. Smith, 102; Quoted in Cattermole, 209-11.
Page 230—Letter of Watson, in B. Smith, 12; Letter of C. Willard, in Barclay, 19; P. Shirreff, 93; Letter of Down, in Scrope, 20; Letter of J. and H. Parks, in B. Smith, 30; Letter of Snelgrove, in Scrope, 27; Letter of Lister, *ibid.*, 19; Letter of Silcox, *ibid.*, 18; Letter of Jones, in *The American Traveller*, 20-1; Letter of Houston, in S. Butler, 85.
Page 231—Letter in S. Butler, 93-5; Letter of Hill, in Barclay, 40; Letter of Jones, in S. Smith, 104; Letter of Watson, in B. Smith, 9; *Canada and the Western States*, II 43-4; In Linton, *Statements from Settlers*, 27; Sockett, 13, and Scrope, 13.
Page 232—Howe, 40, and letter in *The American Traveller*, 22; Bell, 156.

APPENDIX

Page 233—*Quebec Gazette*, June 2, 1834.
Page 234—*News*, July 16, 1853, pp. 29-30; *Ibid.*, August 31, 1850, p. 184.
Page 235—*News*, September 4, 1852, p. 189; *Ibid.*, December 29, 1860, p. 635; *Ibid.*, December 29, 1855, p. 766.
Page 236—Sir S. Fleming, in address before the Canadian Institute, December 17, 1892.
Page 237—W. Butler, 19th Ed., 11.
Page 238—Gourlay, *Emigration and Settlement*, 10; *News*, July 20, 1850, p. 54; *Canada and the Western States*, II 22.
Page 240—Knight, II 358.
Page 241—Barclay-Allardice, 1-8.
Page 242—Moore, 6.
Page 244—Toronto *Mail and Empire*, February, 26, 1935.
Page 245—Maginnis, 50.

BIBLIOGRAPHY

Note—It is intended that this bibliography shall represent largely the items which have been cited or quoted rather than an exhaustive list of available source material. A large amount of printed and unprinted matter which has been consulted has consequently been omitted, as have also been numerous general histories and works of reference.

I. UNPRINTED

(a) *Documents in Public Collections*

Beckwith to Drummond, November 21, 1815. Public Archives of Canada, C. 621, p. 103.
Campbell to Bathurst, Glasgow, February 24, 1815. Public Archives of Canada, Q. 135, p. 106.
Proclamation, February 22, 1815, "British Provinces in North America," Public Archives of Canada, Q. 328, p. 143.
Diary of John Thomson, Archives of Ontario.

(b) *Letters, Journals or Diaries in Private Possession*

Bell, William: "A History of the Christian Church in this Settlement" (Perth, Upper Canada). A large number of closely-written volumes upon this and related subjects are in the possession of the Rev. Mr. Bell's descendants.
Gapper, Mary: Letters, 1828-1842. Written in diary form, a large number of letters descriptive of the Atlantic passage and of pioneer life in Upper Canada are in the possession of Mary Gapper's grand-daughter, Miss Kathleen O'Brien, Toronto, Canada.
Smith, J. T.: "Journal in America." This manuscript volume is in the Burton Historical Collection, Detroit, Mich.
Thomas, Francis: "Journal of a Voyage from London to Quebec, with an Account of the Shipwreck near Cape Ray, on the coast of Newfoundland." (1833). In the possession of his grandson, W. F. Thomas, Esq., Toronto, Canada.

APPENDIX

II. PRINTED

(a) *Acts of Parliament Relating to Passenger Vessels*

The chief Acts regulating conditions of passage in the sailing-ship period are the following:

Act of 1803, 43 Geo. 3, c. 56.
Act of 1817, 56 Geo. 3, c. 83.
Act of 1823, 4 Geo. 4, c. 83.
Act of 1827, 7 and 8 Geo. 4, c. 116.
Act of 1828, 9 Geo. 4, c. 21.
Act of 1835-6, 5 and 6 Will. 4, c. 56.
Act of 1842, 5 and 6 Victoria, c. 107.
Act of 1847, 10 and 11 Victoria, c. 103.
Act of 1849, 12 and 13 Victoria, c. 33.
Act of 1852, 15 and 16 Victoria, c. 44.
Act of 1853, 16 and 17 Victoria, c. 84.
Act of 1855, 18 and 19 Victoria, c. 119.

(b) *Official British, Colonial and American Publications and Reports*

Those italicized appeared in print under the titles given.

Circular issued from the Colonial Office, February, 1818.
Circular issued from the Colonial Office, February 9, 1832.
Colonial Land and Emigration Commissioners' Annual Report, 1848.
Colonial Land and Emigration Commissioners' Annual Report, 1851.
Emigration: Canada and Australia. 1838.
Emigration. Papers Relative to Emigration to the British Provinces in North America. 1847.
Emigration. Papers Relative to Emigration to the British Provinces in North America. 1848.
Emigration. Return to an Address of the Honourable The House of Commons, Dated 7 May 1838. 1838.
Emigration. Return to an Address of the Honourable The House of Commons, Dated 9 July 1839. 1839.
Evidence before the Select Committee of the House of Lords on Colonisation from Ireland, 1847.
Fifth General Report of the Colonial Land and Emigration Commissioners. 1845.
Hansard, 2nd Series, Volume 18, 1828, pp. 962 and 1212.
Papers Relative to Emigration, 1847.

BIBLIOGRAPHY

Report from, and Minutes of Evidence taken before, the Select Committee on Emigration from the United Kingdom. 1826.
Report of the Chief Emigration Agent at Quebec to the Governor-General, 1841.
Report of the Commissioners of Emigration at New York, October 1st, 1847.
Report of the Deer Island Hospital, Boston, for the week ending January 26th, 1848.
Report of the Emigration Officer at St. Andrews, 1847.
Report of the Highland Society of Scotland to a Parliamentary Committee, 1800-3.
Report of the Inspector General of the Province of Canada for 1847.
Report of the Parliamentary Committee on Emigration, 1844.
Report of the Select Committee of the House of Lords on Colonisation from Ireland. 1847.
Report of the Affairs of British North America, by John George Lambton Durham. 1839.
Reports and Correspondence Respecting Emigration to the Colonies. 1839.
Reports, Returns, and other Papers, Presented to the Imperial Houses of Parliament of Great Britain and Ireland, Relating to Canada. (Printed in London, England, and covering the period 1803-1896. The 48 volumes contain a mass of Returns of Emigration, Weekly and Annual Reports, Reports of Emigration Commissioners and Select Committees, Reports of Immigration at Grosse Isle, colonization schemes, and legislation relative to emigration.)
Second Report from the Select Committee on Emigration, Scotland. 1841.
Third Report upon Emigration from the United Kingdom. 1827.

(c) *Newspapers and Periodicals*

It has been considered worth while to particularize the items from the *Illustrated London News* and certain of the older Reviews and Journals.

Albany Advertiser.
Arnprior Chronicle.
Blackwood's Edinburgh Magazine, especially November, 1821, p. 450.
Boston Journal.
Boston Mail.

APPENDIX

Canadian Historical Review.
Chambers' Edinburgh Journal, especially April 13, 1844, p. 228.
Cobourg Star.
Edinburgh Review, especially October, 1802, p. 61; June, 1818, p. 123; June, 1824, p. 315; December, 1826, p. 49; January, 1828, p. 205; and July, 1854, p. 236.
Illustrated London News, especially the following:
"Abolition of the Slave Trade," August 6, 1842.
"The New American Line-ship *Victoria,*" August 12, 1843.
"Emigration to Sydney," April 13, 1844.
"Emigrants on the Way to the Place of Embarkation," December 21, 1844.
"New Mode of Saving Lives from Shipwreck," May 2, 1846.
"Loss of an Emigrant Ship and 240 Passengers," May 8, 1847.
"Wreck of the *Exmouth* Emigrant-ship," May 29, 1847.
"The Emigrant Ship *Artemisia,*" August 12, 1848.
"Burning of the *Ocean Monarch* Emigrant Ship," September 2, 1848.
"Emigration—a Voyage to Australia," January 20, 1849.
"Dreadful Wreck of an Emigrant Ship," March 10, 1849.
"An Emigrant Ship Run Down," July 7, 1849.
"Irish Evictions," October 20, 1849.
"The Tide of Emigration to the United States and the British Colonies," July 6, 1850.
"The *Helena Slowman* Steam-ship," July 20, 1850.
"The Canterbury Association," September 7, 1850.
"Wreck of the *Edmund,*" December 7, 1850.
"The Depopulation of Ireland," May 10, 1851.
"The *Ben Nevis* Packet-Ship," September 4, 1852.
"Emigration from the Isle of Skye," January 15, 1853.
"The *Sovereign of the Seas,*" July 16, 1853.
"Ship Struck by a Whale," April 7, 1855.
"Shipwreck of the Emigrant Barque *John,*" May 19, 1855.
"Liverpool and Australian Navigation Company's Clipper-ship *Royal Charter,*" December 29, 1855.
"Emigration from the North of Scotland," April 25, 1857.
"Wreck of the *Martin Luther* Emigrant Ship," May 2, 1857.
"The *Great Eastern,*" May 30, 1857; June 13, 1857; November 7, 1857; and many other issues covering the construction, launching, completion and maiden voyage of the vessel, up to June 23, 1860.
"The *Great Australia* Clipper-Ship," December 29, 1860.

Kingston Chronicle.
Littell's Living Age, especially September 7, 1850, p. 492.
London *Morning Herald.*
London *Morning Post.*
London *Times.*
Montreal Courier.
Montreal Transcript.
Montreal Pilot.
Miramichi Gleaner.
Montreal Advertiser.
Montreal Herald.
New Orleans Price Current.
New York Express.
Niles' *Weekly Register.*
Ontario Historical Society *Papers and Records.*
Plymouth and Devonport Weekly Journal.
Quarterly Review, especially January, 1819, p. 124; July, 1820, p. 373; July, 1823, p. 338; and March, 1828, p. 539.
Quebec Chronicle.
Quebec Gazette.
Quebec Mercury.
Queen's Quarterly.
Scottish Historical Review.
The Sunday at Home, especially 1880, p. 22; and 1882, p. 28.
Thunder Bay Historical Society *Papers and Records.*
Toronto *Mail and Empire.*
Toronto (York) *Upper Canada Gazette.*
Toronto *Upper Canada Herald.*
Weekly Political Register (Cobbett's).

(d) *Diaries, Narratives, Collections of Letters, Emigrant Guidebooks, and other similar Primary Sources*

Abbott, J.: *Philip Musgrave, or the Memoirs of a Church of England Missionary in the American Colonies.* 1846.
[Abbott, J.]: *The Emigrant to North America.* 1844.
Abdy, E. S.: *Journal of a Residence and Tour in the United States.* 3 Volumes. 1835.
Address of the Irish Emigrant Society of New York to the People of Ireland. 18-?
Alexander, Sir James: *Transatlantic Sketches.* 2 Volumes. 1833.
Alexander, Sir James: *L'Acadie, or Seven Years' Explorations in British America.* 2 Volumes. 1849.

APPENDIX

(The) American Traveller and Emigrant's Guide. 1817.
Anderson, D.: *Canada, or a View of the Importance of the British American Colonies.* 1814.
Arfwedson, C. D.: *The United States and Canada in 1832, 1833 and 1834.* 2 Volumes. 1834.
Ashe, Thomas: *Travels in America Performed in 1806.* 3 Volumes. 1808.
Atkinson, A. F.: *The Present Condition of Upper Canada.* 1849.
Atlantic Crossing, 1835. The diary of James Hopkirk, edited by D. D. Calvin. (*Queen's Quarterly*, March, 1935.)
Aylmer, Lady: *Narrative of the Passage of the Pique across the Atlantic.* 1837.
Bannister, J. W.: *Sketches of Plans for Settling in Upper Canada a Portion of the Unemployed Labourers of Great Britain and Ireland.* 1821.
Barclay, Charles: *Letters from the Dorking Emigrants, who Went to Upper Canada in the Spring of 1832.* 1833.
Barclay-Allardice, R.: *Agricultural Tour in the United States and Canada, with Miscellaneous Notices.* 1842.
[Beaufoy, —]: *Travels through the United States and Canada.* 1828.
Bell, William: *Hints to Emigrants.* 1824.
Bigsby, J. J.: *The Shoe and Canoe, or Pictures of Travel in the Canadas.* 2 Volumes. 1850.
Bingley, William: *Travels in North America from Modern Writers.* 1821.
Birkbeck, Morris: *Notes on a Journey in America, from the Coast of Virginia to the Territory of the Illinois.* 1818.
[Blane, W. N.]: *An Excursion through the United States and Canada during 1822-23.* 1824.
Bonnycastle, Sir Richard: *The Canadas in 1841.* 2 Volumes. 1842.
Bonnycastle, Sir Richard: *Canada and the Canadians.* 2 Volumes. 1846.
Bonnycastle, Sir Richard: *Canada as it Is, Was and May Be.* 2 Volumes. 1852.
Boswell, James: *The Journal of a Tour to the Hebrides with Samuel Johnson, LL.D.* 1785.
Bouchette, J.: *The British Dominions in North America.* 2 Volumes. 1831.
Boulton, H. J.: *A Short Sketch of the Province of Upper Canada,*

BIBLIOGRAPHY

for the Information of the Labouring Poor throughout England. 1826.
Brown, James: *New Brunswick as a Home for Emigrants.* 1860.
[Brown, James B.]: *Views of Canada and the Colonists.* 1844.
Brown, Samuel R.: *The Western Gazetteer; or Emigrant's Directory.* 1817.
Brown, William: *America: A Four Years' Residence in the United States and Canada.* 1849.
Brydone, James M.: *Narrative of a Voyage of a Party of Emigrants, Sent out from Sussex in 1834 by the Petworth Emigration Committee.* 1834.
Buchan, W. F.: *Remarks on Emigration: More Particularly Applicable to the Eastern Townships, Lower Canada.* 183?.
Buchanan, A. C.: *Emigration Practically Considered; with Detailed Directions for Emigrants Proceeding to British North America, Particularly to the Canadas.* 1828.
Buchanan, James: *Project for the Formation of, a Depot in Upper Canada, with a View to Receive the Whole Pauper Population of England.* 1834.
Butler, Samuel: *The Emigrant's Hand-book of Facts Concerning Canada, New Zealand, Australia, Cape of Good Hope, etc.* 1843.
Butler, Sir William F.: *The Great Lone Land.* 1872. (19th edition, 1924.)
"(A) Cabin Passenger": *The Ocean Plague: or a Voyage to Quebec in an Irish Emigrant Vessel. Embracing a Quarantine at Grosse Isle in 1847. With Notes Illustrative of the Ship-Pestilence of that Fatal Year.* 1848.
Calvin, D. D.: *Atlantic Crossing, 1835.* (In the *Queen's Quarterly*, March, 1935.)
Canada and the Western States. 1859.
"(A) Canadian Settler": *The Emigrant's Informant, or a Guide to Upper Canada.* 1834.
Carlisle, Earl of: *Travels in America.* 1851.
Cattermole, William: *Emigration. The Advantages of Emigration to Canada.* 1831.
Chappell, Edward: *Narrative of a Voyage to Hudson's Bay in His Majesty's Ship "Rosamond."* 1817.
Chevalier, Michel: *Lettres sur l'Amérique du Nord.* 2 Volumes. 1886.
Chickering, J.: *Immigration into the United States.* 1848.
Christie, A. J.: *The Emigrant's Assistant.* 1821.

APPENDIX

"(A) Citizen": *Thoughts on Emigration, Education, etc., in a Letter Addressed to the Right Honourable Lord John Russell, Prime Minister of England.* 1847.

"(A) Citizen of Edinburgh": *Journal of an Excursion to the United States and Canada in the Year 1834: with Hints to Emigrants.* 1835.

Cobbett, William: *The Emigrant's Guide, in Ten Letters Addressed to Taxpayers of England, Containing Information Necessary to Persons about to Emigrate.* 1829.

Cobbett, William: *Rural Rides.* 2 Volumes. 1885.

Coke, E. T.: *A Subaltern's Furlough.* 1833.

Continuation of Letters from Sussex Emigrants in Upper Canada for 1833. 1834.

Counsel for Emigrants, and Interesting Information from Numerous Sources. 1834.

Dalton, William: *Travels in the United States of America and Part of Upper Canada.* 1821.

Dartnell, G. R.: *A Brief Narrative of the Shipwreck of the Transport "Premier."* 1845.

Daubeny, Charles: *Journal of a Tour through the United States and Canada, Made during the Years 1837-38.* 1843.

Davis, Robert: *The Canadian Farmer's Travels in the United States of America.* 1837.

De la Fosse, F. M. ("Roger Vardon"): *English Bloods.* 1930.

De Roos, J. F. F.: *Personal Narrative of Travels in 1826.* 1827.

Diary of a Voyage from London to Upper Canada, 1833. (Ontario Historical Society *Papers and Records*, Volume XXIII).

Dickens, Charles: *American Notes for General Circulation.* 1842.

Dixon, James: *Personal Narrative of a Tour through a Part of the United States and Canada.* 1849.

Dobie, W. C.: *Sailing Across the Atlantic 60 Years Ago.* (Thunder Bay Historical Society *Papers and Records*, Volume V).

"Doyle, Martin" (William Hickey): *Hints on Emigration to Upper Canada.* 1832.

Dreadful Wreck of the Brig "St. Lawrence," from Quebec to New York, 1780. 1781.

Duncan, John M.: *Travels through Part of the United States and Canada in 1818 and 1819.* 2 Volumes. 1823.

[Duncan, Mary Lundie]: *America as I Found It.* 1852.

Duncumb, John: *The British Emigrant's Advocate.* 1837.

BIBLIOGRAPHY 265

[Dunlop, William] "A Backwoodsman": *Statistical Sketches of Upper Canada.* 1832.
Emigration. Practical Advice to Emigrants. 1834.
"(An) English Farmer": *A Few Plain Directions for Persons Intending to Proceed as Settlers to His Majesty's Province of Upper Canada, in North America, Containing also a Short Sketch or Journal of the Author's Voyage across the Atlantic in June, 1819.* 1820.
Evans, Francis A.:*The Emigrant's Director and Guide.* 1833.
"(An) Ex-Settler": *Canada in the Years 1832, 1833 and 1834.* 1835.
(The) Extraordinary Black Book. 1831.
Faux, W.: *Memorable Days in America, Being a Journal of a Tour to the United States.* 1823.
Fearon, H. B.: *Sketches of America.* 1818.
Fergusson, Adam: *Practical Notes Made During a Tour.* 1834.
Ferrier, A. D.: *Reminiscences of Canada and the Early Days of Fergus.* 1866.
(A) Few Plain Directions for Persons Intending to Proceed as Settlers to His Majesty's Province of Upper Canada. By an English Farmer. 1820.
Fidler, Isaac: *Observations on the Professions, Literature, Manners and Emigration in the United States and Canada.* 1833.
Finan, P.: *Journal of a Voyage to Quebec in the Year 1825.* 1828.
Finch, J.: *Travels in the United States and Canada.* 1833.
Fitzgerald, James: *A Plan of Settlement & Colonization Adapted to All the British North American Provinces.* 1850.
[FitzGibbon, James]: *A Few Observations on Canada and the Other Provinces of British North America.* 1849.
Fothergill, Charles: *A Sketch of the Present State of Canada.* 1822.
Fowler, Thomas: *The Journal of a Tour through British America.* 1832.
Gannett, Ezra S.: *The Arrival of the "Britannia." A Sermon Delivered in the Federal Street Meeting-House, in Boston, July 19, 1840.* 1840.
Geikie, John C.: *George Stanley, or Life in the Woods.* 1864.
Gesner, A.: *New Brunswick; with Notes for Emigrants.* 1847.
Godley, J. R.: *Letters from North America.* 2 Volumes. 1842.
Gouger, Thomas: *Emigration for the Relief of Parishes.* 1833.
Gourlay, Robert: *A Statistical Account of Upper Canada.* 3 Volumes. 1822.

Gourlay, Robert: *Emigration and Settlement on Wild Land.* 1849.
Grece, C. F.: *Facts and Observations Respecting Canada and the United States of America.* 1819.
Green, Anson: *The Life and Times of the Rev. Anson Green, D.D., 1877.*
Hale, Captain ——: *Instructions to Emigrants.* 1832.
Hall, Basil: *Travels in America in 1827 and 1828.* 3 Volumes. 1829.
Hall, Basil: *Forty Etchings, from Sketches Made with the Camera Lucida in North America in 1827 and 1828.* 1829.
Hall, Francis: *Travels in Canada and the United States in 1816-17.* 1818.
Hancock, William: *An Emigrant's Five Years in the Free States of America.* 1860.
Haw, William: *Fifteen Years in Canada.* 1850.
Head, Sir Francis Bond: *The Emigrant.* 1846.
Henry, George: *The Emigrant's Guide, or Canada as it is.* 1834.
Heriot, George: *Travels through the Canadas.* 1807.
[Hickey, William] ("Martin Doyle"): *Hints on Emigration to Upper Canada.* 1834.
Hill, S. S.: *The Emigrant's Introduction to the British American Colonies.* 1837.
Hodgson, Adam: *Letters from North America, Written During a Tour in the United States and Canada.* 2 Volumes. 1824.
Hopkirk, James: Diary, 1835. Edited by D. D. Calvin in the *Queen's Quarterly*, March, 1935, under the title *Atlantic Crossing, 1835.*
Howe, John: *The Emigrant's New Guide.* 1822.
Howison, John: *Sketches of Upper Canada.* 1821.
Hurd, S. P.: *Information for the Use of Persons Emigrating to Upper Canada.* 1822.
Inches, James: *Letters on Emigration to Canada: Addressed to the Very Rev. Principal Baird.* 1836.
Irvine, Alexander: *An Inquiry into the Causes and Effects of Emigration from the Highlands and Western Islands of Scotland.* 1802.
Jameson, Anna: *Winter Studies and Summer Rambles in Canada.* 3 Volumes. 1838.
Johnson, Samuel: *A Journey to the Western Islands of Scotland.* 1775.
Johnston, F. W.: *Notes on North America.* 2 Volumes. 1851.
Johnston, Thomas: *Travels through Lower Canada.* 1827.

BIBLIOGRAPHY 267

Johnstone, Walter: *A Series of Letters, Descriptive of Prince Edward Island.* 1822.
Johnstone, Walter: *Travels in Prince Edward Island in the Years 1820-21.* 1823.
Journal of a Wanderer. 1844.
Kingston, W. H. G.: *Western Wanderings, or a Pleasure Tour in the Canadas.* 2 Volumes. 1856.
Kohl, J. G.: *Travels in Canada, and through the States of New York and Pennsylvania.* 2 Volumes. 1861.
Lambert, J.: *Travels through Canada and the United States.* 2 Volumes. 1809.
Lamond, Robert: *Narrative of the Rise and Progress of Emigration from the Counties of Lanark and Renfrew to the New Settlements in Upper Canada.* 1821.
Langton, John: *Early Days in Upper Canada; Letters of John Langton.* 1926.
Letters and Extracts of Letters from Settlers in Upper Canada. 1834.
Letters from Canada. 1862.
Letters from Emigrants Sent to Upper Canada by the Petworth Committee in 1832, 1833 and 1837. 1839 (?).
Letters from Settlers in Huron District, C. W. 1842 (?).
Letters from Settlers in Upper Canada. 1833.
Letters from Sussex Emigrants Gone Out from the South Side of the Hills to Upper Canada. 1837.
Levinge, Richard: *Echoes from the Backwoods.* 2 Volumes. 1846.
Lewellin, J. L. *Emigration. Prince Edward Island. A Brief but Faithful Account of This Fine Colony.* 1833.
[Linton, J. J. E.] *Statements from Settlers on the Canada Company Land in the Huron District.* 1842 (?).
[Linton, J. J. E.]: *The Life of a Backwoodsman; or Particulars of the Emigrant's Situation in Settling on the Wild Land of Canada.* 1843.
Logan, James: *Notes of a Journey through Canada.* 1838.
Lucas, Sir C. P.: *Report on the Affairs of British North America, by John George Lambton Durham.* 3 Volumes. 1912
Lyell, Sir Charles: *Travels in North America in the Years 1841-2.* 2 Volumes. 1845.
Lyon, Caleb: *Narrative and Recollections of Van Dieman's Land.* 1844.
M'Donald, John: *Narrative of a Voyage to Quebec and a Journey from thence to New Lanark in Upper Canada.* 1822.

McGregor, John: *British America.* 2 Volumes. 1832.
McKeevor, Thomas: *A Voyage to Hudson's Bay during the Summer of 1812, Containing a Particular Account of the Icebergs and Other Phenomena which Present Themselves in Those Regions.* 1819.
Mackenzie, William Lyon: *Sketches of Canada and the United States.* 1833.
MacLeod, General ——: "Memoirs of His Own Life" (1785), appended to James Boswell's *The Journal of a Tour to the Hebrides with Samuel Johnson, LL.D.* 1785.
McVicar, Robert: *Letters on Emigration from the British Isles, and the Settlement of the Waste Lands in the Province of Canada.* 1853.
Malcolm, J. G.: *An Inquiry into the Expediency of Emigration.* 1828.
Marryat, F.: *Diary in America.* 1839.
Marsden, Joshua: *The Narrative of a Mission, to Nova Scotia, New Brunswick, and the Somers Islands, with a Tour to Lake Ontario.* 1827.
Martineau, Harriet: *Retrospect of Western Travel.* 1838.
Mathison, John: *Counsel for Emigrants.* 1835.
Matthew, Patrick: *Emigration Fields.* 1839.
(The) Mechanic and Labourer's Guide to America. 18–?
Melish, John: *Travels in the United States of America in the Years 1806 & 1807 and 1809, 1810 & 1811.* 2 Volumes. 1812.
Middleton, . E.: *The Well-known North Atlantic.* 192?.
Montule, E.: *A Voyage to North America, and the West Indies in 1817.* 1821.
Moodie, Susanna: *Roughing It in the Bush.* 1852.
Mooney, Thomas: *Nine Years in America . . . In a Series of Letters to His Cousin, Patrick Mooney, a Farmer in Ireland.* 1850.
Moore, George: *Journal of a Voyage across the Atlantic, with Notes on Canada and the United States; and Return to Great Britain, in 1844.* 1845.
Moorsom, W. S.: *Letters from Nova Scotia.* 1830.
Morgan, J. C.: *The Emigrant's Note Book and Guide.* 1824.
Mudie, Robert: *The Emigrant's Pocket Companion.* 1832.
Murray, C. A.: *Travels in North America.* 1839.
Murray, D. A. B.: *Information for the Use of Emigrants.* 1857.

Murray, Hugh: *Historical and Descriptive Account of British North America.* 1839.
Murray, John: *The Emigrant and Traveller's Guide to and through Canada.* 1835.
Myers, J. C.: *Sketches of a Tour.* 1849.
[Need, Thomas]: *Six Years in the Bush.* 1838.
Neilson, Joseph: *Observations upon Emigration to Upper Canada.* 1837.
Observations on the Report of the Emigration Committee of London. 1827.
Observations upon the "Outline of a Plan of Emigration." 1823 (?).
(The) Ocean Plague: or a Voyage to Quebec in an Irish Emigrant Vessel. By a Cabin Passenger. 1848.
[Ogden, John C.]: *A Tour through Upper and Lower Canada.* 1799.
"(An) Old Countryman": *Friendly Advice to Emigrants from Europe, on their Arrival in Canada.* 1834.
Oliphant, Lawrence: *Minnesota and the Far West.* 1855.
Oliver, Andrew: *A View of Lower Canada.* 1821.
Outline of a Plan of Emigration to Upper Canada. 1822 (?).
Palmer, John: *Journal of Travels in the United States of North America.* 1818.
[Philips, George]: *Travels in North America.* 1824.
Picken, Andrew: *The Canadas, as they at Present Commend Themselves to the Enterprize of Emigrants, Colonists and Capitalists.* 1832.
Pickering, Joseph: *Inquiries of an Emigrant.* 1831.
Playfair, Robert: *Recollections of a Visit to the United States and the British Provinces in North America in the Years 1847, 1848 and 1849.* 1856.
Present State of the Canadas. 1833.
Preston, T. R.: *Three Years' Residence in Canada from 1837 to 1839.* 2 Volumes. 1840.
Pryor, Abraham: *An Interesting Description of British America.* 1819.
Radcliff, T.: *Authentic Letters from Upper Canada.* 1833.
Richardson, John: *Eight Years in Canada.* 1847.
Riddell, Walter: *Diary of a Voyage from Scotland to Canada in 1833.* 1932. (Edited by W. R. Riddell).
Robertson, Douglas S. (Ed.): *An Englishman in America, 1785, being the Diary of Joseph Hadfield.* 1933.

APPENDIX

Robertson, John Ross (Ed.): *Diary of Mrs. John Graves Simcoe.* 1911.

Rochefoucauld-Liancourt, Duc de la: *Travels through the United States of North America.* 2 Volumes. 1799.

Rolph, Thomas: *A Brief Account of Upper Canada.* 1836.

Rolph, Thomas: *Emigration and Colonization, Embodying the Results of a Mission to Great Britain and Ireland during the Years 1839, 1840, 1841 and 1842.* 1844.

[Rose, A. W. H.]: *Canada in 1849: Pictures of Canadian Life, or the Emigrant Churchman.* 2 Volumes. 1850. (Edited by the Rev. Henry Christmas).

Schultz, Christian: *Travels on an Inland Voyage through the States of New-York, Pennsylvania, Virginia, Ohio, Kentucky and Tennessee.* 2 Volumes. 1810.

Scrope, G. J. P.: *Extracts of Letters from Poor Persons who Emigrated Last Year to Canada and the United States.* 1832.

Selkirk, Earl of: *Observations on the Present State of the Highlands of Scotland, with a View of the Causes and Probable Consequences of Emigration.* 1805.

Sellar, Gordon: *The Narrative of Gordon Sellar, who Emigrated to Canada in 1825.* 1915.

Shaw, John: *A Ramble through the United States and Canada.* 1856.

[Shirreff, Charles]: *Thoughts on Emigration and on the Canadas as an Opening for it.* 1831.

Shirreff, Patrick: *A Tour through North America.* 1835.

(A) Short Account of the Emigration from the Highlands of Scotland to North America; and the Establishment of the Catholic Diocese of Upper Canada. 1839.

[Smith, Benjamin]: *Twenty-four Letters from Labourers in America to their Friends in England.* 1829.

Smith, Sidney: *The Settler's New Home, or the Emigrant's Location.* 1849.

[Sockett, T.]: *Emigration. A Letter to a Member of Parliament.* 1834.

Stansbury, Philip: *Pedestrian Tour in North America.* 1822.

(A) Statement of the Satisfactory Results which Have Attended Emigration to Upper Canada. 1841.

Steele, M. and E.: *Diary of a Voyage from London to Upper Canada, 1833.* (Ontario Historical Society *Papers and Records*, Vol. XXIII).

Stevenson, Robert Louis: *The Amateur Emigrant.* 1895.

Stewart, Charles: *A Short View of the Present State of the Eastern Townships in the Province of Lower Canada, Bordering on the line 45°: with Hints for their Improvement.* 1817.
Stewart, Frances: *Our Forest Home,* 1889.
Strachan, James: *A Visit to the Province of Upper Canada in 1819.* 1820.
Strachan, John: *Remarks on Emigration from the United Kingdom.* 1827.
Strickland, Samuel: *Twenty-seven Years in Canada West.* 2 Volumes. 1853.
Stuart, Charles: *The Emigrant's Guide to Upper Canada; or Sketches of the Present State of that Province, Collected from a Residence therein during the Years 1817, 1818, 1819. Interspersed with Reflections.* 1820.
Stuart, James: *Three Years in America.* 2 Volumes. 1833.
Sussex Emigrants for Canada. 1833.
Sussex Emigrants in Upper Canada. 1833.
Sutcliffe, Robert: *Travels in North America, 1804-6.* 1811.
Talbot, E. A.: *Five Years' Residence in the Canadas.* 2 Volumes. 1824.
Taylor, C. C.: *Toronto Called Back.* 1886.
Taylor, James: *Narrative of a Voyage to, and Travels in Upper Canada.* 1846.
Thomson, William: *A Tradesman's Travels in the United States and Canada in the Years 1840, 41 & 42.* 1842.
Traill, Catherine P.: *The Backwoods of Canada.* 1836.
Traill, Catherine P.: *The Female Emigrant's Guide.* 1854.
Tremenheere, H. S.: *Notes on Public Subjects Made During a Tour in the United States and Canada.* 1852.
Trollope, Frances: *Domestic Manners of the Americans.* 2 Volumes. 1832.
Tudor, Henry: *Narrative of a Tour in North America.* 2 Volumes. 1834.
View of the Valley of the Mississippi, or the Emigrant's and Traveller's Guide to the West. 1834.
Vigne, G. T.: *Six Months in America.* 1832.
Wakefield, P.: *Excursions in North America.* 1806.
Warburton, Eliot: *Hochelaga, or England in the New World.* 2 Volumes. 1846.
Warr, G. W.: *Canada as It Is. The Emigrant's Friend and Guide to Upper Canada.* 1847.
Watson, William: *The Emigrant's Guide to the Canadas.* 1822.

Weld, Isaac: *Travels through the States of North America.* 1799.
Weston, Richard: *A Visit to the United States and Canada in 1833; with the View of Settling in America. Including a Voyage to and from New-York.* 1836.
"(The) Wife of a British Officer": *Henry; or The Juvenile Traveller.* 1836.
Wilkie, David: *Sketches of a Summer Trip to New York and the Canadas.* 1837.
Willis, N. P.: *American Scenery; or Land, Lake and River Illustrations of Transatlantic Nature.* 2 Volumes. 1840.
Willis, N. P.: *Canadian Scenery.* 2 Volumes. 1842.
Wilson, Charles H.: *The Wanderer in America, or Truth at Home.* 1822.
Wilson, James: *Narrative of a Voyage from Dublin to Quebec, in North America.* 1822.
Wright, Frances: *Views of Society and Manners in America.* 1822.
"(A) Young Emigrant": *Adventures in Canada, being Two Months on the Tobique, New Brunswick. An Emigrant's Journal.* 1866.

(e) *Historical Studies and Works of General Reference*

Anderson, R. and R. C.: *The Sailing-ship.* 1926.
Beauclerk, Lord Charles: *Lithographic Views of Military Operations in Canada under His Excellency Sir John Colborne . . . during the late Insurrection. . . . Accompanied by Notes, Historical and Descriptive.* 1840.
Blair, Walter A.: *A Raft Pilot's Log.* 1930.
Buckman, David L.: *Old Steamboat Days on the Hudson River.* 1907.
Carrothers, W. A.: *Emigration from the British Isles.* 1929.
Chatterton, E. K.: *Sailing Ships.* 1909.
Clark, A. J.: *The Scottish Canadian Pilgrims of the Fifties.* (Ontario Historical Society *Papers and Records*, Volume XXVI.)
Copping, Arthur E.: *The Golden Land.* 1911.
Cowan, Helen: *British Emigration to British North America, 1783-1837.* 1912.
Culliton, J.: *Assisted Emigration and Land Settlement.* (McGill University Economic Studies, No. 9.) 1928.
Cuthbertson, George A.: *Freshwater; a History and a Narrative of the Great Lakes.* 1929.

BIBLIOGRAPHY

Dunbar, Seymour: *History of Travel in America.* 4 Volumes. 1915.
Dunham, B. M.: *The Trail of the Conestoga.* 1924.
Ellms, Charles: *Shipwrecks and Disasters at Sea.* 1856.
Fry, Henry: *The History of North Atlantic Steam Navigation.* 1896.
Gabriel, R. H. (Ed.): *The Pageant of America: A Pictorial History of the United States.* 15 Volumes. 1925-9.
Guillet, Edwin C.: *Early Life in Upper Canada.* 1933.
Guillet, Edwin C.: *Toronto from Trading-Post to Great City.* 1934.
Hammond, John and Barbara: *The Village Labourer, 1760-1832.* 1912.
Hammond, John and Barbara: *The Town Labourer, 1760-1832.* 1917.
Hammond, John and Barbara: *The Skilled Labourer, 1760-1832.* 1919.
Haydon, Andrew: *Pioneer Sketches of the Bathurst District.* 1925.
Hopkins, J. Castell: *Canada, an Encyclopaedia of the Country.* 6 Volumes. 1898.
Jameson, J. F. (Ed.): *Original Narratives of Early American History.* 18 Volumes. 1906-1917.
Johnson, Stanley C.: *A History of Emigration from the United Kingdom to North America, 1763-1912.* 1913.
Johnston, William: *Pioneers of Blanshard.* 1899.
Kapp, Friedrich: *Immigration and the Commissioners of Emigration of the State of New York.* 1870.
Knight, Charles (Ed.): *Old England: A Museum of Popular Antiquities.* 2 Volumes. 185?.
Lubbock, Basil: *The Colonial Clippers.* 1921.
Lucas, Sir C. P.: *Report on the Affairs of British North America, by John George Lambton Durham.* 3 Volumes. 1912.
Maginnis, A. J.: *The Atlantic Ferry: its Ships, Men and Working.* 1893.
Martin, Chester: *Lord Selkirk's Work in Canada.* 1916.
Milburn, William H.: *The Pioneers, Preachers and People of the Mississippi Valley.* 1860.
Oxford and Asquith, Earl of: *Memories and Reflections, 1852-1927.* 2 Volumes. 1928.
Paxson, Frederic L.: *History of the American Frontier.* 1924.

Reynolds, Lloyd G.: *The British Immigrant: His Social and Economic Adjustment in Canada.* 1935.
Riddell, William R.: *Old Province Tales, Upper Canada.* 1920.
Rogers, Stanley: *The Atlantic.* 1930.
Ross, Edward A.: *The Old World in the New.* 1914.
Scadding, Henry: *Toronto of Old.* 1873.
Schouler, James: *History of the United States of America.* 5 Volumes. 1880-2.
Shenston, Thomas: *The Oxford Gazetteer.* 1852.
Skelton, Isabel: *The Backwoodswoman.* 1924.
Smith, W. L.: *Pioneers of Old Ontario.* 1923.
Trevelyan, G. M.: *British History in the Nineteenth Century, 1782-1901.* 1924.
Trevelyan, G. O.: *The Life and Letters of Lord Macaulay.* 2 Volumes. 1876.
Wallace, F. W.: *Wooden Ships and Iron Men.* 1924.
Wallace, F. W.: *In the Wake of the Wind-Ships.* 1927.
Wallace, F. W.: *Record of Canadian Shipping.* 1929.
Webb, Sidney and Beatrice: *The History of Trade Unionism.* 1894.

INDEX

Note—For facility of reference all ships mentioned in the work are indexed alphabetically under that head; similarly an outline of the entire transition from the old land to the new is given under the heads Emigration and Immigration. All other items are indexed alphabetically. Doctors, clergymen, and ship captains are so designated, but distinctions of military rank are omitted except where they aid in distinguishing persons of the same name, or where the Christian name is unknown.

Abbott, Rev. J., 54, 218 fn.
Aberdeen, 238
Adelaide, Aus., 59 fn.
Adelaide Township, 166
Advocate and Canadian Freeman, York, 224
African Slave Trade, 96 fn.
Albany, 190, 193-7, 201, 202
Albany Advertiser, 194
Allan, Sir Hugh, 239
Allan Steamship Line, 239, 240
Ambrose Lightship, 246
Anderson, Rev. Richard, 151 fn.
Annan, 147
Anthony's Nose, 193, 199
Anticosti, 142-3
Antwerp, 131
Apple Island, 143
Arfwedson, C. D., 80 fn., 211
Ashe, Thomas, 182 fn.
Ashley, Lord, *see* Shaftesbury, Earl of
Assiniboia, 207
Assiniboine River, 207
Auckland, N. Z., 59 fn.
Aurora, 210, 229
Australia, emigration to, 24 fn., 29, 32, 59 fn., 88, 117, 227 fn., 233
Aylmer, Lady, 237 fn.
Azores Islands, 50, 122, 134

Baker, William, 227
Baltimore, Md., 180 fn.
Bannister, John W., 6
Barclay-Allardice, R., 241
Barnardo, Dr., 23
Barton, John, 27
Bath, 157
Bath, Marquis of, 28
Bathurst, Lord, 12, 230
Beaufoy, 141 fn., 179, 183 fn.
Beaumont, 153
Beauport, 153

Beckwith, Sir Sidney, 167
Beckwith Township, 22
Belfast, 44, 54, 91
Bell, A., 52 fn.
Bell, Rev. William, 12, 52 fn., 57, 58, 66, 70, 73, 75, 83, 139, 174, 216, 232
Belle Isle, Strait of, 239
Bermuda, 7
Bic Island, 115
Bigsby, Dr. John, 143-4, 154 fn., 237
Bird Rocks, 141
Birkbeck, Morris, 210, 218 fn.
Birmingham, Eng., 38
Bishop's Rock, 246
Black, Rev., 103-4
Black Ball Line, 117
Black Death, 93
Black Rock, 199
Blackwall, 110
Blake, Captain, 100
Blane, W. N., 188 fn.
Bonnycastle, Sir Richard, 119, 165, 188 fn.
Boone, Daniel, 204
Boot, Benjamin, 55
Boston, 87, 95 fn., 180 fn., 184 fn., 234, 237, 238, 241
Boston Deeps, 107
Boswell, James, 2, 43
Boyle, Patrick, 64
Braddock, General, 206
Brazil, 136
Bremen, 151
Brighton, Eng., 240
Bristol, 5, 157, 176
British Navy, structure of ships of, 233, 237 fn.
Brockville, 22, 167, 170, 175, 178, 208, 225 fn.
Brougham, Lord, 6
Brown, James B., 50 fn., 77, 177, 202
Brown, John, 225
Brown, Samuel, 206, 207, 208

275

INDEX

Brown, William, 78, 185, 188, 192, 195-6, 200 fn., 201, 211-12
Brydone, James M., 127
Buchanan, A. C., 13, 23, 24, 35, 39, 48, 53, 54, 57, 71 fn., 157, 158 fn.
Buchanan, James, 6
Buckingham, J. S., 242 fn.
Buffalo, 199, 200 fn., 202, 203, 211, 231
Burns, Robert, 30
Burr, Aaron, 192
Butler, Samuel, 54
Butler, Sir William, 237
Butler's Rangers, 199
Butter Hill, 193
Bytown, see Ottawa

Cabot, John, 67
California, 117, 208, 214, 233
Campbell, John, 12
Campbell, Mrs. —, 165
Canada Company, 26, 41, 159, 212
Canada Creek, 197
Canada, West, see Ontario
Canadian Pacific Railway, 213
Canadian Rebellion of 1837, 216 fn.
Canadian West, 203, 207-8, 213
Canterbury, N. Z., 110
Capelin, Edmund, 176
Capelin, Frederick, 175
Capelin, John, 176
Capelin, Mary, 176
Cape Breton, 12, 13, 99, 127, 141
Cape Clear, 234
Cape Diamond, 153
Cape Horn, 208
Cape North, 141
Cape Ray, 126, 141
Cape Sable, 239
Cape Verde Islands, 244
Caracas, Venezuela, 23
Carillon, 170
Carleton Place, 230
Carlisle, Earl of, 188, 192
Carrigaholt, 130
Carrothers, W. A., 246 fn.
Cartier, Jacques, 141, 142 fn.
Cartwright, Dr. Edmund, 134 fn.
Cartwright, Lieutenant, 133-4
Cascades Rapids, 165, 170
Castle Garden Immigrant Depot, New York, 182, 186-7
Cattermole, William, 39, 52, 53 fn., 224 fn., 227 fn.
Cavan Township, 225, 228 fn.
Cedars Rapids, 165, 166
Ceres, 28
Chambers' Edinburgh Journal, 77

Champlain Canal, 198, 202
Champlain, Lake, 202, 213
Chartist agitation, 6, 227 fn.
Cherry Valley, 199
Cheshire, 111
Chevalier, Michel, 211 fn.
Chicago, 177, 203
China, 117, 211, 233
Chippewa, 199
Choate, Thomas, 209 fn.
Chouéguen, see Oswego
Christie, A. J., 111
Cincinnati, 211
Cirkland, 229
Clare County, 4
Clark, A. J., 59 fn.
Cleveland, 187, 212, 213
Clyde River, 115, 184
Cobbett, William, 30, 31 fn., 41, 49, 52, 56, 76, 84 fn., 99, 210 fn.
Cobourg, 169, 172, 174, 175, 209, 224 fn.
Cobourg Star, 3 fn., 8 fn., 30 fn., 53 fn., 58, 84 fn., 129, 156 fn., 175, 215, 224 fn.
Columbian Agriculturist Association, 23
Columbus, Christopher, 66, 81
Columbus, Ohio, 217
Connaught, 78
Connecticut, 206
Connecticut River, 205
Cook, Captain David, 134-6
Cooper, William, 39
Cork, 7, 44, 45, 46, 90, 96, 100, 147, 176, 225, 236
Corn Laws, 6
Cornish, Captain, 120
Cornwall, 165, 167, 170, 175
Corsley, 28, 230, 232
Coteau du Lac, 165, 167, 169, 170
Courier, York, 224
Crabbe, George, 146
Crimean War, 235, 239
Crow's Nest, 193
Cults, 28
Cumberland, 22
Cunard-White Star Steamship Line, 237, 245, 247
Cunningham, Captain, 105, 141
Cushing, 27

Dana, Richard H., 81
Darnley, Lord, 28, 156 fn.
Daubeny, C., 119
Davenport, 214
Deaves, Captain Henry, 148
Deer Island Hospital, Boston, 184 fn.

INDEX 277

Defoe, Daniel, 93
De la Fosse, F. M., 30 fn.
Delaware, 220
Delaware River, 164, 205
Derby, 5
Dereham Township, 30
De Roos, J. F. F., 189
Detroit, 167
De Vere, Stephen E., 96, 176 fn.
Devonshire, 106, 131
Dickens, Charles, 182, 184, 200 fn., 211 fn., 241-3
Dickens, Mrs. Charles, 241-2
Dickinson, Barnabas, 170
Diesel engines, 247
Disraeli, Benjamin, 4
Ditton, Mrs., 27
Donnolly, Michael, 48-9
Down, John, 228, 230
Downer, John, 227
Downes, Henry, 127
"Doyle, Martin," see William Hickey
Dramatic Line, 117
Draper, W. H., 119
Drummond, Sir Gordon, 167
Dublin, 44, 147, 151
Duff, 165, 169
Duggerna Rocks, 130
Dumfries, 99, 141
Dunbar, Seymour, 214 fn.
Duncan, John, 122-3, 192, 193, 198, 218
Duncumb, John, 198, 200 fn., 201, 202 fn.
Dunham, Mabel, 208 fn.
Dunkirk, 213
Dunlop, Dr. William, 41, 168
Durham, Earl of, 145, 146, 215-6
Durham, Robert, 164 fn.

Eastern Townships of Quebec, 32, 169, 202, 224
East India Company, 233
Eddystone Lighthouse, 107
Edinburgh, 51
Egremont, Earl of, 25-8, 175
Elliot, T. F., 176 fn.
Ellis Island, 182
Emigration, see also Immigration: Incentives to, 1-9, 14, 21; Restriction of, 1-2, 13, 247; State assistance of, 3-4, 20-33, 60-1; Philanthropic assistance of, 8 fn., 18, 20-33; Legislation regulating conditions of, see especially 10-19, 73-6, 96-8, 128, 130, 155, 179 et seq.; Attitude of emigrants towards, 43, 58, 65; Proceeding to the seaport,

43-6; Conditions at the port of sail, 12-13, 34-5, 47-57; Preparations for the voyage, see especially 34-42, 47-65, also 72-6; Inspection of emigrants, 18-19, 63, 65, 146; Emigrant vessels, see especially 10-19, 67-70; Rules of conduct at sea, 27, 68-73; Life at sea, 66-144; Steerage passage, 66-108, 124-44; Cabin passage, 109-44; Storms at sea, 81 et seq.; Shipwreck and other disasters, 124-37; Disease among emigrants, see especially 89-98, also 84-5, 120, 144-56, 162-3, 166, 174-7, 183-4; Fishing off the Grand Banks, 54, 139-40; Approaching America, 138-54, 179-82; Characteristics of seamen, see especially 72, 86-8, 95, 99-108; Customs and traditions of the sea, 62, 99-108; Sailing-vessels, improvement of, see especially 10-19, 119-20, 123, 233-48; Steamships, introduction and development of, 235-48
Emigration Commissioners, New York, 183-4, 187
English Prairie, 210
Erie Canal, 50, 178, 192-203, 211-13
Erie, Lake, 198, 199
Evans, Francis, 40
Ewhurst, 55
Exeter, 49

Fairgrieve, John, 86
Falmouth Light, 131
Fayal, 122-3, 135
Fenton, Thomas, 222 fn.
Ferrie, Adam, 91 fn., 156 fn.
Ferrier, A. D., 139
Fidler, Rev. Isaac, 120, 172, 226
Fife County, 238
Fire Island, 179
Fitzgibbon, James, 173
Fitzroy Harbour, 216
Fitzroy Township, 59-60
Fleming, Sir Sandford, 236
Flores, 134, 135
Fort Douglas, 207
Fort George, 209
Fort Orange, see Albany
Fort Plain, 199, 201
Fort Putnam, 193
Fort Wellington, 167, 174
Forth and Clyde Canal, 235
Foster, Vere, 10, 23
France, 246, 247
French Line, 247

French Navy, 237 fn.
Frome, 157, 222 fn., 228 fn.
Fulton, Robert, 195

Galt, 23
Gapper, Mary, 115, 116, 138, 188-9
Gamblin, 27
Gannett, Rev. Ezra S., 237
Genesee River, 191, 199
Glasgow, 2, 3, 21, 50, 70, 112, 149, 156, 231
Glenmorison, 2
Gordon, Captain Thomas, 134
Gourlay, Robert, 30, 52 fn., 238
Grand Portage, 213 fn.
Grand Trunk Railway, 178
Grant, 165, 169
Grece, C. F., 210 fn.
Green, Rev. Anson, 174
Greenbush, 230
Greene, 27
Greenland, 50
Greenock, 22, 49, 50, 61, 104, 122, 151
Greenwich Village, 192
Greville, Charles, 31 fn.
Grosse Isle, 19, 27, 31, 89, 90, 94-7, 144, 145-54, 159, 183
Guelph, 212
Guillet, Edwin C., 164 fn., 209 fn., 213 fn., 221 fn.

Hale, Captain, 173
Halifax, 103, 152, 239, 241
Hallowell, *see* Picton
Hall's Aberdeen Clippers, 238
Ham's Mills, Cobourg, 174
Hamburg, 151, 238
Hamilton, Ont., 175, 176, 212
Hamilton, Alexander, 192
Hancock, William, 77 fn., 119 fn., 180 fn., 213, 214 fn.
Harwich, 132
Hastings County, 163
Hayes River, 207
Head, Sir F. B., 32 fn., 40 fn.
Hebrides, 1, 2, 43
Hickey, William ("Martin Doyle"), 37, 39, 222 fn., 232
Highland and Island Emigration Society, 28
Highland Society of Scotland, 10
Hill, George, 231
Hill, John, 228 fn.
Hill, S. S., 36
Hill, Sophia, 216 fn., 228 fn.
Hobart, Lord, 10
Hoboken, 192

Hodge, Job, 27
Hogarth, William, 146
Hollaghan, 64
Hoogdensburgh, 170
Hopkins, J. C., 236 fn.
Hopkirk, James, 70, 106, 112-3, 181, 182, 184, 188, 189
Horncastle, 119
Horner, Thomas, 197
Horsley, Bishop, 5
Houston, Matthew, 230
Howe, John, 210, 227 fn.
Howison, John, 165, 172, 189, 218 fn., 229
Hudson, Henry, 234 fn.
Hudson Bay, 204, 221, 235 fn.
Hudson River, 178, 179-203, 211
Hudson's Bay Company, 205, 207
Hull, Eng., 43, 107, 159, 238
Hunt, J., 38
"Huron Tract," 212
Huskisson, William, 96 fn.

Illinois, 178, 210, 218 fn.
Illustrated London News, 6, 34, 47, 61, 77, 110 fn., 124 fn., 129, 131, 134 fn., 234, 240
Immigration, *see also* Emigration: Quarantine and inspection, 95-8, 145-54, 179-83; Reception of immigrants, 28, 95-8, 155-63, 173-7, 179-91; Fraud and dishonest treatment, 156, 158, 162, 165, 173, 181, 185-6, 188-91, 195-6, 218; State assistance, 156-8, 181-4, 186; Philanthropic assistance, 156-7, 173-4, 176-7, 187; Proceeding to the interior, 27-8, 155-79, 192-214; Immigrants' impressions of America, *see especially* 215-32, *also* 155-214 *passim*; Land settlement, 215-32
Inches, James, 41
Indiana, 206, 210, 214 fn., 222, 228, 229
Inglis, John, 227
Inman and International Line, 245
Iowa, 214
Ireland Township, 157
Irish Sea, 45-6, 235
Islay, 129
Italian Liberation, War of, 241

Jameson, Mrs. Anna, 218 fn., 222
Jerome, Frederick, 137
Johnson, Hugh, 149
Johnson, Dr. Samuel, 2, 233
Johnston, Thomas, 104, 139

INDEX

Johnstone, Walter, 99
Jones, C., 218 fn., 231
Jones, D., 230
Jones, William, 64

Kaatskill Mountains, 193
Kansas, 204, 214
Kansas City, 214
Kenmare, 45
Kennoway, 28
Kentucky, 204, 205
Killarney, 7
Kincaid, J., 156 fn.
Kingston, Ont., 167, 169-72, 175-7
Kinshott, Joseph, 176
Kirdford, 227
Knill, Captain, 159
Kohl, J. G., 87 fn.

Labrador, 141
Lachine, 164, 165, 166, 169, 170, 177
Lachine Canal, 162, 177
Lachine Railway, 178
Lachine Rapids, 165
Laidler, Captain, 128
Lanark, Scot., 22
Lanark County, Ont., 3
Lander, 176
Land's End, 107, 131
La Prairie, 202
Largon, 28
Largs, 184
Lasselle, Stanislaus, 214 fn.
Leeds Township, 157
Le Havre, 120
Leith, 43, 73
Leitrim County, 149 fn.
Levinge, R. G. A., 15, 106, 121
Limerick, 7, 44, 56, 127, 129, 147, 151
Lines, Captain, 80 fn., 120
Linton, John, 212
Lister, Thomas, 230
Little Falls, 199, 201
Littledale, Thomas, 136
Liverpool, 17, 18, 34, 45, 46, 47 *et seq.*, 87, 90, 96, 103, 109, 112, 113, 117, 118, 125, 133, 136, 151, 188, 231, 233, 236, 238, 241-2
Lizard Lights, 107, 131
Loch Broom, 59 fn.
Lockport, 199, 202
Logansport, 214 fn.
London, Eng., 8, 16, 44, 49, 50, 60, 123, 126, 132, 161, 231, 234, 236, 240
London, Ont., 222
London Township, 21
Londonderry, 14, 67, 129

Long Island, 179
Long Sands, 132
Long Sault Rapids, 165
Lott, Captain, 133
Louisville, 210, 211 fn.
Lowber, Captain, 64
Lower Canada, *see* Quebec Province
Lubbock, Basil, 18, 67, 244 fn.
Lucas, Sir C. P., 156 fn., 216 fn.
Luddites, 5
Luff, Ned, 176

Macaulay, Lord, 4, 7 fn., 242 fn.
McCormick, Michael, 48
M'Donald, John, 20, 22, 158, 167, 208, 222 fn.
McKee, Martha, 163
McKenney, Thomas L., 194
Mackenzie, William L., 118, 119, 157
McKinnon, Mrs., 43
MacLeod, General, 1
McLeod, Rev. Norman, 59 fn.
Madeira, 236
Maginnis, A. J., 234, 245 fn.
Magrath, Rev. James, 113
Maiden Bradley, 157
Maine, 239
Manchester, Eng., 231
Markham Township, 208 fn.
Marryat, Captain F., 81
Marsden, Rev. Joshua, 103
Marshall, 227
Martin, Captain, 99
Martin, Chester, 208 fn.
Martin (on the *British Tar*), 27
Martin, 90
Massachusetts, 244
Massachusetts Bay, 237
Matthew, Rev., 190
Mayo County, 4
Meath County, 31, 91
Melbourne, Aus., 59 fn.
Mersey River, 45-6, 47 *et seq.*, 59-65, 136
Merston, 39
Mewburn, Arthur, 84 fn.
Mewburn, Dr. John, 84 fn.
Mewburn, Margaret, 84 fn.
Mewburn, Rebecca, 84 fn.
Mexico, Gulf of, 112, 204
Middleton, J. E., 119 fn.
Milburn, William, 206 fn.
Mille Roches, 165
Mills, 206
Minnesota, 178, 204, 213, 214
Mississippi River, Ont., 22, 225 fn.
Mississippi River, U. S., 205, 206, 210, 211, 212, 214, 221, 238

INDEX

Mississippi, State of, 206
Mississippi and Ohio Mail Line, 211
Missouri River, 204, 238
Mitchell, Edgar, 86
Mohawk River, 197, 198, 205
Molson, John, 160 fn.
Monteagle, Lord, 7
Montmorenci Falls, 153
Montreal, 2, 22, 25, 27, 36, 50, 68, 95, 149, 150, 155-64, 167, 175, 176, 177, 183, 199, 202, 213, 224, 239, 244
Montreal Advertiser, 67
Montreal Transcript, 149 fn.
Moodie, Mrs. Susanna, 146-7, 157, 162, 170, 172, 219 fn., 229 fn.
Moon, Mrs., 218
Mooney, Thomas, 9
Moore, George, 186, 242
Morgan, Henry, 128
Morley, Nathan, 176
Morning Chronicle, London, 8
Morrin, Dr., 155-6
Morris, Rev. Charles, 151 fn.
Mudie, Robert, 39, 76
Munster, 78
Murray Firth, 67

Napoleonic Wars, 103; effect upon emigration, 2, 12, 222 fn., 246
Natchez, 206
National Societies, 173
Navigation Laws, 233
Nebraska, 214
Need, Thomas, 182
Nelson, Lord, 40
Nelson Township, 38
Neversink, 179
New Bedford, 244
New Brunswick, 15, 124, 152, 204, 209, 225, 231
Newcastle, Eng., 128
New England, 12
Newfoundland, 50, 54, 89, 93, 96 fn., 101-2, 108, 115, 120, 126-7, 132, 138 et seq., 234
New Jersey, 116, 179
New Lanark, 208
New Orleans, 90 fn., 91, 180 fn., 204, 205, 206, 210, 211, 214
New Perth, see Perth
Newry, 147
New South Wales, 24
New York City, 23, 34-7, 50-1, 64, 87 fn., 90, 112, 114, 116-8, 121-2, 132, 135, 178, 179-193, 198, 203-4, 212-4, 218, 225-6, 228, 234, 236-40, 242, 244, 246-7

New York State, 179-203, 211 fn., 226, 230
Niagara, 167, 171
Niagara Falls, 199, 209
Niagara River, 202
North Carolina, 10
Northiam, 55
Norval Creek, 197
Nottingham, 5
Nova Scotia, 13, 15, 59 fn., 134, 136, 225

O'Brien, E. G., 115
Ogdensburgh, 170
Ohio, 59 fn., 191, 217, 229, 231
Ohio Philanthropic Society, 187
Ohio River, 205, 206, 211, 212, 238
Omaha, 203
Oneida Indians, 199
Oneida Lake, 197
Ontario, *also* Upper Canada and Canada West, 3, 6, 8, 20-22, 25-6, 30, 32, 38, 41, 125-6, 157, 159, 163, 166-78, 197, 199, 201-2, 204, 208-9, 212, 215 et seq.
Ontario, Lake, 165, 197, 202, 209
Orleans Island, 144, 145, 153
Orman, Meredith, 232
Oswego, 172, 197, 202, 212
Oswego Canal, 199
Oswego River, 197
Otonabee River, 22, 209
Otonabee Township, 215, 222 fn.
Ottawa, 170-1, 176, 236 fn.
Ottawa River, 169, 170-1, 177
Owen, Robert, 30
Oxford County, 171, 197
Oxford and Asquith, Earl of, 31 fn.

Paisley, 156, 226, 230
Paisley, Rev., 151
Palisades, 193
Palmer, John, 50, 52, 216
Palmerston, Lord, 156 fn.
Paris, France, 188, 240
Parks, Harriot, 230
Parks, Hester, 73
Parks, James, 55
Parks, John, 73, 230
Partridge Island, 152
Patterson, Henry, 40 fn.
Peacock, William, 161, 162
Peninsular War, 220
Pennsylvania, 164 fn., 208, 210, 228, 230
Pepys, Samuel, 105
Perth, Ont., 21, 208, 232
Peterborough, Ont., 8, 20, 209

INDEX

Peterborough County, 22, 30 fn., 208-9
Petworth, 125
Petworth Emigration Society, 25-8
Philadelphia, 178, 180 fn., 230
Philips, George, 83
Picken, Andrew, 55
Picton, *also* Hallowell, 175
Pictou, N. S., 59 fn., 236
Piermont, 213
Pittsburgh, 211, 228
Playfair, Robert, 80 fn., 120
Plymouth, 131, 134
Plymouth and Devonport Weekly Journal, 134 fn.
Point Levi, 146, 153
Poole, Dr., 19, 31
Poor Law Act of 1834, 5
Port Arthur, 213
Port Hope, 173, 175
Portland, Me., 110
Portree, 43
Portsmouth, 25, 26, 60 fn., 121, 137, 147, 234
Port Stanley, 220
Port Talbot, 220
Potters' Emigration Society, 29
Pounds, John, 60 fn.
Powell, Jane, 227 fn., 228
Powell, Jem, 227 fn.
Poyle Bay, 127
Prayer-book and Homily Society, 61
Prescott, 21, 164-6, 169, 170, 171, 175, 177
Preston, T. R., 121-2
Prince Arthur's Landing, *see* Port Arthur
Prince Edward Island, 22, 38, 99, 141, 218
Prout, T. S., 74
Providence, R. I., 244
Purdy, Samuel, 170

Quarterly Review, 217 fn., 228 fn.
Quebec City, 2, 11, 13-4, 16, 20, 22-3, 27-8, 36-7, 41, 50, 54, 56, 84 fn., 87, 90, 94, 97, 104, 109, 113, 115, 117, 124-31, 133, 144, 145-63, 167, 175, 177, 180, 204, 209, 220, 224, 236, 238-9.
Quebec Chronicle, 151
Quebec Gazette, 90 fn., 128, 148, 156 fn., 158 fn., 159, 160, 170, 173 fn.
Quebec Marine and Emigrant Hospital, 148
Quebec *Mercury*, 22

Quebec Province, *also* Lower Canada and Canada East, 15, 32, 142, 171, 180, 215 *et seq.*, 231-2
Queensbury, 231
"Queen's Bush," 212
Queenstown, 245
Quinte, Bay of, 6

Radcliff, Mrs. William, 58, 113-4, 117, 140, 170
Ragged Schools, 60-1
Raisin River, 167
Rawle, Captain, 131
Read, Captain, 151
Rebeccaites, 6
Red Island Reef, 129
Red River, Canada, 207, 213 fn.
Red River, U. S., 210
Reesor, Peter, 208 fn.
Reform Bill of 1832, 5, 31 fn.
Reid, Robert, 112
Revolutionary War, 193, effect upon emigration, 246 fn.
Rice Lake, 6, 209
Richelieu River, 202, 213
Richibucto, 124
Riddell, Walter, 86
Rideau Canal, 170-1, 177
Rideau River, 167
Rio de la Plata Agricultural Society, 23
Robinson, Captain G. W., 112
Robinson, Peter, 22, 174, 208-9
Rochefoucauld-Liancourt, Duc de la, 171
Rochester, 199
Rose, Rev. A. W. H., 34, 38, 39, 40
Rose Branch, 127
Russell, Lord John, 156 fn.
Rye, Miss, 23

Sailors' chanties, 62, 66, 99, 117, 119
St. Andrew's Rapids, 207
St. Andrew's Society, 173
St. Ann's, 59 fn.
St. Anthony's Nose, *see* Anthony's Nose
St. Charles River, 153
St. Francis, Lake, 165
St. François, 153
St. George's Society, 173
St. John, N. B., 48, 152, 233, 241 fn.
St. John's, lower St. Lawrence, 153
St. John's, Richelieu River, 202, 213
St. John's River, 209
St. Lawrence Canals, 165, 177, 213

INDEX

St. Lawrence River and Gulf, 12, 21, 22, 28, 37, 50, 94, 99, 102, 106, 108, 115, 132, 138-78, 183, 202-3, 205, 209, 238, 239
St. Louis, 206
St. Louis, Lake, 165
St. Michel's, 153
St. Patrick's Society, 173
St. Paul, 210, 214
St. Paul Island, 141-2
St. Peter, Lake, 161
St. Regis, 175
St. Vallier, 153
Salt Lake City, 203
Sandusky, 213
Sandy Hook, 102, 122, 123, 179
San Francisco, 203
Sarnia, 178
Scandinavia, 236
Schenectady, 197, 198, 202, 205
Schoharie Creek, 198
Scoomie, 28
Scott, George, 39
Scott's Mills, *see* Peterborough
Sedlescomb, 228
Selkirk, Earl of, 66, 207, 218
Shaftesbury, Earl of, 23, 60-1
Shakespeare, William, 30, 110, 124
Shannon River, 130
Shawnee Town, 210
Ships: *Accommodation*, 160 fn.; *Affonso*, 136; *Airthy Castle*, 157; *Amy*, 151; *Anglo-Saxon*, 239; *Anna Maria*, 151; *Artemisia*, 60, 61; *Astrea*, 128; *Atlas*, 167; *Aurora*, 159; *Baltic Merchant*, 167; *Ben Nevis*, 235; *Bohemian*, 239; *Boscius*, 117; *Britannia* (sail), 151; *Britannia* (steam), 237, 241-2, 243; *British Tar*, 26, 27, 143, 147; *Brothers*, 151; *Brunswick*, 21, 100, 142, 144 fn.; *Brutus*, 90, 147; *Caleb Grimshaw*, 134-5; *Caledonia*, 21, 171; *Camillus*, 82, 99, 217; *Canadian* (first), 239; *Canadian* (second), 239; *Canadian Patriot*, 159; *Caroline*, 53 fn., 158; *Chancellor Livingston*, 192-3; *Charles Bartlett*, 132; *Charlevoix*, 160 fn.; *Charlotte Dundas*, 235; *Charter Oak*, 234; *China*, 56; *Christopher Columbus*, 234; *City of New York*, 245; *City of Paris*, 245; *Clermont*, 195; *Constitution*, 49; *Corea*, 151; *Cornelius Grinnell*, 234; *Countess of Morley*, 23; *Cumberland Lass*, 54; *Dalhousie*, 170; *David*, 22, 158; *Diana*, 99; *Discovery*, 235 fn.; *Donegal*, 113; *Dorothy*, 167; *Duncan Gibb*, 113, 114, 140; *Edmund*, 130; *Edward*, 128; *Elizabeth Grimmer*, 16; *Ellen Simpson*, 151; *Emily*, 104; *England*, 25, 26; *Enterprise*, 171; *Etna*, 210; *Europa*, 132-3; *Exmouth*, 129; *Fanny*, 122; *Fidelity*, 128; *Florence*, 48; *Floridian*, 131; *Forrester*, 159; *Frances Ann*, 59 fn.; *Friends*, 147; *Frontenac*, 172; *Galatea*, 234; *Ganges*, 151; *Garrick*, 117; *Germanic*, 245 fn.; *Globe*, 237; *Great Australia*, 235, 238; *Great Britain* (Atlantic), 236-7; *Great Britain* (Lake Ontario), 172; *Great Eastern*, 82, 240-1; *Great Republic*, 234; *Great Western*, 236, 242; *Hannibal*, 106; *Harmony*, 159; *Hebe*, 36, 86, 100, 126; *Helena Sloman*, 238; *Hercules*, 28, 147; *Hope*, 70, 79; *Hungarian*, 239; *Importer*, 50, 52; *Indian*, 239; *Ironsides*, 234; *Isaac Webb*, 49, 51, 62, 63; *Isaac Wright*, 49; *James*, 37, 89, 127, 128; *John*, 131; *John Bannerman*, 233; *John Bull*, 159; *John Dennison*, 49, 61, 62, 64 fn., 78, 80, 83, 85, 86, 100, 105, 139, 179, 180, 184; *John R. Manta*, 244; *John Stamp*, 58; *Julius Macgregor*, 16, 53, 77; *Kite*, 236; *Lady Clinton*, 194; *Lady Hood*, 54; *Lady Macnaughton*, 89, 90; *Lancaster*, 86; *Larch*, 95, 151; *Laurel*, 111, 115; *Lightning*, 118, 233, 234; *Lilias*, 151; *London*, 49; *London of London*, 125; *Lord Ashburton*, 95, 96; *Lord Melville*, 25; *Lord Wellington*, 70; *Louisiana*, 211; *Magnet*, 80; *Majestic*, 245; *Marchioness of Breadalbane*, 151; *Margaret*, 128; *Martin Luther*, 133-4; *Mary*, 90, 147, 148; *Mary Ann Bell*, 105, 141; *Matthew*, 67; *Mayflower*, 237; *Mediator*, 119; *Mercury*, 127; *Minerva*, 89; *Minstrel*, 129; *Montezuma*, 64; *Naparima*, 151; *Napoleon*, 100, 120; *New Orleans*, 210; *New World*, 49, 137; *New York*, 120; *Nimrod*, 127; *Normandie*, 246-7; *North Briton*, 239; *Ocean Monarch*, 136; *Onondaga*, 171; *Ontario*, 118; *Ottawa*, 171; *Oxford*, 78; *Panope*, 28; *Patriote*, 160; *Penelope*, 147; *Petrel*, 132; *Pique*, 237 fn.; *Portaferry of*

INDEX   283

Portaferry, 125; *Priscilla*, 147; *Queen Mary*, 122 fn., 247; *Queen of the Ocean*, 136; *Queen of the West*, 49; *Queen Victoria*, 107-8; *Randolph*, 110; *Rebecca*, 139; *Recovery*, 147; *Red Jacket*, 233-4; *Rothiemurchus*, 12, 66, 70, 73, 84; *Royal Charter*, 235; *Royal William*, 236; *St. Andrew*, 121; *St. George*, 112; *St. Mary*, 159; *St. Vincent*, 60, 61, 68; *Samaria*, 237; *Sarah*, 134-6; *Savannah*, 236; *Servia*, 245; *Shannon*, 171; *Sheridan*, 117, 120; *Siddons*, 117; *Sir Henry Pottinger*, 96; *Sirius*, 236; *Snow Sparrow*, 103; *Sovereign of the Seas*, 234; *Spray*, 59 fn.; *Star of the West*, 8, 49, 62, 64; *Tagus*, 133; *Tennessee*, 71, 106, 112, 140, 182 fn.; *Teutonic*, 245; *Thames*, 116; *Thetis*, 147; *Thomas Gelston*, 67; *Titanic*, 248; *Trenton*, 244; *Trinity*, 151; *Triton*, 159; *Ulster*, 14; *Umbria*, 245; *United States*, 170; *Victoria*, 109, 123; *Victory*, 159; *Virginius*, 96, 151; *Voyageur*, 159, 160; *Warrior*, 115-6; *Washington*, 18; *Watchful*, 151; *Waterloo*, 124 fn.; *Wellington*, 209; *Westmoreland*, 37, 159; *West Point*, 49; *William Avery*, 173; *William Fell*, 147; *William IV*, 172; *William M'Gilevray*, 115; *William Thomson*, 118; *Winnepesaukee*, 244; *Yorkshire*, 49
Shirreff, Patrick, 100, 120, 170, 172, 175, 217, 230
Sholto, 90
Sicilian Revolution, 241
Silcog, 232
Silcox, Joseph, 230
Simcoe, John G., 171
Singer, William, 232
Sing Sing, 193
Sioux Indians, 214
Skelton, Isabel, 22 fn.
Skye, Isle of, 10, 43
Slade, Robert, 228
Sligo County, 7, 95, 151
Smart, Henry, 175
Smith, 64
Smith, Benjamin, 210 fn., 228 fn.
Smith, Captain (*Cumberland Lass*), 54
Smith, Captain (*Naopleon*), 100, 120
Smith, Sidney, 53, 196, 218 fn., 228 fn.

Smith Township, 6, 22
Smith, W. L., 149 fn., 171 fn.
Snelgrove, William, 230
Somersetshire, 115, 222 fn.
Sorel, 161
Southampton, Eng., 133, 234, 246-7
Southampton, Penn., 230
Southwold Township, 232 fn.
Spain, 236
Split Rock Rapids, 165
Staffordshire, 29
Standard, Toronto, 176
Staple Cross, 55
Staten Island, 179, 181-3, 184
Steadman, 39
Steele, Ellen, 116
Steelé, Millicent, 116
Stevenson, Robert, 43
Stevenson, Robert Louis, 58, 64 fn., 110 fn., 114, 186, 214, 242-4
Stewart, Frances, 112, 209 fn.
Stewart, Thomas, 112
Strachan, Rev. John, 225
Strickland, Samuel, 30 fn., 115, 125, 140, 141, 166
Strickland, Mrs. Samuel, 212
Stuart, Charles, 20
Stuart, James, 118, 210 fn., 218 fn.
Stuart, Dr. James, 89
Subinacade Lake, 225
Sugar Loaf Mountain, 193
Sullivan County, 226
Sully, 209
Sunday at Home, The, 245 fn.
Susquehanna River, 197, 200 fn., 205
Sussex, 25-8, 55, 175
Sydenham, 212
Sydenham, Lord, 20
Sydney, Cape Breton, 127
Syracuse, 199

Talbot, Edward A., 20, 142-4, 164, 166, 171, 221 fn., 229
Talbot, Richard, 21
Tappan Bay, 193
Taylor, Abraham, 149 fn.
Taylor, C. C., 120
Taylor, George, 149 fn.
Taylor, James, 107-8, 218, 219 fn.
Taylor, Samuel, 149 fn.
Taylor, William, 149 fn.
Taylor, General, 40
Taylor, Rev., 70
Thomas, Francis, 36, 86, 110, 126-7, 132, 146, 161, 171 fn.
Thomson, H. C., 165
Thomson, John, 221 fn.
Thorley, Thomas, 229

Three Rivers, P. E. I., 91
Three Rivers, Que., 161
Tickner, William, 176
Times, London, 8, 96, 97
Toronto, *also* York and Little York, 21, 26, 32 fn., 167, 169, 170, 172, 173-6, 175, 177 fn., 202, 220, 221 fn., 224, 225, 228 fn.
Townagh, 8
Traill, Mrs. Catherine, 111-2, 114-5, 138, 142, 145-6, 162, 170
Treffry, John, 171
Trevelyan, G. O., 7, 242 fn.
Tripp, Mary Jane, 58
Trollope, Mrs. Frances, 184, 242 fn.
Troy, 198, 202
Trussler, Timothy, 38
Turner, Joseph, 184
Turner, Stephen, 86

Uniacke, R. J., 13, 14
United Empire Loyalists, 197
Upper Canada, *see* Ontario
Upper Canada Herald, Toronto, 173
Upton, 27
Utah, 214
Utica, 199, 202

Van Diemen's Land, 3, 24
Venango County, 228
Veness, Harriot, 81, 84 fn.
Veness, John, 84 fn.
Verplank's Point, 193
Vicksburg, 214
Vienna, 223
Vincennes, 206
Virginia, 122, 204

Wake, Captain, 128
Ward's Island, N. Y., 181, 182, 183, 186
Warminster, 157
Warr, G. W., 158 fn., 192
Washington, George, 40
Waterford, 44, 225
Waterloo County, 208 fn.
Watson, John, 209-10, 222, 228, 229
Watson, Mary, 209
Watson, Mary Jane, 110, 228

Watson, Captain, 12
Webb, Charles R., 234
Weehawken, 192
Weld, Isaac, 171
Wellington, Duke of, 40, 90
West, Thomas, 38
Western Islands of Scotland, 8
Western Railway, 202
Weston, Richard, 61, 82, 87 fn., 105, 180, 181, 184-5, 187-8, 206, 208 fn., 210 fn., 212 fn., 218
West Point, 193
Wheeling, 211 fn.
Whitby, Eng., 84 fn.
Whitehall, 202
Whitehaven, 113
Wilkie, David, 174
Willard, Charlotte, 85, 230
Willard, James, 85
Willard, Maria, 85
Wilson, C. H., 91 fn., 210 fn., 215 fn., 221
Wilson, Rev. James, 138, 141 fn.
Wilson, Captain, 130
Wiltshire, 28
Windsor, N. S., 225
Winnipeg, 208
Winnipeg, Lake, 207
Wisconsin, 29, 178, 214
Wolseley, Garnet, 213 fn.
Wood, George, 231
World War, Atlantic sailing-ships surviving at outbreak of, 244; effect on emigration, 247
Wright, William, 66

Yarmouth, N. S., 136
Yarmouth Township, 222
Yonge, 48-9
York, *see* Toronto
York Emigrant Committee, 174
York Emigrants' Asylum, 174, 224
York Society for the Sick and Destitute, 174
York Stranger's Friend Society, 173
York Factory, 205, 207
Yorkshire, 84 fn., 159
Youghall, 147
Youngstown, *also* Young's Town, 202

Supplement

to

THE GREAT MIGRATION

*The Atlantic Crossing by Sailing-Ship
1770–1860*

by EDWIN C. GUILLET, M.A., LL.D.

Including two notable diaries not used in the
original book a quarter of a century ago.

Courtesy New Brunswick Museum, St. John

PROCESS OF CLEARING THE TOWN PLOT AT STANLEY, 1834

Sketches in New Brunswick, 1836

SUPPLEMENT TO
The Great Migration
1962

Among the hazards that are sometimes experienced by authors in dealing with publishers is the editorial alteration of their writing just prior to printing. The original preface to *The Great Migration*, sent with the typescript to New York, was some six or seven pages in length and contained the thoughts of the author on completing his book. This preface was not printed, but instead a short advertising blurb was substituted, so blatant and defective that any author would have been ashamed to have it appear above his name. At the last minute a new but much too short preface was despatched by telegram. It duly appeared, but was only a portion of what had originally been considered necessary to introduce a subject of the magnitude of Atlantic travel in the days of the sailing-ship. Among the many omissions was our indebtedness to the *Illustrated London News* for the finest contemporary illustrations.

This supplement is designed to appear in a sort of final edition of the last 160 copies of *The Great Migration*, published in 1937. Nothing has come to the author's attention in the 25-year interval that would alter any of the conclusions or change his estimate of what was typical or characteristic. A few variations in personal experience are worth recording, but the book remains the only predominantly social history of the Atlantic crossing.

One copy of an emigration booklet that was thought, after long and widespread search in Britain and America, to have disappeared completely was finally located in 1952 in the notable collection of Canadiana of J. G. Ketcheson, Richmond Hill. It was entitled *A Guide for Emigrants from the British Shores to the Woods of Canada* (Dublin, 1834). Its author, Captain George Arundel Hill, was a veteran of Waterloo and among the first settlers in Dummer Township, Peterborough County. Unfortunately his description of his Atlantic crossing was not extensive, possibly because it was a good one and uneventful; in fact the passengers in his ship were so pleased with their passage that they took up a collection and presented the captain with a gratuity at the end of the voyage—the only instance of the kind that the author has seen recorded. The details of the trip up the St. Lawrence by Durham boat are, however, more extensive than found elsewhere for that primitive type of travel.[1]

Perhaps the best general history of emigration is *British Emigration to British North America* by Helen I. Cowan, published in 1928 as one of the series *University of Toronto Studies*. A revised and enlarged edition was produced by Miss Cowan and the University of Toronto Press in 1961.

Numerous other good studies of the subject have appeared before and since, and the present writer is glad to have been able to print, for the first time from the manuscript records, a large part of the Peter Robinson Papers as a portion of *The Valley of the Trent*, the first volume of the Ontario Government series of documentary histories of Ontario regions. Appearing in print in 1957, these materials were among the newly available documents used by Miss Cowan in her revision. Much more might be said of additions to the sources earlier available, but the reader is referred to her excellent Bibliographical Note in the 1961 edition, pages 305-310, and to the remarkably complete notes and references, pages 241-282. I am indebted to Miss Cowan and the University of Toronto Press for permission to reproduce the two full-page illustrations appearing herewith in this supplement.

Two diaries of the Atlantic crossing by sailing-ship add something to *The Great Migration*. John G. Howard of Colborne Lodge, High Park, Toronto, whose munificent gift of parkland to the city is but one reason to honour his memory, made the passage in the cholera year, 1832. To cross from London to York, as Toronto was then called, took him eleven weeks and three days, among the longer recorded passages. The following excerpts from his diary[2] describe the more unique of his experiences, which included fishing and hunting expeditions in small boats at both ends of his voyage. Riotous steerage passengers and a mutinous crew, as well as episodes in which he narrowly escaped drowning, made the passage an exciting one.

---

[1] A summary of these experiences is given in the author's *Pioneer Inns and Taverns*, Volume III, pp. 14-16. The Public Archives of Canada, Ottawa, had Captain Hill's *Guide* photostated when it was brought to their attention, and the author gave his copy of the photostat to the Toronto Public Library. The Ketcheson Collection was sold to Montreal dealers after the death of its owner.

[2] See *Incidents in the Life of John G. Howard, Esq., of Colborne Lodge, High Park, near Toronto; Chiefly Adapted from his Journals*. Toronto, 1885.

DIARY OF JOHN HOWARD, 1832

Describing his Atlantic crossing on the sailing-ship
Emperor Alexander, Captain Boig.

June 26, 1832 . . . We went on board, and began putting things to rights in the cabin. We found that we wanted several things which I ought to have got at Gravesend. The vessel did not sail that night, and the mate assured me that she would not sail before the next evening. We therefore took the opportunity of going on shore again in the morning. We had just made our purchases, and were going to take a walk and call on mother, when a waterman from the pier stepped up and informed us that the ship was under sail. I ran down to the beach, and to my utter astonishment found his words were true. She was sailing away at a rapid rate. We jumped into a boat, and gave the men five shillings. After an hour's hard rowing, we came up with the ship, and sailed on with a fine breeze, coming to anchor off the Nore Light about midnight. The sea around the bow of the vessel appeared illuminated with small blue lights. . . .

On the morning of the 29th we sailed on slowly, passing the Isle of Sheppey about four o'clock in the afternoon. The vessel ran aground on the Spaniard Bank off Herne Bay, which obliged us to wait ten hours for the return of the tide. Some of the passengers took the boat and went fishing and shooting, but they met with very poor sport. About three p.m. a fine breeze sprang up, and Margate, Ramsgate, Deal, and Dover soon appeared in view. Then the wind dropped, and we were opposite the cliffs some hours. The captain, myself, and the rest of the cabin passengers amused ourselves with shooting with my rifle at a bottle slung up to the yard arm. Another gentleman and myself were standing on the poop when the boom jibbed, and nearly swept us into the sea, which put an end to our shooting. The captain caught hold of one of my legs just as I was going over. By the way, the captain turned out a very fine fellow. My sickness being worse than that of anyone else on board, he did everything in his power to make me comfortable. About 11.30 p.m. I went on deck, and distinctly saw a large meteor or ball of fire fall into the sea about three hundred yards ahead of the vessel. . . .

July 4th.—Breakfasted off live mackerel, about 10 a.m. Went out in the boat and shot a puffin with my rifle, and one of our party caught a very curious fish. Our boat became so leaky we could scarcely keep her afloat, so we put back to the ship to get another. I then took my double-barrelled gun, and we went in chase of some divers, one of which I shot; likewise some of Mother Carey's chickens, a very curious web-footed bird, larger than a swallow, with head and bill like a pigeon's. They are never seen on land, and they generally indicate a storm.

We were so intent on our sport that we did not observe that a breeze had sprung up; and, looking round for the ship, we found that she had sailed at least five miles from us. One of the party who had been mate of the ship said the Captain would lay-to, and if we rowed hard we should come up with them in about two hours. This man and myself were the only two that could row. We therefore threw off our coats and fell to work, but all to no purpose, as the ship began to disappear from our view. The gale freshened, and one of us was obliged to take the helm and keep the boat's head to the sea, which now began to run frightfully high. At last a sloop hove in sight. We tied handkerchiefs to our guns and held them up when the boat mounted the billows. We also fired off our guns, and shouted, but they either did not or would not hear us, and sailed past us within half a mile.

We now began to upbraid one another for leaving the ship. I had been lying for some time in the bow of the boat, dreadfully sea-sick, and had resigned myself sullenly to my fate, although the thought of my poor wife almost distracted me. The Doctor was lying by my side; one of the others was wringing his hands, and complaining bitterly against the Captain. I noticed that the boat had sprung a leak, and as well as I could I raised myself up and called to my companions, saying: 'If you are men, cease your wrangling and bail out the boat, or we shall soon go to Davy Jones'.' This had the desired effect, for they were horror-struck at finding so much water in the boat.

I had for some time watched the rigging of the ship as it was fast disappearing from our view, when the rays of the setting sun illuminated the sails, and plainly proved to me that the ship had tacked about. This I communicated to the man at the helm, when, upon looking at her, he perceived that she was bearing down for us. She was at least fifteen miles from us, and the sun was going down, so that we feared we should not reach her that night. We were about a hundred miles from the nearest land, and should the gale increase in the night there was not the slightest chance of saving our lives. Stories haunted my mind about men perishing with want in an open boat.

But erelong the wind began to abate, and we once more commenced rowing. The vessel gained on us very fast. We now took the bearings of the ship as nearly as we could with my pocket compass, in case it should become dark before we came up with her; but we now rowed as it were for our lives. The ship neared and passed us within musket shot. The captain was standing on the poop. I took up my gun and had a great mind to shoot at him, but at that moment we observed our wives imploring him to take us on board. The good ship passed us like a bird on the wing, and her main yard was then laid aback to the mast, and she became motionless with the exception of pitching and rolling.

The captain shouted for us to pull round to the leeward side. I happened to ask the doctor to secure the guns by tying them to the seats of the boat, which very much alarmed him, for I expected the boat would be capsized in boarding the vessel, which it certainly would if it had not been for the captain passing us as he did before he stopped the vessel or lay-to. Thank God we all arrived safe on board at dusk in the evening. The fears of our loved ones on board had been as great as ours, for when it came on to blow the mate went to the masthead with a telescope, but could see nothing of us. We were so benumbed when we were hauled on board that we could hardly stand. We all went to bed as quickly as possible. . . .

July 18th.—This morning about 11 a.m. a party went out in a boat for the purpose of bathing. After they returned a second party engaged the boat for the same purpose, who came back in an hour, took some spirits into the boat, and again pushed off. A breeze sprung up soon afterwards, and we lost sight of them. Towards evening their absence caused alarm, and a boat was sent in quest of them, which returned about half-past ten without any tidings. Lights were hung out at the masthead, and tar tubs were set on fire. We had two small cannon on board, which were loaded and fired. As they sent their thunders across the ocean the sea birds seemed to scream the funeral dirge of our unfortunate companions. The ladies on board were crying. I went to bed about two a.m., and was called up again at three to fire another cannon. As soon as the morning began to dawn the mate went to the masthead, and in about an hour, with the help of a telescope, he observed the missing crew about six miles off. This greatly relieved us, and at six a.m. they came on board, having been absent eighteen hours, and having delayed us eighty miles.

Nothing else of an unusual character occurred until the 24th, when, about 5 a.m., we were awakened by a terrible thumping on the deck, and a cry of 'Fire, fire!' The captain rushed upon deck in his shirt, hind part before, ran to the fore chains, seized the ringleader, dragged him aft, and rope's-ended him. A lot of them ran to the rescue of the man, and got the captain down. They said they were Englishmen and would stick together, and swore they would shoot him, for they wanted neither him nor his crew. They declared that they could work the ship themselves. One of them was about to strike the captain, but the mate seized him, and the captain regained his feet. He ordered the sailors to furl all the sails, telling the rioters they might set them again, for he would not make any sail until all was quiet. This had the desired effect, and restored peace in about two hours.

We—my wife and myself—were both very unwell. I kept my pistols and guns loaded by the bed side, as we expected to hear the ruffians come down the cabin steps, for a set of greater blackguards never sailed out of England. We were in 45° west longitude, and 48° north latitude. Towards evening it blew a gale of wind, and carried away the fore top gallant and royal masts. . . .

August 1st.—At eight a.m., went upon deck. The sailors told me that land was in sight. I had promised a bottle of rum to the first sailor who would point it out to me. It appeared like a cloud. It rained very fast, as it usually does off this coast. About 11 a.m. the fog cleared off, and we could see the land very plainly. It was one of the grandest sights I had ever witnessed. We counted eight icebergs towards the land, and one very large one passed within gun shot of the ship, about the size of St. Paul's Cathedral, London. The sun was shining upon it, which gave it a most brilliant appearance. The captain offered me one of the boats and some competent hands to go out with me shooting and fishing, but I was too unwell to avail myself of his kindness.

The boat pushed off about one p.m., and returned about five, with 250 large codfish alive, which they had purchased for a sovereign. I was rather vexed that I did not go with them, for the wild ducks and geese flew round the boat in great numbers within a few yards. One of the icebergs they passed was about a mile in length, and one of the sailors said he saw a bear upon it, which we did not credit. The fishing boats were moored to the ice, and they caught a great many fish. The scenery at sunset was truly sublime. The mountains in the background with their sombre appearance, and with the clouds passing about half way up them, gave the icebergs a most brilliant appearance on the departure of the god of day. One of the passengers was carried overboard by the main tack, and narrowly escaped a watery grave. . . .

August 10th.—At one p.m. a breeze set in which increased until three p.m. The atmosphere was very foggy, and we were apprehensive of running foul of the Bird Isles, which lie in the Gulf of St. Lawrence. I was very unwell in bed. Towards evening the captain came to my berth and asked me to get up, as I could have a good sight of the land. I arose and went upon deck, but could not remain, and was obliged to go to bed again. About 10 p.m. I heard an unusual noise upon deck, the captain, at the highest pitch of his voice, calling to the sailors to brace up the foreyard, and repeating the order at least a dozen times, as if his orders from some cause or other could not be attended to. Mr. Hill, the mate who was with me in my first trip in the boat, came to my cabin and told me to get up and go upon deck, as there was no doubt but the ship would be lost, for the captain and both mates were drunk and the ship was driving fast upon the rocks.

I dressed myself as quickly as possible and went upon deck. Judge of my feelings when the first object that met my view was the shore, with tremendous rocks running out into the sea, and the breakers dashing over them in a frightful manner. Horror was depicted on almost every countenance, women clasping their children in their arms, and their husbands running about the deck like madmen.

I thank God he has given me confidence and a sort of presence of mind which enables me to act in time of danger. I forced my way to the fore part of the vessel and inquired if the anchor was ready to let go at a minute's notice. It was a beautiful moonlight night, and on turning my head I saw the carpenter sitting on the bulwarks with his axe, ready to cut the anchor-stop if it should be necessary.

My next thought was how to save our lives if the vessel should strike the rocks. I turned my thoughts to the top of the poop, which I think we six male cabin pasengers could easily have removed overboard to form a raft, and with the empty water cans tied round the ladies' waists there was a possibility of saving our lives. We had three good boats, but they would have been crowded and swamped, for there were 162 persons on board, and a great many of them very bad characters. In about half an hour the wind came off the land, and in a few minutes we found ourselves sailing as it were out of the jaws of death.

August 11th.—At eight a.m. went upon deck. We were about eight miles from the shore. We could plainly see the houses here and there along the shore. The wind was against us, and there was a heavy swell. About 10 a.m. passed a bark laden with timber, bound to Greenock. Sent a boat on board to get provisions. The boat returned with only five pounds of tobacco. The bark had been nine days out from Quebec. At five p.m. the island of Anticosti was in sight—a very dangerous coast. At night the revolving light on the lighthouse on the island had a very pretty effect.

August 12th, Sunday.—Still opposite Anticosti, with a foul wind. At 11 a.m. sent a boat off to the *Emperor*, a vessel bound for Liverpool with timber. Got from her two fowls and a pail of potatoes. The crew gave bad accounts of the cholera at Quebec. They had lost six people. We have three or four ill, and if they are not well before we get to the quarantine ground we most likely will have to stay there three weeks. The northern lights were very beautiful every night.

August 13th.—Wind contrary. At 10 a.m. took the pilot on board. He says the cholera is nearly over. Fruit is ripe, except apples. In the afternoon we were off the Seven Islands. We might with a fair wind reach Grosse Isle, the quarantine ground, in 24 hours, but as we get on now we shall not be there for a week. At 10 p.m. saw a beautiful lunar rainbow perfectly white, yet not like the Milky Way.

August 14th.—Wind still contrary. The bold mountains and Cape Chat have been in view the whole of the day. At one time we were very close in shore. The wind from off the land felt extremely warm, and the perfume from the wild flowers was delightful. We were busy getting guns ready to go on shore in the morning. We were very short of provisions, and the wind was still against us.

August 15th.—The boat was lowered, and the captain, myself, the doctor, and seven others well armed, pushed off from the ship, the boat being stored with grog and provisions. I had laid in a good supply of toast and water. We hoisted sail, and stood in for the north shore, about a league to the west of Goose Island. Words will not express my feelings on nearing the iron-bound shore. Huge rocks a hundred yards long by thirty or forty yards high ran out into the sea. Here and there was a stone full of large clefts. Behind, the mountains, covered with spruce firs and white birch trees to the height of several hundred feet, rose like an amphitheatre.

We at last found a landing place, and by laying two oars side by side from the boat to the rocks we all landed. At first I could hardly walk, on account of the motion of the vessel. We began to scramble over the rocks, which were covered with sea weed and marine eggs. We at last gained the land. It was a flat, sandy beach, completely shut in behind the rocks for about a hundred yards wide. It then began to ascend gradually, and from that arose the mountains, apparently about a mile off.

The beach was covered with wild plants, roses, wild gooseberries, everlasting peas—a kind of vetch—together with various flowers, such as I had never seen before. We seemed to have encountered a new climate. I think the thermometer would have registered 90°, while on board the ship we could have borne a great coat. At first we walked about with great caution, expecting to see wild beasts and noxious reptiles; but seeing nothing of the kind, after walking about for several hours, we gained confidence.

The woods were as still as death, and there was no warbling of birds as in England. The mosquitoes and sand flies annoyed us dreadfully, and our faces were literally covered with bites. The sand flies bit a piece out every time they attacked us, and the blood trickled from each bite. Not seeing any game along the shore, I took the bearings with my pocket compass, and the doctor and I struck into the forest. A heavy shower of rain came on that wetted us through, and made it very difficult travelling among the trees. The ground was covered with leaves and moss some inches deep. The trees were blown down across each other to the height of several feet. We were obliged to climb over these, some of which were so rotten as to crumble beneath us.

We chased a very curious bird for some time, which barked something like a dog. It seemed to be a kind of hawk; but hearing the report of two guns in quick succession, and hearing a great shouting we gave up the chase and made the best of our way to the place whence the noise came. The captain had shot a hawk, and one of the others a grouse. While we were talking, another grouse flew past us, which I shot.

We went to the boat to get some refreshment, when eight Indians passed in a canoe. They would not come near us for fear of the cholera. I shot a grouse, a godwit, a dozen snipe and ring plovers; picked about a quart of wild gooseberries, and lost about a pint of blood by the mosquitoes and sand flies. We were hopeful of meeting with deer and bears, which we wanted for provisions, but not the slightest trace of an animal was to be seen.

About four p.m. we put off in the boat with the intent of going on board, as the ship was beating up with a flood tide against a foul wind about 10 miles off. The captain was drunk, as indeed were all the men except the doctor and myself. The sea was so high it came over the gunwale of the boat, so we persuaded the captain to put back and make a fire, and stay all night. There was one bottle of rum left, which I capsized. We gained the shore by getting up to our middle in water. The captain and the sailors rolled about in the sea with their clothes on, and were nearly drowned. The others pulled off their wet clothes and went bathing, which helped to sober them. We started along the beach, and lost two of our number, but by the help of our guns we soon found them again.

We passed four Indian wigwams. We got two of the sailors to take the boat about four miles round to a small bay, or she would have been dashed to pieces. We walked along the shore, and reached the boat about 6.30 p.m. One of the men, in crossing a small creek, was driven out to sea, but saved himself by clinging to the rocks. His feet were badly cut.

The men being now nearly sober, we again put off in the boat, and reached the ship about 8.30 p.m. When we got alongside a great many of the steerage passengers began hooting and hissing. Some of them got out their knives to cut the ropes that held the ladder, saying we should not come on board. One of the most noisy received a blow with the flat part of an oar on his face, which knocked some of his teeth out. This completely silenced them. They had been very mutinous all day, through the captain not being on board. We went to bed as soon as we got on board, and had our bitten faces rubbed with vinegar and water. . . .

August 26th, Sunday, six a.m.—Weighed anchor, and with some difficulty, owing to a foul wind, proceeded as far as the quarantine ground, opposite Grosse Isle. All well on board. The captain ordered all the steerage passengers to prepare themselves to go upon the island for the purpose of airing their bedding and washing their linen. About three p.m. the boats were manned, and the passengers landed. Then they all set to, and the rocks presented a most singular appearance from the various articles of clothing spread about them, and the emigrants in all directions hanging them out to dry. At night they went into a humble shed (for it could not be called by any other name) and spread their beds on the bare ground.

A lamentable occurrence took place this evening. The passengers of the *Minerva*, anchored near us, had performed quarantine, and were returning on board. When they came alongside their vessel the ropes of the davits became entangled with the mast of the boat, and swamped her. From the deck of our ship we could see upwards of twenty persons struggling in the water, only nine of whom were saved. The agony we felt at not being able to render assistance—all our boats being on shore—was extreme. One of our boats, returning from the shore, rowed to their assistance, and succeeded in picking up four, who were taken to the island. One of them, a fine young woman, was in a state of suspended animation. She was quite black in the face when taken from the water, but rubbing her body with brandy restored her, and by the following morning she was quite recovered. An old man and his wife were two of the others who were saved by the crew of our boat. They were completely soaked, and they wept bitterly for the loss of their little boy, who found a grave in the ocean. The other was a little fellow about four years old, brother to the young woman already named, whose lively countenance beamed thankfulness while carried about the shed in the arms of the brave sailor who saved him. I omitted to mention that the young woman named was called upon to lament the loss of a sister who sank to rise no more.

August 28th—This morning our passengers all returned to the vessel in safety. It was a case of thankfulness, for there was not one ill. About two p.m. we weighed anchor for Quebec, but the wind not being favourable we cast anchor at 10 p.m.

August 29th—Weighed anchor at five a.m. and made but little way. At eight arrived opposite the Island of Orleans, and at nine came to anchor at Patrick's Isle, six miles from Quebec, the tide and wind against us. A child had just died of decline, its death hastened by the privations suffered at the quarantine ground. Weighed anchor about four p.m. and sailed slowly up the river. We were transported with the enchanting scenery, particularly with the village at the foot of Montmorency Falls, upon which the sun was shining. At dusk we came to anchor in the basin at the fort, Quebec, after a passage of nine weeks and three days.

30th August, 1832—The Revenue officers came on board, and we waited the arrival of the surgeon, expecting to go on shore today. The captain went on shore to arrange for the child's funeral, which is to take place to-morrow morning.

1st September—A party of us went on shore with the corps about 10 a.m. and were directed to the cholera burial ground. When there we were obliged to wait for several hours for a priest. There were no fewer than seven or eight wagons with rough deal coffins waiting in the hot sun for the said priest. The coffins were nailed together of unseasoned inch-boards. The lids had shrunk and warped so that you could get your hand in, and the stench from them was dreadful. Still we remained until the child was buried. After I was on board I became very ill with a sort of cholera, but cured it with copious doses of tincture of rhubarb.[1]

---

[1] On August 29th, after a passage of nine weeks and three days, John Howard and his wife reached Quebec; and on the 14th of September they were at York (Toronto), eleven weeks and three days from London. Howard was to become Toronto's first city engineer and architect, and his gift of High Park, his home there—Colborne Lodge—and a great collection of art work, surveyors' notebooks, and architectural designs—many of them rediscovered in his desks and cupboards in the summer of 1960—are among Toronto's most notable treasures from the past.

DIARY OF JOHN ROBERTS, 1847

John Roberts' experiences, while not comparable in suffering to those of emigrants in the worst of overcrowded ships, are yet highly typical of the daily miseries which were the lot of most steerage passengers. A member of the family permitted the writer to make a copy of the manuscript, which—if it still exists—is in private possession.

John Roberts's Account from the Time he left Mevagissey [Cornwall] until he reached his Destination.

.... *April 9 Friday Morning*—We had breakfast. After breakfast James & I took a walk on the Quay & we was told that the barg would leave about 11 OClock so we went home & bound up our beds & they were carried up on board the *Clio*. The wind was very fresh & I had a tuff pull. We put it on board & came home again, had some dinner, went & bought some candels & than James, Mary & I walked down to the Ship & went on board. There was a great deal of noise with the children & people so we went & got our beds in order & about eight we went to bed. We had a curtain drawn so that the females could undress without the men seen them. There were some cats on board & they kept a noise all the night. Two or three persons were sick in the night but I did not hear them. The morning came & about five I turned out & saw one woman on the opposite side about to dress. I thought it very curious to see so many in there bedcloths. We had breakfast & after breakfast one of the sealors stept on the atchway, the hatchway gave way & it fell on a boy & hurted him a great deal. The Doctor was sent for & he said no bone was broke so it is all well. We had fried ham for dinner & after dinner Mary felt unwell. There are a great many more on board this afternoon, the wind is about W this afternoon. There are 5 barges alongside, two with balace one with coaks, one with water & one with luggage & Passengers. We have had a great deal of rain to day....

April 13—The Wind W., very rainey all day. All of a bussel, the sailors taking in water. About 3 OClock in the afternoon a boat coming from Padstow with eleven men, she upset & seven were drowned (I was not on shore for the day).

April 14—Very dry, the wind E., three of the men were taken up, the boats belonging to the *Clio* were oisted on board. I thought we should go to sea but we could not get out of the harbour, the *Herald* Steam boat would not take us out because it blew too fresh.

April 15—The wind N.E.N., very dry, the sails loose, every preparation to go to sea. About 5 OClock in the afternoon we weighed anchor with the *Eagle*. They boath worked out of the harbour (& it was a very fine sight) to see them tack & tack. It was laughable to see the passengers sick. I saw one man up to windward sick, & as fast as he would heave up it would blow on him. I stood on the quarter deck all the time she was going out & about 8 OClock I got sick. I went below & went to bed.

Friday Morning April 16—The wind N.N.W., very dry. I got out of bed, went on the deck, about two miles to leward I saw the *Eagle* but I could not see any land (the first time ever I lost sight of land). I felt very curious after been sick so I had a bit of ham & biscuit for breakfast. After that I went on deck but a great many were very sick & I felt unwell all the day. The *Eagle* is about 5 miles to leward & the wind is W.N.W. but not very much. She is going about 4 an hour. I had tea & went to bed. In the night it came on to gale of wind, so much so that she shiped several seas & one broak the glass in the skylight. I was very much affraid at the time but I went off to sleep & in the morning I woke & I was so sick & unwell that I did not turn out of bed for all the day. I had a little grual once, I could not eat anything besides.

April 18 Sunday Morning—I woke but very unwell. I had a little grual for breakfast, & after breakfast (it been Sunday) I begun to think about the chapple & the people that sat in their differant seats & about my Fathers House & if I was home what a good dinner I could make, but all the thinking was of no use. I got out of bed, dressed & went on deck but the weather was very rough & I was so unwell I was obliged to go to bed again & in the night I woke & heard the captain calling take that sail & furl the others & there was so much sea I was affraid she would turn over.

April 19 Monday Morning—I woke & still the ship kept rolling & I was so unwell I did not turn out for the day. James got me a little grual. I eat that but I was not sick for the day but I was very sore with lying in bed & while there I thought let me be so unwell as I may be I would turn out in the morning. I did not sleep much that night, the weather was awful. . . .

April 21 Wednesday Morning—I woke, the wind was the same & very rough, the Ship roled so much that we could scarce lay in our beds. I got out, went on deck & I felt very well. I had an appetite to eat & that was very pleasing to me. In the evening the wind lessened & we had a very fine night.

April 22 Thursday Morning—The wind W.N.W., very fine & dry. I had two eggs for breakfast & went on deck after a wile. A great many persons that had not been out of bed since they left Padstow came on deck this morning & they look'd very pale & some have not been on deck yet. For dinner I had some pastry that is the best meal I have made since I left home (but I hope it will not be the last). After dinner I employed all the afternoon in reading & that was very pleasing so I hope now I shall be more comfortable. In the evening I had a good tea & Mary & I talked about home & the people that were there but I could not stand it long to think that I was by myself but Mary had her Husband & I no one with me, so after we had done talking I went to bed.

April 23 Friday Morning—The wind S. but not much, the weather was very fine. About 10 OClock the Captn had a market for groceries. Tea was sold at 2/ pr lb, Figs 6d, Currants 6d, Sugar 4½, Tobacco 2/6 & so on. In the afternoon the wind increased & the Ship went about 10 miles an Hour, very pleasing to us passengers for her to go so fast with a fair wind. In the evening there was a prayer meeting & it was very comfortable to hear them pray. After the meeting I went to bed. . . .

April 26 Monday Morning—The wind W.N.W., very fresh or a gale, indeed it blew so that it split the topsail though it was double reef & it continued all day, we only carried a double reef topsail & main trisail. The Ship rolled so much that there was no cooking & the passengers was tumbling & the sea wetting of them, it was very laughable to see them.

April 27 Tuesday Morning—The wind N.W. very squalley, under sail of a double reef fore topsail, double reef main topsail & a main trisail. About dinner time we saw a sail a stern with her fore top mast gone. We hoisted our foresail & soon went out of sight of her, nothing occurred any more for the day. . . .

May 1—The wind W. but dry, very cold to day. We had pancakes for dinner but I was very unwell. I thought if I was home I should have some cream, but we had no cows on board so I could not have any.

Sunday Morning May 2—The wind W.S. & a great deal of sea. The Ship rolled so much that we could not sit or stand, a great many men fell & we shiped a great deal of water. The forenoon was whet & the afternoon was dry & sun shine.

May 3 Monday Morning—The wind about W, very strong. We shiped a great deal of water, we could scarce lay in our beds or stand or sit. Three or four men fell with their dinners & lost it, one hurted himself. It was cold with smart hail showers in the Morning, the afternoon was dry. In the evening about 8 it came on so bad we lay to under a double reef topsail & main trisail. . . . We are all obliged to hold fast, to keep us from falling. We cant cook anything, we must eat hard bread & I am very cold. About 7 OClock I went to bed.

May 6 Thursday Morning—I got out & begun to think upon the night that I had passed. I slept a little & dreampt a curious dream about home that is not the first, for I have had a dreem almost every night since I left home. My cloths was whet with the sea comming down the hatchways, I was obliged to put on dry clothes. It is still an awful gale of wind, the wind is about N.W. with hail showers & very cool, no meet cook to day for some.

May 7 Friday Morning—It has been an awful night this last night, I was obliged to take my pillow in the middle of the night & throw it at the bottom of my bed. The sea came down & whetted the pillow & my head. I did not know what to do, I was glad when the day light came to get out. I got out & went on deck. I saw a brig about two miles to winward laying to like us. The wind is about N.W., still a gale & we are still shipping seas at times. I boiled a little rice to day for dinner but James generally cooks. I did it to pass away the time. About 5 the wind lessoned, that was very pleasing to all. About 8 the brig made sail & came up to our stearn & spoke with us. She is bound from Liverpool to New York, called the *Eliza Kate*, she had been out 24 days and us 22 days. After that I went below, I went to bed. As the gale had abated the sealors were employed in getting a few more sails on the Ship. . . .

May 9th Sunday Morning—The wind N. be W., rather squalley. In the morning it rained. The afternoon their was meeting. About 5 a Duck almost lighted on the deck but it flew away again. In the evening there was meeting again by the passengers.

May 10th Monday Morning—The wind N. but it as varied all day. It was very fine in the morning but the afternoon it came on to rain but very mild. This afternoon I walked the deck without holding fast, the first time since I left Padstow. About 9 I went to bed & it was quite a treat to sleep so still, there was scarce any motion in the Ship.

May 11 Tuesday Morning—The wind N.E. About 6 I got out of bed & went on deck to see what I never saw before. The[y] were setting stonisails on her, they put up three on the starboard side. It was a beautiful Morning. About 10 a Man from the yard harm saw a Shark that is the first that any one have seen for the voyage. . . .

May 15 Saturday Morning—The wind N.E.N. but not much, very fine weather. About 10 OClock a calm. To day I made a bread pudding. Last night I put the bread to soak in cold water, this forenoon I cutted it up with Sugar & butter, and put it in a tin with bits of butter on the top, than baked it, but I did not like it as well as fig pudding. This forenoon I saw some Porposes not far from the Ship, they were very large. The afternoon the water became green. I enquired the reason. The[y] told me we was on the Green Bank, that was good news. The wind N.E. but it is very cold.

Sunday Morning May 16—The wind N.E. but very fine weather. The Ship is almost as still when in harbour. About 6 I went on deck & saw hundreds of small murs, they were flying in flocks from 2 or 3 to 50 or 60 and other sorts of Birds. It was as cold almost as I have felt in England. About 8 the Captain got the line & sounding led but could not get any soundage. About 1 OClock he tried & sounded in 40 fathoms of water, the bottom is white sand mixed with small shells but the sand is of a sparry nature. In the afternoon it came on icey fog, very thick & colder than ever. One Fisherman at a great distance at anchor. A child has been ill several weeks but to day it is worse. This afternoon one of the Passengers preached & several attended. In the evening it came on thicker fog & it was bitter cold. About 7 OClock I went to bed to get wharm. . . .

May 17 Monday Morning—As I was laying in bed I heard that the child was ded & also heard that there was several fisherman. . . . The Carpenter is knocking up the empty barrels & binding the staves in bundols. It is very cold to day but very fine weather. At 2 OClock the wind E. & the Ship is going 8 miles an hour. A Man fired & shot a Gul but it floated a stearn. It is comming on very foggy & cold, some large fish alongside but I dont know what sort. In the evening the Child was sewn up in canvis with some clay & carried to the side of the Ship were the burial was read by a Local Preacher, a Passenger, after which it was thrown overboard, after which I went to bed. . . .

May 19 Wednesday Morning—Our Ship under double rccf topsails. To night has been very dirty, a great deal of rain & wind, the wind S & still very foggy. I went on deck about 5½ & it was very foggy & cold, I did not stop long. I went below & sat down, after which I went on deck & boiled some bread for breakfast, before which I felt unwell & it removed it. About 10 I saw a Brig ahead as far as I could see, but we soon caught her. 11½ the Sun begun to open & the Captain said if it cleared we should see land. A few minutes before twelve the fog did clear & there was St. Pauls on the larboard. Happy Land! Happy Land for us on board! The sailors are loosing the sails & hoisting more. Before the fog cleared we was affraid to run to close home on the land, but now it is all speed but the wind is light. A little while after we saw Cape North. This afternoon they are getting the royals on her, they have not been up since we left. The Carpenters are again knocking up the Barrels & there are 7 Vessals in sight, I can see them. There is also Snow on Cape North. The sailors think we shall have head wind but I hope not. If we have a fair wind we shall be up to Quebec on Saturday, but we must leave it to Providence. I also saw a Whale some distance from our Ship. . . .

May 23 Sunday Morning—The wind N.W.N. all against. We have runn'd off from the Land we saw yesterday some distance & now we can see it on both sides with a great deal of snow on it. The Sun is very wharm & the water smooth with a gentle breeze, it is altogether very fine weather. About 12 OClock I had a fig pudding for dinner & I begun to think that our People at home was about their tea because it is 4 OClock home at Mevagissay & I suppose others are walking in the lanes but I suppose I shall be on a Foreign land soon to walk with Strangers but I hope I shall see Mevagissay once more & my old Friends, after which thoughts I went on deck in the Sun to drown it. The wind W.S.W., that is against us. I've seen several whales to day, some at a great distance & some not far from the Ship. In the evening their was Prayer meeting with the Passengers but the air is rather cold. . . .

May 26 Wednesday Morning—Little after 4 I went on deck & enquired how the Ship went. They told me she had been becalm almost all the night. There are mountains with snow on the tops & there are hundreds of Houses for miles along the river, with some land cultivated & it is looking beautiful. About 8 a Child died, it had been unwell ever since it has been on board. . . .

May 27 Thursday Morning—About 1 OClock this morning we anchored in courtenteen ground[1] & about 5 I got out & went on deck to see what could be seen. There are several Houses, a Hospital, Barricks for the Soldiers & there are 36 Ships, Barques & Brigs, all with Passengers. I believe all are Irish & Scotch without us & the feaver with a great many of them are very bad. Yesterday 50 was buried, to day 25 died at the Hospital & a great many on board the Vessals, it is awful to hear the differant accounts. About 3 OClock the Docter came on board, all of us was ordered on deck the fore side of the main mast & a rope was drawn acros. Every one went under so that he might count us. As soon as he had seen all of us pass & he himself went below he said it was a pleasure to come on board such a Ship as us, so he said he would call again in the morning & clear us. The child that died yesterday he said must be carried on shore to the buiring & one of the sailors brought on board some snow. We are very close to the land, this evening I saw some cows & Horses, the first since I left England. . . .

May 29 Saturday Morning—At 2½ we weighd anchor with a little breeze & at 4 I turned out of bed & went on deck & it was a pretty sight to see the Houses of all colours & the Churches with tin roofs & the land so beautifully cultivated. The water fall was the prettiest thing ever I saw. At 6 OClock we let go anchor up to Quebec, the first sight I saw was four Horses working a Boat, than the splended buildings. The Boats was upsat, I saw one Man taken of the bottom of one not far from our Ship. Afternoon I went on shore but it rained, I did not stop long. I brought some cakes & bread & it was quite a trait after eating hard bread so long. The steam boats are splended, they are painted white & very long. All the streets are paved with wood & the wharfs are wood.

May 30 Sunday Morning—The weather is very fine & hot. I've not been on shore to day. Several persons came off to see the people &

---

[1] The quarantine station at Grosse Isle.

amongst them was John Werry. He told me had been waiting in Quebec a week for his Whife & children but they had not arrived. . . .

June 1 Tuesday Morning—Very gloomy & cold. Going up the river there are hundreds of acres of land covered with water but the trees are above. Some places is cultivated & pretty little Houses built. 8½ OClock we got to Surrel. There was brought on board by the inhabitants some boiled fish & Eggs & also bread, ld of fish & bread & made a good breakfast. Surrel is a pretty little place, there are a great many Soldiers there & a beer. After we left Surral the land was a little higher & there was a great deal of cattle on it & houses & a wind mill. The river is narrow & we can see the children & grown persons very plain. At 2 we arrived at Montreal by the *Lady Colborne* for which I paid 3/9 currancy. . . . James & I hired a cart to carry our luggage to Lachine, a distance of 9 miles, to join the Steam boat. There was Houses & Gardens almost all the way from Montreal to Lachine & it was a pretty sight to see apple trees in bloom & every thing looking green. We arrived there about 8 & put our luggage on the quay but went on board to sleep. I slept with the old John Hawe & had a good nights rest.

June 2 Wednesday Morning—Very fine weather & wharm. I went & bought some bread, butter & Eggs, I had the eggs boiled so I could eat them at any time. At 10 OClock we left Lachine & at 12 we arrived at the canal. We had to go in 9 locks, the length of the canal is 16 miles. After we left the canal I saw a great many rafts of timber with sails & some had as many as 16 or 20 men on them. They had a little house on the timber so they might go in out of the rain. . . .

June 3 Thursday Morning—Very fine. I've not slept much to night, I was obliged to sit on a chair, I had no place else to go. It is pretty to see the trees in bloom & the little Islands with trees on them, even the rocks were they are split they trees grow out. I saw the remains of the Houses that was knocked down when the rebelion was.[1] At 7 we arrived at Ogdensburg 100 miles from Lachine. This is a pretty town, here I bought some appels, fine ones, for a penny. At 9 we left for Kingston & going up we calld at Murris Town, Brogville[2] & French Creek. French Creek is 25 miles from Kingston. We arrived to Kingston (15 shillings) at 5 OClock in the Afternoon but I did not go off the Quay as I had to put my luggage in another boat for Cobourg, but I think Kingston is a fine place. There has been a fire here a few days ago & burnt a great deal of flour. Here I left James & his whife. At 7 we started for Cobourg, when night came on I went below. Our boat was full of English, Irish & Germans. I had no place to sleep, I sat on a box until I was very cold, than I begun to walk about the deck.

June 4 Friday Morning—At 4 we arrived at Cobourg (5 s). As soon as I had my luggage on the quay I fell in with a young Man from Wadebridge. I asked him if he knew any one by the name of John Morris. He said he did, he would show me where he lived, so we went to see him. When we came up to the house we was told he had left for Peterborough about a fortnight. I was so cast down I did not know what to do, but as I was going down to the quay again I met with Mr. Mrs. Buridale & the

---

[1] The reference is to the Battle of Windmill Point, near Prescott, in November 1838. Raiders from the United States were driven out of a windmill and adjacent buildings by British regulars and Canadian militiamen. See Guillet, *The Lives and Times of the Patriots*, pp. 132-42.

[2] Brockville.

Daniel Heustis, *Narrative*, 1847
BATTLE OF THE WINDMILL, 1838

three children (they were persons from the Lanceston). They asked me if I had seen the person, I said he was gone away. They told me the[y] had took a house & for me to bring my luggage at there house. I did it, I was quite at home. I changed my clothes & took a walk. Cobourg is a pretty Town & the streets are straight & whide. In the afternoon I went in search of work, the first Shop I went to I got work.

So ends my journal at presant.

THE EMIGRANT'S WELCOME TO CANADA

Courtesy Coverdale Collection, Manoir Richelieu, Quebec

CANADIAN UNIVERSITY PAPERBOOKS

1. *The Canadian Identity* by W. L. Morton,
2. *The Fur Trade in Canada* by Harold A. Innis,

3. *Rideau Waterway* by Robert Legget,
4. *The Politics of Education* by Frank MacKinnon,

5. *Our Living Tradition* edited by C. T. Bissell,

6. *Essays in Canadian Economic History* by Harold A. Innis,

7. *The Bruce Beckons* by W. Sherwood Fox,
8. *The Renaissance and English Humanism* by Douglas Bush,

9. *Democracy in Alberta: Social Credit and the Party System* by C. B. Macpherson,
10. *The Birth of Western Canada* by George F. G. Stanley,

11. *Rhythm in the Novel* by E. K. Brown,
12. *Between the Red and the Rockies* by Grant MacEwan,

13. *Champlain* by N. E. Dionne,
14. *The Life and Times of Confederation* by P. B. Waite,

15. *In Search of Chaucer* by B. H. Bronson,
16. *The Great Migration* by Edwin C. Guillet,
17. *A Prophet in Politics* by Kenneth McNaught,

18. *Democratic Government in Canada* by Robert MacGregor Dawson,

www.ingramcontent.com/pod-product-compliance
Lightning Source LLC
Chambersburg PA
CBHW052010070526
44584CB00016B/1697